NORTH AMERICAN CRIMINAL GANGS

NORTH AMERICAN CRIMINAL GANGS

Street, Prison, Outlaw Motorcycle, and Drug Trafficking Organizations

Edited by

Tom Barker

CAROLINA ACADEMIC PRESS

Durham, North Carolina

Library of Congress Cataloging-in-Publication Data

Barker, Thomas.
North American criminal gangs : street, prison, outlaw motorcycle, and drug trafficking organizations / Tom Barker.
p. cm.
Includes bibliographical references and index.
ISBN 978-1-61163-071-8 (alk. paper)
1. Gangs--North America. 2. Prison gangs--North America. 3. Motorcycle gangs--North America. 4. Drug traffic--North America. I. Title.

HV6439.N67B37 2012
364.106'6097--dc23

2012015545

CAROLINA ACADEMIC PRESS
700 Kent Street
Durham, North Carolina 27701
Telephone (919) 489-7486
Fax (919) 493-5668
www.cap-press.com

Printed in the United States of America.

To Addie, who brought new meaning, love and
joy into our world.

Contents

Acknowledgments

The author would like to thank his Canadian friend, Karan Katz. Without your help this project would not have been possible. I would also like to thank the staff of Carolina Academic Press, especially Beth Hall. Your guidance and help smoothed out the laborious publishing process. As always, I express my gratitude to BSJ, who made it all possible.

North American Criminal Gangs

Chapter 1

Introduction

I. Overview

Over the years, several textbooks have been published on gangs; however, their focus has been primarily on male youth gangs in the United States. This is a worthwhile but narrow approach to the study of gangs, especially adult criminal gangs, such as institutionalized street gangs, prison gangs, outlaw motorcycle gangs (OMGs) and drug trafficking organizations. These latter gangs are defined by their criminal activity, often organized crime such as drug trafficking, and not the age of the members (see Table 1.1). "Youth gangs," a media constructed label, is and always was for the most part, a misnomer and a narrow approach to the study of gangs. Frederick Thrasher's seminal study of gangs classified the gangs studied as forty-seven percent ranging in age from 11–17, 37 percent ranged in age from 16–25, and the oldest gangs (four percent) in his study ranged in age from 21 to 51 (Thrasher, 1963).

In recent years, the upper age limit of gang members has risen along with the nature of their criminal activities. The National Youth Gang Center reports that over 60 percent of all youth gang members in the United States are adults 18 years of age or older and that these gangs are involved in crime for profit (i.e., criminal gangs). Further confusion occurs in the accepted definition of street gangs such as the "consensus Eurogang definition" agreed to by "100 gang researchers in the United States and Europe" (Klein, 2005: 136). For this group "a street gang is any durable, street-oriented youth group; whose own identity includes involvement in illegal activity." Klein further states that his definition of street gangs distinguishes them from "prison gangs, terrorist groups, motorcycle gangs and adult criminal organizations" (Klein, 2005: 136). Street gangs, such as the Bloods, Crips, Gangster Disciples, Latin Kings, MS 13, the Avenues, the 18th Street, etc., at one time in their evolution were primarily youth gangs engaged in serious crime on an occasional basis but today they are not adolescent youth gangs. They are serious and violent criminal gangs and becoming more so. The same can be said for the other gangs we examine. According to the latest findings from the 2011 National Gang Threat Assessment prepared by the National Gang Intelligence Center, street, prison, and outlaw motorcycle gangs are expanding, evolving and posing an increasing threat to U.S. communities (see Box 1.1).

In addition to the evolution from youth gangs, many street gangs have evolved into criminal gangs from other benign beginnings. The National Gang Intelligence Center

Table 1.1 2011 Estimated Gang Membership

	Members	Gangs
Street	1,140,344*	30,313
OMGs	44,108	2,965
Prison	231,136**	n/a
TOTAL	1,414,578	33,278

* Based on 2010 and 2011 NGIC (National Gang Intelligence Center) and NDIC (National Drug Intelligence Center) data.
** Based on reporting from 32 States.
Source: 2011 National Gang Threat Assessment.

(2009) points out that the Chicago-based Gangster Disciples, Black P. Stones, and the Latin Kings formed as organizations for political and social reform during the 1960s. Today, they are violent national and international adult criminal gangs heavily involved in narcotics trafficking and other forms of organized crime. Montreal Canada's first black gang, the Master Bs, composed of Haitian immigrants, was formed as a protection group against the racist skinheads and neo-Nazi gangs prevalent in Montreal. Many

---

Box 1.1 2011 National Gang Threat Assessment—Key Findings

- There are approximately 1.4 million active street gangs (criminal organizations formed on the street), prison gangs (criminal organizations that originated within the penal system and operate within correctional facilities), and outlaw motorcycle gangs (organizations whose members use their motorcycles as conduits for criminal enterprises) members in more than 33,000 gangs operating in all 50 states, the District of Columbia, and Puerto Rico.

- Gangs are responsible for an average of 48 percent of violent crime in most jurisdictions and up to 90 percent in several others.

- Gangs are increasingly engaging in non-traditional gang-related crimes like alien smuggling, human trafficking, and prostitution, as well as white-collar crimes like counterfeiting, identity theft and mortgage fraud ... primarily due to the high profitability, and much lower visibility, risk of detection, and punishment than drug and weapons trafficking.

- Gang members are acquiring high-powered military-style weapons and equipment, which poses a significant threat because of the potential to engage in lethal encounters with law enforcement and citizens alike.

- Gangs are becoming increasingly adaptable and sophisticated, employing new and advanced technology—including social networking websites—to carry out criminal activity discreetly and connect with other gang members, criminal organizations, and potential recruits around the country and around the world.

Canadian Aboriginal gangs began as protection groups or as social groups to express cultural identity. Gordon (2000) suggests, "Analysts and policy makers should view the phenomenon [gang/group] along a continuum ranging from groups of friends who spend time together and who occasionally get into trouble, to more serious, organized criminal groups or gangs." That is the approach taken in this book as we focus on the right left end of the continuum—organized criminal groups or gangs.

The book also takes the approach that gangs should be examined in a comparative way. Street gangs, prison gangs, outlaw motorcycle gangs, and drug trafficking organizations are not unique to the United States. For that reason, we examine gangs in a North American context—the United States, Canada and Mexico. There are many similarities among the U.S. gangs and those in Canada. Street gangs in both countries are most common in the country's economically deprived groups—minority groups, such as African Americans, Hispanics and recent immigrants in the United States; and minority groups such as Aboriginals and recent immigrants (blacks, Hispanics, Asians, etc.) in Canada. All three countries have prison gangs and outlaw motorcycle gangs , and the American-based OMGs—the Hells Angels, Bandidos, Outlaws—are a major source of organized crime in Canada. Our discussion of Mexican gangs will be somewhat limited, due to a lack of published information; however, several prison gangs operate in the United States and Mexico, two American-based outlaw motorcycle gangs have chapters in the United States and Mexico, and the major Mexican drug trafficking organizations distribute illegal narcotics to the United States and Canada.

Super Gangs

"Super gangs" evolved after the crack cocaine trade put into place the necessary organizational structure of leader, treasurer, enforcer, runner and foot soldiers to put the drugs on the street (Venkatesh & Levitt, 2000). These "super gangs" require social networks far beyond the scope of adolescent youth gangs to engage in crime for profit. This structure also ensures that youths and youth gangs are important to the adult criminal street gangs. The criminal street gangs use "youth" gangs and young "wannabe" as the foot soldiers to carry out their criminal schemes. For example, it is well documented that notorious street gangs such as the Los Angeles-based Hispanic street gang, the Avenues, which is controlled by the Mexican Mafia prison gang, has small cliques of young gang wannabe that are "tolerated, monitored, and often encouraged and counseled" (Rafael, 2007: 154). The larger gang recruits the good earners and talented criminals from these youth groups. When the time comes the adult criminal gangs tell the youngsters to join or stop gang banging.

The structure of the criminal gang takes on the aspect of a career and path for socioeconomic mobility for poorly educated inner-city youths in the United States, and Aboriginal youths in Canada, with the only available jobs being menial minimum wage jobs with no career advancement. The likelihood of moving up the ladder of criminal advancement is low but it remains a powerful draw for those blocked from more socially acceptable careers. Thus, some of the reasons for the movement of large U.S. urban gangs into the underground economies of drug trafficking—dues from members, "street taxes" from independent illegal operators, and legitimate businesses such as grocery store owners, gypsy cabs, and service providers such as auto or plumbing repair—is the lack of opportunity in more socially accepted economic spheres:

> I want to have me a car man, you know man, have my shit on, live in a nice place where all them people working downtown live, you know, you ain't got no trash on the streets, everyone's driving the Lexuses and the Benzes. You think they come back to this shit [he says pointing to the housing project in which he resides]. Fuck no, nigger! They ain't worried about getting no heat, no food on their plate. I'm tired of hustling man, want the good life. (A Black Kings [pseudo name for Chicago street gang] member quoted in Venkatesh & Levitt, 2000:448).

II. What Exactly Is a Gang?

For a policy maker or a criminal justice professional, the definition of a gang is more than an academic exercise. The definition of gang, in effect defines the nature and extent of the gang crime problem and the development of policies and strategies to deal with gang criminal behavior. The gang definition that criminal justice professionals use defines for the purposes of prosecution and punishment who is and who is not a gang member, and what criminal co-offenders will be classified and prosecuted as criminal organizations. For these reasons, we begin with a legalistic definition that defines criminal gangs as adult groups of three or more persons who engage in criminal activity for profit on a continuing basis. "On a continuing basis" is an ambiguous term, however, it makes clear that the acts/behavior of the group is intended to last longer than one or several occurrences. The group comes, or came together, to commit a series of similar criminal acts. Using this definition we can classify adult criminal gangs into two categories: **Single Purpose** criminal gangs that come together for single criminal activities of short duration, such as gangs of robbers, burglars, car thieves, gambling/cheating schemes, corrupt police gangs or otherwise legitimate actors that engage in illegal schemes that are occupationally related, such as health care providers who engage in Medicare fraud, brokers who engage in mortgage fraud, investment bakers engaging in Ponzi schemes, etc. Single purpose criminal gangs have limited supporting networks and organization, and the criminal activity they engage in is only constrained by opportunity and inclination. Typically, single purpose gangs have little or no continuity—arrested members are not replaced.

Aggressive law enforcement action against single purpose criminal gangs usually eliminates them. The single purpose gang does not endure with the turnover of members, that is, unless the single purpose gang morphs into an organized criminal gang. **Organized** criminal gangs, on the other hand, have extensive supporting networks and long histories of criminal activity, a defined membership, and use violence in the furtherance of their criminal behavior and quest for power, examples include adult street gangs, prison gangs, outlaw motorcycle gangs and drug trafficking organizations (DTOs). These gangs have a higher degree of organization because of the nature of their criminal activities. For example, to engage in drug trafficking on a consistent basis there has to be a network to import and distribute the drugs. Once distributed the drugs must be sold and the proceeds collected; someone has to protect the organization and keep out competitors; the money must be laundered; and members paid. As we shall see, a complex organization is necessary for members of the Mexican Mafia prison gang to run drug trafficking activities in Southern California from the California supermax prison in Pelican Bay. The Aryan Brotherhood, another prison gang, needs organization so that members in the federal supermax prison in Florence, Colorado can have inmates killed in a prison in Pennsylvania or run a bank in Miami. Consider the organization necessary for Mara Salvatrucha (MS 13), a street gang founded in Los Angeles, to send members from El Salvador to set up chapters in the Northeast United States.

Not all **organized** adult criminal gangs will have the extensive communication networks to operate with the sophistication of the Mexican Mafia, the Aryan Brotherhood, Mara Salvatrucha, and the Hells Angels, but many street gangs, particularly the "super gangs" of Los Angeles and Chicago, are multi-generational gangs that have gone national and survived numerous prosecution attempts to eliminate them. The complexity and organization of these criminal gangs means that aggressive law enforcement action against organized criminal gangs cripples them but seldom eliminates them. They have continuity — there is always someone waiting to fill the ranks after leaders are sent to prison or killed.

Organized adult criminal gangs such as street gangs, prison gangs, and outlaw motorcycle gangs are unique within the category of organized criminal gangs because they share common characteristics. These criminal gangs make a clear distinction between themselves and others—they are truly "outsiders" in society. They express this distinction with symbols, colors, tattoos, argot, and dress. They also share the distinctive characteristics of all criminal gangs. The members of these groups are involved in various types of crime for profit and violence, or they have the potential for violence.

Typically, organized criminal gangs have some hierarchal organizational structure. Some go so far as to have strict rules and regulations in the form of constitutions or bylaws that dictate such things as membership requirements, duties of members, initiation rites, and discipline. Furthermore, street gangs, prison gangs, and outlaw motorcycle gangs have physical, psychological, and social boundaries that define who is and who is not a member of the group. Often included in the physical boundaries are racial and ethnic distinctions among gang members. In addition, these gangs have geographical areas that they consider their own with non-members excluded from these areas. The "territory" is where the gangs conduct their illegal business and is often defended through intimidation and extreme forms of violence.

In many cases, as we stated earlier, the organized criminal gangs we examine formed as social groups or protection groups, which evolved into criminal organizations with one purpose—crime for profit. For example, the violent street gang—the Crips, evolved in the United States from a 1960s social protest group. The Mara Salvatrucha, known as the "most dangerous gang in the world," evolved in Southern California as a protection group. More specifically, members of MS 13 were immigrants from El Salvador and Central America who were attempting to protect themselves from the deprivations of Mexican and black gangs already in the Southern California area. The notorious prison gang the Aryan Brotherhood, evolved from a group of white prisoners in California seeking protection from black prisoners. Even, the infamous international outlaw motorcycle gang—the Hells Angels, evolved from a group of disgruntled WWII veterans. On the other hand, some criminal gangs, such as the Mongols Motorcycle Gang, the Breeds Motorcycle Gang and drug trafficking organizations, began as criminal groups and have remained so throughout their history. When possible we will discuss the evolution of these gangs and explain how criminal gangs come to evolve from social groups into criminal organizations. Now, we will provide illustrative, not exhaustive, examples of single purpose and organized criminal gangs. For organized criminal gangs we will, when possible, identify geographical reach (local, regional, national, and international) and alliance/s. We will also divide street gangs into Los Angeles and Chicago based/influenced gangs. A more thorough examination of each criminal gang, and the divisions, will come in succeeding chapters.

III. Selected Examples of Single Purpose Gangs

(Crimes of short duration, limited supporting network, not sustaining)

Mortgage Fraud Gang—A Schenectady, New York man was sentenced to 27 months in prison for his role in mortgage fraud scheme. He pled guilty and admitted that, through the use of fraudulent loan applications, settlements, appraisals, and other false statements, and documents, he and the other participants in the scheme were able to fraudulently cause a Delaware bank to finance the sale of residential properties in amounts well in excess of their actual value, and that he and the other participants then used the proceeds of the loans to purchase the properties in much lower amounts and retained the bulk of the funds. (*FBI-Albany Division Press Release*, 2010)

Ponzi Scheme Gang—Three men calling themselves the Three Hebrew Boys promised massive returns based on investments in the foreign currency exchange market, or FOREX. For a contribution of a few thousand dollars, investors were supposed to have their homes, cars, college tuition, credit card bills, and other financial obligations paid off. Instead, the Three Hebrew Boys used some of the incoming money from new investors to pay their outstanding obligations. With the rest, they purchased a private jet, luxury suites at the Carolina Panthers and Atlanta Falcons stadiums, a fleet of cars—including two Mercedes roadsters each valued in excess of $100,000—homes in Florida, condominiums in Atlanta, and a $900,000 party bus, among other things. (*FBI-Columbia Division Press Release*, 2010)

Armored Car Robbers Gang—Three member of a Portland, Oregon family were indicted for the theft of $3 million from armored cars. The father, a driver, allegedly staged two robberies, and his son, a receiving and shipping clerk, allegedly stole money from the vault. The third member of the gang was the wife of the driver who allegedly participated in laundering the money. The three allegedly concealed the cash by purchasing money orders that were used to pay of their living expenses. They also obtained numerous credit cards using false names, false income figures, false employers, and other false financial information. They then allegedly used those credit cards to pay their living expenses, and paid the resulting credit card bills with money orders purchased for cash. (*Department of Justice Press Release.* FBI-Portland, Oregon, December 7, 2010*)*

Police-Involved Insurance Scam Gang—A Philadelphia Highway Patrol Officer and a tow truck driver solicited people to be involved in staged or completely fictitious accidents to defraud insurance companies of more than $450,000. (*FBI-Philadelphia Division Press Release,* April 21, 2011*)*

Health Care Fraud Gang—A total of 21 individuals were arrested in Detroit for a $14.5 million Home Health Care Fraud scheme. Those arrested owned and operated home health care agencies that were to provide private home health therapy services to Medicare beneficiaries. The services provided were unnecessary and/or were never performed. (*FBI-Detroit Division Press Release,* December 7, 2010)

Federal Grant Money Fraud Gang—An elementary school superintendent and two San Diego State Imperial Valley college professors were charged with fraud in the use of federal grant money from the National Science Foundation and the U.S. Department of Education. (*Department of Justice Press Release.* FBI-San Diego Division November 30, 2010)

Police Gang and Citizen Conspiracy—Three Prince George county police officers and six other defendants were charged with corruption, drug trafficking and firearms violations. Maryland liquor store-owners paid the police officers to insure the safe transport and distribution of untaxed cigarettes and alcohol. A second indictment charged that police officers and citizens were involved in a conspiracy to distribute cocaine and firearms. (*FBI-Baltimore Division Press Release,* November 15, 2010)

Police Gang Escorting Drugs—Two Laredo, Texas police officers conspired with drug traffickers to escort cocaine-loaded vehicles through Laredo. (*Department of Justice Press Release. Southern District of Texas,* April 11, 2011)

Illegal Sports Bookmaking Gang—A University of San Diego assistant basketball coach and two former players were indicted for bribery, illegal bookmaking, and drug distribution. Allegedly, one of the players indicted took a bribe to influence the result of a game and solicited another player to affect the outcome of USD basketball games. The group is also charged with managing sports books, collecting outstanding gambling debts, and distributing marijuana. (*Department of Justice Press Release. Southern District of California,* April 11, 2011)

NYPD Officer Member of Drug Dealer Robber Gang—An eight-year veteran NYPD officer was arrested and accused of being part of gang that committed more than 100 robberies of drug dealers. The robbery crew included four in-laws of the officers. The officer supplied the robbery gang with N.Y.P.D. raid jackets, badges, bullet-resistant vests, and handcuffs. (Sulzeberger, A. G. & Baker, A. (May 6, 2010). "Police Officer Accused of Helping Gang Rob Drug Dealers." *New York Times)*

Texas Department of Public Safety (DPS) Employee Part of Gang Selling Driver's Licenses—The DPS employee and four co-conspirators pled guilty to unlawfully providing Texas driver's licenses for cash. (*Department of Justice Press Release. Southern District of Texas,* May 6, 2011)

IV. Selected Examples of Organized Criminal Gangs

(Extended supporting networks, organization, and long histories)

Drug Trafficking Organizations

Berly Drug Trafficking Organization (DTO)—Following an 18-month investigation by a combined task force composed of federal, state, and local law enforcement agencies, eight people were arrested for operating a DTO in Nashville, Tennessee. The DTO, known as the Berly DTO, was running cocaine and marijuana from Mexico through Ontario, California to the final destination of stash houses in Tennessee. They were using 18-wheeler trucks and reportedly were delivering a 100 pounds of pure heroin into Nashville every month. (Bellinger, M., "Police Bust Cocaine Ring in Nashville." *NewsChannel5.com,* February 1, 2011)

Khat Drug Trafficking Organization—Eighteen naturalized U.S. citizens from Somalia were arrested in May 2011 for being involved in an international Khat trafficking conspiracy. Khat is a flowering plant native to tropical east Africa, Somalia, Yemen, and the Arabian Peninsula, with leaves that contain the drug cathinone, an addictive stimulant with effects similar to but less intense than methamphetamine or cocaine. The FBI alleges that the Khat DTO used human couriers to transport Khat into the United States from England, Canada, and Holland. The drug would then be distributed via couriers and the postal system to at least 15 states, including California, Washington, Tennessee, New York, and the Washington, D.C.-metro area. The proceeds from the drug sales would be transmitted to others in England, Kenya, Somalia, and Uganda. (*FBI-Washington Field Office Press Release,* May 19, 2011)

Toledo Drug Trafficking Organization—In May 2011, 20 Toledo, Ohio individuals were indicted for bringing at least 20 kilograms of heroin from Mexico and California to be distributed in Toledo. The drugs once brought to Toledo were supplied to mid-level distributors for sale. (*FBI-Cleveland Division Press Release,* May 10, 2011)

Baltimore Drug Trafficking Organization—In February 2011, two defendants were convicted of conspiring to distribute and possessing to distribute marijuana, and cocaine. The defendants were involved in a DTO that received marijuana, heroin, and/or cocaine from the Gulf and Los Zetas Mexican drug cartels, which they distributed on the east side of Baltimore, Maryland. (*Department of Justice Press Release. District of Maryland,* February 8, 2011)

Street Gangs

Los Angeles-Based or Influenced Street Gangs

Crips (National African American Street Gang)

San Diego, California—Thirty-eight members of three Crip gang sets—Insane Crip Gang, Deep Valley Crips, and Crook, Mob, Gangsters—and a Limited Liability Company (LLC) were charged with "using a corrupt enterprise to conduct a pattern of racketeering activity, namely prostitution of minors and adults, use of facilities of interstate commerce to promote prostitution, drug trafficking and other gang-related crimes." The racketeering enterprise had been in existence for at least six years when the arrests were made. (*Department of Justice. Southern District of California Press Release*, April 18, 2011)

Los Angeles, California—Two Crip leaders—Alphonso E. Foster, age 41, and leader of the Grape Street Crips and Kim V. Walker, age 47, a leader of the Santana Block Crips—were sentenced to life in prison without parole for their roles in a PCP distribution conspiracy that distributed PCP throughout South Los Angeles and the East Coast. Foster and Walker had opened a graffiti removal business in San Bernardino as a front to obtain the precursor chemicals necessary to produce PCP. Ten other Crip members were convicted in the conspiracy and received sentences of 4 to 25 years. (*Department of Justice. Central District of California Press Release*, February 4, 2011)

Salt Lake City, Utah—Seventeen members of the Tongan Crip Gang, also known as TCG, were charged in a 29-count federal indictment that alleges that the gang is a criminal organization engaged in acts of violence to enhance the gang's prestige and to protect and expand the gang's operation. The indictment alleges that TCG is a multigenerational street gang that has terrorized neighborhoods in the Salt Lake Valley for years through robberies, shootings, and violent assaults. (*Department of Justice. District of Utah Press Release*, May 12, 2011)

Nashville, Tennessee—Jamal Shakir, 34, a member of the Rollin 60s Crips based in Los Angeles was sentenced to 16 life sentences to be followed by an additional nine consecutive life sentences for nine murders resulting from him being the "kingpin" of an interstate drug trafficking operation which operated in Los Angeles, Nashville, Memphis, Oklahoma City, and other cities. (*Department of Justice. Middle District of Tennessee Press Release*, December 7, 2009)

Bloods (National African American Street Gang)

Los Angeles, California—Operation Red Dawn was executed by federal state and local law enforcement agencies in May 2011 against the Black P. Stones (BPS) street gang, a set of the Bloods street gang. Seventy-five members and associates of the gang were arrested. Twenty-one members ranging in age from 25 to 59 were arrested for federal statutes related to possession and conspiracy to possess and distribute methamphetamine and crack cocaine. (*FBI-Los Angeles Division Press Release*, May 16, 2011)

Santa Maria, California—A multi-agency task force (federal, county, local) arrested nine members ranging in age from 23 to 51 of two Central Coast street gangs—Six Deuce Brims Bloods and the Northwest (Santa Marie) street gang. The Northwest Street

Gang is the largest Hispanic street gang on the Central Coast and is affiliated with the Mexican Mafia Prison Gang. [An unusual criminal conspiracy between a black and Hispanic street gang.] The defendants were arrested on a variety of federal and state charges related to narcotics trafficking, firearms sales, and violent crimes in the communities. (*FBI-Los Angeles Division Press Release,* May 3, 2011)

Brooklyn, New York—Nine members of the Nine-Trey Gangsters, also known as the Bugout Boyz, a set of the Bloods ranging in age from 21 to 33, were indicted for racketeering, murder, drug distribution, and firearms offenses. All of the defendants were charged with conspiracy to distribute cocaine and heroin. The investigation revealed that the gang operated for at least 12 years on Sterling Place in the Crown Heights neighborhood of Brooklyn, where they controlled four apartment buildings that they used as a focal point for crack cocaine and heroin dealing. (*FBI-New York Field Office Press Release,* August 25, 2010)

Nashville, Tennessee—Twenty-six Bloods were indicted under the RICO (Racketeer Influenced and Corrupt Organizations) Act . The charges included conspiracy to distribute, and possessession with intent to distribute, crack cocaine, cocaine, hydromorphone, and marijuana. One of those indicted was the father of an indicted Blood member. The father was the co-founder of the Galaxy Star Drug Awareness and Gang Prevention Center located in Nashville. He allowed the Bloods to use his facility to conduct gang meetings, and he and another Galaxy Star employee provided gang members with fraudulent documentation of court-ordered community service hours in exchange for money. (*Department of Justice. District of Tennessee Press Release,* June 24, 2010)

Baltimore, Maryland—In an unusual twist to street gang prosecutions, a female member and leader of the Tree Top Piru Bloods (TTP) was sentenced to 30 years in prison for the murder of a victim who was wearing the wrong gang colors. Michelle Hebron a.k.a. Michelle Hell, age 25, testified that she was a member of the TTP and regularly met with other gang members to discuss gang business and helped the gang spread throughout Maryland. (*Department of Justice. District of Maryland Press Release,* June 23, 2010)

Mara Salvatrucha, "MS 13" (National and International Hispanic Street Gang)

Flushing, New York—The leader of the New York state chapters of MS 13 street gangs and the leader of the Huntington, New York chapter of MS 13 were convicted of murder in aid of racketeering for the killing of a suspected member of the Bloods street gang. The two MS 13 members were driving through the streets of Flushing, New York looking for rival gang members to kill when they spotted their victim standing outside a store with a friend. The victim was wearing a red sweatshirt, the color of their bitter rival the Bloods. The two MS 13 members exited their car and ran up and shot the victim, who was not a gang member, three times in the head, killing him. MS 13 is the largest street gang on Long Island and has a chapter in Queens. In the past two years the U.S. Attorney's Office for the Eastern District of New York has obtained convictions for 100 MS 13 members and ten clique leaders. (*FBI-New York Field Office Press Release,* March 14, 2011)

Columbia, South Carolina—Two members of MS 13, illegal aliens living in Houston, Texas were hired by an individual in Honduras to kill a man living in West Columbia, S.C. The two gang members drove the thousand miles from Houston to Columbia and executed the victim and drove back to Houston. Two weeks later the Houston police arrested one of the shooters, who still had the murder weapon in his possession. The two gang members were illegal aliens who had been deported before, one six times. They were convicted of murder for hire, illegally possessing a firearm as an illegal alien, and illegally re-entering the United States after being deported. (*FBI-Columbia Division Press Release,* February 11, 2011)

Washington, D.C.—Two MS 13 members were sentenced to life in prison for conspiracy to participate in a racketeering enterprise, conspiracy to and committing murder in aid of racketeering, witness tampering, murder, and assault with a dangerous weapon in aid of racketeering. One of those convicted, Juan Carlos Moreira, a native of El Salvador, resided in Silver Springs, Maryland. He was the leader of the Sailor Locos Salvatruchos Westside (SLSW) clique of Mara Salvatrucha. Moreira was born in El Salvador where he was "jumped in" to the SLSW clique. In 1998, Moreira and four others entered the United States illegally. In 2000, Moreira founded the SLSW clique in Maryland. His duties as leader of the "First Word" of the Maryland SLSW clique included leading clique meetings, representing the clique at general and regional meetings, and collecting dues. (*FBI-Baltimore Division Press Release,* September 14, 2010)

Charlotte, North Carolina—The first MS 13 member to receive the death penalty for murder in aid of a racketeering offense was Alejando Enrique Ramirez Umana, age 25, an illegal alien who came to Charlotte to assist in reorganizing the Charlotte MS 13 clique. Umana killed two brothers in a Greensboro, N.C., for disrespecting the gang by calling their gang signs "fake." The investigation of MS 13 after the two murders resulted in 24 convictions of 24 members of the Charlotte clique. (*FBI-Charlotte Division Press Release,* July 27, 2010)

Atlanta, Georgia—Twenty-six members of MS 13, ranging in age from 19 to 30, were named in a 29-count indictment that alleged that the defendants conspired to participate in the affairs "of MS 13, an international violent criminal organization with approximately 10,000 members in various nations in North America, through a pattern of racketeering activity, which included multiple crimes of murder, attempted murder, kidnapping, and robbery in metropolitan Atlanta." The indictment stated that MS 13 has been in Atlanta since at least 2005 and has staked out Gwinnett and DeKalb Counties as its territory. (*FBI-Atlanta Division Press Release,* March 04, 2010)

Los Angeles, California—In June 2009, the first indictment in Los Angeles against MS 13, led to the indictment of 24 MS 13 members, ranging in age from 20 to 40. The defendants were charged with participating in a racketeering conspiracy that included murder, conspiracy to commit murder, extortion, robbery, narcotics trafficking, and witness intimidation over a period of 15 years. The indictment also charged Alex Sanchez, a former member of MS 13 and anti-gang crusader, who at the time of the indictment was Executive Director of "Homies Unidos," with racketeering offenses, including murder. Homies Unidos was a non-profit organization that supposedly used public and private contributions for gang intervention efforts. (*FBI-Los Angeles Division Press Release,* June 24, 2009)

18th Street Gang (National and International Hispanic Gang)

Greenbelt, Maryland—Seven members of the 18th Street Gang, ranging in age from 20 to 35, were indicted for a RICO conspiracy to participate in a racketeering enterprise which engaged in murder and attempted murder, including the murder of three individuals in Maryland and two individuals in Washington, D.C., armed robberies, and obstruction of justice. The indictment alleges that the national and international violent street gang is divided into subsets called cliques, including the Shatto Park Locos, Hollywood Locos, and Hoover Locos. Eighteenth Street members operate according to certain rules, which include: to attack and kill persons suspected of belonging to rival gangs; to remain loyal to the gang; and to not cooperate with law enforcement when they are investigating gang members. The rules are enforced by punishments by the gang that include a physical beating known as a "36" (beating for 36 seconds). Serious transgressions result in the murder of the gang member. *(FBI-Baltimore Division Press Release,* October 20, 2010)

Los Angeles, California—A combined task force of federal, state and local law enforcement agencies arrested 27 members of the 18th Street Gang on June 25, 2009. The indictment alleges that the 18th Street Gang is one of the oldest, largest, and most heavily entrenched gangs in Southern California. The gang is divided into cliques that have spread coast to coast. The indictment alleges that the gang traffics in narcotics and firearms and engages in murder, assault, robbery, illegal gambling, and prostitution. The criminal activities often take place at illegal after-hours clubs known as "casitas." The casitas are often located in residential neighborhoods where the gang members use intimidation to keep area members from notifying authorities. (*Bureau of Alcohol, Tobacco, Firearms, and Explosives. Los Angeles Field Division. ATF Press Release,* June 25, 2009)

Los Angeles, California—Thirty-nine members and associates of the 18th Street Gang were indicted for operating a racketeering enterprise responsible for the October 2007 attempted murder of a street vendor near McArthur Park that resulted in the fatal shooting of a 3-week-old infant. They were also charged with participating in a racketeering conspiracy that involved acts of violence, narcotics distribution, money laundering, and violent crimes in aid of racketeering. The 39 defendants were members and associates of the Columbia Lil Cycos (CLCS) set. It is alleged that the lead defendant was the Shot Caller of the CLCS, which is controlled by a Mexican Mafia member serving a life-without-parole sentence at the federal supermax prison in Florence, Colorado. The CLCS charged narcotics dealers in their territory "rent" (a percentage of their illegal profits) to sell drugs and for protection. Street vendors were also charged "rent." A criminal defense attorney was indicted for laundering the illegal proceeds of the CLCS and transferring approximately $27,500 into the Mexican Mafia member's prison account. According to the indictment, the defense attorney and the Mexican Mafia member were partners in several businesses, including a limousine service, a liquor distributor, and a real estate holding corporation. The death of the 3-week-old infant was the result of the botched shooting of a street vendor who refused to pay the $50 rent. The Mexican Mafia was incensed over the infant's murder and ordered the murder of the 18th Street Gang member responsible. Eighteenth Street members took the shooter to Mexico on the pretext of hiding him from the police. Instead, his fellow gang members took him to a remote area and strangled him, but he survived. (*Department of Justice. Central District of California Press Release,* June 16, 2009.)

Avenues (Regional Hispanic Street Gang)

Highland Park, California—Between 1995 and 2001, the Avenues street gang of Highland Park began a crusade to drive African Americans out of their neighborhoods through intimidation, violence, and murder. The FBI field office in Los Angeles broke new ground when they investigated this Hispanic street gang for violations of federal hate crimes statutes and applied criminal laws that had only previously been used against white supremacists groups like the KKK. The FBI conducted numerous interviews of gang members both inside and outside of the California prison system and in Arizona, Illinois, Florida, and El Salvador. They were able to elicit the assistance and cooperation of actual gang members who revealed that the Avenues had a deep-rooted policy of assaulting and killing African Americans to terrify them into leaving the neighborhood. Additionally, dozens of African American victims, who were casual citizens or non-gang members gave statements to the FBI describing their violent encounters with the gang. The trial against the Avenues commenced on June 21, 2006 concerning the murder of three African American males, and dozens of violent assaults against other African Americans. On August 1, 2006, the federal jury reached guilty verdicts for all the defendants—Gilbert "Lucky" Saldana, Alejandro "Bird" Martinez, Fernando "Sneaky" Cazares, and Poririo "Dreamer" Avilia—on all counts. (*FBI. Facts and Figures, 2010–2011*)

Los Angeles, California—Eighty-eight members and associates of the Avenues street gang were indicted as part of a criminal enterprise that engaged in a host of criminal acts, including murders, attempted murders, narcotics trafficking, robberies, extortions, money laundering, and witness intimidation. Five of the gang members were charged with the murder of a Los Angeles County Sheriff's deputy. The indictment alleged that there were numerous conversations and meetings between Avenues members and incarcerated Mexican Mafia members where the two gangs discussed such things as the amount of "taxes" or "rent" the Avenues extorted from drug sellers would go to the Mexican Mafia. A selected portion of the "taxes" would be deposited into the Mexican Mafia member's prison bank accounts. The two gangs, a street gang and a prison gang, plotted to smuggle drugs and cell phones into California prisons and jails. (*Department of Justice. Central District of California Press Release,* September 22, 2009)

Varrio Hawaiian Gardens Gang (Local Hispanic Street Gang)

Los Angeles, California—Operation Knock Out was at the time the nation's largest ever action against gangs. Fourteen hundred federal, state, county, and local law enforcement officers entered the City of Hawaiian Gardens on May 21, 2009, searching for 147 defendants for a variety of federal RICO offenses. Fifty of those defendants were members and associates of the Varrio Hawaiian Gardens Gang. This multigenerational Hispanic gang had been terrorizing the City of Hawaiian Gardens, and been trafficking in drugs and committing violent crimes for over 50 years. Also included in the indictments were members and associates of the East Side Paramount, 18th

Street, Morton Town Stoners, Santanas, Carmelas, Varrio Grape Street Watts, and Compton T-Flats street gangs, as well as the Nazi Low Riders, a white supremacist prison gang. The investigation leading to the gang sweep began after the fatal shooting of a Los Angeles Sheriff's deputy, Jerry Ortiz, in 2005. Deputy Ortiz was killed while attempting to arrest a Hawaiian Gardens gang member who was a suspect in the shooting of an African American man. The shooter was arrested, convicted, and sentenced to death but the investigation into the gang continued. The Nazi Low Rider member arrested supplied methamphetamine and heroin to the Hawaiian gang. (*FBI-Los Angeles Division Press Release,* May 21, 2009; *Department of Justice. Central District of California Press Release,* July 8, 2009; and *FBI-Los Angeles Division Press Release,* January 10, 2011)

Chicago-Based or Influenced Street Gangs
Gangster Disciples (National African American Street Gang)

Racine, Wisconsin—Ten members of the Gangster Disciples street gang, ranging in age from 20 to 39, were charged with federal RICO offenses related to distribution of controlled substances and firearm offenses. This is part of a long-time law enforcement effort against the Racine Gangster Disciples that first formed in Racine in the 1990s. (*Department of Justice. Eastern District of Wisconsin Press Release,* January 26, 2011)

Seattle, Washington—Three members of the Deuce 8 set of the Black Gangster Disciples were sentenced for federal crimes. Thomas L. Callandret, 23, of Seattle was sentenced to three years in prison and three years of supervised release for possession of crack cocaine with intent to distribute. Dimitrius Tinsley, 21, of Seattle was sentenced to six years in prison and three years of supervised release for conspiracy to distribute BZP—a synthetic substance similar to Ecstasy (MDMA). Avery Roberto Scharer, 23, of Seattle, was a co-conspirator in the BZP distribution. He was sentenced to 18 months in prison and three years of supervised release. (*FBI-Western District of Washington Press Release,* January 15, 2010)

Chicago, Illinois—Eight Gangster Disciple members, ranging in age from 19 to 36 were arrested for federal and state drug and firearms trafficking around the Cabrini-Green housing project on Chicago's north side. (*FBI-Chicago Division Press Release,* June 16, 2010)

Little Rock, Arkansas—Antoine Demetris Baker, the governor of the Gangster Disciples in Southwest Little Rock, was sentenced to four concurrent life sentences without parole for ordering the murder of a witness who was going to testify in court against him and inform law enforcement officers of Baker's drug activities. (*Department of Justice. Eastern District of Arkansas Press Release,* October 15, 2009)

Minneapolis, Minnesota—A former Minneapolis police officer was sentenced to 12 months in prison for supplying restricted police information to a member of the Gangster Disciples for $100. The transaction took place in the former officer's police squad car while he was working an off-duty security job. The disgraced officer used the car's computer to obtain the information. (*Department of Justice Press Release. District of Minnesota Press Release,* September 22, 2009)

Vice Lords (National African American Street Gang)

Grand Rapids, Michigan—Nine gang members—eight Vice Lords and one Four Corner Hustler (a Vice Lords off-shoot)—ranging in age from 30 to 43, either pled guilty or were convicted at trial for 20 robberies in the greater Lansing area. They called themselves the "Fallen Angels" because the leader was connected to several others on a rap music label called "Fallen Angels Records." The robberies were committed to help fund their aspiring rap music careers. (*FBI-Detroit Division Press Release,* February 11, 2011)

Indianapolis, Indiana—Members of the Vice Lords of Gary, Indiana, moved to Indianapolis to establish a drug trafficking organizations. The enforcer for the gang, Michael Jackson, 30, was sentenced to 30 years for conspiracy to possess with intent to distribute crack cocaine, and cocaine. Wiretaps revealed that Jackson told the other members of the DTO that he would shoot rival drug dealers and their children. (*FBI-Indianapolis Division Press Release,* December 14, 2010)

Chicago, Illinois—A joint FBI/Chicago Police Department code named Operation Blue Knight led to the arrests of nearly 100 members and associates of the Traveling Vice Lords street gang. The gang ran around the clock retail sales of crack cocaine and heroin on Chicago's west side in an area known as KO. The operation stored packaged drugs in common areas and residences. "Runners" distributed the packaged drugs to "managers" who supervised the drug operation at KO. The managers distributed the drugs to "pack workers" who worked shifts selling the drugs to customers. The managers then collected the proceeds of the drug sales at KO. State charges were filed against 65 defendants, including four juveniles. Thirty-one defendants, ranging in age from 20 to 63, were charged with various narcotics distribution charges. (*FBI-Chicago Division Press Release,* November 27, 2010)

Nashville, Tennessee—Nine Vice Lord members were indicted for commission of violent crimes in furtherance of racketeering activity. The crimes they were charged with included murder, kidnapping, assault with a dangerous weapon, attempted murder, conspiracy to possess firearms in relation to violent crimes, the use and carrying of firearms in violent crimes, and conspiracy to distribute drugs. (*Department of Justice. Middle District of Tennessee Press Release,* October 27, 2009)

Latin Kings (National Hispanic Street Gang)

Hammond, Indiana—Six members of the southeast region of the Latin Kings, ranging in age from 23 to 44, were indicted for conspiracy to engage in racketeering activity and conspiracy to possess with intent to distribute cocaine and marijuana. The indictment alleged that the southeast region of the Latin Kings was responsible for at least 15 murders. (*Department of Justice Office of Public Relations Press Release,* April 20, 2011)

Chicago, Illinois—The highest-ranking national leader and three other high-ranking leaders of the Latin Kings were convicted of racketeering conspiracy and other charges involving narcotics trafficking and violence in numerous neighborhoods in Chicago's north, south, and west sides. Testimony at trial revealed that:

- The Latin Kings had its origins in Chicago's west side Little Village community and spread throughout Chicago and Illinois and established branches in other states.

- The Latin Kings has 10,000 members in Illinois alone.
- The hierarchy of the Latin Kings was organized as follows:
  Carona—The highest-ranking national leader and responsible for overseeing illegal activities of all factions of the street gang.
  Supreme Regional Inca—In charge of all Latin Kings in Illinois.
  Incas—Chapter leaders who acted with some autonomy but adhered to the rules and hierarchy of the Chicago gang.
- The Latin Kings extorted a "street tax" on non-gang members who engaged in criminal activities in their territory.
- Issued an "SOS"—shoot on sight or smash on sight—on anyone cooperating with law enforcement.
- Twice a month the proceeds from powdered cocaine funded a "Nation Box," a kitty by the regional hierarchy to purchase weapons and ammunition, and pay for funeral and attorney fees for gang members.
- Conducted the gang's affairs through a series of laws and policies, some of which were codified in a "constitution," as well as a "manifesto," and the 26 Street Rules (a three-page list of 26 rules establishing procedures for homicides, security, and the sale of counterfeit identification documents).
- Attended regular meetings, known as "demos" when held by Nation officers. At "nation demos" they discussed, planned, and otherwise engaged in criminal activity, including violent crimes, narcotics distribution, and obstruction of justice.
- Initiated members by causing them to endure physical assaults conducted by other members at various gang-related gatherings.
- Managed the procurement, transfer, use, concealment, and disposal of firearms and dangerous weapons to protect gang-related territory, personnel, and operations, and to deter, eliminate, and retaliate against competitors and other rival gangs and individuals. (*FBI-Chicago Division Press Release*, April 6, 2011)

Newburg, New York—Thirty-one members of the Newburg chapter of the Latin Kings were indicted for conspiracy to distribute narcotics and using, carrying, and possessing firearms during and in relation to the Newburg Latin Kings drug distribution conspiracy. Eleven of the defendants are charged with committing and attempting to commit violent acts, including murder as part of the Newburg Latin Kings criminal activities. The indictment alleged that the Newburg Latin Kings are governed by a council of five officers, referred to as crowns (collectively, Crown Council). The Crown Council wielded great power and directed punishment, known as "violations," against members who were determined to have committed transgressions. In some instances, the Crown Council used meetings to order attacks on individuals and rival gangs. (*FBI-New York Field Office Press Release,* February 10, 2010)

Long Island, New York—Thirteen members of the Huntington and Brentwood subset of the Long Island Latin Kings, were indicted for a series of violent gang-related activities, including conspiring to shoot members and associates of rival gangs—the Crips, Southside Posse, Zulu Nation, and MS 13—as well as other individuals who "disrespected" the Latin Kings. The investigation included a confidential informant who recorded conversations at gang meetings and with other Latin gang members. (*FBI-New York Field Office Press Release,* October 14, 2010)

Dallas, Texas—The leader of the Almighty Latin King and Queens Nation (ALKQN) in Texas and one of his enforcers were sentenced to life in prison for using a firearm to commit murder in relation to a drug trafficking crime and one count of a conspiracy to distribute and possess, with intention to distribute, cocaine and marijuana. The two counts of murder resulted from a drive-by shooting in Big Spring, Texas. Six people were shot with an AK-47, two died, including a female who was 26-weeks pregnant. In all, sixteen Latin Kings pled guilty to the drug conspiracy charges. (*FBI-Dallas Division. Press Release,* May 13, 2010)

Boston, Massachusetts—A leader of the Chelsea Latin Kings was sentenced to 25 years on charges of being a felon in possession of ammunition, assault on a federal officer, and discharging a firearm in connection with a crime of violence. The Latin King leader shot at two Chelsea police officers, one was also a Special Federal Officer working with the FBI's North Shore Gang Task Force. The gang member had three previous convictions for crimes of violence or drug trafficking, and therefore qualified as an Armed Career Criminal (ACC) under federal law. Federal law imposes a mandatory 15-year sentence on anyone who qualifies as an ACC and is convicted of being a felon in possession of a firearm or ammunition. Federal law also makes it a crime to assault a federal officer while he is engaged in official federal duties and imposes a mandatory 10-year sentence, on and after the other sentence, for discharging a firearm in connection with a crime of violence. (*FBI-Boston Division Press Release,* August 26, 2009)

Cleveland, Ohio—Thirty-four members and associates of the Cleveland Latin Kings were indicted in a DTO that distributed heroin, cocaine, and crack cocaine that extended from Cleveland to New York to the Dominican Republic and crossed all racial and ethnic lines. (*FBI-Cleveland Division Press Release,* August 13, 2009)

Prison Gangs

Black Guerilla Family (National Black Prison Gang)

Baltimore, Maryland—Four leaders of the Black Guerilla Family (BGF) pleaded guilty to a conspiracy to conduct and participate in the activities of the BGF, a racketeering enterprise. The BGF is a nationwide prison gang operating in prison facilities and major cities throughout the United States. The gang was founded in California in the 1960s and introduced into the Maryland correctional system in the mid-1990s. It is the largest prison gang in Maryland and has an active street presence in Baltimore City. BGF members arrange to have drugs, tobacco, cell phones, food, and other contraband smuggled into Maryland prison facilities. On occasion, the BGF recruits and pays employees of prison facilities, including corrections officers, to assist BGF members in the smuggling of contraband, the collection of intelligence, and in the concealment of BGF's criminal activities. BGF members use violence and threats of violence to coerce incarcerated persons to pay protection money to BGF, to enforce the BGF code of conduct, and to increase their control of the Baltimore City drug trade and the underground "prison economy" in Maryland correctional facilities. Intercepted phone conversations recorded one of the BGF leaders arranging a meeting of 100 BGF members at a city park in Baltimore as well as arranging for the smuggling of contraband into correctional facilities through the use of couriers and corrections employees. (*FBI-Baltimore Division Press Release,* May 02, 2011)

Baltimore, Maryland—A former correctional officer with the Maryland Department of Public Safety and Correctional Services was sentenced to six months in prison for her part in the extortion of money from the mother of an inmate in the DOC (Department of Corrections). The BGF member called the victim and said her son owed money for cigarettes, liquor, and gambling, and she needed to send money for her son's protection. She complied and then received increasing demands. The distraught mother sent 27 payments totaling $7,030 to addresses in Baltimore and six payments totaling $4,250 to the address of the former correctional officer before notifying the FBI. (*FBI-Baltimore Division Press Release,* August 18, 2009)

Mexican Mafia (Hispanic Prison Gang)

Los Angeles, California—Fifty-five members and associates of the 38th Street Gang were charged with RICO violations on behalf of the gang and participating in murders, murder plots, attempted murders, narcotics trafficking, robberies, extortion, and witness intimidation. The racketeering count alleges 250 overt acts, many of them violent crimes, including assaults on rival gang members and law enforcement officers. The 38th Street Gang, one of Southern California's oldest, is controlled by the Mexican Mafia prison gang. The Mexican Mafia demands "taxes" for the 38th Street Gang and gives authorization for the gang to engage in certain criminal acts, such as extortion and murder. Members of the 38th Street Gang allegedly extorted legitimate businesses, including vendors at the Alameda Swap Meet, with some of the money going to the Mexican Mafia. Gang members also allegedly distributed narcotics at the Swap Meet and taxed drug dealers to sell narcotics there. (*Department of Justice. U.S. Attorney's Office. Press Release,* February 1, 2011)

San Diego, California—Maurico Mendez, 37, was sentenced to 318 months for conspiracy to conduct enterprise affairs through a pattern of racketeering activity and brandishing a firearm during the commission of a crime. Mendez in pleading guilty admitted joining the Mexican Mafia prison gang and participating in robbery, kidnapping, extortion, and drug dealing. He also admitted to performing a home invasion robbery during which he brandished a firearm to prevent the occupants from fleeing. A multi-agency task force investigating San Diego Hispanic street gangs and their ties to the Mexican Mafia arrested him. (*Department of Justice. Southern District of California Press Release,* December 3, 2010)

Los Angeles, California—Twenty-one members and associates of the Chino Sinners street gang were indicted for the distribution of narcotics and weapons in the City of Chino. The indictment alleges that the Chino Sinners were affiliated with, and under the control of, the Mexican Mafia. The street gang members were bringing heroin into the state prison system for a Mexican Mafia member. The indictment alleges that the Mexican Mafia member sent messages from inside the California Institution for men in Chino to street gang members directing the importation of heroin and other controlled substances into the prison. (*FBI-Los Angeles Division Press Release,* June 16, 2010)

Los Angeles, California—Eight members of the Puente-13 street gang were indicted for federal RICO offenses charging that they engaged in federal racketeering and narcotics offenses. According to the indictment Puente-13 was formed in the City of La Puente approximately 60 years ago. Puente-13 is aligned with the Mexican Mafia, as indicated by the "13" in the gang's name and controlled by Mexican Mafia member Rafael Munoz Gonzales. (*U.S. Drug Enforcement Association Press Release,* June 9, 2010)

Riverside, California—Twenty members of a local Hispanic street gang, the Eastside Riva (ESR), were indicted for engaging in the trafficking of methamphetamine and other federal offenses that include hate crimes targeting African Americans. The ESR is controlled by the Mexican Mafia and pays "taxes" or "rent" to the prison gang. The 20-year-old local street gang has approximately 500 members and claims territory on the east side of the City of Riverside. The indictment alleges that ESR members use MySpace.com to communicate about gang business, and they use rap music videos and recordings to deliver messages of violence and intimidation. ESR is alleged to be hostile to the presence of African Americans in ESR territory, even if they are not affiliated with a gang. One of those indicted is a 45-year-old Mexican Mafia member, currently incarcerated on attempted murder charges, who allegedly issues directives to senior ESR members on topics including "tax" collections and drug distribution in ESR territory. (*FBI-Los Angeles Division Press Release,* January 27, 2010)

Los Angeles, California—Ten members of the Florencia 13 (F 13) street gang that controlled the unincorporated areas south of Los Angeles and certain areas such as Huntington Park were convicted of federal RICO offenses and shootings of African Americans. Testimony at trial revealed that F 13 was a criminal enterprise controlled by an incarcerated member of the Mexican Mafia and Mexican Mafia members on the street. Leaders of the F 13 collected taxes or "rent" from gang members and others who engaged in criminal activities in F 13 territory, in return for Mexican Mafia protection when they went to prison and jail. Testimony also revealed that F 13 indiscriminately targeted African Americans who were seen in their neighborhoods. (*FBI-Los Angeles Division Press Release,* January 12, 2009)

Nuestra Familia (Hispanic Prison Gang)

Sacramento, California—Four Nuestra Familia (NF) members were sentenced to prison (25 years; 33 years, four months; 36 years, eight months; and 40 years) in 2001 for running a long-term drug conspiracy (2004 through 2007) for the Nuestra Familia prison gang. They were part of 22 defendants arrested in 2007 as a result of federally funded, multi-year, multi-jurisdictional investigation of the Nuestra Familia prison gang's street operations that spanned 15 cities, five counties, three states (Ohio, Utah, and Hawaii), and Mexico. One of those convicted acted as a channel between the gang's street regiment and leaders in Pelican Bay State Prison, the headquarters of the Nuestra Familia. (*Department of Justice. Eastern District of California Press Release,* May 25, 2011)

Sacramento, California—Eight members or associates of the Nuestra Familia pleaded guilty to conspiracy to distribute methamphetamine and cocaine. Testimony revealed that NF exerted control over street-level Norteno gang members engaged in drug trafficking and violent crime. NF members and their associates were responsible for the

distribution of large amounts of illegal controlled substances, including methamphetamine, cocaine, marijuana, and Ecstacy throughout the Eastern and Northern Districts
of California with supply lines from Mexico and distribution channels throughout the
United States. (*Department of Justice. Eastern District of California Press Release*, March
28, 2011)

Fresno, California—Thirty-six members and associates of the Nuestra Familia were
indicted for conspiracy to distribute methamphetamine and cocaine in the California
counties of Kings, Fresno, Kern, Tulare, Monterey, Stanislaus, Merced, Sacramento,
and Madera. (*Department of Justice. Eastern District of California Press Release*, August
31, 2010)

Sacramento, California—A Stockton, California member of the Nuestra Familia
was sentenced to 20 years after his conviction for engaging in a large-scale cocaine,
methamphetamine, and marijuana conspiracy. The criminal enterprise was the Mario
Diaz Drug Trafficking Organization (DIAZ DTO) that distributed large amounts of illegal controlled substances, including methamphetamine, cocaine, marijuana, and Ecstasy throughout the Eastern and Northern Districts of California with supply lines
from Mexico and distribution channels reaching to U.S. cities, including Warren, Ohio
and Atlanta, Georgia. The DTO used a Mazda Millennium equipped with a hidden
compartment that was designed to conceal large quantities of controlled substances
and transport drug proceeds while avoiding law enforcement detection. (*Department
of Justice. Eastern District of California Press Release*, May 17, 2010)

Texas Mexican Mafia (Hispanic Prison Gang)

San Antonio, Texas—Three members of the Texas Mexican Mafia (TMM) were
found guilty of conspiring to violate the federal RICO statute. Specifically, the TMM
members committed 22 murders, robbery, and extortion, plus distributed heroin
and cocaine. (*Department of Justice. Western District of Texas Press Release*, May 20,
2010)

Lubbock, Texas—Two high-ranking TMM members in command of the Texas Mexican Mafia in San Angelo and Abilene, Texas pleaded guilty and were sentenced to
lengthy prison sentences. One, who held the ranks of captain and lieutenant who was
responsible for managing the TMM's distribution of methamphetamine in San Angelo,
Abilene, and throughout North Texas received 120 months in prison. The other, second in command, was sentenced to 210 months in prison for for distribution and possession with intent to distribute methamphetamine. They were two of the 15 members
and associates of the Texas Mexican Mafia who were indicted for the operation of major
methamphetamine trafficking operation. All 15 defendants pleaded guilty. (*Department of Justice. Western District of Texas Press Release*, May 20, 2010)

Texas Syndicate (Hispanic Prison Gang)

McAllen, Texas—Three members of the Texas Syndicate (TS) prison gang were sentenced to life imprisonment for committing violent crimes in aid of racketeering
(VICAR). One of the murders they committed was of a fellow TS member who did

not kill a rival gang member he was ordered to kill. (*Department of Justice. Southern District of Texas Press Release,* January 6, 2011)

Dallas, Texas—Twenty-one members and associates of the Texas Syndicate were sentenced to lengthy prison terms for their part in a conspiracy to distribute and possess to distribute cocaine. The cocaine was imported into the U.S. on military transport flights from Columbia to Ft. Bliss, Texas. The drugs were trafficked from south Texas and Mexico to Dallas and Decatur, Illinois. (*Department of Justice. Northern District of Texas Press Release,* February 5, 2007)

Barrio Azteca (Hispanic Prison Gang and Transnational Criminal Organization)

El Paso, Texas—Thirty-five members of the Barrio Azteca (BA) prison gang and transnational criminal organization were arrested and charged with a variety of federal racketeering charges including kidnapping, extortion, drug distribution, and murder. Twelve of those arrested were charged with the 2010 slayings of a U.S. Consulate employee, her husband and the husband of another U.S. Consulate employee in Juarez, Mexico. (*FBI-El Paso Division Press Release,* March 09, 2011)

Raza Unita (Hispanic Prison Gang)

Corpus Christy, Texas—Three current or former jailers and two members of the Raza Unita prison gang were charged with conspiracy to bribe public officials. The jailers were charged with smuggling cell phones into jail facilities. (*Immigration and Customs Enforcement Press Release,* April 21, 2011)

Houston, Texas—Fifteen members and associates of the Raza Unita (RA) prison and street gang were indicted for trafficking cocaine and methamphetamine and possessing firearms unlawfully and during the commission of drug trafficking offenses. (*FBI-Houston Division Press Release,* April 23, 2009)

Los Hermanos de Pistoleros (HPL) (Hispanic Prison Gang)

Houston, Texas—A leader of the Los Hermanos de Pistoleros prison and street gang was sentenced to 300 months in prison for his part in a conspiracy to possess with intent to distribute cocaine and laundering millions of dollars in drug proceeds together with 23 other HPL members and associates. The HPL leader also forfeited eight real estate properties, multiple high-end vehicles, numerous pieces of expensive jewelry, and $4.5 million dollars in cash. The HPL members and associates smuggled cocaine into the U.S. from Mexico, stored the contraband in Laredo and Houston stash houses and transported and distributed the cocaine to HPL members and associates in Texas. (*FBI-Houston Division Press Release,* September 28, 2009)

McAllen, Texas—An HPL leader was sentenced to life imprisonment without parole for conspiracy to possess with intent to distribute cocaine. His conviction and the conviction of 14 other HPL members and associates arose from an investigation into a series of home invasions and carjackings by the defendants to obtain cocaine and methamphetamine. The gang was selling the drugs they stole. (*Drug Enforcement Administration News Release*, August 26, 2008)

Aryan Brotherhood (White Supremacist Prison Gang)

Los Angeles, California—In 2006, two Aryan Brotherhood (AB) leaders were sentenced to life imprisonment without parole [the two leaders were already serving life without parole sentences, but the jury could not unanimously agree on the death penalty] for ordering a white-on-black race war that led to the death of two inmates in a Pennsylvania prison. The six-month trial that led to their conviction and sentence was the result of a 110-page indictment unsealed in October 2002 containing racketeering charges alleging a series of murders and violent attacks designed to preserve the power of the white, prison-based criminal enterprise. The indictment alleged that AB members had committed 16 murders and 16 attempted murders in an effort to control drug trafficking, gambling, and extortion in the prison systems. Thirty-six AB members were convicted of a variety of RICO offenses. (*Department of Justice. Central District of California Press Release*, September 15, 2006)

Albuquerque, New Mexico—A member of the Aryan Brotherhood was sentenced to 150 months in prison for committing violent crimes in aid of racketeering. He conspired to commit murder in order to gain entrance to and maintain and increase his position in the Aryan Brotherhood in New Mexico. (*FBI-Albuquerque Division Press Release*, March 24, 2011; *U.S. v Benjamin Raymond a/k/a/ "Big Ben." Criminal No. 07-748 MCA.*)

Beaumont, Texas—Two members of the Aryan Brotherhood of Texas (ABT) were charged with violent crimes in aid of racketeering (shooting a man). According to the indictment, the ABT was established in the early 1980s within the Texas prison system and is modeled after the Aryan Brotherhood established in 1964 in California. (*Department of Justice. Eastern District of Texas Press Release*, March 31, 2011; *U.S. v. Bodine & Manning. No. 1:11 CR 37*)

Outlaw Motorcycle Gangs (OMG)

Hells Angels MC (National and International OMG)

Rochester, New York—The vice-president and sergeant-at-arms of the Rochester Hells Angels (HA) were charged with assault with a dangerous weapon in aid of racketeering for beating a man with a baseball bat for allegedly threatening the HAMC. The indictment states that the Rochester HA is a criminal organization whose members function as a continuing unit (enterprise) for the purpose of facilitating criminal activity, including narcotics trafficking and murder. (*Department of Justice. Western District of New York Press Release*, April 29, 2011)

Denver, Colorado—On July 28, 2010, Gunnison County law enforcement officers encountered 15 to 20 Hells Angels partially driving eastbound in the westbound lane. They were stopped and the police found a .44 caliber revolver in the waistband of an HA vice-president. He was charged with being a felon in possession of a firearm. (*U.S. Attorney's Office Press Release*, August 30, 2010)

Paducah, Kentucky—The President of the Fulton County Kentucky Chapter of the Hells Angels pleaded guilty to distributing methamphetamine in the Western District of Kentucky. The Hells Angels president sold the amphetamine to a person working undercover for the Kentucky State Police and the U.S. Drug Enforcement Administration. (*U.S. Drug Administration Press Release*, December 17, 2009)

Las Vegas, Nevada—In October 11, 2006, the plea negotiations stemming from the violent fight between the Hells Angels and the Mongols MC in Harrah's Casino and Hotel in Laughlin, Nevada on April 27, 2002, came to a close. The violent altercation left three dead and 16 injured. The Hells Angels were charged with operating as part of a racketeering enterprise pursuant to a conspiracy and causing the violent assaults. There were six Hells Angels members who entered pleas. (*Department of Justice. District of Nevada Press Release*, October 11, 2006)

Outlaws MC (National and International OMG)

Washington, D.C.—The national president of the American Outlaw Association (Outlaws) motorcycle gang was sentenced to 20 years in prison for leading a violent criminal organization. The Outlaws' national president oversees a highly organized criminal enterprise with a defined, multi-level chain of command. As national president, the defendant declared war on the Hells Angels and ordered violent acts on rival gang members. At trial he was convicted of conspiracy to commit racketeering and violent acts. There were 24 Outlaw and three Pagan members charged in the original indictment; thus far, 20 have pled guilty or were convicted at trial. The 24 Outlaw members, including numerous leaders, came from multiple states—Wisconsin, Maine, Montana, North Carolina, Tennessee, South Carolina, and Virginia. The three Pagan members came from Virginia. Court records indicated that the Outlaws planned and executed violence against several rival motorcycle gangs. In one incident the Pagans OMG joined the Outlaws in an assault against rival gangs. During a charitable event known as the Flood Run, Outlaw members brutally beat Hells Angels members and stole their patches or colors. Court testimony also revealed that the Outlaws regularly distributed narcotics and used firearms or other dangerous weapons. (*Department of Justice Press Release*, April 8, 2011; *FBI-Washington Field Office Press Release*, June 15, 2010)

Washington, D.C.—Fourteen members of the Outlaws Motorcycle Gang pleaded guilty in Detroit, Michigan to charges including violent crimes in aid of racketeering, illegal drug distribution and firearms violations. The defendants were Outlaw leaders, members and associates from Outlaw chapters in Fort Wayne, Indiana and Indianapolis, as well as areas of Detroit including Eastside, Detroit Westside, Downriver, and Bay City. Several of the defendants were charged with assaulting members of the Hells Angels. (*Department of Justice Press Release*, July 30, 2009)

United States Marshals' Service—Randy Mark Yager, the regional president of the Outlaws Motorcycle Gang was placed on the U.S. Marshals' list of 15 "most wanted" fugitives. He was one of 17 Outlaw members indicted by a Wisconsin federal grand jury in June 1997 for violations of the RICO statutes. The offenses included murder, arson, possession and use of explosives, possession and trafficking in counterfeit U.S. currency, robbery, burglary, trafficking in stolen motor vehicles, and narcotics violations. (*U.S. Marshals' Service Press Release*, December 17, 2004)

Bandidos MC (National and International OMG)

Lubbock, Texas—Twenty-eight defendants were indicted in 2009 for operating a major methamphetamine trafficking organization in west Texas, Arizona, and in the Modesto, California area. Among the 28 defendants were the president and founder of the Aces and Eights OMG, a support club for the Bandidos OMG, a Nomad Bandidos member and two Hockley County Sheriff's deputies. The president of the Aces and Eights OMG and the Bandidos members put up the cash and recruited other members of the conspiracy, often other members of the Aces and Eights MC, to go to Modesto to purchase large quantities of methamphetamine and then transport the meth to Levelland, Texas. The Aces and Eights president and the Bandido member would distribute it throughout the South Plains area of Texas for sale. The two Hockley County deputy sheriffs gave the conspirators sensitive law enforcement information and deterred other law enforcement officers from investigating the DTO. (*FBI-Dallas Division Press Release*, February 12, 2010; *FBI-Dallas Division Press Release*, July 10, 2009; *Department of Justice. Northern District of Texas Press Release*, November 5, 2009)

Bellingham, Washington—The 65-year-old president of the Bellingham Chapter of the Bandidos OMG was sentenced to four years in prison for conspiracy to violate RICO statutes. The Bandido leader sold methamphetamine and marijuana to an undercover informant on four occasions and sold guns to the informant on one occasion. (*U.S. Attorney's Office. Western District of Washington Press Release*, November 17, 2006)

Whatcom County, Washington—The national president of the Bandidos OMG was sentenced to 20 months in prison, three years of supervised release and a $10,000 fine for RICO conspiracy. The Bandido leader had to move out of Whatcom County, Washington during his supervised release. The Bandido leader sanctioned and approved of the criminal acts of gang members. He admitted to encouraging his 17 co-defendants to commit the crimes of witness tampering and motor vehicle trafficking. All 18 defendants, Bandido members and associates, have pleaded guilty. Those who pleaded guilty included a Bandido national president, the Bellingham chapter president, the national regional secretary, national sergeant-at-arms, Bellingham Chapter secretary treasurer, and the Missoula, Montana chapter president. (*U.S. Attorney's Office. Western District of Washington Press Release*, October 6, 2006; *U.S. Attorney's Office. Western District of Washington Press Release*, June 10, 2005)

Pagans MC (Regional OMG)

New York—Seventeen members and associates of the Pagans MC (PMC) were indicted for murder conspiracy, violent crimes in aid of racketeering, drug distribution, firearms offenses and witness tampering. According to the indictment, two defendants were at one time president of the Long Island Pagans chapter and one was a member of the Pagans national governing body known as the "Mother Club." At one point Pagan members engaged in a conspiracy to use grenades to kill members and associates of the

Hells Angels. Members and associates, according to the indictment, conspired to distribute cocaine, and used, carried, and possessed firearms in furtherance of their trafficking crimes. (*U.S. Attorney Southern District of New York Press Release*, September 15, 2010)

Charleston, West Virginia—Fifty-five Pagan members and associates were indicted for kidnapping, racketeering, robbery, extortion, and conspiracy to commit murder. The indicted Pagans came from chapters in West Virginia, Kentucky, Virginia, Pennsylvania, New York, New Jersey, Delaware, and Florida. There were five Pagan officers indicted, including the national president and the national vice-president. The charges included an allegation that the Pagan national vice-president and other members conspired with a prison guard to kill an inmate suspected of cooperating with law enforcement. (*Department of Justice. Southern District of West Virginia Press Release*, October 6, 2009; *U.S. District Court For the Southern District of West Virginia. Charleston Grand Jury 2008. September 29, 2009 Session.*)

A Word of Caution

Making estimates about the number of gangs, chapters of gangs and gang membership is an inexact science. Criminal gangs—street, prison, or outlaw motorcycle gangs—do not maintain accurate records or detailed information on members for obvious reasons. Therefore, at times throughout the book there may be divergent or contradictory estimates of gangs, chapter of gangs, or members of gangs by different agencies or individuals.

References

Gordon, R. M. (2000). Criminal business organizations, street gangs, and "wanna-be" groups: A Vancouver perspective. *Canadian Journal of Criminology.* January:39–60.

Klein, M. W. (2005). The value of comparisons in street gang research. *Journal of Contemporary Research.* 21(2):135–152.

National Gang Threat Assessment: Emerging Trends-2011 (2011). *National Gang Intelligence Center.* GPO.

Rafael, T. (2007). *The Mexican Mafia.* New York: Encounter Books.

Thrasher, F. (1963). *The Gang: A Study of 1,313 Gangs in Chicago.* Chicago: University of Chicago Press.

Venkatesh, S. A. & Levitt, S. D. (2000). "Are we a family or a business?" History and disjuncture in the urban American street gang. *Theory & Society.* 29(4):427–463.

Chapter 2

Street Gangs

I. Street Gangs—
An Introduction

Although every large urban U.S. city has a gang problem, Los Angeles and Chicago are recognized as the most prominent American street gang cities. The major street gangs, particularly those alluded to as "super gangs," are either based in these two cities or were founded or started in these two cities. Therefore, the major U.S. street gangs can be categorized as Chicago-based/influenced or Los Angeles-based/influenced. Furthermore, the majority of the gangs in these cities have divided themselves into alliances or loose confederations.

In California, the Hispanic gangs divided themselves into Surenos (southerners) and Nortenos (northerners) based on allegiance to the Hispanic prison gangs the Mexican Mafia or the Nuestra Familia. In Chicago, the alliances are not restricted to ethnic or racial distinctions only. According to the Chicago Crime Commission (CCC, 2006), in the mid-1970s the Latin, African American, and Caucasian gangs in Chicago merged into the "People" and the "Folks" nations or alliances. Those not merged into the People and Folks nations/alliances were referred to as Independents. Incarcerated members seeking protection formed the alliances in the penitentiary system and maintained them upon release. The People and Folks alliances became rivals and enemies and "represented" or identified themselves in several ways. The "People" gangs represented to the left, that is, wearing hats with visors to the left side; earrings in the left ear; the left shoe tied in a certain way; the left pant leg cuffed, etc. Gangs in the "Folks" alliance represented to the right side.

The Chicago Crime Commission identifies the seven largest street gangs in Chicago as the Gangster Disciple Nation (Gangster Disciples and Black Disciples), Black Gangsters or New Breeds, Latin Kings, Black P. Stone Nation, Vice Lords, Four Corner Hustlers, and Maniac Latin Disciples. U.S. Marshal Ed Farrell, opines "We [Chicago] have the biggest gang problem in the country. There are many more gang members per citizen than anywhere else in the country" (Thomas and Bass, October 8, 2009). The Chicago-based/influenced gangs are not solely a Chicago problem because in the 1970s and 1980s many of the gangs began moving outside Illinois and have now become a national problem.

II. Chicago-Based/Influenced Street Gangs

Folks Nations/Alliances

Black Gangster Disciples	Black Disciples
Gangster Disciples	Imperial Gangsters
La Raza	Spanish Cobras
Latin Eagles	Latin Disciples
Maniac Latin Disciples	Simon City Royals
Spanish Gangster Disciples	Two Sixters
International Posse	

People Nations/Alliances

Black P. Stone	El Rukns
Gaylords	Latin Counts
Kents	Vice Lords
Spanish Lords	Bishops
Latin Kings	Mickey Cobras

Gangster Disciple Nation (National Street Gang —Alliance: Folks)

 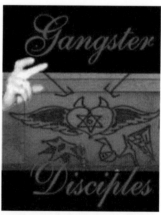

Source: The Department of Justice (www.justice.gov/criminal/ocgs/gangs/street.html).

Symbols and Identifiers—the six-point star, a common identifier of all gangs in the Folk nation; the numeral "6" or three "6" numerals in a triangle form, pitchforks, heart with wings, a tail and horns, a three-point crown, numerals "74" or "274" signifying "GD" or "BGD."

The Chicago Crime Commission (2006) divides the Gangster Disciple Nation (GDN) into two separate gangs, the Gangster Disciples and Black Disciples. The Department of Justice in their 2009 National Gang Threat Assessment does not make this division

---

Box 2.1 Phoney Philanthropy

Not since Al Capone ruled Chicago in the 1920s, authorities say, has the city seen a more sophisticated band of criminals than the Black Gangster Disciple Nation street gang.

And like Capone, a gregarious criminal who courted politicians, police, and the press, Gangster Disciple leader Larry Hoover cultivated an almost mythical aura around himself in the lower South Side neighborhoods dominated by his gang.

Known as "King Larry" or "The Chairman," Hoover became a legend by the early 1990s, even though he had been locked away in an Illinois prison since 1973, serving two life sentences for murder.

At Hoover's direction, the 30,000-member gang organized rap music concerts. It started a political action committee to register voters and support candidates in city elections. The gang marketed casual wear, some of it with Hoover's prison number on it.

So successful was the Gangster Disciples' effort to appear legitimate that Hoover won the support of community activists and politicians, including former Mayor Eugene Sawyer, in a 1993 parole bid.

It was all a façade, say state and federal law enforcement authorities. Behind that exterior, authorities say, lay a $100 million-a-year drug business organized like a corporation. Under Hoover, who presided over the empire from his prison cell, was a complex chain of command that included a board of directors and officials called governors and regents—some 6,000 in all—responsible for keeping the drugs flowing to the streets of Chicago neighborhoods and suburbs, as well as the state prisons.

Source: Modified from Gibeaut, J. (1998). Gang Busters. *ABA Journal.*

---

and only lists the Gangster Disciples. In any event, there is no disagreement that the Gangster Disciples is one of the largest "super" street gangs in the United States. The CCC states that the Gangster Disciple Nation was founded in the early 1960s when the Black Disciples, under the leadership of David Barksdale, merged with the Gangster Nation led by Larry Hoover. After the merger Barksdale became the supreme leader and Hoover second in command. In 1969, Barksdale was shot by a rival gang member and died from his injuries in 1974. After Barksdale's death Hoover became chairman of the board and ran the Gangster Disciple Nation until he was convicted of multiple murders and sentenced to six life terms and imprisoned in the ADX Super maximum prison in Florence, Colorado.

The Department of Justice (2009) states that the GDN is structured like a corporation and led by a chairman of the board. The Department of Justice (DOJ) estimates that the Gangster Disciple Nation has a membership of 25,000 to 50,000 mostly African American males from the Chicago metropolitan area. The CCC (2006) reports that the Chicago Police Department has identified 36 GDN factions in the city. The gang through a national expansion is active in 110 cities in 31 states. The gang's main source of income is street-level distribution of cocaine, crack cocaine, marijuana, and heroin. The gang, according to the DOJ, is also involved in assaults, auto theft, firearms violations, fraud, homicide, the operation of prostitution rings, and money laundering.

Black Gangsters or New Breed (Regional Street Gang— Alliance: Independents)

Symbols and Identifiers—New Breed gang members wear black and gray colors and often wear sports apparel with a "G" on it such as the Green Bay Packers and the Georgetown Bulldogs. Their symbols include a winged heart with a combination of crossed pitchforks, devil's horns and/or tail, letters "LLL," representing Love, Life and Loyalty; Roman numeral III, a sword, a shotgun.

The New Breeds street gang originated in the late 1980s or early 1990s, initially as a splinter group from the Black Gangsters (one of the three factions of the original Black Gangster Disciple, the other two being the Gangster Disciples and the Black Disciples). The New Breeds ultimately absorbed the Black Gangsters back into the gang, operating under the new name, "New Breeds." The New Breeds are primarily located on the west side of the Chicago and have an estimated membership of over 4,000.

The main territory is a combination of four Chicago housing projects: Grace Abbott Homes, Robert Brooks Homes and Brooks Extensions, Loomis Courts and Jane Adams Homes, along Roosevelt Road, and the K-town area of Chicago's west side. The gang has a presence in the Chicago suburbs of Aurora, Peoria, Robbins and Rockford. It is reported that the New Breed Gang has branches in Milwaukee, Wisconsin; Indianapolis, Indiana; Atlanta, Georgia; and New Orleans, Louisiana. The gang has a defined rank structure with a "don" at the top. The don controls the entire gang. Under the Don in descending order are "kings," "princes," "godfathers" "generals," "field marshals," "lieutenants," and "soldiers."

Latin Kings (National Hispanic Street Gang—Alliance: People)

Source: The Department of Justice (www.justice.gov/criminal/ocgs/gangs/street.html).

Symbols and Identifiers—Black and gold colors. Symbols include the letters "LK," "ALK" (Almighty Latin King) or "ALKN" (Almighty Latin King Nation)

or "ALKQN" (Almighty Latin King and Queen Nation in some areas outside of Chicago), a five-point crown, lions, a five-point star of cross with five rays and the numeral "5."
Other letter symbols are:
   A.L.M.I.G.H.T.Y. (A Love Measured In Great Harmony Towards Yahve)
   A.D.C. (Amor De Carona/King Love)
   A.M.O.R. (Term used to show love and respect for one another and it is
      an acronym for Almighty Masters of Righteousness)
Their motto is—Once a King, Always a King
Salute—clenched fist to the chest that means "I will die for you."
Source: CCC, 2006.

According to the Chicago Crime Commission, the Latin Kings are the oldest and largest Hispanic led gang (CCC, 2006). They formed in the mid-1950s or 1960s in the Humboldt Park area of Chicago. The original reason for formation was to act as a protection group against black street gangs. The National Gang Intelligence Center (NGIC, 2009) reports that the original philosophy was to overcome racial prejudice and create an organization of proud "Kings." However, as is common with many gangs originally formed for protection purposes, they soon evolved into a criminal organization.

The NGIC says that the evolution and expansion into crime came under two umbrella factions—the Motherland (Chicago) and the Bloodline (New York). Latin King members associating with the Motherland faction also identify themselves as the Almighty Latin King Nation (ALKN) and make up 160 chapters operating in 158 cities in 31 states. The ALKN faction is estimated to have 20,000 to 35,000 members. A Chicago Latin King, Luis Felipe, formed the Bloodline faction when he was incarcerated in the New York State correctional system in 1986. The Latin Kings identifying with the Bloodline faction call themselves the Almighty Latin King and Queen Faction (ALKQN). The membership of the ALKQN is estimated to be 2,200 to 7,500, divided among several dozen chapters operating in 15 cities in 5 states. Although the Latin King membership is primarily Hispanic it includes Caucasians, African Americans, and immigrant groups from the Middle East, Poland and Asia, prompting the label of the Latin Kings as a "Rainbow" gang.

In Chicago, their rivals are the Gangster Disciples and Hispanic gangs aligned with the Folk nation. The Latin Kings, particularly the ALKQN's in New York, have portrayed themselves as a community organization, an attempt at public relations to mask their true nature as a criminal organization. The gang is heavily involved in the street-level distribution of powder cocaine, crack cocaine, heroin, and marijuana.

Black P. Stone Nation (National Street Gang—Alliance: People)

Source: The Department of Justice (www.justice.gov/criminal/ocgs/gangs/street.html).

Symbols and Identifiers—Colors are red, black and green. The gang's symbols include:
Five Point Star—Represents their affiliation to the People alliance. The five points also represents, according to gang lore, "Five highest principles known to man: Life, Truth, Peace, Freedom, and Justice."
Crescent Moon—Represents peace and unity
"All seeing eye"—360 degrees of pure wisdom, knowledge and understanding.
21 Stone Pyramid—Represents the "Main 21," or original governing body, and the 21 branches of the Black P. Stone Nation.
Rising Sun—Represents "a nation on the rise, a new day, a new era of time and the light that shows the way."
"Circle 7"—7 surrounded by a circle broken into four parts representing Birth, Life, Mortality and Death. Seven is considered the perfect number known to man.
Source: CCC, 2006.

The CCC (2006) reports that the Black P. Stone Nation is the second largest Chicago street gang with a membership of 20,000 in Chicago and over 3,000 in prisons throughout the United States. The NGIC (2009) estimates that there are 6,000 to 8,000 members. As pointed out earlier, making estimates about the number of gangs, chapters of gangs and gang membership is an inexact science. The gang was originally formed by a group of neighborhood friends in 1959 in the Woodlawn Community on Chicago's west side. The original name was the Blackstones in reference to what they considered their territory—63rd–67th and Blackstone. The group originally formed as a protection group against the other gangs in the area. Once again, we see that over time a protection group of neighborhood youths evolved into a criminal gang. As the group evolved, the name changed from the Blackstones to the Blackstone Rangers until the 1960s when the now criminal gang became known as the Black P. Stone Nation. The majority of the members are African American males from the Chicago Metropolitan area, although the gang is present in Arkansas, Florida, Georgia, Indiana, Iowa, Kentucky, Massachusetts, Michigan, Minnesota, Mississippi, Missouri, New Jersey, New York, Ohio, South Carolina, South Dakota, Tennessee, Texas, Wisconsin, and Virginia (CCC, 2006). There are also Black P. Stone Bloods in Los Angeles and Oakland, California, who are majority black and have no ties to the Chicago faction. The gang's main source of income is the street-level distribution of cocaine, heroin, marijuana and methamphetamine.

Vice Lords (National Street Gang—Alliance: People)

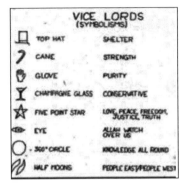

Source: The Department of Justice (www.justice.gov/criminal/ocgs/gangs/street.html).

Symbols and Identifiers—Colors are red and black. Symbols include: Five point representing the People nation, a crescent, a Playboy bunny with bowtie, glove, martini glass, dice dollar signs and circle with fire.

According to the Chicago Crime Commission (2006), the Vice Lords were formed in the St. Charles, Illinois reformatory by a group of African American inmates from the North Lawndale area of Chicago. The name "Vice Lords" was chosen from a dictionary meaning of the word "Vice" meaning "to hold tightly" or "keeping it tight and not letting go." As the young gangsters were released they returned to the Lawndale area and began recruiting. By 1964, the Vice Lords had evolved into a criminal gang involved in robberies, thefts, assaults, batteries, intimidation and extortion. Also in 1964, the Vice Lords in a public relations effort changed the gang's name to the Conservative Vice Lords (CVL) and created the Vice Lords Nation. The CVL was advertised as a community outreach group. A common practice by criminal gangs, including outlaw motorcycle gangs, as they attempt to rehabilitate their image. The CVL established recreational areas for neighborhood youths, such as teen centers, which were used as CVL meeting places after hours. In 1970, two CVL leaders received a $275,000 grant from the Rockefeller Foundation. It soon became clear that the CVL was using its community outreach image as a front for their illegal activities. In truth, the CVL was introducing drugs into the community and extorting protection money from business owners. Several business owners who refused to pay protection money were murdered. A federal investigation into the fraud/misuse of grant monies led to the arrest and incarceration of several CVL leaders.

The Chicago Police have identified 3,600 Vice Lord members, but other estimates run as high as 30,000 to 35,000 members. Membership is predominately African American. The NGIC (2009) reports that the Vice Lord Nation operates in 74 cities in 28 states, primarily in the Great Lakes region.

Four Corner Hustlers (Regional Street Gang— Alliance: People)

Symbols and Identifiers—Colors include black and gold, black and red, or black and white. Symbols include the numeral "4" with letters "C" and "H" combined with a black diamond, a five-point star, cane, top hat, Playboy bunny, dollar signs and dice.

The CCC (2006) reports that the Four Corner Hustlers are one of the largest Chicago street gangs but does not provide an estimate of membership. The gang was founded on Chicago's west side in the 1970s and soon after allied themselves with the Vice Lords. The Four Corner Hustlers have expanded their territory throughout Chicago's south side and the far south suburbs. The gang has been identified in several other Illinois cities and towns and the neighboring states of Indiana and Wisconsin. The gang is predominately African American and allied with the Vice Lords. The CCC reports that in addition to assaults and murders their criminal activities include armed robbery, extortion, drug trafficking, renting out drug turf to independent dealers, prostitution, firearms sales and laundering money through businesses owned by the gang.

Maniac Latin Disciples (Regional Street Gang— Alliance: Folks)

Symbols and Identifiers—Colors are black and red or black and gold. Their symbols include a heart with horns and tail, pitchforks, monks and backwards swastika.

The CCC (2006) reports that the Maniac Latin Disciples aka Latin Disciples are believed to have originated in the mid-1960s. At that time Albert "Hitler" Hernandez led them and their symbol was the backward swastika. The gang joined the alliance the United Latin Organization (ULO) that was formed to fight off the expansion efforts of the Latin Kings. They later joined the Folk nation to resist the Latin Kings.

The gang's sphere of influence is in the Humboldt park area of Chicago, the Chicago suburbs, and numerous outlying Illinois cities including Elgin, Joliet and Rockford. The CCC also reports that the Maniac Latin Disciples have been reported in several unnamed mid-west and southern states. The gang consists of a mix of Hispanic, Caucasian and African American members. Their main criminal activity is the sale of illegal narcotics.

Chicago Caucasian Street Gangs (Local Street Gangs)

C-Notes (Alliance: Folks)

This street gang is thought to have formed in the 1950s by Italian youths. It changed its philosophy to white supremacy in the 1970s. Their philosophy changed again in the

1980s and the gang joined the Folks nation. The gang's territory is exclusively in Chicago. Membership is primarily Caucasian and Hispanic.

Almighty Gaylords (Alliance: Folks)

This northside Chicago gang formed in the late 1950s by Italian youths and also evolved into a white supremacist gang. They dropped their white supremacist philosophy in the 1980s when they joined the People alliance. The CCC reports that they have lost membership in recent years but still operate on a small scale on Chicago's north side.

Popes (Alliance: Folks on the Northside of Chicago and People on Chicago's Southside)

This Caucasian gang was formed in the 1970s on Chicago's north and south sides to protect their turf from Hispanic gangs. They are allied with the Simon City Royals, the oldest Caucasian Chicago Street Gang.

Simon City Royals (Alliance: Folks)

The CCC (2006) reports that this gang is probably the oldest predominately Caucasian street gang in Chicago. They were formed as a protection group against Hispanic gangs moving into their area. The gang was one of the original members of the Folks alliance, and they have strong ties to the Black Gangster Disciples.

III. Los Angeles-Based/Influenced Street Gangs

African American Street Gangs

Bloods (African American National Street Gang)

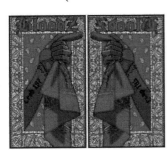  

Source: The Department of Justice (www.justice.gov/criminal/ocgs/gangs/street.html).

Symbols and Identifiers—Color is red. Members wear red bandannas or rags. The most common tattoo is P for "Piru" or B for "Blood" or CK for "Crip Killer" or "Cop Killer." The gang crosses out "C" in words as a disrespect for Crips.

The National Gang Intelligence Center (2009) reports that the Bloods is an association of structured and unstructured street gangs that have adopted a single-gang culture. The original Bloods grew out of a Crips set—the Piru Street Boys, in Compton, Los Angeles. The Piru Street Boys Crips set broke with the Crips after a violent internal conflict in 1971 and set up their own gang, the Bloods. The two gangs have been bitter enemies since then. Since their 1971 split from the Crips they have expanded into virtually all 50 states. The Royal Canadian Mounted Police (RCMP) report that there are several Canadian street gangs with the name Bloods, but the RCMP can find no connection to the American Bloods. For example, the Ottawa Police Service reports that the most prominent gangs in their jurisdiction are the "Crips" and the "Bloods," and these gangs are composed of members from 57 different nationalities (Callaghan, Campbell-Waugh, 2008). This mixed nationality certainly raises doubts about their ties to U.S. gangs of the same name. Even in the United States, there is no formal leadership structure that controls all the Bloods gangs. The East Coast branch of the Bloods, the United Blood Nation, was formed in Rikers Island Jail in New York City in 1993. Individual Bloods sets have their own hierarchical structure and identifiable levels of membership. On occasion, different Bloods sets in the same area are often in conflict with each other. The Black P. Stone Bloods set in Los Angeles has had violent disagreements with other Los Angeles Blood Sets.

Bloods membership is estimated at 5,000 in Los Angeles and up to 35,000 throughout the United States; most members are African American males. The gang's primary source of income is street-level distribution of cocaine and marijuana.

Source: The Department of Justice (www.justice.gov/criminal/ocgs/gangs/street.html).

Crips (African American National Street Gang)

Symbols and Identifiers—The color is blue. Blue bandannas and rags. The gang uses the letter "C" in place of "B" in writing in disrespect for Bloods. Crips call each other "Cuzz." Members wear the tattoo "BK" for "Blood Killers."

The NGIC (2009) reports that the Crips, like the Bloods, is a collection of structured and unstructured gangs that have adopted a common gang culture. However, when the Crips were founded in 1969 by a 15-year-old black youth, Raymond Washington, in Los Angeles, they were one gang. Legend has it that Washington was influenced by the Black Panthers and wanted his new gang to emulate their revolutionary ideology and act as community leaders and protect their neighborhoods. Stanley "Tookie" Williams, another young thug, supposedly met Washington in 1971 and started his own Westside Crips, modeled after the revolutionary ideology fostered by Washington. Whether or not this is true, Washington and Williams formed an alliance and expanded their territory as the Crips evolved into a violent drug-dealing street gang. Both men, Washington and Williams, generally considered co-founders of the Crips met violent deaths. A gang rival in 1979 murdered Washington. Williams was convicted of four brutal murders and after a lengthy stay on California's death row was executed in 2005.

Co-Founders of the Crips

Raymond Washington
Born—August 14, 1953
Los Angeles
Died—August 9, 1979
Murdered

Stanley "Tookie" Williams
Born—December 29, 1953
Shreveport, Louisiana
Died—November 13, 2005
Executed

Source: The Department of Justice (www.justice.gov/criminal/ocgs/gangs/street.html).

Hispanic Street Gangs

Surenos and Nortenos Alliances

The Hispanic street gangs have divided themselves into alliances or movements known as Surenos ("Southerners" in Spanish) and Nortenos ("Northerners" in Spanish) under control or influenced by allegiance to competing Hispanic prison gangs. The Surenos in California are under the direct control of the Mexican Mafia prison gang; the Nortenos owe allegiance to the Nuestra Familia (Our Family) prison gang. As stated earlier, the California Hispanic alliances do not include African American or Caucasian gangs as the Folk and People alliances do in Chicago-based or influenced gangs. In fact, the Mexican Mafia, the oldest prison gang in the United States came into being as a protection group to protect California Hispanic inmates from the violent acts of black and white inmates. The Mexican Mafia has since then allied themselves with the Aryan Brotherhood prison gang and is bitter enemies with the Black Guerilla Family prison gang. The anti-black animosity of the Mexican Mafia has led to violent acts, including murder of African Americans in areas controlled by Sureno gangs.

The original Mexican Mafia members were from southern California and considered the recent immigrants who settled in the rural, agricultural areas of northern California to be weak and viewed them with contempt. They referred to those Hispanic gang members who worked for them as Surenos or southerners and treated them with disrespect and violence. Northern California Hispanic inmates formed their own prison gang known as Nuestra Familia and called themselves Nortenos. The dividing line for Surenos and Nortenos is generally viewed as the city of Delano or Bakersfield.

All California Hispanic (Mexican American) street gangs claim allegiance to the Surenos or Nortenos, except the powerful and violent Fresno Bulldogs. Mara Salvatrucha (MS 13), the national/international "super gang" founded in Los Angeles by Salvadorans does not claim allegiance to either the Surenos or Nortenos alliance, but identifies with the Mexican Mafia for reasons to be explained later. In California, there are no separate and distinct Surenos or Nortenos gangs, instead there is a loose rank structure composed of well-known veteranos (veterans) or "shot callers" who direct the activities of the individual gangs in their street activities. Outside California there are separate street gangs that identify with the Sureno movement and identify themselves as "Surenos," "Sur Trece," "Sur," "Sur 13" or some other derivative of Sureno. They may or may not be affiliated with the California Sureno movement or even know a Mexican Mafia member. California Surenos often identify themselves as "foot soldiers" for the Mexican Mafia and identify themselves or their gang with the number "13" (the 13th letter in the alphabet is M) as a sign of allegiance to the Mexican Mafia and wear blue bandanas. The Sureno gangs are a feeder system for the Mexican Mafia where they are a pool for the prison gang to recruit, cultivate and develop future Mexican Mafia members. The Nuestra Familia identify themselves with the number "14" (the 14th letter in the alphabet is N) and use the Norteno gangs as their feeder system and wear red bandanas. In prison, the Sureno and Norteno gangs come under the strict control of their respective prison gang.

The California Hispanic "super gangs"—18th Street, Mara Salvatrucha, Florecnia 13, and 38th Street identify themselves as Surenos.

Source: The Department of Justice (www.justice.gov/criminal/ocgs/gangs/street.html).

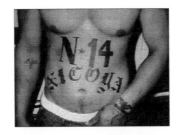

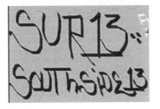

Source: The Department of Justice (www.justice.gov/criminal/ocgs/gangs/street.html).

18th Street (National and International Hispanic Street Gang—Alliance: Surenos)

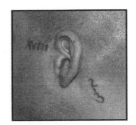

Source: The Department of Justice (www.justice.gov/criminal/ocgs/gangs/street.html).

Symbols and Identifiers—Wear blue for Surenos and sometimes wear gray and black (Raiders) colors. Most common tattoos are number 18 (XVII, XV3); 666; numbers (213) for the Los Angeles area code and Diesiocho (Spanish for 18) and the letters BEST (Barrio 18th Street).

Undocumented Hispanic immigrants and mixed race youths formed the 18th Street Gang in the 1960s because mixed ancestry Hispanic youths were not allowed to join

---

Box 2.2 Columbia Lil Cycos (CLC)

The Columbia Lil Cycos (CLC) is the largest clique of the 18th Street Gang, and this clique has the dubious distinction of being the first L.A. street gang to be prosecuted by the federal government under the RICO act. Anthony "Coco" Zaragoza, the chief enforcer for the CLC, and Frank "Puppet" Martinez, an incarcerated member of the Mexican Mafia, were convicted of racketeering and murder charges in 2002 and sentenced to life in prison without parole. The investigation began in the late 1990s and revealed that Martinez controlled the drug trade in the MacArthur Park neighborhood through the leaders of the Columbia Lil Cycos. In all, 24 members and associates of the CLC were convicted, including Zaragoza's former wife and father. The Lil Cycos offered protection in exchange for kickbacks on drug sales and legal and illegal vendors and split it with Puppet Martinez.

Source: Rosenzweig, D. (December 24, 2002).

---

the Clanton Street Gang composed of members who were American citizens from a pure Hispanic background. The mixed race youths formed their own gang and because they lived on 18th Street that was the name they chose for the gang. The 18th Street location is in the notorious Rampart area of Los Angeles. The gang was the first Hispanic gang to break the racial membership barrier. This led to a rapid rise in membership. Today, the gang is composed of loosely associated sets or cliques each led by an influential member.

Membership is estimated at 30,000 to 50,000 members in 44 cities and 20 states in the United States and internationally located in Mexico, Central America, and Canada. There are reportedly 30 clikas (sets or cliques) of the 18th Street Gang in Los Angeles alone. The NGIC (2009) reports that in California 80 percent of the gang's members are illegal aliens from Mexico and Central America. Although the gang's members are primarily Hispanic, some sets, particularly outside of California have African American, Caucasian, Asian and Native American members. The gang is sometimes referred to as "The Children's Army" because of their proclivity to recruit elementary and middle-school youths to do the "gang's work"—sell and distribute drugs. The gang is also considered by many law enforcement authorities to be one of the most violent street gangs in the world. The most violent is their bitter rival—MS 13.

In California, the shot callers of the individual 18th Street sets report to the Mexican Mafia representative for the area who is often serving a life without parole prison sentence. The gang collects "taxes" from any business (legitimate and illegitimate), including street vendors, shop owners, prostitutes, and drug dealers. A portion of the "taxes" is given to the Mexican Mafia shot caller (see Box 2.2).

The gang's major source of income is street-level distribution of cocaine and marijuana, and, to a lesser extent, heroin and methamphetamine. The 18th Street Gang is engaged in national and international drug trafficking with ties to the Mexican and Colombian drug cartels.

Florencia 13 (Regional Hispanic Street Gang— Alliance: Surenos)

Symbols and Identifiers—Color is blue for the affiliation with the Surenos. Prominent tattoos are F 13, FX3, EFE13, EFEX13, SSF13, and 213 for Los Angeles area code.

Box 2.3 Operation Joker's Wild

Operation Joker's Wild, at the time the largest gang takedown in American history, was the result of a three-year investigation of the Florencia 13 (F 13) street gang conducted by the Los Angeles High-Intensity Drug Trafficking Area (HIDTA) Task Force composed of agents and officers with the Los Angeles County Sheriff's Department; the Drug Enforcement Administration (DEA); the Bureau of Alcohol, Tobacco, Firearms and Explosives (BATF); U.S. Immigration and Customs Enforcement (ICE); the Los Angeles Police Department; IRTS-Criminal Investigation Division; the Federal Bureau of Investigation and the Los Angeles County Probation Department. Six area police departments (Bell Gardens Police Department, South Gate Police Department, Long Beach Police Department, Torrance Police Department, Baldwin Park Police Department and the Azusa Police Department) and the United States Marshals Service-Regional Fugitive Task Force assisted in the operation.

There were four indictments returned by a federal grand jury against 102 members and associates of Florencia 13 for federal and state criminal charges, including federal RICO charges of drug trafficking, attempted murder, murder, and extortion. As of February 4, 2010, 94 defendants had been convicted, either at trial or as a result of guilty pleas. Five of the defendants received sentences of life in prison without parole.

Evidence at trial revealed that the criminal activities of the gang were controlled by an incarcerated member of the Mexican Mafia prison gang and gang leaders on the street. F 13 leaders on the street collected taxes or "rent" from gang members and others who engaged in criminal activity in F 13 territory, in return for Mexican Mafia protection when they went to prison or jail. Trial testimony also revealed that F 13 members acting on orders from the Mexican Mafia targeted African Americans who lived in F 13 territory. These innocent victims were beaten and killed as a result of racial hatred, leading the judge to comment "[Florencia 13 gang members] preyed on victims because they were black and for no other reason but racial motive."

Sources: U.S. Attorney's Office, Central District of California, Press Release No. 07-138, October 30, 2007; ATF News Release April 24, 2009; Department of Justice Press Release January 12, 2009; Department of Justice Press Release February 4, 2010.

Florencia 13 (F 13) is the second largest Hispanic gang in Los Angeles and considered to be the strongest gang in South Central Los Angeles. The gang originated in Los Angeles in the 1960s and gang membership is estimated at more than 3,000 members (NGIC, 2009). The gang operates primarily in California but has been reported in Arkansas, Missouri, New Mexico, and Utah. As is common for all California Sureno gangs, F 13 is subordinate to the Mexican Mafia with clique shot callers reporting to their Mexican Mafia member representing the area (see Box 2.3 on the previous page).

Mara Salvatrucha [MS 13] (National and International Hispanic Street Gang—Alliance: Surenos)

Source: The Department of Justice (www.justice.gov/criminal/ocgs/gangs/street.html).

Symbols and Identifiers—Tattoos include "Mara Salvatrucha," "Mara Salvatrucha 13," "MS 13," and "MS XII." The number "13" shows allegiance to La Eme or the Mexican Mafia. Colors are blue and white from the flag of El Salvador. The color blue also signifies that they are members of the Sureno alliance. The most common gang hand sign is created by extending the index and finger fingers with the middle and ring fingers folded into the palm with the thumb covering the folded fingers. The hand sign is referred to as the "Devil's Horn" and shown on the next page.

Mara Salvatrucha (MS 13) is considered to be the largest and most violent and dangerous street gang in the world. Salvadoran immigrants fleeing the U.S.-backed civil war against insurgents in El Salvador during the 1980s formed the gang. The Salvadoran im-

Source: The Department of Justice (www.justice.gov/criminal/ocgs/gangs/street.html).

migrants were not accepted by the existing Latino gangs, particularly the 18th Street Gang, so they formed their own gang as a protection against the Hispanic gangs. The newly established Mara Salvatrucha gang members were "green lighted" (targeted for murder) by the allied Latino gangs in Los Angeles setting off a violent war between the gangs. According to Brenda Paz, a 17-year-old informant who provided most of what is known about the inner workings of MS 13 before she was murdered by the gang, the Mexican Mafia, realizing that the war was bad for business, offered a truce (Logan, 2009). The Mexican Mafia's first offer was the standard agreement with the other Latino gangs—protection in prison and on the streets in return for a cash tribute. Mara Salvatrucha turned them down, saying that they did not pay tribute to anyone. The Mexican Mafia, in a move to stop the war, made a counter offer. In exchange for Mexican Mafia protection, Mara Salvatrucha would agree to let the Mexican Mafia have the use of Mara Salvatrucha's best hit man when the Mexican Mafia needed someone killed on the streets. Mara Salvatrucha agreed and became known as La Mara Salvatrucha Trece, or MS 13. In spite of the truce, MS 13 and the 18th Street Gang continued to be bitter enemies and still are in the United States and in Central America. However, as a Sureno gang, MS 13 could operate relatively safely with the other gangs in Los Angeles.

Since its founding in Los Angeles in the 1980s, MS 13 has expanded throughout the United States and internationally into Canada, El Salvador, Guatemala, Honduras, and Mexico. The FBI estimates that there are 10,000 in 42 states and the District of Columbia. The largest concentrations of MS 13 appear to be in: Southern California, 20 cliques with over 4,000 members and associates; New York City, 24 cliques with almost 2,000 members and associates; and the Northern Virginia/Metropolitan D.C. area with 21 cliques and over 5,000 members and associates. The FBI estimates that there are 60,000 MS 13 members in El Salvador, Guatemala, and Honduras. MS 13 has become such a problem that the FBI created the MS 13 National Gang Task Force. This task force targets MS 13 and the 18th Street Gang. At the same time, the FBI instituted the Central American Fingerprint Exploitation (CAFÉ) initiative that acquires fingerprints from the Central American region and merges those fingerprints and the associated criminal records into the Integrated Fingerprint Identification System (AFIS). The MS 13 Task Force increases and speeds the flow of information and intelligence, coordinates investigations, and helps state law enforcement identify the gang in their states. The FBI also created a Transnational Anti-Gang or TAG initiative to coordinate activities against MS 13 and 18th Street gangs with El Salvador and other Central American countries (see Box 2.4). This international cooperation is important because MS 13 leaders in El Salvador send members into other countries to set up cliques, commit

---

Box 2.4 Transnational Anti-Gang Initiative

Two FBI agents are permanently stationed in San Salvador, working along-side 20 investigators and 10 analysts from the Policia Nacional Civil, or PNC, the national law enforcement agency of El Salvador, to share intelligence information across Central America and the U.S.

Source: FBI. (10/10/07).

---

murders or other criminal activities. Recently, trial evidence revealed that MS 13 leaders in El Salvador sent a leader to run what was called "The Program" in the Charlotte and Greensboro, North Carolina area (FBI Press Release March 04, 2011).

MS 13 is a particularly ruthless and violent gang with ties to the Mexican cartels. Their violence shows few bounds:

> They've severed the fingers of their rivals with machetes…. brutally murdered suspected informants, including a 17-year-old pregnant witness [Brenda Paz] … attacked and threatened law enforcement officers…. committed a string of rapes, assaults, break-ins, auto thefts, extortion and frauds across the U.S…. gotten involved in everything from drug and firearms trafficking to prostitution and money laundering … and are sowing violence and discord not just here in the U.S. but around the world. FBI 07/13/05.

On December 23, 2004, MS 13 gunmen intercepted a city bus in Chamelecon, Honduras and sprayed the passengers with automatic weapons killing 28 passengers, including seven children. MS 13 was protesting the recent crackdown on the gang. In Newark, New Jersey on August 19, 2007, six MS 13 members and associates forced four college students to kneel facing a wall and then shot them in the head execution style killing three. In 2007, 13 members of the MS 13 clique Thompson Place Locos Salvatruchos (TPLS) were indicted for killing three people and attempting to kill seven more. An MS 13 member and an illegal alien from El Salvador was charged in San Francisco with the murder of a father and two sons following a minor traffic accident in June 2008. The murderer of Chandra Levy, the government intern who was having an affair with a congressman in 2001, was an illegal immigrant from El Salvador and a member of MS 13. At the time he was charged for her murder in 2006, he was in prison serving ten years for attacking two other women.

Avenues (Local Hispanic Street Gang—Alliance: Surenos)

Symbols and Identifiers—The gang's insignia often tattooed on their bodies is a skull with a bullet hole in it and wearing a fedora, and they call each other "skulls." Gang members display the letter "A" for Avenues or the interlocking "L-A" for "Los Avenidas." They also wear baseball caps from teams such as the Oakland Athletics, Atlanta Braves, and Los Angeles Dodgers whose team insignias include an "A" or "L.A." As with all Surenos gangs, Avenues gang members use the various forms of "13" such as "13," "X3," or "XIII" on their clothing or in tattoos.

The Avenues gang is estimated to have between 400 to 700 members. Compared to the "super gangs" in Los Angeles, they are not very big but they have had a very violent criminal history that belies their size and includes: the murder of a three-year-old child that drew comments by the President of the United States, several Avenues members becoming shot callers for the Mexican Mafia, ethnic cleansing activities against African Americans living in their territory, the first Los Angeles street gang to be prosecuted under the RICO Act; the first time that federal hate crime statutes were used against a street gang; human smuggling; and violent attacks on and murder of law enforcement officers.

The Avenues were started by brothers named Flores in the 1940s as a social club of guys who hung out with one another, settling fights with their fists. By the late 1960s the social club evolved into a criminal street gang with strong ties to the Mexican Mafia, settling fights with violence and firearms and acting as drug traffickers and hit men for the notorious prison gang.

The gang takes its name from the avenues crossing Figueroa Street in the Highland Park area of Los Angeles. As the gang grew, the members formed into cliques based on where the members lived. The first clique was the Cypress Avenues, then the 43rd Aves, Avenues 57 and lastly the extremely violent Drew Street clique. In time, the Drew Street clique became the most violent clique and the producer of the most revenues for the "big homies" of the Mexican Mafia.

The Avenues street gang received national attention for what became known as the "wrong way" shooting. A vehicle containing a family of five, including three young children, returning from a birthday party and looking for a short cut home turned down a dead end alley in the Cypress Park neighborhood of Los Angeles in the early morning hours of September 17, 1995. Unbeknown to the innocent family, a group of Avenues gang members were lying in wait for rival gang members. The gangsters opened fire on the vehicle as the stepfather tried to back out of the alley, killing a three-year-old girl and wounding her younger brother and the stepfather. Several days after the shooting, then President Bill Clinton went on national TV and condemned the shooting and murder and promised federal monies to fight gangs in Los Angeles. Two years later three Avenues gang members were sentenced to prison terms of 54 years and eight months to life for the shootings (Krikorian, August 02, 1997). In 2006, four members of the Aves 43 clique of the Avenues street gang were convicted in the first federal use of the hate-crime statute against a street gang (Pelisek, August 2, 2006). Each of the defendants received two consecutive life sentences. The Aves 43 gang was accused of conducting a six-year campaign between 1995 and 2001 against African Americans in their territory on orders from the Mexican Mafia. The street gang members threatened, intimidated, and beat African Americans who made their homes in Highland Park. Aves 43 members killed three black men for no other reason than the color of their skin. In 1999, a 38-year-old black resident was shot to death as he parked his car. The next year, a 28-eyear-old black male was shot in the head three times as he waited for a bus. The third victim, a 20-year-old mixed race male, was attacked in his bed and shot twice in the head.

Tony Rafael, Mexican Mafia expert and author of the definitive book on the Mexican Mafia prison gang, states that the "policy of ethnic cleansing" was issued by Mexican Mafia "shot caller" Alex "Pee Wee" Aquirre, a former Avenues member serving a life sentence in the federal penitentiary in Marion, Illinois (Mock, 2006). The reason for the "green light" (kill on sight) on African Americans in territories controlled by Surenos street gangs is the long-standing war between the Mexican Mafia and the African American prison gang Black Guerilla Family.

Two years later, in 2008, 70 members and associates of the notorious Drew Street clique of the Avenues were indicted by a federal grand jury for RICO offenses. The lead defendant in the indictment was an Avenues shot caller put into that position by the Mexican Mafia. He acted on the orders of a Mexican Mafia "made man" incarcerated in California's supermax Prison at Pelican Bay. The Avenues shot caller collected "taxes" from narcotics traffickers and then paid a portion of the "taxes" to the Mexican Mafia boss. The gang also raised funds for the Mexican Mafia by conducting armed home invasion robberies and collecting extortion payments from area businessmen. The prosecutor in the first case in 2005 against the Avenues and the Mexican Mafia stated in his opening statement to the jury: "The connection between the Mexican Mafia and the Avenues is so strong that it's tough to tell where the Avenues end and the Mexican Mafia begins (Rafael, 2007)." In another Avenues trial, a member of the Avenues testified that "everybody in the Avenues is obligated to the Mexican Mafia. Not every gang runs that way, but Avenues does. We have five members in the Mexican Mafia." (Rafael, 2007).

While the members of the Drew Street clique were awaiting trial, two members of the Avenues walked up behind Los Angeles County Sheriff's Deputy Juan Able Escalante and shot him in the back of the head. The 27-year-old deputy and father of three was getting in his car to go to work at the county jail. The deputy, in all probability, did not see his assailants coming. The resulting investigation of Deputy Escalante's murder led to a September 2009 indictment of 88 members of the Avenues street gang. In addition to the deputy's murder were allegations that the Mexican Mafia was trying to reorganize the Drew Street clique after the 2008 indictment. The indictment alleging threats of violence against law enforcement officers cited a February 2008 attack in which Avenues members opened fire on Los Angeles Police Department officers with handguns and an assault rifle.

The majority of the defendants indicted in the 2008 and 2009 cases have not gone to trial as of this date, therefore, we will have to wait to see the final impact on the Avenues street gang. However, the "ethnic cleansing" of African Americans in Latino communities that have Sureno gangs under the control of the racist Mexican Mafia prison gang continues. One can argue that the need to remove the possible drug trafficking competition of African American street gangs is also a factor behind the violence directed toward African Americans. In any event, the Varrio Asuza 13 street gang in the City of Asuza, California, a predominately Latino working community of 46,000 of Los Angeles County is the second street gang to be prosecuted under the federal hate-crime statutes for civil rights violations.

Varrio Azusa 13 (Local Hispanic Street Gang— Alliance: Sureno)

Symbols and Identifiers—Azusa 13 gang members wear black or blue items that display some version of the "A" symbol commonly associated with the Atlanta Braves, Oakland Athletics, or Los Angeles Angels. They wear belt buckles that display the letter "A" and athletic shoes that have the letter "A" or the number "13" and "Vara" written on them. Azusa gang members have the tattoos "Azusa," "A13," "SUR," "VAR," "SVG," "Canyon City," and "Bright Lights Big City," on their bodies. Of course, the number "13" in their name and tattoos represents that they are a Surenos gang with allegiance to the Mexican Mafia.

In February 2011, 45 members of the Varrio Azusa 13 street gang were indicted for numerous violations of the federal RICO statute and a nearly 20-year conspiracy to violate the civil rights of African Americans in the City of Azusa, California. According to the indictment, the Varrio Azusa 13 is a multi-generational gang formed in the 1960s. The gang claims as its territory the entire City of Azusa, which is located within the eastern San Gabriel Valley region of Southern California. The membership of the gang is estimated at 400. The gang controls the drug distribution and other illegal activities within the City of Azusa under the control of the Mexican Mafia.

The indictment details a wide range of crimes, including acts of violence (ranging from battery to murder), drug trafficking, robbery, burglary, carjacking, witness intimidation, kidnapping, weapons trafficking, and hate crimes directed against African Americans who reside or are present in the city of Azusa. Gang members have sprayed "Get out N" on residences and businesses. U.S. Attorney Andre Birotte, Jr. was quoted as saying that for 15 years gang members have assaulted, chased, and robbed blacks as well as vandalized their property in a "crime spree to drive African Americans out of the city of Azusa" (Quinones & Winton, June 8, 2011).

IV. Street Gangs in Canada

Organized criminal street gangs in Canada are nowhere near the problem that they are in the United States. The Criminal Intelligence Service Canada (CISC), Canada's national agency for gathering and sharing crime information, in their 2006 report states that there are 300 street gangs in Canada with an estimated 11,000 members and associates. The 2010 CISC Annual Report on Organized Crime reports that street gangs have increased since 2006, but does not give a number. The CISC further opines that street gangs have only become a real crime problem since the formation of cocaine smuggling and distribution networks in the 1980s (CISC, 2006:22). In many Canadian cities, street gangs only became a crime problem in the last 15 to 20 years. For example: Ottawa, the second largest city in the Province of Ontario and the fourth largest city in the country, did not formally recognize that street gangs were emerging in the city until 2001 (Callahan & Campbell-Waugh, 2008). At that time the Ottawa Police Service formed a two-person gang investigation unit and found that there were eight gangs

---

Box 2.5 Canadian Street Gang Characteristics

Some common characteristics among Canadian and U.S. street gangs include specific gang identifiers and paraphernalia, a common name or identifying sign or symbol, induction rituals, and a rigid or loose code relating to the conduct and duty of members and associates. The composition of Canadian street gangs varies in terms of total membership, gender, and age and is generally determined by the demographics of the community. While some gangs are ethnically homogeneous, there are also those with a diverse multicultural base. Those from a similar ethnic background tend to operate within a fixed area and are generally found in lower income urban area (prevalent in the Prairies, Toronto, and Montreal). Further, some street gangs are based on familial relations or friendships while others are hierarchical in nature with mutual cells and more complex networks. While commonly associated with the cities, street gangs are not exclusive to urban centres and are also active in rural areas, on Aboriginal reserves, and correctional facilities. Criminal groups commonly identified as street gangs are primarily active in street-level crime and trafficking of illicit commodities. They are commonly at the retail end of organized crime. Most of the profit from street gang criminality is directed towards maintaining a particular life style.

Source: CISC, 2010:19.

---

with approximately 100 members. The criminal street gangs in Canada are Aboriginal, Asian, black, and multi-ethnic gangs with some gangs with U.S. ties such as MS 13, 18th Street, and the Latin Kings. However, the CISC (2010) cautions that some Canadian street gangs "have borrowed or copied the name of well-known international gangs such as the U.S. 'Crips' or 'Bloods' but no known international affiliation actually exists." The Canadian street gangs share, for the most part, the same characteristics as U.S. street gangs (see Box 2.5).

The criminal activities of these street gangs include illegal drug distribution, the sex trade, robberies, home invasions, and to a lesser extent, fraud and counterfeiting of currency and merchandise. Street gang involvement in the sex trade is national and includes street-level prostitution, escort agencies, and exotic dancing establishments. Gangs recruit women, including minors, into the sex trade and transport them to various locations across Canada. The Canadian criminal street gangs predominately engage in the street-level trafficking of cocaine, marijuana, and synthetic drugs. The street gangs get their drugs from other Canadian organized crime groups such as outlaw motorcycle gangs and Italian and Asian crime groups. The gangs are involved in a drug dealing system known as "Dial-a-Doper" where customers phone their dealer at a predetermined number and then the dealer sends a driver to deliver the drugs like a pizza delivery. The CISC (2006) reports that the majority of the crime proceeds support the lavish lifestyle of the gang members. However, some launder the money and purchase legitimate businesses. The CISC (2006) identified the street crime problem by Canadian province and territory.

Provincial and Territorial Overview

Territories (3)

(Populations in thousands—Statistics Canada 2010)

Yukon Territory

Capital: Whitehorse
Population: 34.5

Nunavut

Capital: Iqaluit
Population: 33.2

According to the CISC (2010), there are no identified street gangs or gang activity in these two territories.

Northwest Territories

Capital: Yellowknife
Population: 43.8

Members of Alberta-based street gangs are involved in the street-level distribution of various drugs in Yellowknife. The Crazy Dragons, an Asian-based street gang started by the children of Vietnamese immigrants in Edmonton, Alberta, in the 1990s have been identified as one of the gangs operating in Yellowknife (Quenneville, June 22, 2007). A second Alberta criminal street gang distributing drugs in Yellowknife is the notorious White Boy Posse *(Edmonton Journal,* March 28, 2008*)*. White Boy Posse is a 50- to 100-member street gang under the control of the Hells Angels Motorcycle Gang, which follows a white supremacist ideology and uses the swastika in the tattoos and other gang paraphernalia.

Provinces (10)

Ontario Province

Capitol: Toronto
Population: 13,210.7

The CISC (2006) reports that there are approximately 80 street gangs in Toronto and an additional 95 street gangs in the regions of Ontario—York, Peel, Waterloo/Kitchener, Thunder Bay, Niagara Falls, and Ottawa. Their main source of illegal income comes from street-level trafficking of cocaine, crack cocaine, marijuana, and Ecstasy. Street gangs are also involved in street level prostitution and some in the production of pornography. The street gangs in the Greater Toronto area are involved in gun violence with frequent drive-by shootings, attempted murders, and murders.

Jamaican Shower Posse Gang—The Jamaican Shower Posse (JSP) gang is not a street gang, but it has dealings with Canadian street gangs. The JSP is an international drug trafficking organization that supposedly has ties to Jamaica's ruling political party. At one time, the Jamaican Shower Posse U.S. faction, organized by Vivian Blake in Brooklyn, New York, in the 1980s, reportedly operated drug bases in more than 20 U.S. cities (Wallace, 2010). Sometime in the early 1980s the Jamaican Shower Posse established a drug base in Toronto. The Jamaican Shower Posse is discussed here because the Toronto Police discovered a connection between this DTO and street gangs during Project Corral a law enforcement action against Toronto street gangs in 2009.

Falstaff Crips and the Five Point Generals—The Toronto Police launched Project Corral in August 2009 after an escalation of street gang violence in the city. The targets were two rival Toronto street gangs, the Falstaff Crips and the Five Point Generals. The investigation lasted until May 2010 when 1,000 police officers from throughout Ontario executed 105 search warrants in the City of Toronto, arresting 78 street gang members, and seizing cash, guns, and drugs (Vallis, 2010). The investigation revealed that the Jamaican Shower Posse was supplying drugs and guns to both street gangs. The JSP was bringing drugs into the Greater Toronto Area from the United States, the Dominican Republic, Jamaica, and Panama for the street gangs to sell on the street. Canada is attempting to deport 12 Jamaican nationals because of their suspected involvement in the Jamaican Shower Posse.

MNE and 400 Crew—One year earlier, 1,000 police officers, including the Toronto Police and 38 tactical units from across the Ontario province, executed the largest street gang operation in Ontario's history, Project Fusion. Project Fusion's raids against three gangs—MNE (an acronym for the neighborhoods of Markham and Elington) and the 400 Crew, based at 400 McCowan Rd—resulted in the arrest of 125 gang members and the seizure of $431,000 in cash, 34 handguns, 19 kilos of cocaine, 344 grams of crack cocaine, 29 kilos of marijuana, 30,000 Ecstasy pills, and 41 grams of Oxycotin (Lamberti & Doucette, April 2, 2009).

MS 13—Although the majority of the Canadian street gangs are local or national with few ties to United States gangs (even those who have adopted U.S. gangs' names such as the Crips and the Bloods) it appears that MS 13 has moved into Canada. In 2007, MS 13 was reported in Vancouver, Montreal, Toronto, and to a lesser extent in Edmonton and Calgary (Global National, May 2, 2007). In 2008, the Toronto police arrested 17 people with ties to MS 13, when they learned of a plot to kill a law enforcement officer. The gang, as in the U.S., is exclusively Hispanic and is located in the west side of Toronto's downtown.

Driftwood Crips—The target of the law enforcement operation Project Kyrptic was the well-organized, violent black gang the Driftwood Crips from the Ontario Housing community of Driftwood Court in the Jane and Finch section of North York. As is true for the U.S. Crips, whose name they use, the members wear blue and are enemies of the Canadian Bloods, who also use the U.S. Bloods name without any affiliation. The Driftwood Crips are also enemies of other Crip gangs such as Toronto's Mount Olive Crips and the Stovetop Crips. The police task force raids that culminated from Project Kryptic took place in the early morning hours of June 13, 2007. More than 80 members and associates of the Driftwood Crips, including their leaders, were arrested and charged with a variety of crimes. It was not learned until two years later that the police informant, a Driftwood Crips member who gave the information that led to the raids, committed several violent felonies, including the murder of a bystander during a gang gunfight, while he was acting as a police informant (Powell & Small, December 23, 2009). Unfortunately, the police often "shake hands with the devil" to penetrate the secret world of criminal gangs.

More than 700 Toronto police officers were involved in the raids that seized 30 kilograms of cocaine, several kilograms of hashish oil, and marijuana, and three dozen guns. Six of those arrested were current or former employees of Toronto's Pearson International Airport cargo and ramp staff. The current and former airport employees were charged with helping the street gang members smuggle guns and drugs into Canada.

Adwick Blood Crew—In 2006, the Toronto Police Chief when asked about the spike in the number of gun-related violent acts in the city was quoted as saying, "The fact that street gangs are now emerging in our city is a problem for us" (Dube, 2006). The number of guns coming from the United States was also seen as a contributing factor. This followed a violent year in Toronto where 37 out of 55 murder victims were killed by guns. As a response, the Toronto police conducted Project Flicker targeting the Adwick Blood Crew. The police operation seized 15 firearms, including a MAC-11 machine gun. The Adwick Blood Crew was reportedly formed in the mid-1990s on Toronto's west side to counter the expansion of the Crips. The Bloods name was chosen because the Bloods are the Crips mortal enemy in the United States.

Quebec Province

Capital: Quebec City
Population: 7,907.4
Largest City: Montreal
Population: 3,859,316

The CISC (2006) states that there are approximately 50 established or emerging street gangs in Quebec province with the most sophisticated and criminally oriented gangs in Montreal and the urban areas. For the most part, the gangs are homogeneous, such as having primarily Caribbean or Hispanic composition. The gangs may have the same name, but they operate independently. The gang's primary illegal activities are drug trafficking and the sex trade. Some gangs, particularly those in Montreal, have ties to organized crime groups such as the Italian Mafia and the Hells Angels. Although Quebec City is the capital, Montreal (estimated 2011 metro population of 3,859,316) is the largest city in Quebec and the second largest city in Canada; therefore, we will examine street gangs in Montreal. The Service de la Ville de Montreal (SPVM), Montreal's municipal police, believes that there are 20 major gangs within the territory of Montreal, divided into two distinct groups (the Reds and the Blues). An assistant SPVM police chief opines that the nature of Montreal's street gangs had changed in the last 25 years. In 1985, 70 percent of the street gang members were juveniles and 30 percent were adults. In 2005, the situation is the "complete reverse" (Anon., December 16, 2005).

Reds and the Blues Alliances—Brassard (March, 2011) states that Pie-IX Boulevard in Montreal acts as the dividing line between the territories of the Reds (Bloods) and Blues (Crips) street gangs in Montreal. The street gangs under the Red banner call themselves Bloods after the L.A. gangs of the same name. The Reds are gangs that occupy the eastern point of the island of Montreal. The Blues, the gangs under the Blue banner, are west of the Pie-IX division line and call themselves Crips, also after the L.A. gang of the same name.

Master Bs—Montreal's first black gang, the Master Bs, composed of Haitian immigrants, was formed in the 1980s as a protection group against the racist skinhead and neo-Nazi gangs prevalent in Montreal (Brassard, March 2011). The name came from the nickname of the founder Beauvoir Jean aka "Maitre Beauvoir" (Master B). Beauvoir Jean is now a social worker counseling youths against joining gangs. As often happens this protection group soon turned into a street gang involved in prostitution, drug trafficking, extortion and robbery. The Master Bs quickly spread throughout North Montreal.

Bo-Gars—During this same time period, another Haitian immigrant street gang developed in North Montreal, the Bo-Gars. The gang started as a school fight club, where the young kids would play a game where teams of boys would change sides each day and fight each other. They were not criminals but groups of boys play fighting. The name Bo-Gars was chosen because the English translation is roughly "good-looking guys" according to the founder. It wasn't long before groups of the Bo-Gars began acting as soldiers for the Master Bs and became criminal street gangs. Over time, internal disputes between the Bo-Gars and the Master Bs led to the ascendency of the Bo-Gars. They are now the ascendant gang in the Reds.

Crack Down Posse—The Haitian immigrant neighborhoods west of the division line had emerging gangs that were smaller and less organized than the Master Bs and the Bo-Gars. One of these gangs, the Crack Down Posse (CDP), formed an alliance among the other gangs to challenge the Master Bs and the Bo-Gars. This alliance was called "les Blues" either because they wanted to identify with the L.A. Crips or because the subway line that ends in their territory is called the Blue Line. It wasn't long before the Bo-Gars began forming an alliance of street gangs in their area and called it the Blues. It appears that the identification of the Blues as Crips and the Reds as Bloods after the L.A. gangs of the same name is only symbolic as reported by the RCMP.

Mafia and the Hells Angels Alliances—In recent years the Reds and the Blues have formed ties with other organized crime groups in Montreal, including the Mafia and the Hells Angels. The Blue alliance with its closer proximity to downtown Montreal has close relations with the Hells Angels who supply them with drugs. This relationship is primarily due to a Haitian-born black named Gregory Wooley aka "Picasso." The extremely violent Wooley was actually a member of the Red alliance, at one time a member of both the Master Bs and the Bo-Gars. Wooley formed his own gang the Syndicate and became close friends with the equally violent leader of the Montreal Nomads Chapter of the Hells Angels, Maurice "Moms" Boucher. Wooley became an associate of the Hells Angels and then a patched member of the Rockers MC, a puppet/support gang of the Hells Angels, leading to the erroneous conclusion by many that he is the first black full-patched member of the Hells Angels. Wooley is alleged to be the gangster that formed the relationship between the Hells Angels and the Crips, allowing the street gangs and the Hells Angels to control the drug trade in Montreal. The Red alliance formed ties with the Rock Machine MC, the bitter enemies of the HAMC.

Operation AXE (February 12, 2009)—The SPVM had at least four operations against the city's street gangs. Operation AXE is important because it established that there was a working relationship between the Crips street gang, the Syndicate (a street gang formed by Hells Angels Associate George Wooley), and the outlaw motorcycle gang criminal organization, the Hells Angels.

The police operation, the largest in Montreal history, began at 6 a.m. ET when more than 700 police officers from the RCMP, Quebec Provincial Police, and police officers from the cities of Montreal, Lava, and Longueuil, began executing 63 search warrants in Quebec and Ontario provinces. At the end of the operation, 55 adults had been arrested (49 men and six women). Among those arrested were George Wooley, the Syndicate street gang founder and HAMC associate, a former Canadian Olympic weightlifter and the father of a Montreal police officer. Wooley was arrested in prison where he was serving time for a previous conviction. He was charged with gangsterism (engaging in crime for the profit of a criminal organization), becoming the first person in Canada to be charged with gangsterism a second time. According to SPVM, the police seized:

25 firearms, along with clips and munitions
41 kilos of cocaine
2,300 rocks of cocaine
11 kilos of hashish
225 kilos of marijuana
hundreds of pills of various sorts (steroids, speed, etc.)
and more than $675,000 in cash

Twenty-two of those arrested were charged with gangsterism along with conspiracy to commit murder, arms possession, cocaine trafficking, crack production, conspiracy to import cocaine, and possession with the intent to distribute.

British Columbia Province

Capital: Victoria
Population: 83,363
Largest City: Vancouver
Population: 747,281 Metro area—2.37 million

There are approximately 20 street gangs in the Lower mainland, Vancouver area, of British Columbia province, primarily engaged in drug trafficking (CISC, 2006). These gangs obtain their drugs from the Hells Angels MC, Asian, and independent organized crime groups. The gangs often use the "dial-a-dope" distribution system mentioned earlier. There are Crips and Aboriginal gangs in Victoria and Vancouver, but it appears that the multiple ethnic gangs and Indo-Canadian gangs are the most serious crime problems. Fueling the gang problems in the province is the powerful home-grown marijuana know as "B.C. Bud." Trafficking in B.C. Bud is estimated to be a $7 billion dollar-a-year industry. We will now discuss the United Nations Gang, the Red Scorpions, the Independent Soldiers, and the violent Indo-Canadian gangs.

United Nations Gang—John Morton, the Assistant Secretary of the U.S. Immigration and Customs Enforcement (ICE) Agency of the Department of Homeland Security calls the British Columbia-based UN Gang a transnational criminal organization whose drug smuggling operation includes the United States, Mexico, Venezuela, Colombia, India, Vietnam, Australia, and Great Britain (Morton, 2011). The UN Gang, according to Morton, exports large quantities of B.C. Bud into the United States, sells it, and then uses the revenues to purchase cocaine abroad that is then smuggled into British Columbia and sold throughout Canada. Hundreds of pounds of cocaine are imported into British Columbia every month.

Since December 2005, U.S. ICE-led operations against the UN Gang have resulted in the seizure of 2,169 pounds of marijuana, 335 kilograms of cocaine, two pounds of crack cocaine, four pounds of methamphetamine, five firearms, and approximately $2 million dollars. Following a joint operation by U.S., Mexican, and Canadian law enforcement authorities, the leader of the UN Gang, Clay Roueche, was sentenced in 2009 to 30 years in prison in the United States District Court in Seattle, Washington after pleading guilty to exportation of cocaine, importation of marijuana, and conspiracy to launder money.

The British Columbia-based UN gang was formed by drug peddler Clay Roueche in 1997 and adopted its name because of the variety of nationalities that became members, including Iraqis, Chinese, and Guatemalans. The gang may have started out as street thugs who stole cars and robbed stores, however, by the early 2000s the gang had swelled in membership and became involved in more serious crimes: arms trafficking, extortion, home invasion, money laundering, and murder. Under Roueche's leadership the gang became a multi-million dollar organization and global drug distributor. The bitter enemy of the United Nations gang is the Red Scorpions.

Red Scorpions—The Red Scorpions is another multicultural British Columbia-based street gang. They are identified by "RS" tattoos on their arms and neck and their colors are red and black. According to the Abbotsford, British Columbia police, the gang members, contrary to common expectations, come from middle class families (Jiwa, 2009). They are involved in dial-a-dope operations and have been known to give out free crack cocaine and a phone number, saying "Please call us if you want us to sell you cocaine" (CBC News, August 19, 2008). The phone number was reportedly manned 24 hours a day. The Red Scorpions are one of the most violent gangs in British Columbia. Red Scorpion members, including one of the founders, a Vietnam native, were the assassins in what is called the Surrey Six murders, where four drug dealers and two innocent witnesses were killed in 2007. Several Red Scorpion and United Nations gang members have been killed in their bloody war.

The gang was formed in 2000 by a group of young criminals in a youth detention facility. The gang started out as a criminal organization wanting to become involved in the drug trade. The gang has steadily grown since 2000 and is considered one of the largest criminal gangs in the Vancouver metro area.

Independent Soldiers—Four of the six victims of the Surrey Six murders committed by the Red Scorpions gang were Independent Soldiers (IS) gang drug dealers. The murders are believed to be in retaliation for a Red Scorpion drug dealer murder by Independent Solders. Although there are reports that the Independent Solders were originally an Indo-Canadian gang that "morphed" into a multi-racial criminal gang (Gandia, 2008) a convicted kidnapper claims to have founded the Independent Solders in 2004 as a clothing company (Bolan, September 14, 2009). The Independent Soldiers do have a patented line of clothes and stores where the clothes are sold. Whatever, founding story is correct, today, the Independent Soldiers are a multi-ethnic, violent criminal street gang heavily involved in drug trafficking with several chapters in the metro Vancouver area. The members wear red, black and white colors and have tattoos of "Independent Soldiers" on their forearms.

Indo-Canadian Street Gangs—The Indo-Canadian street gangs are composed of South Asians (India) who have immigrated to Canada. One of the earliest gangs the "Indo-Canadian Mafia" was formed in the mid-1990s. A branch of the gang was the Elite Hit Squad, which would get $15,000 to $20,000 a killing. The gang imported heroin from India that they distributed and sold in the Vancouver area. In the late 1990s and early 2000s, they were ranked as the most powerful criminal organizations in British Columbia (Ghosh, 2010). A remarkable aspect of these violent gangs is that they were of Punjabi Sikh descent from middle class families with well-educated parents.

Alberta Province

Capital: Edmonton
Population: 730,372 Metro—1,034,945
Largest City: Calgary
Population: 953,628

There were approximately 30 street gangs reported in Alberta Province in 2006, primarily involved in drug trafficking (CISC, 2006). The Edmonton police report that there are 18 "criminal networks" (street gangs) operating in the Edmonton area (Barlow, 2007). Ten of these gangs were identified by name: the Asian Street Gangs—Crazy Dragons and the Crazy Dragon Killers; GTC (Get the Cash); North End Jamaicans; West End Jamaicans; Southside Boys; the white supremacist White Boy Posse; and the Aboriginal gangs—Alberta Warriors, Indian Posse, and the Redd Alert. The Independent Soldiers from British Columbia have also been reported in Edmonton. The violent Winnipeg African Mafia street gang now has a presence in parts of Alberta.

Aboriginal Street Gangs—Aboriginal (Native Canadians) street gangs are active in the western provinces of Canada, particularly in the cities of Calgary and Edmonton in Alberta Province, Regina and Saskatoon in Saskatchewan Province, and Winnipeg in Manitoba Province (CISC, 2004). They are involved in street level drug trafficking with drugs usually supplied by Asian-based criminal organizations or the Hells Angels motorcycle gang. In Alberta, the predominately Aboriginal gangs are the Alberta Warriors, the Redd Alert, and their bitter enemy the Indian Posse. These gangs recruit members from Aboriginal population in the urban and rural communities, correctional institutions and on reserves (reservations). The CISC (2004) reports that the Aboriginal gangs are very violent and "generally involved in opportunistic, spontaneous and disorganized street-level criminal activities, primarily low-level trafficking of marijuana, cocaine, and crack cocaine, and, to a lesser extent, methamphetamine." They are also involved in prostitution, burglary, robbery, assaults, vehicle thefts, and illicit debt collection from other crime groups such as the Hells Angels. One Canadian gang expert opines that the difference between Aboriginal gangs and other Canadian gangs is that "almost all have grown up in severe poverty. It is not just a little bit of poverty, but it's very, very deep deep grinding poverty, and they grow up in families where they don't just know where the next meal is coming from, or maybe the family is homeless" (Delaney, 2010).

African Mafia Street Gang—The African Mafia street gang was formed in Winnipeg in 2004 by young men who had immigrated to Canada from war-torn regions of eastern Africa, such as Ethiopia, Somalia, Sudan, and Sierra Leone. The Winnipeg Police Services say that the original gang has split into three factions—the African Mafia, Da Pittbull Army (DPA) and the All 'bout Money (ABM)—and is expanding into parts of Alberta Province (Turner, 2010). This extremely violent street gang is primarily engaged in the trafficking of crack cocaine. There have been eight African Mafia members deported from Canada since the gang was formed. The last member deported had 22 criminal convictions, including assault, robbery, and assaulting a police officer, between 2004 and 2008 (CBC News, January 12, 2011).

Manitoba Province

Capital: Winnipeg
Population: 684,100

The CISC (2006) reports that there are 25 street gangs in Manitoba Province with most concentrated in the Winnipeg area and some in the rural areas and the Aboriginal reserves. Winnipeg has at times been called the gang capital of Canada. Winnipeg and Edmonton have bounced back and forth as the "Murder Capital" of Canada and are ranked 2nd and 3rd for the dubious distinction of being the "most dangerous city in Canada" (2009 Maclean's National Crime Rankings). In 2011 Winnipeg was the most violent major metropolitan area in Canada (Anon, 2011). The Canada West Foundation (2007), a charitable research institution serving the four western provinces (Alberta, British Columbia, Manitoba, Saskatchewan), reports that street gang activity is a large problem for Winnipeg and turf warfare between the gangs is a growing concern (Wilkie & Berdahl, 2007). The report goes on to say that street drug activity, predominately dealing crack and crystal meth, is present and wide-open in most neighborhoods.

The African Mafia, mentioned earlier, is originally a Winnipeg street gang, and it splintered off from another Winnipeg gang, the Mad Cowz. The split supposedly occurred over avenging the slaying of a 14-year-old Mad Cowz drug dealer by the rival gang, the B-Side or Broadway Boys, an Aboriginal gang formed in 2000 in Winnipeg's West Broadway area (Markosun's Blog, October 17, 2010). There was also a disagreement over the distribution of funds from the drug sales fueling the split.

The Central gang (CTL), a multi-cultural gang, was formed in 2002 when the Deuces gang was disbanded. Members wear black and white sweaters or jackets with "Central" or "CTL" on the back. They have been linked with the Aboriginal prison gang the Manitoba Warriors, which was founded in 1992 by incarcerated Aboriginals as protection against biker and Aryan gangs. The Native Syndicate, another Canadian prison gang, has chapters in Winnipeg and is the enemy of the Central gang. The Central gang is bitter enemies with the Indian Posse, an Aboriginal street gang originally formed in Winnipeg. The Indian Posse and the Manitoba Warriors are bitter enemies. The depth of this bitterness is demonstrated by a shooting in Winnipeg. A 16-year-old Indian Posse member shot his 27-year-old brother, a Manitoba Warrior member, in their grand-mother's house (McIntyre, 2011). The victim survived the shooting. The Indian Posse is now one of the largest street gangs in Canada.

Saskatchewan Province
Capital: Regina
Population: 204,512

Twenty-one street gangs have been identified in Saskatchewan Province (CISC, 2006). The largest group of gangs are Aboriginal criminal adult gangs: Native Syndi-cate, Indian Posse, Redd Alert, Saskatchewan Warriors, Crazy Cree, Mixed Blood, Tribal Brotherz, and West Side Soldiers (CISS, 2005). Twenty-two percent of all Cana-dian gang members are Aboriginals and most of the Regina gang members are First Nation (W-Five Staff, May 16, 2009). There are also Aboriginal youth gangs: Crips, Junior Mixed Blood, Indian Mafia Crips, and North Central Rough Riders. Accord-ing to the CISS (2005), Saskatchewan has the highest concentration of youth gang members in Canada. The gangster lifestyle appears to be an attractive alternative for Aboriginal youths who are subjected to extreme poverty, violence, absent parents, and urban migration combined with blocked opportunities and substance abuse (CISS, 2005).

Joining a Canadian Aboriginal gang appears to follow similar steps as joining a United States youth or criminal gang. The recruit must have a gang sponsor who is re-sponsible for his loyalty and suitability. Then the recruit must meet three require-ments:

1. The prospective member must perform a series of acts—vehicle thefts, as-saults, robberies, etc.—called "strikes." The CISS reports that most of the crimes in Saskatchewan are strikes committed by new members trying to in-crease their status in the gang.
2. The recruit must produce "paperwork" or a copy of their criminal record.
3. There is some sort of initiation ceremony usually a "beating in" or "jumping in" process where the prospective member is beaten by other gang members for a certain period of time.

In Saskatchewan and in the United States most of the adult gangs have evolved over time and have become involved in more organized criminal activity such as drug traf-ficking (CISS, 2005).

Atlantic Provinces: Nova Scotia, New Brunswick, Newfoundland and Labrador, Prince Edward Island

The four Atlantic Provinces are generally considered to be crime free with few gangs. The CISC (2006) reports that ten street gangs have been reported in Nova Scotia, seven in New Brunswick, and none in Newfoundland and Labrador or Prince Edward Island. Those gangs identified are typically involved in low level street-level drug trafficking of cocaine and crack cocaine.

References

Anon. (December 16, 2005). Cops take aim at street gangs. *Gazette Montreal.*

Anon. (07/21/2011). Manitoba records highest crime rate among the provinces: Statistics Canada. *Canadian Press.*

Barlow, E. (January 4, 2007). Alberta gangs everywhere say police. *Edmonton Sun.*

Bolan, K. (September 14, 2009). Founder of Metro Vancouver's Independent Soldiers our on parole. *Vancouver Sun.*

Brassard, J.B. (March 2011). Montreal Gangs Following in the Footsteps of LA Gangs? *Montrealites Justice.*

Callahan, G.K.; Campbell-Waugh, M. (2008). How are gangs evolving in your city. *Gazette.* 70(2): 12–13.

CBC News. (August 19, 2009). Violent Red Scorpion gang busted in Victoria. *CBC News.*

CBC News (January 12, 2011). Winnipeg street gang member deported. *CBC News.*

CCC. (2006). The Gang Book. *Chicago Crime Commission.*

CISC. (2004). *Report on Organized Crime.* Criminal Intelligence Center Canada. Ottawa

CISC, (2006). *Report on Organized Crime.* Criminal Intelligence Center Canada: Ottawa.

Criminal Intelligence Service Saskatchewan (2005). 2005 Intelligence Trends: Aboriginal-based gangs in Saskatchewan.

CISC. (2010). *Report on Organized Crime.* Criminal Intelligence Center Canada: Ottawa.

Delaney, J. (April 1, 2010). Aboriginal gangs spreading across Canada. *Epoc Times.*

Department of Justice (2009). *2009 National Gang threat Assessment.*

Dube, R.C. (January 2, 2006). Toronto struggles with rising gun violence. *USA Today.*

Edmonton Journal (March 29, 2008). Edmonton police smash gang feeding Hells Angels Edmonton. *Canada.com.*

FBI. (10/10/07). FBI going global on gangs, new partnerships target MS 13.

Gandia, R. (May 22, 2008). B.C. gang expands to Edmonton. *CNews.*

Ghosh, P.A. (August 5, 2010). Indo-Canadian gangsters shatter "model minority" stereotype. *International Business Times.*

Gibeaut, J. (1998). Gang busters. *ABA Journal.*

Global National. (May 2, 2007). Violent Hispanic gang spreading in Canada. *Canada.com.*

Jiwa, S. (November 16, 2009). Red Scorpion gang suspect arrested with $100,000 cash and drugs. *Digital Journal.*

Krikorian, G. (August 02, 1995). Gang members sentenced in "wrong way" shooting. *Los Angeles Times.*

Lambert, R. & Doucette, C. (April 2, 2009). Toronto gangs hit in massive raids. Cops seize weapons, drugs; arrest 125. *The Toronto Sun.*

Logan, S. (2009). *This is for the Mara Salvatrucha.* New York: Hyperion.

Markosun's Blog. (October 17, 2010). Winnipeg's Criminal Gangs.

McIntyre, M. (05/21/2011). Young gang member sentenced to two years for shooting brother. *Winnipeg Free Press.*

Morton, J. (May 17, 2011). Statement before the U.S. Senate Committee on the Judiciary. Subcommittee on Immigration, Refugee and Border Security.

NCIC (2009). National Gang Intelligence Center.

Pelisek, C. (August 2, 2006). Avenues gang members meet the end of the road. *Law Weekly.*

Powell, B. & Small, P. (December 23, 2009). Creba killer was a police tipster. *Inside-thestar.com.*

Quenneville, G. (June 22, 2007). Drug gang may be targeting high school students. *Northern News Services.*

Quinones, S. & Winton, R. (June, 8, 2011). 51 Indicted in Azusa gang's "terrorizing" of blacks. *Los Angeles Times.*

Rafael, T. (2007). *The Mexican Mafia.* New York: Encounter Books.

Rosenzweig, D. (December 21, 2002). Gang enforcer gets life term in prison. *LA Times.*

Thomas, P. & Bass, S. (October 8, 2009). Gangs turn Chicago streets into a battlefield. *ABC News.*

Turner, J. (January 21, 2010). African Mafia Street Gang. *CBC News.*

Vallis, M. (May 4, 2010). Massive police raids executed across Ontario: Project Corral. *National Post.*

Wallace, K. (May 5, 2010). Police raids reveal links to powerful Jamaican Shower Posse Gang. *National Post.*

Wilkie, K. & Berdaht,L. (September 2007). Hard times: a portrait of street level social problems in western Canada. *Canada West Foundation.*

W.-Five Staff. (May. 16, 2009). City of Gangs: Regina grapples with gang problem. *CTV News.*

Readings

1. Valdez, A. (Fall, 2005). Mexican-American Youth and Adult Prison Gangs in a Changing Heroin Market. *Journal of Drug Issues:* 843–867.
2. Arana, A. (May–June 2005). How the Street Gangs Took Central America. *Foreign Affairs.*
3. Grekul, J. (2008). Aboriginal Gangs and Their (Dis)placement: Contextualizing, Recruitment, Membership, and Status. *Canadian Journal of Criminology and Criminal Justice.*
4. Friesen, J. (June 18, 2011). The Ballad of Daniel Wolfe. *The Globe and Mail.* Permission granted by the *Globe and Mail.*

Reading 1.
Mexican American Youth and Adult Prison Gangs in a Changing Heroin Market*

*Avelardo Valdez***

This article focuses on the interaction between the larger community's drug markets and youth and adult prison gangs, and the process that leads to specific adverse consequences both to the youth gangs as organizations, and to individual members. Described is the emergence of a restructured heroin market dominated by an adult prison gang. A major consequence of this was the increasing use of heroin among Mexican American gang members and their transformation from autonomous youth gangs to extensions of the adult prison gangs or their demise. Data was collected from 160 members of 26 Mexican American youth gangs and key informants in San Antonio. Findings focus on organizational rules, drug market transformations, consequences on members, and the impact of heroin on the gang's organization. Discussed is how the dominance of prison gangs is related to the increased incarceration and recidivism rates of Mexican Americans and declining economic opportunities for urban minorities.

Introduction

The participation in the drug market by youth street gangs is best understood as part of a constellation of economic and social activities that comprise the informal economy of urban minority communities (Fagan, 1996; Jackson, 1991). The increasing presence of minorities in the drug market in this country during the last 30 years (1970–2000) has coincided with economic restructuring (Wilson, 1975; Wilson, 1990). These economic changes exacerbated the misdistribution of wealth and have produced greater inequality and, as a by-product, increased poverty, joblessness, and welfare dependency in urban minority neighborhoods. As a result, low-income immigrants and minorities including youth gangs in interaction with adults have taken advantage of the economic opportunities in different sectors of the informal economies.

Previous studies offer insights into the participation of minority youth and gangs in the illegal drug market, especially during the cocaine and crack epidemic in New York during the 1980s and 1990s (Curtis, 2003; Hamid, 1990; Williams, 1989). Studies specifically on gangs have focused on their participation in street-level heroin and other drug distribution markets (Bullington, 1977; Hagedorn, 1998; Moore, 1978;

* © 2005 *Journal of Drug Issues;* Permission granted by *Journal of Drug Issues.* Copyright of *Journal of Drug Issues* is the property of Florida State University/School of Criminology & Criminal Justice and its content may not be copied or emailed to multiple sites or posted to a listserv without the copyright holder's express written permission.

** Funding for this study was provided by the National Institute on Drug Abuse (RO1 DA 0864). I would like to thank Richard Arcos and John Alvarado for their assistance on this research.

Sanders, 1994). Some researchers report that gangs are well organized drug trade enterprises and are responsible for the majority of the drug distribution business in these markets (Padilla, 1992; Skolnick, Correll, Navarro, & Rabb, 1990; Taylor, 1990). Other researchers have found that gangs are not the major perpetrators of illegal drug trade and that the connection between street gangs and drug sales and related problems is overstated (Fagan, 1996; Hagedorn, 1998; Maxson, 1995). However, as Venkatesh (1997, p. 83) states there is still a gap in the "attention to the ways in which street gangs interact with other groups (adults) and institutions in its neighborhood."

This article focuses on the interaction between the larger community's drug markets and youth and adult prison gangs and the process that leads to specific adverse consequences, both to the youth gangs as organizations and to individual members. The interest here is in the patterns of change and continuity of gangs and community over time. This article describes heroin use and dealing among Mexican Americans within the context of San Antonio, Texas. Discussed are the gang's initial prohibition of heroin use and its enforcement through a "no heroin rule." As well, we discuss the emergence of a restructured San Antonio heroin market dominated by an adult prison gang. Furthermore, we examine the effects of this changing heroin market controlled by the prison gang on gang member's heroin use and other personal consequences. Lastly, the paper explores how the gang's organizational rise and fall is influenced within the context of this changing heroin market.

Heroin Use, Selling, and Dealing in the Barrio

The Mexican American drug using population has been characterized in the literature as having a clear preference for heroin and other opiates and nearly universal use of intravenous injection as the route of administration (Bullington, 1977; Casavantes, 1976; Desmond & Maddux, 1984; Moore, 1978; National Institute of Justice, 1996). As a result of this pattern of drug use within this population, a distinct heroin subculture developed over the last 50 years in southwestern cities and towns among Mexican American users or "tecatos." The term tecato tends to denote a chronic or career heroin user with a criminal orientation and repeated involvement with the criminal justice system (Quintero & Estrada, 2000; Ramos, 1995; Valdez, Kaplan, & Cepeda, 2000). As a result, tecatos have developed a distinct street identity that revolves around a "pachuco" lifestyle characterized by heroin use, criminality, incarceration, unique style of dress and tattoos, and social networks. They have traditionally been stigmatized and socially isolated from the larger Mexican American and Anglo community. Despite this lifestyle, they tend to remain integrated into family and neighborhood networks more so than heroin users from other groups (i.e., Puerto Ricans, Blacks and especially Whites). For these and other reasons, investigators have described Mexican American heroin users as "clannish" (Casavantes, 1976) even within their own neighborhoods and in the prison system.

Mexican Americans have traditionally dominated the opium, morphine, and heroin trade since before World War II (Bullington, 1977; Desmond & Maddux, 1984). This early period corresponds with increased numbers of Mexicans immigrating to the United States. Within this market, Mexican Americans had an advantage in the drug trafficking business over others in that they shared a common language and ethnic background with drug wholesalers in Mexico's border regions and interior.

The proximity of Mexico, a major source of heroin in the United States, has made heroin more accessible to users in South Texas than to other regions of the U.S. In 1988, the Office of National Drug Control Policy (ONDCP) pursuant to the Anti-Drug Abuse Act designated the southwest border of the U.S. as a high intensity drug trafficking area (HIDTA). These areas are identified as having the most critical drug trafficking problems that adversely impact the United States (Office of National Drug Control Policy, 2003; United States Government Printing Office, 2001). For instance, South Texas, which shares a 2,000-mile border with Mexico that is one to two counties deep, is identified as a primary staging area for large-scale binational narcotic trafficking operations.

Although not conclusive, sources tend to agree that exclusive networks of multigenerational family members and friends carry out heroin distribution activities in Mexican American communities (Moore, 1978; Valdez & Mata, 1999). Some of these networks are small and their operations limited to specific southwestern cities, whereas others are larger, national drug networks. Even though South Texas is primarily a staging area for large-scale shipments of narcotics to the north; heroin, cocaine, marijuana and prescription drugs "spill over" and flood the local market (Valdez, Cepeda, Kaplan, & Yin, 1998). As a result, Mexican American heroin users in these southwestern communities have little difficulty making purchases from neighborhood-based dealers, at local bars, private residences, on the streets or more recently by home delivery services.

There have been few studies on Mexican American drug use and selling/dealing especially among youth gang members (Bullington, 1977; Sanders, 1994; Valdez & Sifaneck, 2004). The sparse existing literature suggests that most Mexican American street gangs are involved in drug markets as low-level sellers, with only a minority engaged in profitable, mid-level drug enterprises. Moore's (Moore, 1978) study discusses the participation of adult gangs within the drug market of East Los Angeles. Moore states, "drug dealers did employ members ... in a hierarchy that included non-addicted dealers, addicted dealers (who in turn would supply addict-pushers who sold heroin for use rather than profit), and finally the consumer addict" (1978, p. 85). Her findings suggested that it was usually individual older gang members who used other gang members to market the drugs to the street consumer.

In a previous article that focused on the role Mexican American gangs and members have in the drug market, a fourfold typology emerged based on two dimensions: (1) the gang's organizational structure defined by involvement in drug dealing and (2) the individual gang member's role in using, selling, and dealing drugs (Valdez & Sifaneck, 2004). The typology encompasses a wide range of connections and intersections between gangs, their individual members, and the selling of illegal drugs within the wider distribution system. A major finding of this study was that most gang members are user/sellers and are not profit-oriented dealers. It found that there were seven highly entrepreneurial and organized criminal gangs among the 26 gangs that are the subject of this research. It also suggests that adult prison gangs and criminal family members may play important roles in member's drug dealing activities. This study builds upon this earlier work by focusing on the role of adult prison gangs and the larger drug markets on the transformation of Mexican American youth gangs in San Antonio.

Methods

This research evolved from a study of gang violence among Mexican American gangs in South Texas sponsored by the National Institutes of Health (NIH), National Institute on Drug Abuse (NIDA). The focus of the study was to identify and distinguish the relationship between gang violence and drug use among male gangs. The term "youth gang" is used in this study to refer to groups of adolescents who engage in collective acts of delinquency and violence and are perceived by others and themselves as a distinct group. Moreover, the group has a structured hierarchy with rituals and symbols (colors, signs, etc.) and is associated with a territory.[1]

The study used multiple methods, including ethnographic field observations, focus groups, and life history/intensive interviews with 160 male gang members (Yin, Valdez, Mata, & Kaplan, 1996). The study was delimited to two areas of the city's Mexican American population encompassing centers of commerce and residency for the group. The area also has the highest concentration of delinquent behavior and Mexican American gang activity as well as underclass characteristics (Kasarda, 1985). This delimitation was based on ecological data such as the U.S. Census, criminal justice data, public housing statistics, and previously published governmental reports and studies:

After identifying two study areas, two indigenous field-workers began the social mapping of these communities, using systematic field observations and recording extensive field notes. Using Wiebel's (1993) indigenous outreach model, field-workers were selected based on their knowledge and familiarity with the targeted community and their ability to provide entree to groups of Mexican American juvenile gang members. The social mapping stage of the study lasted approximately six months, although fieldwork and collection of field notes was a continuous process lasting a total of four years. Social mapping assisted in the identification of gangs and where the target groups congregate, such as public parks, public housing spaces, playgrounds, recreational centers, downtown areas, neighborhood businesses, and specific neighborhoods. In conducting this initial fieldwork, field-workers were able to establish an ethnographic presence (Sifaneck & Neaigus, 2001) and maintain a high visibility within the targeted community to help legitimize the project in the community. After this was accomplished, the field-workers began to make contacts with the gang members, gain their trust, and obtain access to their social networks. The primary goals of the field-workers were to establish rapport with the gang members, maintain nonjudgmental attitudes and promote candid and accurate reporting by respondents during data collection and the interview process. Respondents were assured that information disclosed would be held in the strictest confidentiality as protected by NIH federal guidelines. Much of the data collected on the gang's drug selling activities and that of the adult prison gangs was usually triangulated to insure truthfulness and assure accuracy. This was particularly the case in descriptions of sensational events such as gunfights or murders that often had to be pieced together from various persons.

---

1. In the literature there are very different definitions of what constitutes an adolescent gang (Klein, 1971; Miller, 1975; Moore, 1978; Yablonsky, 1962) often based on the researcher's relationship to the gang and source of information. The definition used in this study is based on our experiences in working with gangs in San Antonio.

After gaining access, rapport, and trust, field-workers began to collect observational data based on gang hangouts mentioned previously. Results of this fieldwork were recorded in daily field notes that were shared and discussed with the research team. All efforts were made not to use information from school officials or police agencies in order to not associate the project with these authorities. Attention was focused on the primacy of developing and maintaining networks and a research presence in these communities and among the gangs in these areas.

The fieldwork resulted in identifying all 26 active juvenile gangs and their respective rosters in this area whose cumulative membership totaled 404 persons.

The validity and accuracy of gang rosters were checked using at least three of four collateral sources: "gatekeepers," gang member contacts, key respondents, and field-workers' observations. Gatekeepers are those who control access to information, other individuals, and places (Hammersley & Atkinson, 1995). Field-workers were able to acquire information for initially classifying membership (leader, core, peripherals), gang type, and to delineate the gang's territory (neighborhood). Using this information, a stratified sample was designed that generated the 160 gang members interviewed for this study (See Yin et al., 1996 for a detailed description of this sampling procedure.). Approximately 10 gang members originally selected refused to be interviewed, giving us a refusal rate that is not any more different from those of more conventional surveys. A monetary incentive of $40 was provided to the gang member for participating in the interview. In order to protect the identities of the study participants, actual names of the gangs and gang members were known only to the field-workers and the project administrator. Any reference to individual members or organizations was based on pseudonyms or an identification number assigned by the administrator. Fictitious names were given to all geographic and other physical locations. Formal consent forms were required of all the participants as well.

For the purpose of this paper emphasis will be on drug selling and drug use information elicited from the 160 respondents at various points during the life history/intensive interview, field notes, and informal interviews. Focus group data on drug markets was limited given they were conducted during the initial months of the study when drug markets were not a primary focus. The cross-sectional interview consisted of both closed- and open-ended responses and took approximately two hours to administer. Embedded in the formal interview were scenario questions on the respondents' gangs' organizational structure and two major illegal activities (Page, 1990). The latter scenario included specifics on the activity such as the types of drugs sold, individual in charge, the subject's participation and the distribution of profits. Specifically, an open-ended question was asked regarding whether the gang's illegal activities were connected in any way with adults or "veteranos" outside the gang. If so, they were asked to probe for ages, activity, frequency, relatives, etc. From this data, the role of the prison gangs in the drug market emerged. A closed-ended question elicited data on the gangs' frequency of dealing during the last year as well. Individual level data was also collected by asking respondents their frequency of drug selling during the last year as well as the characteristics of their customers.

The field-workers conducted less formal on-the-spot ethnographic interviews focused on specific topics that emerged throughout the fours years of the study. The emergence of the heroin market was one such theme that we began to focus on particularly toward the latter part of the research. These field interviews were conducted with study respondents and others in the community knowledgeable about gangs and the drug market such as social service agency representatives, public housing residents, recreational workers, and small store owners. Field interviews were also conducted with five veteran prison gang members who were long-time acquaintances of one of the staff members. These key informants provided valuable information on the drug market. Field notes based on these interviews were taken by the field-workers. There were also weekly debriefing sessions between the principal investigator and field-workers where information on the drug markets were discussed. For instance, if there had been a murder in the community the session might focus on who were the individuals involved, gang involvement, and if it was drug related. The field note and life history/intensive interview data were combined into an electronic qualitative database. The data was then analyzed and contextualized for themes and commonalities.

Based on these data, four classifications of Mexican American gangs were constructed from the analysis (Valdez, 2003). The classifications of the 26 gangs include criminal adult-dependent gangs (4), criminal nonadult dependent gangs (5), barrio-territorial gangs (12), and transitional gangs (5). The gangs were classified by five dimensions: illegal activities, gang organization, drug-use patterns, adult influences, and violent behavior. This analysis produced four polythetic classes of gangs that share an overall similarity around these different dimensions (Bailey, 1994). However, these are not absolute categories and demonstrate fluidity in that some gangs may change from one type to another over time.

Sample Characteristics

Formal respondents consisted of 160 male gang members ranging in age from 14 to 25 years with a mean age of 19. Approximately 43% of the respondents reported living in single head of households with a large proportion living with mothers (39%). Only 21% were living in households where both parents were present. The remaining 37% were currently living by themselves, friends, or other relatives including grandparents, wives, uncles, and aunts. Interestingly, 31% of the subjects reported having children. Only 26% reported being currently enrolled in middle or high school. Sixty eight percent reported having lived or currently living in public housing. Almost the entire sample of gang members had used marijuana and cocaine in their lifetime. Approximately three fourths reported lifetime use of benzodiazepines (e.g., rohypnol). Close to half reported using speedballs, psychedelics, and heroin. Current substance (last 30 days) use patterns indicated 75% of these respondents were using marijuana, and half reported using cocaine. A fourth currently used speedballs, benzodiazepines, and heroin. Among the current heroin users, 58% were noninjectors (i.e., sniffing/snorting) and 42% injectors.

Evidence of increasing heroin use was observed in a two-year follow-up pilot study on this population where self reported data revealed 43% of the noninjectors had transitioned to injecting (Valdez, Mata, Codina, Kubicek, & Tovar, 2001). Yet another follow-up study conducted eight years after the original sample was interviewed demonstrated a pattern of increased heroin use. In conducting this follow-up study, a random sample of 80 original gang members was relocated and administered a short questionnaire. Of this sample, approximately half reported using heroin during this interim period. Further evidence of this increasing heroin use is based on the constant contact with this population through several other studies conducted by this research team in this community. One of these was a Centers for Disease Control (CDC) study that focused on the females associated (i.e., girlfriends, siblings, relatives, etc.) with the original male gangs.

Findings

Gang's Prohibition against Heroin Use

Mexican American street gang members in this study voice ambivalent attitudes towards tecatos. Although Chicano adult heroin users have been an integral part of the criminal scene in the barrios, they are marginally accepted by other participants such as gang members, juvenile delinquents, car thieves, drug sellers and dealers, "coke heads," and alcoholics. Tecatos have a reputation even among these networks as being untrustworthy and unreliable. Once a heroin user becomes addicted, this person needs to generate approximately $40 to $100 a day to avoid experiencing withdrawal distress. Acquiring the drug becomes the driving force of their existence. As a result, addicts spend most of their time in criminal or quasi-criminal activities related to generating resources to purchase drugs. This includes shoplifting; committing burglaries; fencing stolen merchandise; and scamming friends, neighbors, and relatives for money. Additionally, addicts spend much of their time in the complex process of locating and obtaining their drugs from numerous sources in the communities. This eventually leads to arrests and sporadic periods of incarceration for these individuals.

However, young gang members are reluctant to completely reject tecatos because many are often immediate and extended family members, neighbors, and friends. Therefore, many gang members know firsthand how an addict's behavior negatively impacts the lives of family and friends. Many have personally experienced how their heroin dependent fathers, older brothers, or, in some cases, mothers discard their family obligations, caring about little but feeding their addiction (Valdez et al., 2000). One gang member stated, "You can't trust them (addicts), they'll steal from their own mothers."

As a result of such experiences, most gangs actively discourage the use of heroin through a "no heroin" rule that prohibits the use of heroin among its members. Nearly 70% of the respondents report that their gang had such a rule as part of the informal bylaws. The sanctions for violating the rule varied from a verbal warning to a severe beating. One gang member explains the no heroin rule in his gang:

> The rules were just something everybody knew. It was just understood that heroin was not allowed. If a person was known to have done heroin and the gang leadership found out about it then a violation would be given to the gang member who was accused of doing heroin. The punishment depended on how bad the violation was.

It is clear from our field research that sanctions vary across the different types of gangs and depended on the status of the gang member within the organization.

The Chicano Dudes, a criminal nondependent gang, is one of the gangs in the study who had a strict no heroin rule. Members of this gang remarked that they did not want to be known as "a bunch of spray heads and tecatos." This gang was one of the largest in the city at the start of this study with a membership of approximately 150 persons. The gang was organized into five different sets (cliques or subgroups) found throughout the Mexican American community. This was especially the case in outlying areas of the barrios where many families were being relocated as result of the closing of several housing projects. The gang's principal set was located in one of the housing projects that remained open.

In the beginning of our study, the Chicano Dudes held weekly meetings. Among other business, the leadership would give out violations and sanctions to those members who allegedly used heroin. First time violators would just get a verbal warning. If the heroin use persisted, the leadership would order that the member be given a "calentada" (beating) by three to six members of the gang.

However, not all the gangs had a no heroin rule nor was the rule always enforced among those that had one. For instance, the Nine-Ball Crew, an adult dependent criminal gang, did not enforce such a rule because many of its members, including the leader, were selling heroin. Thus it was not in the gang's interest to have this kind of restriction on their membership. In some cases, senior members of some gangs (popularly identified as the older gangsters, or "OGs") used heroin despite the gang's no heroin rule. As one member stated, "They (OGs) don't listen to no one anyway." Their OG status seemed to give them special privilege. However, this exception to the rule encouraged other gang members to use heroin as they realized that they might not be given the sanctions associated with this violation.

Prison Gangs and the Drug Market Transitions

The drug market in San Antonio's Mexican American community has been a highly diversified marketplace with various actors operating at different levels within this market. Exclusive networks of multigenerational family and friends carry out these drug activities. Some of these networks are small, and their operations limited to San Antonio. Others are larger, organized drug networks with connections in Mexico and other cities throughout the United States. Although a hierarchical structure exists in this drug market, there has always been space for individual entrepreneurs to operate. Mexican American drug users in San Antonio looking to buy the more popular drugs (e.g., marijuana, cocaine, and heroin) do not have any difficulty locating a seller or dealer in the immediate community. This may be less so for Black or White drug users. Additionally, a robust market exists for prescription drugs that enter the United States through the loopholes in the U.S./Mexico laws. This results in an abundant influx of such drugs as tranquilizers, painkillers, diet pills, and other drugs used recreationally by Mexican Americans (Valdez et al., 1998).

The South Texas drug market has four organizational levels. These include large-scale distribution enterprises with links to well-known Mexican suppliers, intermediate dealers who buy large quantities, smaller dealers, and user/sellers (Valdez & Sifaneck, 2004). The user/sellers sell small affordable quantities to barrio recreational drug users and addicts. Gang members in this study deal drugs at all levels except at the large-scale level that is restricted for older, well-established dealers with Mexican connections. Most gang members are found at the user/seller level and only sell drugs to reduce the costs associated with their own drug use. For the most part, this activity consists of selling small quantities of marijuana and cocaine to friends and acquaintances. This is usually very loosely organized with individuals engaged in freelance rather than organized drug entities. The barrio-territorial and transitional gangs tended to fall into this category, while the other gang types were more likely to function as intermediate or small dealers. The relationship, however, between gang membership, gang organization, drug use, and drug distribution is constructed along a complex dimension in this community (Valdez & Sifaneck, 2004).

The city's heroin market radically changed when a Mexican American prison gang, Pura Vida, entered into this marketplace in the early 1980s. Pura Vida was one of three prison gangs with a presence in San Antonio's criminal scene. At the time of the study, the other two prison gangs operated in areas outside the territories where the gangs and gang members for this study were recruited.[2] The 1990s experienced a dramatic increase in incarceration and recidivism rates in Texas and the United States, largely as a result of federal and state drug laws passed during the last three decades (Gray, 1998). Thus, the American prison population increased to approximately two million persons during the 1990s. Young Hispanics and Blacks disproportionately comprised the majority of this incarcerated population in the U.S. (Harrison & Beck, 2003). Eventually, this incarcerated population returned to communities that offered little economic opportunity, particularly for ex-felons.

Pura Vida was formed by Mexican American inmates from San Antonio in penal institutions in the Texas Department of Corrections in 1984 allegedly to protect themselves from White supremacists and Black nationalists groups. In 1992 Pura Vida was reported to have approximately 700 members in the Texas prison system; this number increased to 1,425 in 1998 (Comyn, 1999). This group rapidly became the largest gang in the Texas prison system and was known for their wide range of criminal activity in the prisons including extortion, drug sales, and murder.

According to interviews with ex-felons, when members of Pura Vida began to be released (paroled) from penal institutions, they organized themselves into a criminal network outside the prison. Under the leadership of members still inside the system, Pura Vida began to engage in drug dealing, extortion, fencing stolen property, and other illegal activities throughout South Texas. Pura Vida's presence was most visible on the west side of San Antonio, home for many of the parolees before being incarcerated. Neighborhoods in this area are characterized as having the highest concentration of low-income persons of Mexican origin in the city. It was within this community, particularly in the city housing projects, that they established their presence in the drug marketplace.

During the course of this study (1995–1999), Pura Vida gradually gained control of a large portion of the heroin and cocaine market in large areas of the west and south

2. One of these gangs was initiated by Mexican American prisoners from El Paso and the other by inmates from the Rio Grande Valley and other parts of South Texas. At the time of the study, although there was some competition among the gangs, neither gang posed a threat to the control that Pura Vida on the west or south side of San Antonio.

sides. The control of the heroin market has been accomplished through a highly regimented vertical organization using ex-felons recruited in the prisons and connections in Mexico. The organizational structure is along paramilitary lines with a president, vice president, general, captains, lieutenants, sergeants, and soldiers. They communicate to outside members through personal visits from relatives who relay directives, written material, and, in some cases, cryptic phone calls.

Independent drug dealers are allowed to sell in these geographic areas, but they are assessed a 10% surcharge, known as el diez por ciento, on all drug sales by the gang. Pura Vida members enforce the surcharge through intimidation, physical threats, violence, and murder. In one highly publicized incident, Pura Vida soldiers killed an independent heroin dealer who had refused to pay his diez por ciento. What made this incident so shocking was that the dealer's teenage daughter, boyfriend, and friends who were not involved in the drug market were also murdered. Weeks later the perpetrators of these killings were found, mysteriously murdered, their bodies dumped on the outskirts of the city.[3]

The Consequences of the Changing Heroin Market on Youth Gangs and Members

Increased Use of Heroin

Part of Pura Vida's success in this market was a result of its well established heroin connections in Mexico, organizational structure, and members' loyalty and commitment. Once they acquired these characteristics, they began to market the drug, just like any retailer or wholesaler. Pura Vida consciously targeted heroin sales to two vulnerable populations: delinquent nongang youths and gang members. They did this by making the drug more accessible, lowering the prices, offering higher purity levels and using gang members and peers as sellers. One young heroin user commenting on the accessibility of heroin said, "You can get it anywhere in the neighborhood, from all kinds of people. Even young kids can get it for you." One gang member reported how easy it was to score a $10.00 paper to snort a few lines of heroin to party or when they were just "kicking back." Increased purity allowed users to ingest the drug in ways other than through injecting, a practice that was still frowned upon by most gang leaders and members. As a result, snorting heroin (or "sniffing") slowly became an acceptable alternative among many gang members, particularly as its availability increased within this population.

While heroin use increased, for many members it still retained the ambiguous status of the past. In contrast, the use of marijuana and cocaine was highly normalized among gang members in this study. Many smoked "weed" (marijuana) continuously throughout the day. Marijuana use is highly associated with gangs and other delinquent juveniles in many low-income minority neighborhoods. One field-worker notes, "These guys smoke marijuana while walking to school, cruising, and even during pick-up basketball games at neighborhood playgrounds. It's just common behavior." Intranasal use of powdered cocaine is also an acceptable part of the gang member's lifestyle. The use

---

3. This information was gathered initially from fieldwork and later confirmed by police reports and articles that appeared in the San Antonio Express-News during this period.

of cocaine is usually reserved for parties and special occasions, such as a concert or sporting event. Cocaine is also used when a gang member has acquired some unexpected cash (usually through some illegal activity) and decides to share his good fortune with his "homeboys"(a vernacular term for close friend).

About a quarter of the gang members interviewed report using heroin in the last 30 days. Approximately 42% of these were injectors, and the rest reported intranasal use (sniffing or snorting). As mentioned previously, heroin was a highly stigmatized drug that was associated with being a tecato when the study began. In a focus group for the noninjecting project, one participant described tecatos as "dirty, sick, and always scratching themselves." Persons who were heroin addicts were chastised by gang members even though tecatos were part of the street scene in these neighborhoods. In fact, many gang members had older adult relatives who were heroin addicts. These attitudes about heroin users changed as gang members began to increase their noninjecting use of heroin. This was done either by snorting it or "shabanging," a method in which a solution of heroin and water is prepared and sprayed into the nasal passages with either a syringe or an eyedropper.

Co-Optation and Recruitment of Gang Members by Adult Prison Gangs

Another consequence of the dominance of the heroin market by Pura Vida in San Antonio is the practice of recruitment and co-optation of members of the youth gangs. Pura Vida has recruited gang members either as independent sellers or as more formal associates of the gang. The association may range from a "probationary" or "apprentice" status to a full-fledged member. Many delinquent barrio youths have been eager to join the Pura Vida, given the prison veteran's warrior-like status within the street culture of San Antonio's barrios. The "pinto" (prison veteran) is seen by many as having a highly disciplined code of conduct and a philosophy of life attuned to the values of many street-oriented young men. In addition, many of these delinquent youths assume that by joining Pura Vida, they would have access to more lucrative illegal enterprises and increased levels of protection from other street rivals.

Most young gang members were initially recruited into Pura Vida when they were sent to Texas state correctional facilities. Upon entering the system with a street reputation as "un vato firme"(a stand-up and trust worthy person) they would likely be approached by them to join. Several gang members comment that, "It's hard to not join and keep your allegiance to your street gang when you're locked up." Those who have tried to resist have had to suffer some serious consequences. An example of this is what happened to a member of the Chicano Dudes, a gang that for many years has tried to maintain independence from the prison gangs. Sammy, one of the secondary leaders of the Chicano Dudes, was sent to an adult correctional unit outside of San Antonio that was controlled by the prison gang. Sammy continued to "sport the gang's colors" in prison, even after being warned repeatedly by Pura Vida not to do so. The wearing of the gang's colors symbolized his continuing alliance to his street gang. As result of his refusal to yield, Sammy was severely beaten by the prison gang. One gang member said, "They were just sending a message to the Chicano Dudes."

Because of this type of intimidation and violence, most gang members in state prisons agree to join or at least provide "esquina" (loyalty) to Pura Vida or one of the other Chicano gangs that control that facility. In the prison, they develop a close solidarity with the organization and participate in the group's illegal activities. They are also tutored on Pura Vida philosophy, codes of conduct, and principles of the organizations. Upon release from prison they become the "soldados" (foot soldiers) of Pura Vida and usually do not return to their street gang.

Another common mechanism of recruitment is kinship. Gang members who are recruited into Pura Vida often have a close relative—a brother, father, uncle, or cousin—already in the gang. Such persons may have been active in Pura Vida activities outside of prison, but because of age or inexperience, have not been admitted. However, if a relative (who is a member of prison gang) were to put his word and reputation on the line for this prospective gang member, he will be admitted. Gang members recruited in this way often prove to be extremely loyal.

The case of Jaime, the leader of the Nine-Ball Crew, illustrates the influence of family on the recruitment of gang members. Jaime's stepfather, a high-level member of Pura Vida, controlled the drug trafficking for the prison gang in the neighborhood in which the gang was located. Jaime mentioned in interviews the respect he had for his stepfather and the position he had in Pura Vida and his ambition of eventually becoming a member. By the end of the research project, Jaime, as well as many other gang members, had been recruited by Pura Vida mostly through familial ties, such as cousins, uncles, and brothers.

Another way a youth gang member may become an associate of Pura Vida is by being identified as someone who is "moving" (selling) large amounts of drugs in the neighborhood. Word spreads that a gang member has the reputation or potential to be a "good hustler" or a "good earner." This gang member will be approached by Pura Vida and told that he must start to pay the 10% fee for dealing in their territory or suffer the consequences. Some gang members, however, are given the option of selling directly for Pura Vida. This means they do not have to pay the diez por ciento and will be afforded the physical protection of the gang. This does not make them a full-fledged gang member, but it does provide an associate status.

Pura Vida also recruits associates into their organization by "fronting" drugs to potential earners. Fronting is a technique that is commonly used by drug dealers. It is somewhat similar to giving credit to someone. Pura Vida will front drugs to a gang member and in turn is obligated to pay his debt after the drugs are sold. If the gang member does not pay his full debt in the manner agreed upon, then he may be forced to continue to sell for Pura Vida even after his debt is paid. Many times just the intimidation that Pura Vida wields in the neighborhood obligates individuals to sell for them. The positive aspect of fronting for the gang member is that he now has the protection of the prison gang from rival youth gangs and other adult criminals in the same area.

Personal Consequences for Gang Members

As described in the interviews and focus groups, heroin is a drug that allows users to feel relaxed, particularly as compared to cocaine that makes them feel "too wired." As noted, many gang members often began to use heroin intranasally during the course of the study. Many mentioned that this route was preferred over injecting because of a belief that it would allow them to control their use and avoid addiction. As the follow-up data mentioned earlier indicated, transitioning to injecting had adverse consequences for these gang members. Many of those that began to inject became dependent (addicted), a status that led to personal problems and impaired functioning with respect to obligations as gang members.

Once they transition to drug injecting these young adults engage in other exceptionally high-risk health behaviors. Our data indicates that over half of those who inject have shared a needle with another user and over 80% of them have shared a cooker, filter, or rinse water with another user. These behaviors make these individuals much more susceptible to infection with HIV, hepatitis B and C viruses, and other blood-borne pathogens.

Gang members that are addicted begin to engage in compulsive drug-seeking behavior that is irresponsible and indifferent to their responsibility as gang members. Moreover, they become unable to sustain nonheroin related personal relationships. They begin to engage in crimes that are geared towards getting resources to buy drugs, such as burglary, shoplifting, low-level drug selling (for one's own profit), and other less "gang related" crimes. This behavior invariably leads to conflicts with the gang's leadership who often continue to enforce the no heroin rule. This rule becomes increasingly more difficult to enforce because large numbers of the members are using heroin. In some gangs, the leadership itself was using heroin. In these circumstances, the leadership has no moral authority to enforce the no heroin rule.

Some gangs experience such critical numbers of members drifting away to the heroin tecato subculture that the gang's viability was threatened. The gang that best illustrates this transformation is the Chicano Dudes. Follow-up data and qualitative fieldwork estimated that approximately thirty of the hard-core members became addicted to heroin during the course of the study. This gang initially had a very strict no heroin rule; however, as the leadership and OGs began using and selling large quantities of heroin, the rule was no longer enforced. Heroin use has become so prevalent among this gang that it has acquired a reputation among other gangs as a "bunch of tecatos" and has nearly disintegrated.

Another major consequence of heroin use among members is the disproportionate incarceration rate compared to nonusers. Many heroin users are arrested and incarcerated for two primary reasons. One is directly associated with the selling and dealing of heroin. A gang member who sells heroin eventually will get "snitched on" by a disgruntled customer, a neighbor, or even a fellow heroin dealer who is trying to rid himself of competition. One of these persons will turn his name over to law enforcement, an action that often ends in his arrest. The other reason for arrest and incarceration is due to the high volume of burglaries, robberies, and car thefts they commit. While incarceration has a negative effect on the individual, it has an even more detrimental impact on the organization of the gang as many of its members and leaders are removed from the community.

Little information is available on the drug use patterns of Pura Vida members, but there is a general impression that these members are using marijuana, cocaine, and heroin. When asked about their drug use, one informant responded:

They use the same as the street gangs members, only difference is that they have a little more control. They're not going to be driving around with jale (drugs) on them. These guys will get messed up on the weekend.

Specific Effects of Heroin on the Gang's Organization

Those most influenced by the changing heroin market are independent nonadult controlled gangs that sell heroin and cocaine in areas that correspond to their territory. Most of the drug selling and dealing that occurs is carried out as a gang enterprise with profits distributed to the gang as an organization. One of these, the Nine-Ball Crew, located in one of the major housing projects in San Antonio, is distinct from other adult gangs in its direct familial ties to Pura Vida through adult relatives of the gang's leadership. When the prison gang began its solidification of the heroin trade, the Nine-Ball Crew also expanded its drug trade in its own territory. The gang found itself in direct competition with Pura Vida's drug trade. One would surmise that this would lead to a serious conflict between these two entities; however, this was minimized because the leader's stepfather was one of the heads in the prison gang.

This gang is now one of the major allies of the prison gang and is used by them against other youth gangs who refuse to cooperate with them. For example, the leader of the Chicano Dudes, one of the largest gangs in the area, was shot by a Nine-Ball Crew member for refusing to pay Pura Vida a percentage of his profit. This assassination attempt (hit) was a tactic by the Pura Vida to solidify their control of the heroin trade within a specific area.

Another gang eventually co-opted by the prison gang was Varrio La Paloma (VLP), an older, established gang, and one of the few whose former members include parents and relatives. This is a nonadult dependent criminal enterprise gang. The distribution and dealing of drugs was largely controlled by the leader of the gang and his close gang associates. The associates were older, hard-core members including two of his brothers. These individuals had connections to wholesale drug distributors that were associated with independent adult criminals with ties to Mexico. The actual drug dealing was conducted by other gang members who were fronted the drugs by the gang's leadership. The majority of the profits were turned over to the heads that pass them on to the leader of the VLP.

Pura Vida began to demand the diez por ciento from gang members selling heroin in what they determined was their territory. A compromise was reached by consistent supply of heroin. In the settlement, the VLP would be allowed to continue to sell cocaine and marijuana without any disruption or surcharge, but they would pay the diez por ciento on heroin. There were several members who refused and were consequently beaten or murdered by prison gang members. In one instance, a gang member, "Shorty," refused to deal for them or pay the surcharge. As a result, the "green light" was given to prison gang members to authorize his murder. Our source described the incident:

> Three men were sent to kill Shorty, but when the hit men met him they were shot and killed by him. Shorty was wounded during the gunfight. He was hit once in the thigh, once in the lower back, and once in the lower leg.

Shortly after the gunfight, while recovering from his wounds, he stated, "I work hard selling drugs, and I'm not going to share my profit with no one." One month later, another attempt was made on his life. His brother and uncle were killed, but Shorty survived.

There were a couple of gangs that successfully stood up to Pura Vida and maintained their independence. One of these was the Chicano Dudes, whom the prison gang has over the years attempted to control. The leader of the gang, Mark Sanchez, resisted through his own violent behavior and the loyalty of several hardcore members who, refused to be intimidated. Only recently did this independence begin to waiver after Sanchez was seriously wounded in an aborted attempt on his life by a rival gang associated with Pura Vida. The ability and willingness of the Chicano Dudes to stand up to the adult prison gang financially benefited those members who were involved in the gang's drug dealing operations. In the case of this gang, it ceased operating as a youth gang and focused almost entirely on its drug business. Nongang drug business activity was further depleted through many of the member's heroin use and addiction.

Several gangs experienced a complete dissemination as result of heroin addiction. A critical number of the leaders and members become either heavy users or addicts. Many of these then became unable to fulfill their obligations to the gang. Unable to provide protection to their members or defend their territories from encroachment by other gangs, they become easy prey for rival gangs. Other factors associated with the complete transformation of these gangs can be attributed to intimidation and coercion by the prison gangs.

After successfully taking over a neighborhood, Pura Vida actually discourages gang activities that would draw the attention of law enforcement to the neighborhood. The notes from one of our field-workers illustrates:

> On one occasion while doing fieldwork in the Comanche Homes at the Kauff-man Center, I witnessed a beating that was administered by the Pura Vida. Three guys in their early twenties walked straight up to this young male, about 17 years old, and just started kicking him and hitting him with their fists. The young man did not offer much resistance. I took a step forward to intervene when immediately I was held back by one of the community workers who told me that it was a "camalito" thing and not to get involved.

In another incident, a young member had fired a gun the night before and "tagged" a housing office building. Later that evening Pura Vida ordered a beating of this young man. From the perspective of Pura Vida, this man's behavior had unnecessarily brought the police into the neighborhood, thereby disrupting their drug trade. Following the beating, there was no more tagging in the area for at least a couple of months.

Discussion and Conclusion

This article has demonstrated how within the context of San Antonio, a Mexican American adult prison gang has been able to dominate the heroin market and other street-based drug sellers and dealers such as youth gangs. A major consequence of this was the increasing use of heroin among Mexican American gang members and the transformation of many of these from autonomous youth gangs to extensions of the adult prison gangs or their demise. This transition is accomplished through the co-optation of gang members as in the case of the Nine Ball Crew or, in some cases, by outright violent coercion, threats, and abuse.

Gangs most susceptible to the latter were those gangs or gang members selling heroin and cocaine in specific areas that adult prison gangs self-identified as their territories. These areas tended to be located within or around public housing projects, where homes of many recently released convicted felons returning from state and federal prisons are located. Others highly susceptible to heroin use and co-optation by Pura Vida were the barrio-territorial and transitional barrio gangs comprised of user/sellers primarily buying for personal consumption, and selling a portion of the drugs to offset the costs associated with their drug use. This user-seller behavior has been observed with some consistency across the different types of illegal drugs in varied geographic contexts (Andrade, Sifaneck, & Neaigus, 1999). Many of these polydrug users began to use heroin more frequently and became addicted.

The prison gang's monopoly of the heroin market constrained and narrowed other actor's participation in this market including nonprison gang affiliated adults. They transformed the heroin market from one that was a highly diversified marketplace with a wide array of individual entrepreneurs operating independently toward a more corporate-dominated market place (Venkatesh, 2000). They were able to create a demand for their product by encouraging the use of heroin through noninjecting methods, which was perceived as less of a risk than injecting. They controlled the distribution by elimination of the competition and dictating market prices. However, unlike the situation in New York when the sudden change from a restricted and controlled market in the 1970s to a fully deregulated market increased use of cocaine and spawned intense competition for territory and market share (Fagan, 1996, p. 59), the opposite occurred in San Antonio. That is, in a restricted and controlled market environment where competition decreased, heroin increased. Gang members energies thus, became focused on criminal and quasi-criminal activities related to generating resources to purchase heroin. In many cases this behavior led them away from their responsibilities as gang members. Thomas (1991) suggests a similar phenomena occurred in New York where the demise of Puerto Rican and Black youth gangs in the 1960s was linked to a heroin epidemic during this period.

A few youth gangs were able to maintain their autonomy either by not selling heroin or resisting through violence (Valdez, 2003). The latter was the case with La Poloma Blanca and the Chicano Dudes, who were two of the few to resist the adult prison gang. La Poloma was able to do it because of its strong ties to nonprison gang adult criminals and other community-level resources embedded in specific neighborhoods. These gang members come from what Joan Moore has identified as "cholo families,"which are families with a street orientation, incarceration histories, and drug use. The Chicano Dudes were able to resist the prison gang through the defiant behavior of the gang's leaders and hardcore members who were willing to use violence and mobilize other resources to defend their commitments.

Regardless of the heroin market's transformation, the role of youth gangs in this drug market was never very substantial. Based on these findings, we concur with gang researchers that have argued that gangs have a "negligible role" in drug distributions

(Curtis, 2003; Decker, Bynum, & Weisel, 1998; Fagan, 1996). Klein (1995) in particular has argued that few gangs are involved in drug selling and dealing as organizations
that share profits with its members. In the data presented here only seven gangs were
organized, criminal, drug dealing enterprises. Except for two of these gangs, they either were co-opted by the prison gang or ceased to exist. However, what is emerging
in San Antonio is a mechanism for the transition of selective youth gang members to
adult organized crime groups. This finding is different from most gang researchers
who argue that there remains a disjunction between adolescent and adult groups
(Fagan, 1996; Moore, 1992). This linkage may be occurring because of the critical
mass of offenders being released from prison in these and other minority communities that correspond with the declining opportunities in formal job markets (Pettit &
Western, 2004).

In conclusion, drug markets seem to have their most pernicious impact when they are
organized and dominated by corporate style drug dealing organizations rather than more
street level sellers and dealers such as youth gang members. The existence of corporate
style dealers such as adult prison gangs in economically marginalized communities is
more likely to market drugs like heroin that have higher profit margins. As demonstrated
by this study, corporate style dealers in these types of drug markets may also lead to
greater levels of hard drug use and addiction by young gang members. This seems to
contribute to the breakdown of community-based institutions including the economy,
family, and peer-based friendship groups such as gangs. The extent to which this happens in similar communities in different regions of the U.S. and other places in the world
needs further study.

The methodological limitations of our study need to be acknowledged. Common with
other ethnographic and qualitative studies, the generalizability of the results is limited to
communities with similar characteristics. Even then, ethnographic studies of drug dealing and markets often arrive at seemingly contradictory findings in relatively similar communities (Hagedorn, 1998; Taylor, 1990). South Texas, with its proximity to Mexican
trafficking operations, may present so special a context that replication of our findings
would be problematic. Another limitation may revolve around issues of reactivity, even
though we had during the course of this research no indication that this was a problem.
Much of this we attribute to the rapport established by the indigenous field-workers and
an understanding by the subjects that we were not making any judgments on their drug
use or criminal activities. Nonetheless, deeper and more extended qualitative research
needs to be initiated in other cities with gang members and drug markets of other eth-
nicities in order to further evaluate the significance of the findings from this single study.

References

Andrade, X., Sifaneck, S. J., & Neaigus, A. 1999. Dope sniffers in New York City: An
    ethnography of heroin markets and patterns of use. *Journal of Drug Issues*, 29(2),
    271–298.

Bailey, K. D. 1994. *Typologies and taxonomies: An introduction to classification tech-
    niques.* Thousand Oaks, CA: Sage Publications.

Bullington, B. 1977. *Heroin use in the barrio*. Lexington, MA: Lexington Books.

Casavantes, E. J. 1976. *El Tecato: Social and cultural factors affecting drug use among chicanos* (Rev ed.). Washington, DC: National Coalition of Spanish Speaking mental Health Organizations.

Comyn, J. 1999. *Gangs in Texas: 1999.* Retrieved August 15, 2003, from http://www.oag.state.tx.us/AG_Publications/pdfs/1999gangs.pdf.

Curtis, R. 2003. The negligble role of gangs in drug distribution in New York City in the 1990s. In L. Kontos, D. Brotherton, & L. Barrios (Eds.), *Gangs and society: Alternative perspectives* (pp. 41–61). New York: Columbia University Press.

Decker, S. H., Bynum, T., & Weisel, D. 1998. A tale of two cities: Gangs as organized crime groups. *Justice Quarterly*, 15(3), 395–425.

Desmond, D.P., & Maddux, J. F. 1984. Mexican American heroin addicts. *American Journal of Drug & Alcohol Abuse*, 10(3), 317–346.

Fagan, J. 1996. Gangs, drugs, and neighborhood change. In C. R. *Huff (Ed.), Gangs in America* (2nd ed.) (pp. 39–74). Thousand Oaks, CA, US: Sage Publications, Inc.

Gray, M. 1998. *Drug crazy: How we got into this mess and how we can get out*. New York: Routledge.

Hagedorn, J. M. 1998. *The business of drug dealing in Milwaukee* (Report). Thiensville, WI: Wisconsin Policy Research Institute.

Hamid, A. 1990. The political economy of crack-related violence. *Contemporary Drug Problems*, 17(1), 31–78.

Hammersley, M., & Atkinson, P. 1995. *Ethnography: Principles in practice*. London: Routledge.

Harrison, P. M., & Beck, A. J. 2003. *Prisoners in 2002* (Bulletin No. NCJ 200248): Bureau of Justice Statistics, Office of Justice Programs, U. S. Department of Justice.

Jackson, P. I. 1991. Crime, youth gangs, and urban transition: The social dislocations of postindustrial economic development. *Justice Quarterly*, 8, 379–397.

Kasarda, J. D. 1985. The severely distressed in economically transformed cities. In A. Harrell & G. Peterson (Eds.), *Drugs, crime and social isolation*. Washington, D.C.: The Urban Institute Press.

Klein, M. 1971. *Street gangs and street workers*. Englewood Cliffs, NJ.: Prentice Hall.

Klein, M. W. 1995. *The American street gang: Its nature, prevalence, and control*. New York: Oxford University Press.

Maxson, C. L. 1995. Street gangs and drug sales in two suburban cities (Research in Brief). Rockville, MD: US Department of Justice, Office of Justice Programs, National Institute of Justice.

Miller, W. B. 1975. *Violence by youth gangs and youth groups as a crime problem in major American cities.* (Report to the National Institute for Juvenile Justice and Delinquency Prevention). Washington D.C.: Department of Justice.

Moore, J. 1978. *Homeboys: Gangs, drugs, and prison in the barrios of Los Angeles.* Philadelphia, PA: Temple University Press.

Moore, J. W. 1992. Institutionalized youth gangs: Why White Fence and El Hoyo Maravilla change so slowly. In J. Fagan (Ed.), *The ecology of crime and drug use in inner cities*. New York: Social Science Research Council.

National Institute of Justice. 1996. *1995 drug use forecasting: Annual report on adult and juvenile arrestees.* Rockville, MD: National Institute of Justice, Office of Justice Programs, U. S. Department of Justice.

Office of National Drug Control Policy. 2003. *Southwest border HIDTA.* Retrieved September 10, 2003, from http://www.whitehousedrugpolicy.gov/hidta/southwest.html.

Padilla, F. M. 1992. Becoming a gang member. In *The gang as an American enterprise* (pp. viii, 198). New Brunswick, N.J.: Rutgers University Press.

Page, B. 1990. Shooting scenarios and risk of HIV-1 infection. *The American Behavioral Scientist,* 33, 478.

Pettit, B., & Western, B. 2004. Mass imprisonment and the life course: Race and class in U.S. incarceration. *American Sociological Review,* 69(2), 151–169.

Quintero, G. A., & Estrada, A. L. 2000. Cultural models of masculinity and drug use: "Machismo," heroin, and street survival on the US-Mexico border. Tuscon: The University of Arizona.

Ramos, R. 1995. An ethnographic study of heroin abuse by Mexican American in San Antonio, Texas. Austin: Texas Commission on Alcohol and Drug Abuse.

Sanders, W. B. 1994. *Gangbangs and drive-bys: Grounded culture and juvenile gang violence.* Chicago, IL: Aldine.

Sifaneck, S. J., & Neaigus, A. 2001. The ethnographic accessing, sampling, and screening of hidden populations: Heroin sniffers in New York City. *Addiction Research and Theory,* 9, 519–543.

Skolnick, J. H., Correll, T., Navarro, E. N., & Rabb, R. 1990. The social structure of street drug dealings. *American Journal of Police,* 9(1), 1–41.

Taylor, C. S. 1990. *Dangerous society.* East Lansing, MI: Michigan State University Press.

Thomas, P. 1991. *Down these mean streets.* New York: Vintage Books.

United States Government Printing Office. 2001. *Drug trafficking on the southwest border.* Retrieved March 29, from http://www.house.gov/judiciary/72144.pdf.

Valdez, A. 2003. Toward a typology of contemporary Mexican American youth gangs. In L. Kontos, D. Brotherton, & L. Barrios (Eds.), *Gangs and society: Alternative perspectives* (pp. 12–40). New York: Columbia University Press.

Valdez, A., Cepeda, A., Kaplan, C. D., & Yin, Z. 1998. The legal importation of prescription drugs into the United States from Mexico: A study of customs declaration forms. *Substance Use & Misuse,* 33(12), 2485–2497.

Valdez, A., Kaplan, C. D., & Cepeda, A. 2000. The process of paradoxical autonomy and survival in the heroin careers of Mexican American women. *Contemporary Drug Problems,* 27(1), 189.

Valdez, A., & Mata, A. G. 1999. Life histories of four Chicano heroin injecting drug users in Laredo. In M. O. Loustaunau & M. Sanchez-Bane (Eds.), *Asi es la vida: Life, death, and in-between on the US-Mexico border* (pp. 1–32). Westport, CT: Bergin & Garvey.

Valdez, A., Mata, A. G., Codina, E., Kubicek, K., & Tovar, S. 2001. *Childhood trauma, family stress, and depression among Mexican American gang non-injecting heroin users: An exploratory study.* San Antonio: Final Report to the Hogg Foundation Submitted by the Center for Drug and Social Policy Research, The University of Texas at San Antonio.

Valdez, A., & Sifaneck, S. J. 2004. Getting high and getting by: Dimensions of drug selling behaviors among U.S. Mexican gang members in South Texas. *Journal of Research in Crime and Delinquency*, 41(1), 82–105.

Venkatesh, S. A. 1997. The social organization of a street gang activity in an urban ghetto. *American Journal of Sociology*, 103(1), 82–111.

Venkatesh, S. A. 2000. *American project: The rise and fall of a modern ghetto.* Cambridge, MA: Harvard University Press.

Wiebel, W. 1993. *The indigenous leader outreach model: Intervention manual.* Rockville, MD.

Williams, T. M. 1989. *The cocaine kids.* Reading, MA: Addison Wesley.

Wilson, J. Q. 1975. *Thinking about crime.* New York: Basic Books.

Wilson, J. Q. 1990. Against the legalization of drugs. *Commentary*, 89(2), 21–28.

Yablonsky, L. 1962. *The violent gang.* New York: Macmillan.

Yin, Z., Valdez, A., Mata, A., & Kaplan, C. D. 1996. Developing a field-intensive methodology for generating a randomized sample for gang research. *Free-Inquiry Special Issue: Gangs, Drugs, and Violence*, 24(2), 195–204.

Reading 2.
How the Street Gangs Took Central America[*]

Ana Arana

While Washington Slept

Last December, a bus driving through the northern city of Chamalecon in Honduras was stopped by gunmen. The assailants quickly surrounded the bus and opened fire with their AK-47s, killing 28 passengers. The attackers, police later revealed, had been members of a notorious street gang known as Mara Salvatrucha (or MS 13) and had chosen their victims at random. The slaughter had nothing to do with the identities of the people onboard; it was meant as a protest and a warning against the government's crackdown on gang activities in the country. (U.S. officials subsequently arrested Ebner Anibal Rivera-Paz, thought to be the mastermind of the attack, in February in the Texas town of Falfurrias.)

The attack and the subsequent arrest were only the latest sign of the growing power of Central America's gangs and their ability to shuttle between their home countries and the United States. In the past few years, as Washington has focused its attention on the Middle East, it has virtually ignored a dangerous phenomenon close to home. Ultraviolent youth gangs, spawned in the ghettos of Los Angeles and other U.S. cities,

* Reprinted from *Foreign Affairs.* 84(3) (May–June, 205): 98–110. Reprinted by permission of FOREIGN AFFAIRS (84 (3) 2005). Copyright (2011) by the Council on Foreign Relations, Inc. www.ForeignAffairs.com. [Editor's Note: The images that accompanied this original article have intentionally been left out.]

have slowly migrated south to Central America, where they have transformed themselves into powerful, cross-border crime networks. With the United States preoccupied elsewhere, the gangs have grown in power and numbers; today, local officials estimate their size at 70,000–100,000 members. The *marabuntas,* or *maras,* as they are known (after a deadly species of local ants), now pose the most serious challenge to peace in the region since the end of Central America's civil wars.

Nor is the danger limited to the region. Fed by an explosive growth in the area's youth population and by a host of social problems such as poverty and unemployment, the gangs are spreading, spilling into Mexico and beyond—even back into the United States itself. With them, the *maras* are bringing rampant crime, committing thousands of murders, and contributing to a flourishing drug trade. Central America's governments, meanwhile, seem utterly unable to meet the challenge, lacking the skills, know-how, and money necessary to fight these supergangs. The solutions attempted so far—largely confined to military and police operations—have only aggravated the problem; prisons act as gangland finishing schools, and military operations have only dispersed the gangs' leadership, making bosses harder than ever to track and capture.

If Central America is going to make a stand, it must do so quickly. And it must take a new approach, one that is multilateral, combines police work with prevention, and attacks the region's underlying ills.

Only such a multipronged approach has a chance of stemming the growth of the *maras.* Fortunately, the necessary expertise already exists: in the United States, cities such as Boston and San Jose have managed highly successful antigang campaigns that could be emulated south of the border. The problem for Central America is one of political will, funding, and timing. Washington can help with all three, and should do so. Not only does the problem threaten the United States, but it started there, too.

In the Ghetto

The roots of the *maras'* presence in Central America can be traced back to 1992. In the aftermath of the Los Angeles riots, police there determined that most of the looting and violence had been carried out by local gangs, including Mara Salvatrucha, then a little-known group of Salvadoran immigrants. (*Mara* is slang for "gang," and *trucha* "trout.")

California implemented strict new antigang laws. Prosecutors began to charge young gang members as adults instead of minors, and hundreds of young Latin criminals were sent to jail for felonies and other serious crimes. Next came the "three strikes and you're out" legislation, passed in California in 1994, which dramatically increased jail time for offenders convicted of three or more felonies.

In 1996, Congress extended the get-tough approach to immigration law. Noncitizens sentenced to a year or more in prison would now be repatriated to their countries of origin, and even foreign-born American felons could be stripped of their citizenship and expelled once they served their prison terms. The list of deportable crimes was increased, coming to include minor offenses such as drunk driving and petty theft. As a result, between 2000 and 2004, an estimated 20,000 young Central American criminals, whose families had settled in the slums of Los Angeles in the1980s after fleeing civil wars at home, were deported to countries they barely knew. Many of the deportees were native English speakers who had arrived in the United States as toddlers but had never bothered to secure legal residency or citizenship.

The deportees arrived in Central America with few prospects other than their gang connections; many were members of MS 13 and another vicious Los Angeles group, the 18th Street Gang (which took the name Mara 18, or M-18, in Central America). Local governments—which were desperately trying to rebuild after a decade of civil strife—had no idea who their new citizens really were the new U.S. immigration rules banned U.S. officials from disclosing the criminal backgrounds of the deportees.

The result, predictably, was a disaster. At first, few Central American officials paid attention to the new arrivals. But the returnees, with their outlandish gang tattoos, their Spanglish, and their antiauthoritarian attitudes, soon made themselves noticed. Shortly after their arrival, crack cocaine was introduced to El Salvador, and related arrests, which had been in the single digits in 1995, climbed to 286 three years later. By 1999, terms such as "crack babies" and "crack dens" had become as common to Salvadoran newspaper readers as they were to readers in Los Angeles. The same trend, meanwhile, occurred in Honduras and Guatemala. "We had these guys arriving in fresh territory and they did what they knew how to do best," said Lou Covarrubiaz, a former San Jose police chief turned police trainer in El Salvador.

In the following years, the deportations continued. As more and more hard-core gang members were expelled from Los Angeles, the Central American *maras* grew, finding ready recruits among the region's large population of disenfranchised youth (according to the United Nations, 45 percent of Central Americans are 15 years old or younger). In El Salvador (a country of 6.5 million people), the gangs now boast 10,000 core members and 20,000 young associates; in Honduras (with a population of 6.8 million), the authorities estimate the gang population at 40,000. Their median age is just 19 years old, although their leaders are often in their late 30s and 40s.

Today, the gangs regularly battle each other and the police for control of working-class neighborhoods and even entire cities. Fifteen municipalities in El Salvador are believed to be effectively ruled by the *maras*. Soyapango, a gritty working-class neighborhood of San Salvador that was once home to leftist guerrillas, is now the subject of a fierce turfwar between M-18 and MS 13. Municipal bus drivers have refused to traverse the area since three of their colleagues were killed by gang members in April 2004, and an estimated 300 families fled the neighborhood last year.

M-18, with its connections to the U.S. 18th Street Gang (which the FBI calls a "mega-gang"), is far better organized than its local rival, but in both cases, the *maras* function as surrogate families—albeit ultraviolent ones—for their members. Often recruiting children as young as nine, the gangs initiate their members with beatings: three older members will punch and kick a recruit nonstop for 13 seconds. Once they recover, the new junior gang members engage in robbery or petty crime or serve as lookouts for older members. Their more seasoned comrades, meanwhile, engage in drug dealing, burglaries, and contract killings. The *marai* members also act as foot soldiers for pre-existing drug-trafficking networks and for international car-theft rings and run sophisticated alien-smuggling operations. Thanks to their work, overall crime has increased dramatically throughout the region. Honduras today has a murder rate of 154 per

100,000—higher even than Colombia's, where, despite an ongoing civil war, the murder rate is just 70 per 100,000.

The Strong Hand

In 2002, the embattled Central American republics began to fight back. The charge was led by Honduras, where Ricardo Maduro, a Stanford graduate, was elected president in November 2001 on a get-tough platform. Maduro, whose son had been killed in an attempted kidnapping in 1997, introduced a series of "zero tolerance" laws empowering the government to imprison people for up to12 years merely on suspicion of gang membership (often determined simply by the presence of distinctive tattoos, which members wear on their necks, arms, and legs).

Maduro's *"mano dura"*("strong hand") approach had an immediate impact, and El Salvador soon adopted a similar program. Many young gang members were quickly pulled off the streets and thrown into prison. Within a year, the Honduran prison system had swelled to 200 percent beyond capacity, leading to several prison riots in April 2003 and May 2004. Guatemala, Panama, and Nicaragua are now considering similar policies.

Despite initial signs of success, however, human rights groups bitterly criticized the new hard-line approach, and local governments soon began to realize what U.S. officials had learned in the early1990s: that tough legislation alone cannot fix the gang problem. Central America was trying to arrest itself out of its gang trouble without providing the sorts of social and educational programs that can keep kids out of gangs in the first place or persuade gang members to defect. According to Covarrubiaz (the former San Jose cop), get-tough programs "work temporarily, but do not address the real problems."

This soon became obvious throughout the region. The *maras* retaliated against the crackdown by launching a wave of random violence. Shortly after the introduction of the new antigang laws, they began killing and beheading young victims; at least a dozen decapitated bodies were found in Honduras and Guatemala, grisly symbols of the *maras'* undiminished power. As gang leaders were jailed, new leaders sprang up to take their places. Ms-13 and M-18 also began to scout abroad for more hospitable terrain, turning their sights first on Mexico and then back on the United States.

Homeward Bound

In Tapachula, a Mexican city on the Guatemalan border, the *maras* began to prey on poor immigrants heading north to enter the United States illegally. Maiming and killing these undocumented workers became a sort of marketing message for the gangs: it sent a warning that only those who paid gang-connected "coyotes" (who often charge $5,000 to $8,000 a head) to smuggle them into the United States would make it alive.

Meanwhile, MS 13 set up shop in seven Mexican states, from Chiapas, in the south, all the way up to Tamaulipas, on the U.S. border. According to the Mexican National Migration Institute, MS 13 quickly established working relationships with a number of new Mexican drug cartels, helping them wrest control of various U.S. drug markets from more established smuggling rings. As they expanded northward, meanwhile, the *maras* left in their wake what had become their traditional trademark: the tortured bodies of young women.

In the last two years, Central American members of MS 13 have begun to return to the United States itself. This time, however, they are appearing in nontraditional areas, ranging from New York City to suburban Maryland and Massachusetts—anywhere there are significant Salvadoran populations. Local authorities are often unaware of the newcomers' actual identities, assuming that they come from Southern California. Once ensconced, the gangs grow quickly, using their connections to alien-smuggling rings to ensure a steady supply of recruits. Many of their new members are children who were left behind in Central America when their parents moved illegally to the United States in the1980s and1990s. Now they are rejoining their parents—but often after they have already been recruited by the *maras* in the rough neighborhoods where they grew up.

MS 13 may have originated in the United States during the early 1980s, but the gang that has recently returned to the country is much more dangerous than its original incarnation. The group has grown more sophisticated and developed a taste for (and skills with) more high-powered weaponry (AK-4JS, left over from the recent civil wars, are easily obtained in Central America). At the same time, in the Washington, D.C., area, where MS 13 now has an estimated 5,000 members, it has begun using machetes (the traditional weapon of the Central American peasant) as a favorite killing tool.

Throughout the United States, the returning *maras* have quickly engaged in a variety of criminal enterprises. "They are not sophisticated enough to move into financial crime," said one U.S. official, "but they can earn a lot of money hauling people into the United States." The gangs engage in car theft and other types of robbery and traffic in stolen documents, marijuana, cocaine, and methamphetamines, using children as couriers and to distract the police. "Having community kids dressing like them and organized in small cliques can deflect attention from the big guys," said Detective Tony Moreno of the Los Angeles Police Department.

Besides the usual problems caused by such activity, the *maras* have recently raised other, more specific security threats. In September 2004, U.S. officials grew concerned when Honduran authorities reported sighting in Tegucigalpa a known al Qaeda operative named Adnan G. El Shukrijumah, and rumors circulated of a meeting between the jihadists and the *maras*. Central American officials quickly denied that any such meeting had taken place. But the danger of such a link being established remains very real: "If they can smuggle people looking for a job [into the United States]," said Joe Torres, an immigration official, "they can smuggle people interested in terror."

Blame Game

As the Central American gangs have grown, so has the argument over who is to blame for them. Some Central American government officials have accused the United States of inflicting the problem on them, comparing Washington's deportation of gang members to the 1980 Mariel boat lift, when Fidel Castro supposedly emptied his prisons and shipped the inhabitants north to Miami. Meanwhile, U.S. officials, including Los Angeles Police Chief William Bratton, think the Central Americans should shoulder the problem alone and favor continued deportations. Such mutual recriminations are typical of the debate over gang problems and help explain why the affected countries have yet to develop a united front to deal with them.

It is unrealistic, however, to expect any of the tiny Central American countries, with their fragile governments, to take the lead in organizing a multilateral approach; that role can only be played by the United States. Yet so far Washington has proved reluctant to take that job. Part of the problem is that for the last 15 years U.S. policy toward Central America has essentially been limited to immigration and drugs, and thus the gang problem has fallen through the administrative cracks, with no agency attempting to formulate or oversee an integrated approach. Responsibility for tracking gang activity domestically falls to several different parts of the U.S. government. The FBI has national oversight over any criminal activity associated with violent street gangs. But MS 13's involvement in alien smuggling has also brought it within the jurisdiction of the Border Patrol and the Immigration and Customs Enforcement agency, both divisions of the Department of Homeland Security that track crimes committed near or involving the border.

U.S. law enforcement agencies do all have access to the National Crime Information Center, a federal database that lists gang members who have served prison terms. But according to Wesley McBride, president of the California Gang Investigators Association, a more effective nationwide database of all gang members (convicted and unconvicted) is needed, as well as a standard definition of what gangs are and what constitute gang crimes. As McBride told the Senate Judiciary Committee last year, "no federal agency collects or disseminates gang-crime statistics or demographics in order to establish the true picture of gangs." A national gang intelligence center, to be headed by the FBI, will be established at FBI headquarters in Washington, D.C., next year. But to be effective, such an operation would have to be able to coordinate information from across Central America.

In the meantime, different regions within the United States are tackling the *mara* problem differently, with varied results. A hard-line approach being pursued in Virginia has been criticized by gang experts because it focuses on suppression alone and does not include the two other elements necessary to stamp out gangs: intervention and prevention. "If you do not do the three at the same time, you lose the momentum," said Moreno of the LAPD. Maryland, on the other hand, is following a more effective process: police there have united with a community and educational task force to introduce a tough law enforcement program coupled with a strict intervention element. The Maryland program features both effective policing and after-school programs that can prevent young kids from joining gangs, as well as intervention programs that encourage members to leave their gangs and protect them from retaliation after they do.

Most experts agree, however, that today's most effective approach comes from Los Angeles—the city where the *maras* originated (not to mention many other U.S. gangs, including the infamous Crips and Bloods). Los Angeles has experimented with every type of antigang effort. Prosecutors there were the first to launch a federal racketeering case against a gang (the18th Street Gang) under the tough Racketeer Influenced and Corrupt Organizations (RICO) statute. California attorneys used the statute to send more than a dozen gang leaders to federal prison for life without parole and to dismantle the so-called Mexican Mafia. Police have also taken advantage of new laws that forbid gang members from congregating in known hangouts.

Los Angeles' current approach draws on more than just force. Bratton, the police chief, has warned other U.S. cities not to follow the strategy California used against the gangs in the 1990s,when it focused exclusively on law enforcement. "We think of prison as punishment, but in many instances we're just reinforcing their loyalty to the gang," Bratton said. "To them prison is like going to finishing school." This realization was brought home in 2002,when city crime statistics shot up after a wave of gang members who had been sent to jail in the early 1990s were suddenly released and hit the streets. Local law enforcement officers began to rethink their get-tough approach. "We still don't have enough money, but at least we all agree now that you have to focus on all angles at the same time," said Father Gregory Boyle, a community activist. "You use suppression today and intervention tomorrow and it won't work. It would be like saying, I will feed you today, but I won't clothe you."

As Los Angeles discovered, to be effective, law enforcement has to work with everyone in a community. Accordingly, in 2003, the city's police department created task forces called Community Impact Action Teams that paired local, state, and federal law enforcement agencies with citizen watchdog groups and clergymen, who best knew the neighborhoods. Probation and parole officers were also brought into the effort, as well as representatives from local school districts and city and state prosecutors. The program, which mimicked a similar effort in San Jose, has already had a dramatic impact: crime statistics in January 2005 were down 14 percent from a year earlier.

Come Together

So far, Central America has yet to adopt such a multifaceted approach, nor have the countries there learned to work together or with the United States—despite the fact that the gang problem affects all of them. Instead, El Salvador and Honduras continue to pursue their *mano dura* policies. Meanwhile, the region's more deep-seated problems—such as dysfunctional politics, rampant corruption, drug smuggling, intense urban poverty, and overpopulation—remain untouched, and the *mano dura* campaigns are only taking attention and resources away from the fight against these larger ills.

Central American governments have also used their highly publicized crackdowns on youth gangs to avoid action on another urgent priority: strengthening local democratic institutions. Since the end of the Central American civil wars in the early1990s, judicial, legislative, and social reforms have stalled amid partisan infighting, and local political debates remain split along the same left-right fault lines that caused bloodshed two decades ago.

Corruption also remains a persistent scourge and has helped prevent a more effective antigang strategy from emerging. In Guatemala, the Anti-Narcotics Operations Department (the local equivalent of the U.S. Drug Enforcement Administration) had to be dismantled in November 2002 after investigators found that 320 of its officials were in the pay of local criminals. Guatemala's parliament has also refused a UN offer to help it fight organized crime, rejecting the establishment of a UN-appointed investigative commission. It is no coincidence that many criminal syndicates there are run by retired military officers with political connections.

The United States needs to help Central America craft a multi-level and multicountry approach to its gang problem. In January 2005, the U.S. Justice Department quietly created an FBI task force to deal with MS 13. The new group will coordinate activities with immigration officials, the Bureau of Diplomatic Security, the U.S. Marshals Service, the Federal Bureau of Prisons, the Drug Enforcement Administration, and the Bureau of Alcohol, Tobacco, Firearms, and Explosives, as well as local law enforcement agencies. In a positive first step, the task force has introduced new regulations that will permit U.S. officials to inform their counterparts in Central America about the criminal backgrounds of future deportees. Other signs, however, are less promising. The top-heavy task force has only focused on law enforcement so far. To be successful, the group must be made more international and have its ambit expanded to include helping strengthen Central American institutions. To ensure that the strategy is comprehensive, the gang task force should also include representatives from educational and social services departments.

Regional options effective in one country should be replicated in others. El Salvador's national police, for example, have benefited from reforms suggested and training provided by the U.S. Justice Department's International Criminal Investigative Training Assistance Program (ICITAP). In the last five years, ICITAP has helped El Salvador focus on community policing and improve internal and external communications. As a result, El Salvador is now the only country in the region with a working national emergency police response system, a computerized crime analysis and deployment network similar to that used by the New York City Police Department, and an Intranet that connects the precincts internally. Emphasizing such functions was a departure for ICITAP, which usually focuses on intelligence gathering. But it helped El Salvador's police force learn how to serve the community—a lesson the police badly needed. ICITAP also helped El Salvador tighten controls on petty corruption, which had bled budgets, and set up an internal affairs department, which removed 5,000 corrupt cops in three years. Similar tactics should be used in neighboring countries.

The region should also implement a three-pronged approach to gangs, one that includes prevention, suppression, and intervention. Prison systems must be transformed so that they no longer serve as training grounds for new gang members. In California, police now avoid placing competing gangs in the same facilities. Central America should do the same, to avoid the sort of clashes that recently occurred in Honduras and El Salvador when M-18 and MS 13 members were thrown into the same prisons.

School programs should also be developed to prevent young people from joining gangs in the first place. To help pay for them, the United States can teach Central America to harness its business sector to fund after-school programs and job training for low-income youth. In El Salvador, the government has already convinced private groups to fund witness protection programs and jobs for former gang members who choose to join the mainstream. Such efforts should be promoted at a regional level.

To facilitate suppression, police should focus heavily on hard-core gang members who refuse to give up their criminal lives. Central American legislators should introduce antigang and antidrug measures that make it a felony to engage in related activities within a mile radius of schools, which are currently prime recruiting grounds for the *maras*. Probation officers should also be brought into the circle of active antigang officials, since keeping close tabs on gang members after they leave prison is important. U.S. and Central American law enforcement agencies should also exchange information on people smugglers. And Central American leaders should offer reassurances that they will prosecute those caught bringing illegal immigrants to the United States.

Washington should also help Central America's various police forces establish an integrated computer system that tracks criminals across borders, incorporating data on people smugglers as well. And U.S. immigration policies must be formally changed to provide information on the criminal records of all deportees. Some observers have even suggested that the United States could help bear the brunt of the gang problem by having Central American gang members serve their prison terms in the United States.

Together, such tactics have a chance of stemming the onslaught of Central America's *maras*. The reforms should be instituted as quickly as possible, however. With every day that governments wait, the gangs grow in strength and the danger they pose becomes greater. If Central America hopes to escape the chaos of its past and finally make the transition to stable, democratic governance, it needs to act fast to tackle the *maras*. And the United States must help.

Reading 3.
Aboriginal Gangs and Their (Dis)placement: Contextualizing Recruitment, Membership, and Status*

Jana Grekul & Patti LaBoucane-Benson

Interviews with ex-gang members, police officers, and correctional service personnel suggest that the risk factors for involvement in gangs are abundant for Aboriginal youth and young adults. Aboriginal ex-gang members report the burden of discrimination and labelling based on race, in addition to the structural inequality and lack of opportunity reported as causal factors to gang involvement by gang researchers. Disadvantaged and disillusioned, encouraged by gang-involved family and friends, Aboriginal youth turn to gangs for a sense of identity and purpose. Interestingly, decades after their formation, groups such as the Indian Posse, Manitoba Warriors, Alberta Warriors, and Native Syndicate may not only be relegated to the outskirts of legitimate society but are also marginalized within the criminal world, in their organization and behind bars. Understanding Aboriginal gangs requires consideration of contextual factors, including the presence and interaction of precursors to gang involvement. These factors contribute to their pronounced presence in prisons and the suggestion that despite decades of existence they are relegated to street gang status.

* Reprinted from *Canadian Journal of Criminology and Criminal Justice*. 2008, 50(1): 59–82. Reprinted with permission from the Canadian Journal of Criminology and Criminal Justice.

Introduction

Gang research in the United States abounds (Chesney-Lind and Shelden 1992; Fong 1990; Fong and Buentello 2001; Huff 1990; Klein 1971; Sanchez-Jankowski 2003; Spergel 1995; Spergel and Curry 1995, Yablonsky 1959), but there is a relative paucity of Canadian research on the topic. Until recently, most of our policies and programming for gang prevention and intervention was informed by either media accounts of gang activities or information from the United States. Yet media sensationalization and differences between the countries in history, ethnic and cultural composition, government policies, health and educational apparatuses, gun control, drug legislation, and policing testify to the inadequacy of relying solely on these sources of information.

This is not to detract from Canadian studies on the topic. The first recorded work was a study of juveniles in street gangs in Toronto by Rogers (1945); since that time, several works have added to the growing field (Fasilio and Leckie 1993; Gordon 1995, 1998, 2000; Joe and Robinson, 1980; Kelly and Caputo 2005; Mathews 1993, 2005; Young 1993). Much of the academic work conducted in the area emerged in the early 1990s (Fasilio and Leckie, Gordon, Mathews, Young). One of the more recent contributions to the field is the creation of a typology by Gordon (2000), which delineates six types of groups that fall under the gang spectre.

These studies establish the fact that gangs are not new to Canada, and that the current concern expressed by communities, governments, law enforcement agencies, and criminal justice system personnel is symptomatic of the latest in a wave of gang concern (Young 1993). Public concern may partly explain the number of government research projects and publications on the topic of gangs, which adds to the cumulative understanding of youth groups, gangs, offenders, prison life, and factors that contribute to delinquent behaviours (Fasilio and Leckie 1993; Gordon 1993; Jones, Roper, Stys, and Wilson 2004; Mathews 1993; Mellor, MacRae, Pauls, and Hornick 2005). In addition to the media focus, there is evidence for this latest concern in the number of specialized gang units created in police detachments across the country in recent years (Gang Unit 2005; Symons 1999), and the passage of Bill C-24 by the federal government in 2002 that provides a legal definition of a criminal organization.

This growing concern seems at least partly based on an increase in gang-related activities. The Correctional Service of Canada and law enforcement agencies nationwide report increasing gang membership and activities on the street and behind bars (Correctional Services Alberta 2003; Gang Unit 2005; Mellor et al. 2005; Nafekh 2002). Media reports, however, fuel the concern by sensationalizing the criminal activities of these groups (Fasilio and Leckie 1993), and the popularization of "gangsta" imagery by movies, television, and music hold the public at once fascinated by and terrified of gang activities. Gangs warrant our attention because people are being victimized, and youth are being lost to organized and not-so-organized groups that lead to lives marred by crime, violence, injury, jail time, and sometimes resulting in death.

While the body of research on gangs is slowly growing, information on Aboriginal gangs in Canada is virtually non-existent, with the exception of a handful of research studies produced through government agencies (Dickson-Gilmore, Dickson-Gilmore, and Whitehead 2003; Mercredi 2000; Nafekh 2002) and a master's thesis from Simon Fraser University (Giles 2000). Ovid Mercredi provided the federal government with a critical report on Aboriginal youth gang members in the federal correctional system, while the Royal Canadian Mounted Police released a report describing the infrequent occurrence of organized crime among Aboriginal groups in eastern Canada (Dickson-Gilmore et al. 2003). The lack of research on Aboriginal gangs is a glaring omission in the literature. Particularly disturbing is the reported link between Aboriginal street gangs and their prison counterparts (Gordon 1998; Kelly and Caputo 2005; Mercredi 2000).

Aboriginal over-representation in Canadian prison populations is a long established fact, with approximately 3% of the general population representing about 17% of the federal carceral population (Bell 2002; Hamilton and Sinclair 1991; Linden 2000; Royal Commission on Aboriginal Peoples 1996), as is the existence of Aboriginal prison gangs (Correctional Services Alberta 2003; Gordon 1998; Kelly and Caputo 2005). High recidivism rates combined with over-representation of Aboriginals in prisons suggests that the prison-street gang link for this population is significant and literally institutionalized. Institutional authorities have taken steps to deal with street and prison gangs without the benefit of academic scholarship to guide intervention. Early intervention led to the unintentional officially induced proliferation of gangs across the nation.[1] Any efforts to address Aboriginal (or other) street gangs must also take into consideration the strong links between the two types of gangs, especially in recruitment.

The ways in which the gang threat is portrayed and constructed in the media and by agents of social control affects gangs, their members, and members of the public. Part of the construction of gangs in the media and by politicians is stereotyping by ethnic group. We read and hear of the Asian gang problem, the problem of Jamaican Blacks in the East, and Aboriginal gangs in the Prairies. We do not often hear of Caucasian or white gangs. The White Boy Posse in rural Alberta never makes newspaper headlines. Racial and ethnic stereotyping leads to racial profiling and creates increased misunderstanding, labelling, mistrust, and hostility between groups.

However, by lumping these groups together and referring to them as pieces in a multi-ethnic gang mosaic (i.e., whether they are Asian or Aboriginal, society is faced with ethnic hoodlums wreaking havoc on mainstream society), we conflate the uniqueness of each group. It may be that the ethnic gangs referred to, and the white gangs we seldom hear of, are at base caused by different processes and express themselves differently. Lumping all these groups together, and attempting to deal with them all in the same way, may prove futile.

This paper briefly explores the definition(s) of gangs, describes characteristics of several Aboriginal gangs in Canada, and places these groups into a typology of gang

---

1. The Correctional Service of Canada progressed through three stages of dealing with gang members behind bars. Initially, denial of the gang problem led to proliferation of gang activities in the absence of official response to the situation. This phase also involved transfer of gang members to institutions across the country, which resulted in increased proliferation of gang members behind bars (increased recruitment) and an increased street gang presence in cities previously untouched. Next, CSC attempts to separate and segregate gang members seemed to aggravate the problem, sending the message that gangs would be accommodated, resulting in more creative attempts of segregated gang members to assert their dominance in prisons. Finally, in the third stage, CSC is researching and developing programs and policies to target the root causes of gang involvement.

types. In the process, we posit causal explanations for Aboriginal gang recruitment and membership and suggest that the interaction of risk factors (and corresponding lack of protective factors) make Aboriginal youth more susceptible to gang recruitment than other at-risk youth. Prison over-representation for this group compounds the situation, making gang affiliation an almost expected outcome for increasing numbers of Aboriginals, particularly since the street gang-prison gang connection is pronounced for this population. Our objective in explicating the links between extreme marginalization and gang involvement is not to dismiss the situation as insurmountable but rather to illuminate specific risk factors as a first step toward the creation and implementation of prevention and intervention approaches that directly address the needs of Aboriginals. Finally, we suggest that the use of typologies in conjunction with recognition of the importance of regional and ethnic differences draws attention to the important role of context in understanding the gang phenomenon more generally.

Defining "Gangs"

Critical to the cumulative understanding of youth groups and gangs is the debate surrounding the definition of a gang. One view is that gang is a judgmental and overly negative term applied indiscriminately by adults to groups of adolescents ranging from friends hanging out who occasionally get into trouble, to more serious organized criminal gangs (Mathews 2005: 204). Loosely referring to groupings of youth and young adults as gangs neglects the fact that associating with friends is an important part of adolescent development—that important stage where young people learn to exert their independence from family by forming healthy relationships with peers.

Kelly and Caputo (2005) describe the evolution of gang definitions in the literature, from early definitions that focused on the expressive nature of loosely formed groups of adolescents whose membership was a source of status, to definitions that emphasized level of organization, nature and role of leadership, and use of violence. Canadian researchers have developed several typologies of gangs to assist in the definition, recognition, and classification of groups (Gordon 1995, 2000; Mellor et al. 2005). The rationale behind typology creation is that prevention and intervention are facilitated by the identification of groups with similar characteristics.

Static and standard definitions are problematic for service providers and researchers because they do not illuminate the more complex aspects of gang structure, activity, and membership. Further, different regions in our country have gang issues that are particular to the specific area or region, based on factors such as the socio-economic status of the area and the ethnic and age composition of members (Gordon 1998). Research and agency documents indicate that gang problems in Toronto are different from those in Winnipeg or Vancouver (Gordon 1998). While there are similarities in basic causes and processes of gang formation that characterize gang members across the nation, the specific form the group takes depends in part on the region of the country in which it is located (Gang Unit 2005; Mathews 2005: 205; Mellor et al. 2005: 1; Symons 1999: 126). No single theory or definition can account for the pluralistic or heterogeneous gang/group phenomenon in contemporary Canadian society (Mathews 1999: 4). It follows that gangs in Canada must be defined in the local context if policy and programming are to proceed effectively.

Method

Our data derive from two larger projects dealing directly with Aboriginal prison gangs and street gangs. Open-ended, face-to-face interviews with three ex-gang members living in the community and six incarcerated ex-gang members were conducted. These individuals were affiliated with a number of different Aboriginal gangs. The focus of the interviews was risk factors of youth who are gang-involved or at risk of gang involvement, including information on recruitment and desistance from gang-related activities. Participants were asked to recall their personal experiences of joining a gang, life in the gang, and the process of leaving the gang. Extensive and detailed field notes were taken during most interviews; others were taped and transcribed (with identifiers removed). Interviews lasted 30–40 minutes.

An internal intelligence report provided to the researchers by the Edmonton Police Service (EPS) Gang Unit and face-to-face, open-ended interviews with two members of the EPS—one a member of the Gang Unit, another a resource officer working in high schools in the city—provided information on the numbers of active gangs, active gang members, gang structures and hierarchies, membership (age, race, gender), youth at risk, criminal activities, recruitment, and changes in the nature of gangs over time. We also drew on interviews with police officers and ex-gang members (male and female) recorded in the documentary film Gang Aftermath (2005) produced by one of the authors of this paper.

In addition, 25 individuals from federal correctional facilities in the Prairie Region were interviewed face to face, over the phone, or through a self-administered questionnaire. Staff interviews were conducted with individuals who were available and willing to speak with us during our visits to the correctional facilities. Interviewees include people who work as security and gang intelligence officers, placement and program officers, correctional officers (1 & 2), native liaison workers and coordinators, and parole officers. In addition, four elders were interviewed.

Experience ranged from one year working in the system to 30 years of correctional experience. Many of the respondents indicated daily contact with gang members in the institutions. Some who worked in Aboriginal-specific programs indicated they were involved in developing institutional policies and programs that prohibited gang activities in their centres, ranges, and/or programs. Two of the institutions have ranges that deal specifically with the gang issue: in one case the Intensive Monitoring Range separates gang members from general population inmates, in another a range is set aside for inmates who want to leave their gangs.

Methodological challenges in studying the gang phenomenon are numerous. As Gordon points out (2000: 46), a gang census is not available to researchers or criminal justice system personnel. Membership is fluid and difficult to monitor; without an accurate estimate of the population under study, sample representativeness becomes an issue. In addition, it is difficult to find gang and ex-gang members who are willing to speak openly about these issues with any type of authority figure, including researchers.

Our interviews began with two ex-gang members who run an intervention and prevention program in the community. From there, our sample expanded. In this exploratory study we discovered characteristics shared by many Aboriginal gang members and, while not representative or generalizable in the truly scientific sense, these observations provide insight into a relatively "unresearched" field and provide a foundation for future research.

Results: Aboriginal Street Gangs and Wanna-Bes

Not all Aboriginal youth turn to gangs. But for Aboriginal families specifically in the Prairie provinces, gangs are real; youth are being recruited into this lifestyle on the street and in prisons, leaving school and family behind to take on the gangster identity. Further, when young Aboriginals choose to take on a personae generated by African-American gangs, they lose their connection to their people and their identity as a Cree, Blackfoot, Lakota, Dene, Metis, etc. This migration to gang lifestyles by young men and women, therefore, can have serious consequences to the individual, family, and entire community. In the *Gang Aftermath* (2005), Detective Doug Reti (RCMP) states,

> I have never witnessed gang activity so pronounced as I have seen it here, in the community I am in [Hobbema, Alberta]. At such a young age also. We are seeing kids young as 9 and 10 as runners, as young as 13 doing drive-by shootings and carrying weapons and so forth.

The ex-gang members interviewed presented with numerous tattoos associated with gang life and reported that the group they affiliated with had colours. Further, they spoke at length about childhood experiences of poverty and dysfunction and the thrill and sense of belonging that gang life offered them. An ex-gang member speaks about the effect gangsta music and movies had on him as a young boy:

> I got all mine [role models] from movies ... I found that [movie] Blood In Blood Out ... watched it ... It was straight gangster, man ... It was awesome, man ... [I thought] that's it, right there (*Gang Aftermath* 2005).

Another young man talks about being a child in the inner city of Edmonton and how poverty was a precursor to his gang affiliation:

> When I look around [at the place I grew up] ... this was the community league for the hood—this is where gang members came, the drug dealers, the drunks, drug addicts, the people from the street ...
>
> [When I was 10] that was a hard thing to deal with—having Mom taking off and not being there ... you get up in the morning, sometimes she would be there, sometimes she wouldn't. When she was there, she wouldn't be up to get us ready for school, to cook us breakfast. I would slap something together for me and my little brother, get my little brother dressed, and away we went.

[That's how I grew up], seeing my mother and stepfather fight a lot—that's how they handled their problems, by yelling, swearing, screaming, and physically assaulting one another. So I thought, OK, that's how I deal with things (*Gang Aftermath* 2005).

The gang lifestyle appears to offer an alternative to lives filled with helplessness and hopelessness.

Gordon (2000), in his research on known gang members in the Greater Vancouver area, identifies several groups that seem to attract the "gang" label, three of which are relevant to our discussion. Street gangs, groups of young people, mainly young adults, are semi-structured. The main purpose of street gangs is planned and profitable criminal behaviour or organized violence against rival groups. These groups have identifiable "markings," including a name, clothing, colours, and a desire to be seen by others as gang members. "Wanna-be" groups are loosely structured and engage in spontaneous social activity, as well as impulsive, exciting criminal activity, including collective violence against other groups of young people. These groups are not as structured, organized, or permanent as the street gangs and criminal business organizations—the third group, comprising primarily older, more educated males who keep a low profile in their lucrative criminal behaviours (2000: 48). Before addressing the structure of Aboriginal gangs, however, let us first examine more closely what respondents have to say about precursors to gang involvement and implications for the structure that Aboriginal gangs tend to take.

Family Dysfunction and the Search for Identity

Family plays a role in gang involvement in two main capacities: as an arena of dysfunction that can lead youth to gang involvement and as a direct source of recruitment. In other words, family problems can push young people into the gang lifestyle, while family members who are already gang-involved pull youth in the direction of gang involvement. Two comments are representative of many respondent stories:

My family was involved in the gang lifestyle. My mother was a prostitute. I was taken away from her at 7. I started doing petty crime and moved up to selling drugs by age 12. I hung around with a group of other kids, mostly my cousins (ex-gang member).

I grew up in Saskatoon and was surrounded by family members who were gang members. Other than this, I had no real connection to my family otherwise. They were alcoholics or drug addicts. I had no role models and no support in the community (ex-gang member).

Damaged or weak family relationships contribute, then, to gang involvement. Invariably respondents indicate that the gang acts as, or promises to act as, a substitute family, filling the void left by family backgrounds marked by violence, substance abuse, and crime. Children longing for a sense of identity and belonging are pushed into the welcoming arms of gangs. One ex-gang member confirms the importance of family problems to gang involvement:

The kinds of kids that are attractive to gangs are street kids without close family. These kids want love and respect, and the gang provided that family for them. Kids within the family services system are really attractive to gangs.

Correctional staff concur: "Gangs offer members the opportunity to feel a sense of self-worth, a sense of identity." "The gang is a substitute family." "A gang provides companionship, support, protection."

Family Recruitment

Family and peers can also contribute to gang involvement:

My family was involved in the gang lifestyle (ex-gang member).
  The strongest link in a gang is when it is made up of the people that you grow up with (ex-gang member)
  It is expected, if a family member is a member, that the remaining family members will either join that particular gang or do things for the gang (correctional officer).

A police officer with the Gang Unit offers this insight:

On the reserves, the recruitment is not only along ethnic but along familial lines. They are closely connected, which makes it difficult from an enforcement perspective to deal with. The Asian gangs are not really recruited along ethnic lines—there are just as many white members as Asian members.

Peers: Support, Protection, Loyalty

Many gangs begin as a group of ethnically homogeneous friends, family members, or acquaintances who, as the group grows and criminal activities increase, make alliances with other groups and individuals (Gordon 1998; Mathews 2005). The literature and our data provide support for this concept of gang formation, which begins with a "group of friends hanging out" (often with no intention to commit crimes) that evolves into a group of wanna-bes, then changes into a street gang.

It ends up being that people end up being part of a gang. But they start out, a lot of times, particularly with the Aboriginal gangs, as just a group of children who band together because they don't have the family support or the role models or they are being muscled or intimidated by other groups so they start out well meaning, just a group to keep each other safe (correctional officer).
  There is a loyalty to the person or people who get you out [off the street]. When you have nothing to live for, you have nothing to die for (ex-gang member).
  The guys that get you off the streets are someone that you will do anything for, and that is how these kids get involved. They then go and repeat the process by "flipping" someone else and the process continues (ex-gang member).

As long as they [the gang leaders] get their respect [recruits], they're theirs (ex-gang member).

When they are surrounded by family and peers already involved in a gang, recruitment becomes a possibility for many Aboriginal youth. Peers can actually push some youth into gang associations out of a need for protection. One ex-gang member relates a situation from his youth where his city neighbourhood "had problems" with a nearby neighbourhood so he "started his own crew to protect himself." He states, "Most kids joining a gang are attracted to the lifestyle because it provides them with protection from other gang members and from life."

Protection from the perspective of our correctional sample refers to muscling and intimidation that is prevalent behind bars. Protection from "life" might refer to abuse and family dysfunction, but it might also refer to structural problems like poverty.

Structural Inequality

Aboriginals are not alone in their experience of structural inequality. However, understanding the manner in which sources of structural inequality interact for this group can help direct prevention and intervention programming for them.

School

Aboriginal people are attending universities in record numbers; the rate of high school completion is higher today than 10 years ago. Between 1981 and 2001, the percentage of Aboriginal persons 15–24 attending school increased by two-thirds to over half, only slightly lower than for the general population (Aboriginal Edmonton 2005). Nevertheless, Aboriginal drop-out rates are still far above the national average. While 29% of adults in Edmonton's general population have not completed high school, 43% of Aboriginals are in the same situation (2005: 37). This figure indicates that another source of legitimate support and opportunity is absent for a significant proportion of Aboriginal youth. One respondent recalls being called "just a dumb Indian who would never amount to anything" by one of his school teachers. Another ex-gang member offers additional insight: "The young kids that become involved have little connection to the outside. The problems start within the family and get magnified through poverty, lack of education, and racism."

Work

Lower levels of education and a lack of post-secondary education translate into problems finding well-paying employment. Aboriginal people face unemployment rates two to three times as high as for the total population (Lindsey, Beach, and Ravelli 2006: 199). Disparity in mean and median income is pronounced. In 2000, average employment income for a working Aboriginal person was $21,485, compared to $32,183 for the average working Canadian. Median employment income was only $16,040 for Aboriginals, compared to $26,111 for the total population (ibid.). High rates of unemployment among Aboriginal people are another indicator of structural inequality. Legitimate money-making options may be absent or in short supply for Aboriginal youth and young adults. Joining a gang appears to be a lucrative venture, as the following quotes reveal:

> Reserves are especially easy targets for potential recruitment because the kids in reserves want to be perceived as cool. These kids have nothing or are very poor, and the gang members seem to be the best alternative (ex-gang member).
>
> Kids on reserves are the target for gangs (ex-gang member).
>
> I grew up on a reserve surrounded by gang members. My family was involved and sold drugs. I started drug running at 12 and started selling at 14. I wanted the money (ex-gang member).
>
> On the reserve, gang members were attractive because they had money, and what they had looked like a good life, an opportunity to get away from the environment of the reserve (ex-gang member).

Systemic Discrimination

The broader context for this discussion is based in the recognition of systemic discrimination that manifests itself in the social structure. Cultural conflict, poverty, lack of opportunity, and lack of power contribute to a cycle in which Aboriginal people are imprisoned for criminal behaviours that may be the outcome, in part, of structural inequality. Imprisonment perpetuates the problems, since, once one is released, the same structural issues prevail. Recidivism is a likely result, and the cycle continues. Stigmatization and labelling by authorities—teachers, police officers, or correctional staff—exacerbates the problems. While youth from other ethnic minority groups also experience racism and inaccurate labelling, in conjunction with the litany of structural issues described earlier, Aboriginal youth may face compounded risk. Labelled "trouble-makers" and "gang bangers" on the street and in prison, Aboriginals deal with two powerful labels: Aboriginal first, and through stereotyping, gang member. A broader historical context marred by colonialism, discriminatory government practices, and residential schools contributes to a situation where the label stigmatizes and propels the labelled further into a life of deviance; the label can in effect produce further deviant and criminal behaviour.

One of the ex-gang members recalls the police calling his group of friends a gang, so they "began to act that way" and identify as a gang. He recollects the experiences of labelling and racism. "The police are not trusted because of a history of racism, like finding gang members, taking off their shoes, and leaving them in rival gang territory."

Systemic discrimination reaches fruition in over-representation of Aboriginals in the criminal justice system. Certainly this disproportion contributes to the prevalence of Aboriginal gangs behind bars, which also has implications for street gang presence and recruitment. As a staff respondent from Bowden Institution claims, "When released, these guys are expected to hook with the parent organization to fulfil their obligation." According to another staff member, "Lots are recruited within prisons—they leave and become active in street gangs." An ex-gang member states, "The majority stay [with the gang] when they leave prison because sooner or later they will be back in prison and will need protection and support."

History and Structure of Aboriginal Gangs

Gangs offer members the opportunity to feel a sense of self-worth, a sense of identity.

> With the Redd Alert, lots of them found recognition in gangs. They hadn't had that before—they were abused, put down all their lives. They got in the gang and had a name. "I'm somebody." They got recognition and a sense of belonging (staff member).

Aboriginal gangs have developed extensive hand signals, language, and artwork, including tattoos specific to their gangs. They wear certain colours and in many ways mimic the more established American gangs such as the Bloods and Crips, using identifying marks as powerful and symbolic labels that reinforce group membership. As an ex-gang member states, "When it comes to Aboriginal youth that are involved, it comes down to identity—they try to be black." This reinforcement is often compounded by media constructions and sensationalization of the gangsta lifestyle. This individual also points out that Aboriginal gangs use hand signals and colours more than, for example, "Asian gangs."

Although Aboriginals sometimes model themselves on American gangs, it is not clear whether they are organized groups. Street gang members are less educated than members of criminal organizations and are economically disadvantaged. They also experience ethnic marginalization, domestic violence, ineffective parents, poverty, inability to obtain income, lack of a father figure, additional dependent siblings, and isolation from the larger community (Gordon 2000: 51–52). Interview data presented earlier support these factors as especially salient characteristics of the lives of Aboriginal youth.

Some evidence for the lack of organization comes from our interviews, although reports conflict. Noticeably, ex-gang members were reluctant to comment on gang structure. Respondents did agree that gang structure varies from group to group. But there is some disagreement on the actual form that gang structure takes. One staff member suggests that it is explicit: "The upper echelon tends to be the decision makers, the lieutenants pass on the tasks, the sergeant-at-arms assigns the tasks, and the enforcers/strikers carry out the tasks and are the muscle." Some liken it to a political or military organization. According to one staff respondent, "The Warriors, for instance, are becoming much more organized in their political structure—they are modelling their organization more toward Biker groups." Others disagree: "Aboriginal gangs don't have structure like Biker groups" (staff member). In addition three staff from the Saskatchewan Penitentiary point out that Aboriginal gangs change their structure and leadership almost daily. One of the ex-gang members put it succinctly: "This isn't organized crime we're talking about, it's Aboriginal street gangs, which are not the same as organized groups."

In prison, organization is affected when leaders are transferred or sent to segregation. On the street, organization is affected when leaders are sent to prison. The discrepancy in reports may be a result of different experiences with different gangs, some more structured than others. Or some ex-gang members may feel more free to talk about personal experiences in the gang, but not want to reveal information that directly affects or relates to the group itself. In other words, as a result of fear or respect, some secrets are best left untold—even for ex-gang members. But one ex-gang member does say this: "Leadership changes all too often. There are too many chiefs and not enough Indians. Everyone wants to run the show. With organized crime groups, there is one boss and everyone knows it."

Official sources corroborate some of what our respondents report. Groups such as the Redd Alert, Indian Posse, Alberta Warriors, and the Native Syndicate fit Gordon's description of street gangs.

Crime for profit (though less organized than in criminal organizations) and violence characterize these street gangs. For example, the Indian Posse of Winnipeg was unorganized initially but became more organized over time (Correctional Services Alberta 2003). This gang is involved in low-level organized street crime, including drug trafficking, assaults, and break-and-enters. Dependent on more structured criminal organizations for their drugs, Indian Posse members are involved in street-level dealing. As is characteristic of other Aboriginal street gangs, the Indian Posse is very active in correctional institutions, using fear, violence, and intimidation to recruit members and exercise control (Correctional Services Alberta).

Both the Manitoba Warriors and the offshoot Alberta Warriors are considered street gangs, although their strength appears to come primarily from their activities and recruitment in prisons. Both touted as being on the organized end of the street gang continuum, these groups—which started off as Aboriginal political groups—have ties to more organized criminal organizations such as outlaw motorcycle groups. The Redd Alert, on the other hand, which originated in Edmonton, is an offshoot of the notorious Edmonton Northside Boys (Correctional Services Alberta 2003). But interviews suggest the group originally comprised Aboriginal young people who wanted to offer a legitimate alternative to youth: a clean lifestyle with a focus on positive, pro-social alternatives to deviant and criminal behaviours. With time, the group changed its mandate, particularly as members found themselves in prison and requiring protection from other prison groups. Again, very active in correctional institutions, the Redd Alert developed in response to aggressive institutional recruitment by gangs such as the Indian Posse and the Manitoba and Alberta Warriors. The Redd Alert evolved into an alternative for Aboriginals being forcefully recruited into these other groups. Over time, its focus has become the opposite of its original intent.[2]

Street gangs, their prison affiliations, and wanna-be groups are relatively fluid, gaining or waning in strength and numbers as membership changes and in response to enforcement strategies (Correctional Services Alberta 2003; Mathews 2005; Yablonsky 1959). One example is the Northside Boys, a group comprising primarily Aboriginal youth ranging in age from 13 to 21, very active in the late 1990s. They most closely resemble Gordon's wanna-bes, groups younger than the other groups in his typology and

---

2. This history of the Redd Alert is based on an interview with two staff members who work closely with Aboriginal gang members. We have summarized their detailed description of the history of this group.

involved in less organized behaviour. Bullying, violence, and opportunistic crimes are the mainstay of wanna-bes. Without specific objectives, wanna-be group members tend to fit the profile of hardcore young offenders (Gordon 2000: 53). Reports indicate that the Northside Boys were easily intimidated by career criminals in the correctional system and were primarily a "friendship group" without real leadership structure, loosely organized, and with little involvement in organized crime.

Clearly more research is required into gang structure. Evidence suggests that less organization is characteristic of Aboriginal groups. Some studies (Kelly and Caputo 2005) and official sources (Correctional Services Alberta 2003) indicate that Aboriginal gangs are used by more organized criminal business organizations to carry out "street work," placing Aboriginal groups on the disorganized end of a continuum of group organization. Our suggestion is that not only in the legitimate world of work, but also within the world of crime, structural inequality, poverty, and discrimination relegate Aboriginal youth to the more disorganized, less lucrative criminal opportunity structures. They do not make up the bulk of the criminal business organizations, which are more lucrative and enduring, and are more likely to be found in the street-level groups and the wanna-be groups, which are less stable, organized, and established.

Prevention and Intervention

The causal factors we have identified in Aboriginal street gangs and wanna-be groups can inform policy and programming used in dealing with them. Although the focus of this paper is not a detailed development of programming, two programming opportunities in this area can be effective: (1) preventative programs, which focus on youth at-risk, dealing with precursors to gang involvement, and (2) intervention programming for individuals committed to a criminal/gang lifestyle, who are usually already serving time. The programs deal with the same problem, only at different stages.

In the case of wanna-be group formation, and in the early stages of the formation of possible street gangs, policies and programs that directly target the structural issues mentioned earlier would be most appropriate. Targeting street gang members is more difficult, but still possible. Street gang members who have already been exposed to the seeming benefits of street gang life might need more coaxing to leave. In dealing with these individuals, ex-gang member mentors can effectively intervene. Ex-members are real-life examples of the good that can come from leaving the gang.

Prevention within prisons entails dealing with protection and the desire for money. Long-term offender programs can help with intervention by encouraging inmates to face the precursors (issues relating to family, substance abuse, violence) to their involvement. Gang intervention in prison, including provision of special units for members attempting to leave the life, is a promising means of reducing gang activities both inside and outside prison walls. If prisons are a source of recruitment—and our interviews indicate that they are—then intervening in prison gangs could lead to a reduction of members on the street (after release).

Discussion

This exploratory study into Aboriginal gangs in the Canadian Prairies offers insight into precursors to gang involvement and the application of a typology to criminal groups. Aboriginal gang members experience structural inequality, racism, discrimination, family dysfunction, substance abuse, and violence—all indicators of marginalization. Their marginalization, including lack of school and work opportunities, compounded by institutional labelling, makes the gang lifestyle an attractive option. Recruitment by family members on reserves is significant, making gang life the preferable option in many cases, a family business of sorts signalling gang life as a functional response to generations of economic, social, political, and educational inequalities.

Every possible indicator of structural inequality and discrimination works against many Aboriginal youth to make gangs an attractive alternative to lives filled with hopelessness and despair. It is true that other youth experience despair as well. Black youth in the inner city of Toronto are similarly tempted by the gangsta lifestyle. The Vietnamese child of immigrant parents may experience alienation, language barriers, and the parents' obligation to work long hours in order to make ends meet. Here, quick money made available through gangs and drugs may be appealing. The Caucasian youth from Richmond Hill may experience substance abuse or sexual abuse. All are faced with factors that could lead to crime and gang involvement. Our point, however, is that within Aboriginal communities, the risk factors interact with and exacerbate each other in the lives of these young people and are compounded by physical separation from society (living on reserves), cultural loss, and lack of cultural identity. Aboriginal youth may be among the most marginalized in a sub-population of marginalization (i.e., at-risk youth and gang-involved youth generally). When the perception is created that all ethnic gangs are alike, we lose sight of the uniqueness of groups that, while sharing criminal involvement, arise out of different contexts and conditions, are often organized differently, and vary in function and form. While there are many similarities among and between gangs, it is the existence of these differences that is obscured in public discussions of the problem.

For Aboriginals, the interaction of these indicators of structural inequality with each other, with community and cultural breakdown as a result of historical, economic, and political processes, and with systemic discrimination results in Aboriginal over-representation in prisons. Aboriginal prison gangs appear to be a permanent part of the carceral landscape in the Prairies. This fact in itself not only indicates marginalization but may also indicate that Aboriginal gang members experience multiple forms of marginalization, which can reach fruition in their imprisonment. A concentration of established precursors to gang involvement reflected in high rates of imprisonment and the institutionalization of Aboriginal prison gangs sets this population apart. Furthermore, preliminary evidence indicates that, when placed on a continuum of gang types, Aboriginal gangs fall on the "unorganized" end of the continuum. These are not groups marked by the structure of well-established criminal organizations. Although Aboriginal gangs have existed for decades, they have not attained the level of sophistication characteristic of organized crime groups. Despite their longevity, their increasing numbers, and their pronounced presence in prison populations, Aboriginal gangs are still relegated to the status of street gangs and wanna-be groups, known for their violence, their semblance of structure based on African American gangs, their conflict with other groups, and their lack of sophistication. Members are individuals who have been relegated to the outskirts of the legitimate and illegitimate opportunity structures in Canadian society. They are "double failures" as evidenced by their presence in Prairie prisons. Our primary objective in this paper was to explicitly describe these types of marginalization as an important first step toward creating and implementing policies and programs that deal directly with the needs presented by this group, and with their location in a typology of gang types. Research on gang-related programming, including the description and evaluation of programs developed and implemented by members of the Aboriginal community, may be the next logical step for future research in this area.

Whether these processes and characteristics are specific to this particular population and this particular region of the country remains to be seen in future research. Aboriginal gangs stand out for their extensive and excessive use of violence, their prevalence in Prairie correctional facilities, and their functional utility as substitutes for institutions damaged by colonial legacies, structural inequality, and marginalization. These processes seem to set Aboriginal gangs apart in the gang landscape, displaced in a land that was once theirs.

References

Aboriginal Edmonton
    2005   December   A Statistical Profile of the Aboriginal Population of the City of Edmonton. Edmonton Urban Aboriginal Accord Initiative.

Bell, Sandra J.
    2002   Young Offenders and Juvenile Justice: A Century after the Fact. Scarborough: Thomson Nelson. Canada 1996 Report of the Royal Commission on Aboriginal Peoples. Vol. 3. Ottawa: Royal Commission on Aboriginal Peoples.

Chesney-Lind, M. and R. Shelden
    1992   Girls, Delinquency and Juvenile Justice. Pacific Grove, CA: Brooks/Cole.

Correctional Services Alberta
    2003   Special Interest Offenders. Edmonton: Alberta Solicitor General.

Dickson-Gilmore, E.J., Jane Dickson-Gilmore, and Chris Whitehead.
    2003   Aboriginal Organized Crime in Canada: Developing a Typology for Understanding and Strategizing Responses. Ottawa: Research and Evaluation Branch, Royal Canadian Mounted Police.

Fasilio, R. and S. Leckie.
    1993   Canadian Media Coverage of Gangs: A Content Analysis. Users report 1993–94. Ottawa: Ministry of the Solicitor General.

Fong, Robert
    1990   The organizational structure of prison gangs: A Texas case study. Federal Probation 54(1): 36–46.

Fong, Robert S. and Salvador Buentello.
    2001   The detection of prison gang development: An empirical assessment. Federal Probation 55(1): 66–70.

Gang Aftermath, dir. Francis Campbell
	2005	Bearpaw Media Productions. Native Counselling Services of Alberta.
Gang Unit
	2005	Overview of the current gang situation in the city of Edmonton. Edmonton: Edmonton Police Service.
Giles, Christopher M.H.
	2000	The History of Street Gangs in Winnipeg: 1945–1997: A Qualitative Newspaper Analysis of Gang Activity. Master's thesis, Simon Fraser University, Burnaby, BC.
Gordon, Robert M.
	1993	Incarcerated Gang Members in British Columbia: A Preliminary Study. Victoria: Ministry of Attorney General.
Gordon, Robert M.
	1995	Street gangs in Vancouver. In J. Creechan and R. Silverman (eds.), Canadian Delinquency. Scarborough: Prentice Hall.
Gordon, Robert M.
	1998	Street gangs and criminal business organizations: A Canadian perspective. In K. Hazlehurst and C. Hazlehurst (eds.), Gangs and Youth Subcultures: International Explorations. New Brunswick, NJ: Transaction Books.
Gordon, Robert M.
	2000	Criminal business organization, street gangs and "wanna-be" groups: A Vancouver perspective. Canadian Journal of Criminology (January): 39–60.
Hamilton, A.C. and C.M. Sinclair
	1991	Report of the Aboriginal Justice Inquiry of Manitoba. Vol. 1: The System and Aboriginal People. Winnipeg: Queen's Printer.
Huff, C.R.
	1990	Gangs in America. Newbury Park, CA: Sage.
Joe, D. and N. Robinson
	1980	Chinatown's immigrant gangs. Criminology 18: 337–345.
Jones, Dean, Vince Roper, Yvonne Stys, and Cathy Wilson
	2004	Street Gangs: A Review of Theory, Interventions, and Implications for Corrections. Ottawa: Research Branch, Correctional Service of Canada.
Kelly, Katharine, and Tulio Caputo.
	2005	The linkages between street gangs and organized crime: The Canadian expe rience. Journal of Gang Research 13(1): 17–30.
Klein, M.
	1971	Street Gangs and Street Workers. Englewood Cliffs, NJ: Prentice Hall.
Linden, Rick
	2000	Criminology: A Canadian Perspective. 4th ed. Toronto: Harcourt Brace.
Lindsey, Linda L., Stephen Beach, and Bruce Ravelli
	2006	Core Concepts in Sociology. Toronto: Pearson.
Mathews, F.
	1993	Youth Gangs on Youth Gangs. Ottawa: Solicitor General Canada.
Mathews, F.
	1999	Girls' use of violence and aggression. Orbit 29(4): 10–15.

Mathews, Fred
  2005   Youth Gangs. In John A. Winterdyk (ed.), Issues and Perspectives on Young
         Offenders in Canada. 3rd ed. Toronto: Thomson Nelson.
Mellor, Brian, Leslie MacRae, Monica Pauls, and Joseph P. Hornick
  2005   Youth Gangs in Canada: A Preliminary Review of Programs and Services. Cal-
         gary: Canadian Research Institute for Law and the Family, prepared for Pub-
         lic Safety and Emergency Preparedness Canada.
Mercredi, Ovide W.
  2000   Aboriginal Gangs: A Report to the Correctional Service of Canada on Abo
         riginal Youth Gang Members in the Federal Corrections System. Ottawa: Cor
         rectional Service.
Nafekh, Mark
  2002   An examination of youth and gang affiliation within the federally sentenced
         Aboriginal population. Ottawa: Research Branch, Correctional Service of
         Canada.
Rogers, K.H.
  1945   Street Gangs in Toronto: A Study of the Forgotten Boy. Toronto: Ryerson
         Press.
Royal Commission on Aboriginal Peoples
  1996   Bridging the Cultural Divide: A Report on Aboriginal People and Criminal
         Justice in Canada. Ottawa: Minister of Supply and Services, Canada.
Sanchez-Jankowski, Martin
  2003   Gangs and social change. Theoretical Criminology 7(2): 191–216.
Spergel, Irving A.
  1995   The Youth Gang Problem: A Community Approach. New York: Oxford Uni-
         versity Press.
Spergel, Irving A. and G. David Curry.
  1995   The National Youth Gang Survey: A research and development process. In
         Malcolm W. Klein, Cheryl L. Maxson, and Jody Miller (eds.), The Modern Gang
         Reader. Los Angeles: Roxbury Publishing.
Symons, Gladys L.
  1999   Racialization of the street gang issue in Montreal: A police perspective. Cana-
         dian Ethnic Studies 21(1): 124–138.
Yablonsky, L.
  1959   The delinquent gang as a near-group. Social Problems 7: 108–117.
Young, M.
  1993   The History of Vancouver Youth Gangs: 1900–1985. Master's thesis, School
         of Criminology, Simon Fraser University, Burnaby, BC.

Reading 4.
The Ballad of Daniel Wolfe*

Joe Friesen

For two decades, the Indian Posse and gangs like it have wreaked havoc on native communities. To understand how and why, look at two of its key figures, Winnipeg's Wolfe brothers—their broken childhoods, criminal ascent, bloody mistakes and ultimate reckonings, one of them fatal. In a special investigation, retraces a Canadian tragedy.

The guards at Regina Correctional Centre had just finished the evening cell check when Daniel Wolfe tapped his younger half-brother on the shoulder and told him to get ready. The escape was on.

Small and wiry, with long hair and glasses, Daniel had been anticipating this moment for four months. He'd realized there was a two-metre blind spot at the end of the long corridor that housed the prison unit—a place not covered by the security camera. So that was where he'd decided to dig.

Using nail clippers, he'd unscrewed the cover of a heating vent directly beneath the camera. Then he and his half-brother, Preston Buffalocalf, had started prying and scraping at the wall behind it with a kind of mini-crowbar they'd made by breaking off a piece of a metal table.

They would dig for an hour each night after dinner, while other inmates did calisthenics to distract the guards. It had taken a month and a half just to get through the steel plate at the back of the heater. Then it was weeks of chipping away at the cinder block with a homemade chisel. They stuck a piece of fabric from a winter coat behind the grill to hide their progress. And they flushed the dust and debris down the toilet.

"I thought that we'd get caught in the act. All the banging, all the noise, the dust all over us," Mr. Buffalocalf says.

Accused murderers almost never break out of jail. But Daniel, awaiting trial and facing the certainty of life in prison, had thought about little else since his arrest in January, 2008.

Daniel was a leader—and not only in the prison block. Although he had barely a Grade 6 education, he was sharp, often charming, and ruthless. When he was just 12, he and his older brother had founded a gang that became the largest in Canada, with a manifesto that called for reclaiming native pride by force. While still in their teens, they were burning through hundreds of thousands of dollars from an expanding criminal empire.

The Wolfe brothers are the most intriguing figures among a generation of native youth devastated by the impact of gangs. In the past two decades, thousands of young native men in Western Canada, on reserves and in cities, have been affected through

---

* Reprinted from *Saturday's Globe and Mail*. June 18, 2011. Reprinted with permission from *The Globe and Mail*. Copyright *The Globe and Mail*. Joe Friesen is a reporter for *The Globe and Mail*.

personal involvement or family association or as a victim of gang crime. The groups' promotion of drugs, prostitution, robbery and murder have damaged communities and destroyed lives.

It all began with one family, the Wolfes, and the family they created—the Indian Posse. In a lengthy investigation, The Globe and Mail has reconstructed their story through more than two dozen interviews with gang members, relatives, lawyers and police, as well as court transcripts and Daniel's prison letters. Richard Wolfe, Daniel's older brother and fellow Indian Posse founder, spoke at length for the first time since his own release from prison.

1976: Born under a Bad Sign

Susan Creeley was drinking the night Daniel Wolfe was born. She says she drank almost every night in those days, the summer of 1976. Just 18, she finished an entire bottle of Five Star whisky before giving birth at a Regina hospital. Daniel was small and weak, three months premature. He was her second son. Her first was Richard, a year older. They were each named for their father, Richard Daniel Wolfe.

Ms. Creeley is now 53, and sober since 1999. She has a job and has immersed herself in native spirituality. But at age 5, like thousands of other native kids, she was taken away to residential school, where she suffered sexual and physical abuse.

"It has made my life a miserable life," she says. "I started drinking heavily when I was 12, 13 years old. That was killing the pain." At that age, she escaped the school and ran to the city. She survived on welfare, living with her sister, until she met her future husband: "He was old enough to drink and I wanted to go drinking. That's what I wanted to do, any place, any time."

A few years after Daniel's birth, they moved to Winnipeg. Ms. Creeley and her husband, also a residential-school survivor, struggled with poverty and addiction. Their home was loving but often violent.

From time to time, Daniel and Richard were taken to foster homes. They always ran away—sometimes back home, more often to the streets.

Richard, who was released from the penitentiary last fall after serving 15 years, says he and his younger brother were inseparable as kids. Daniel was the risk-taker with the infectious sense of humour. Richard was ambitious and thoughtful.

They would stay out late, completely unsupervised. When they were 8 or 9, the boys and a few friends were at a department store downtown at closing time. They hid under a pile of coats until the store emptied and had the run of the toy department until they were discovered by a guard.

A year or two later, they stole a van and drove from Winnipeg to Regina. While Richard took the wheel, he remembers, Daniel crouched on the floor to operate the gas pedal. They had been gone a week when the police caught up to them.

Richard says he was arrested 20 times before he was 12 years old.

"I remember when the cops used to bring them home, I'd say, 'Okay,'" Ms. Creeley says. "I more or less let them live their own lives. Whenever a problem came at me, I picked up the bottle."

One moment that left an indelible mark was the day the Wolfe brothers saw their mother in hospital, beaten black and blue by their father. "We were pissed off," Richard says. "We both wanted to hurt him. I think he took off to Saskatchewan after that.… Every time I tried to find out where he was, people said he's on the street or he's drinking."

1988: The Advent of the Indian Posse

The gang that would brutalize so many Canadian native communities was born in the Wolfe family home on a summer's day in Winnipeg in 1988. There were seven founding members, all of them native and from similarly poor families. They lived in the neighbourhood just south of the rail yards that divide Winnipeg. Daniel, 12, was the youngest.

They hit on the name "Posse" while flipping through the pages of a hip-hop magazine. They chose Indian, rather than native, much the way black rap groups often defiantly labelled themselves with the N-word. "It was about us Indians sticking together at the time. Because we were looked down on," Richard says. "We were living under the same roofs, had the same struggles: No food in the fridge. Empty beer bottles in the house. People coming over for hours at a time at night and you don't even know who the hell they are."

Richard was 13 when he bought his first handgun. He took it to school tucked in to the back of his pants. Soon he was keeping an AK-47 hidden in a heating vent at home. "Even back then, I was skipping classes and doing scores. Every time I had to report back to the youth [correctional] centre, I always had money and dope on me. Sometimes, if I had to drive there, I stole a car," Richard says.

The brothers' academic career ended shortly after that. But their criminal careers were just taking off.

They got their start in car stereos. The going rate was $100 and there was a buyer in Chinatown. From there, they graduated to break-ins and armed robbery, in which they excelled.

"When we first started dealing with [the Indian Posse], they were pretty much just robbery crews. They were doing bingo halls, gas bars, convenience stores, banks," Winnipeg Police Constable Nick Leone says. "Even back then, they were very violent, as far as street gangs went."

Gangs are a fact of life in many cities today. But that wasn't always the case. An academic study found almost no mention of gangs in Winnipeg from the demise of the Dew Drop Gang around 1950 until the mid-1980s, just before the dawn of the major native gangs: the Indian Posse, the Manitoba Warriors and the Native Syndicate. As the Posse's origins show, there was an influence from the era's African American gang images. But mainly it was the situation of urban aboriginal populations, which included people who were overwhelmingly poor, with significant drug, alcohol and domestic violence problems. The children of that generation formed gangs, surrogate families, to fill the void.

In 1991, at 15 and 14, Richard and Daniel started selling drugs. "That's when we had to start making money to pay the rent," Richard says. "The stereos were good for cash to buy [sneakers] and stuff, but to actually have a house we needed to move up and make some money." They moved to a rented house away from their mother, who admits now that she was lost in a fog of drugs and alcohol.

The Posse spread quickly to the north and west ends of Winnipeg, where it faced rivals. Like any business, it was either grow or die, Richard says. He remembers IP members taking one independent-minded rival for a ride one night. They drove to some woods out of town, handed him a shovel and told him to dig his own grave. They'd seen bikers do this. "That really works, you know," Richard says. The man survived, but his gang was theirs.

Daniel had an even more direct approach to conflict, Richard says. Although drive-by shootings were common in those days, Daniel thought they were "soft." He preferred "walk-bys."

After expanding across Winnipeg, the gang made its next breakthrough on the reserves. In the remote communities of Canada's North, drugs sold for three to five times their price in the city. With almost universal unemployment and widespread despair, the market was insatiable. And as the Posse's brand grew, kids eagerly joined up.

"You [didn't] even need to make recruiting trips to these reserves," Richard says.

1994: Where Did All the Money Go?

By the time Richard was 19, he was making $15,000 to $30,000 a week, roughly a million dollars a year. The people under him were expected to "kick up" 35 per cent of what they made selling drugs. He was also running the gang's prostitution business. Richard (who was higher in the gang than Daniel at the time) says he disapproved of prostitution, but the money was too good to pass up. The gang muscled out the existing pimps, improved the women's take from 25 per cent to 40 per cent and made $3,000 to $5,000 a night running 10 girls.

Of course, there were costs associated with all that income. Some was used to rent gang houses and set up a fund to pay defence lawyers. Richard admits he also had a weakness for gambling. But police say one of the puzzling aspects of the IP has been its inability to develop the more sophisticated techniques of traditional organized crime.

"There's no discipline to save cash and accrue assets. No education to rely on for cash management," says Sergeant Mike MacKinnon of Winnipeg's organized-crime unit. "You might pull them over and they'll have $10,000 or $15,000 on them, but at the end of the day that's money already spent.... We haven't seen anyone moving up into buying large condos or anything like that. They still live in the neighbourhoods they always lived in."

Richard, who left the gang years ago, is quiet when asked where all the money went. Is there a Swiss bank account? He chuckles.

He says they used to talk about investing in youngsters who could go to university and infiltrate the police force and the Crown's office. As with many organizations, recruiting and promoting the right people was a challenge. Daniel was one of the gang's top recruiters, but he complained in a prison letter to Richard in 2000 that there were "too many fucked-up people recruiting fucked-up people." It was causing "a lot of shit," he said.

IP recruits, Richard says, are often kids with disastrous home lives, out on the street late at night, looking for any place to belong. They might be tough enough to survive the initiation, but they bring their own baggage. It's better to find a smart kid: "The smart guy can be a tough guy when the time comes, but not vice versa," he says. "The smart guys usually stay out of gangs, though."

On the whole, street gangs occupy the bottom rung of the organized-crime pecking order. They handle high-risk tasks such as street-level drug dealing and they pay steep prices to buy drugs from higher up the food chain. And even in the underworld, as at every other social level in Canada, natives are discriminated against, according to one study: They're relegated to less lucrative, less enduring criminal opportunities.

1995: All the Wrong Moves

Richard Wolfe settles into a booth at a Regina pizza place wearing dark glasses, and orders a small Hawaiian pizza. In person, he is a large, imposing presence, though with a quiet demeanour. His extensive tattoos peek out from the sleeves of his black shirt, which is buttoned to the top in the style of a 1990s Los Angeles gangster.

Most young IP recruits start with a small tattoo on one hand, which they receive once they complete their first mission. Richard has four shields tattooed near his neck. Three shields is the sign of a captain, someone with roughly 25 people under him. He won't say what four means.

His personal downfall happened very quickly, he explains. In 1995, the owner of a Winnipeg pizza joint owed him $60,000 and wasn't paying. Word went around in criminal circles that Richard had no credibility. His reputation was at stake.

He called the pizza place and made an order for delivery: Hawaiian. He was expecting the pizza box to contain his $60,000, in cash. But he also decided to send a message: When the delivery car came, he ambushed it and opened fire. The driver survived, and Richard was arrested for attempted murder.

Before the trial, Daniel tried to come to his big brother's rescue. He took a sawed-off shotgun to the homes of two witnesses, threatening to kill them if they testified. They reported him and Daniel was sentenced to two years for attempting to obstruct justice. Richard got 19 years, an exceptionally long sentence for attempted murder. When he was led out of the courtroom, he recalls, a line of police stood and applauded.

The shooting was stupid, he says now. Normally underlings handle debt collection. "I lost my cool. There were lots of people mad at me for that."

Daniel served his time, then soon wound up back behind bars. In 1999, he went down for armed robbery, sentenced to eight years.

Prison was nothing new for the Wolfe brothers. Daniel had first gone to jail in 1989, aged 13, and averaged nearly a sentence a year until he turned 19. Each time, he met people inside, and the force of his personality drew them to the Indian Posse. It's no wonder recruitment was good: aboriginal people make up 22 per cent of admissions to sentenced custody (by 2007–08 numbers), despite being only 3 per cent of the population. They also make up 21 per cent of youth-gang members.

By the late 1990s, the Indian Posse had more than 1,000 members, perhaps as many as 3,000. And they weren't alone. The other large aboriginal gangs—the Native Syndicate, primarily in Saskatchewan, and the Warriors in Alberta, Saskatchewan and Manitoba—had several hundred each.

Prison officials tried to dilute the gang's influence in Manitoba jails by sending some IP members outside the province, including Richard and Daniel. But that only helped the gang expand nationally, first across the Prairies and then to B.C and Ontario.

Although the first IP members were all native, expansion brought cultural mixing. The first person to break the colour barrier was Ron Taylor, a black kid who knew the Wolfe brothers in Winnipeg. His gang nickname used the N-word—affectionately, Richard claims. (Mr. Taylor was murdered in prison in 2005.) Richard says he had no problem with letting in non-natives. Daniel wasn't so sure. In a 2006 letter, he wrote, "Every other family's numbers are up except ours [so] we had to swallow some of our pride and open the door. So now we got white, black, might as well say all nations … Bro I never thought this would happen."

2007: A Bloody Day in Saskatchewan

In the summer of 2007, after Daniel was released from his latest round in prison, he moved to his mother's reserve, Okanese, just north of Fort Qu'Appelle, Sask. Police say he was on a recruiting mission.

On Sept. 20 that year, according to court testimony, Christina Cook, 61, returned to Fort Qu'Appelle from a trip to find her daughter and some friends at her home. A few minutes later, two men kicked open the front door. One wore a red bandana over his face. He held a .22-calibre rifle. Jesse Obey was sitting on a couch directly in front of the door. All he saw was the gun barrel, he later testified. The first bullet went through his cheek and blew out his teeth. The next hit the left side of his torso.

The shooter took a step past him to the bedroom, where Ms. Cook and several others were sitting. Sitting across from her, Michael Itittakoose's white hoodie exploded with red. She scrambled to find the phone.

Onc of the attackers yelled, "Shoot the old lady, she's calling the cops." The shooter swivelled toward Ms. Cook, and in a fraction of a second, her husband, Marvin Arnault, dove across the room and threw her to the ground.

He asked if she was hurt. No, Ms. Cook replied, she was okay. "You know I love you," her husband said. "Look after the boys."

"Are you hurt, Marvin?" she asked.

He said, "I think so." Mr. Arnault, 51, died at the scene.

Percy Pascal, a friend of the family, was shot nine times and somehow survived. Cordell Keepness took three bullets, including one through the hand.

The gunman lowered his weapon and stepped toward the door. He had fired more than 20 shots. Two people were dead, three others wounded.

"That'll teach them to mess with IP," he said.

2007–08: Backed into a Corner

RCMP Major Crimes Corporal Rob Zentner arrived at the house about three hours after the shooting. He was shocked by what he found.

"There was blood staining on the floor, on the walls. You could see that it had been hysteria in the house. People obviously ran all different directions," he says. "You could follow their footprints where they had run, and there was bullet holes in the wall and cartridge casings and bullet fragments on the ground."

For Cpl. Zentner and the rest of the team assembled to investigate the murders, the first step was figuring out what prompted it.

They knew the gunman had mentioned the IP, Cpl. Zentner says. Mr. Pascal, who was in hospital recovering from his wounds, had a Native Syndicate tattoo on his face. It seemed clear that it was a gang shooting.

Witnesses told them that Mr. Pascal had exchanged words earlier that night with a man at a hotel bar. The man had a tattoo that said "Red 'til Dead," an Indian Posse slogan. Fort Qu'Appelle, a mainly Native Syndicate town, was not friendly territory for the IP. There was an escalation of insults. Mr. Pascal asked the man if he knew that the IP and Native Syndicate were at war.

It looked as though there would be a fight, but Mr. Pascal and company left. A bartender told police that he overheard the man say afterward, "They don't know what's coming for them." Surveillance footage revealed the man was Daniel Wolfe.

The RCMP now knew they were looking at an experienced criminal. Getting a conviction would be difficult.

The investigators say they decided in January, 2008, that they needed an undercover operation to extract a confession from Daniel: They arrested him and, while he sat in one police cruiser, another cruiser pulled up with an undercover officer handcuffed in the back seat. The uniformed officer in front got out, opened the trunk and made a show of displaying a seized Uzi to his colleagues.

Daniel was then brought inside and interviewed. The RCMP detective told him that Gerard Granbois, suspected of driving Daniel to the shooting scene, had already confessed what happened that night. Daniel said very little. The detective left the room.

Daniel, who was being watched on video, immediately whipped around the desk to see what was on the laptop. He opened a file headed "Granbois Re-enactment" and watched several seconds of Mr. Granbois's (genuine) video statement to police, in which he described the route they had taken the night of the murders. Daniel hurried back to his side of the desk when the detective returned.

Later, he was taken to a two-person cell, which was already occupied by the undercover officer.

"You a biker?" Daniel asked. The undercover told him he was a biker associate and that he was carrying some guns when he got pulled over. He asked what Daniel was in for.

Daniel told him that he was screwed. He had seen the evidence against him and he was going down. "They're gonna give me life," he said. "Fuck, I'll be 60, man. That's a long fucking time."

He explained about the driver who had been interrogated. "Wonder if he rolled?" the undercover said.

"Yeah, he rolled," said Daniel. He pointed his finger and thumb in the shape of a gun—he should have killed Mr. Granbois and his 15-year-old accomplice when he had the chance, he said. He knew he had screwed up. The police would have had nothing on him: Not a hair found at the scene, no saliva, no murder weapon.

Daniel said his heart had been pounding when he looked at the detective's computer, but he quickly calmed down. Anxiety was pointless. He knew he was finished.

"That's the life of a gangster," he said.

2008: The Great Escape

After four months of digging, it was Sunday, Aug. 24, 2008, when Daniel announced the time had come. Mr. Buffalocalf went quickly to gather blankets and sheets from inmates. They removed the heater cover and smashed through the remaining bricks with a shower rod. The hole was open for the unit's 17 inmates, nine of them accused of murder. Despite a tip from a police informant that Daniel and company were going out "like in the movies," none of the 76 corrections officers who moved through the unit detected anything.

"It was a good moment. It was one of those Titanic moments," Mr. Buffalocalf says, smiling.

Daniel went first. He crawled through the hole and emerged on a narrow ledge three metres above the exercise yard. He shuffled over to an adjacent wall and clambered up, draping blankets over the coils of razor wire to protect himself before jumping to the ground below.

Mr. Buffalocalf went next. He remembers the adrenalin surging through him. He could barely breathe. He hauled himself to the top of the wall, then balked at the six-metre drop. Daniel waved at him from the ground.

"He just told me to jump," Mr. Buffalocalf says. "Luckily, I didn't get hurt."

There were still two fences to climb and perimeter guards to avoid. They didn't wait for the four inmates who followed them, but just started running. Mr. Buffalocalf had jogged in the exercise yard and done push-ups for a month to get in shape for this. After five minutes, he was wishing he had trained harder.

Daniel was way ahead of him, running across farm fields on the outskirts of Regina. It was dark, but the ground was flat for miles around and they were worried they would be spotted. They alternated walking and running for about eight kilometres, following the railway tracks and ending up in the city's east end. They hung around back alleys, drank water from a garden hose and racked their brains for a place to stay.

They found a ride to Brandon, Man., within a few hours and spent a fretful, paranoid night in a garage. By morning, Daniel had become the RCMP's top priority.

2008: Outlaw on the Run

Daniel considered trying to kill the witnesses who could convict him, but decided against it, Mr. Buffalocalf says. Instead, they made their way to Winnipeg. They were so exhausted by the escape that they rested for a week before doing anything. Their first public outing was to a house party.

"The best part? The girls, man, the girls. There were lots. Coming and going," Mr. Buffalocalf says. Women were enthralled by Daniel's outlaw aura.

But there were few places to hide. Police in several provinces were squeezing anyone associated with the Indian Posse. They never stayed anywhere for more than two nights. Mr. Buffalocalf eventually made up his mind to head for Saskatchewan. He thought he could survive in the bush. But the police caught up to him first, surrounding the apartment building in Winnipeg where he was staying.

It was over. He called Daniel to say goodbye. Daniel was on his cellphone, watching the standoff from a block away.

"I told him I loved him. I told him to hide, to get out of town," Mr. Buffalocalf remembers. Daniel continued to elude police for a third week. Tales of possible sightings and futile police raids made him something of a folk hero. His lawyer, Estes Fonkalsrud, listened to the media coverage, wondering whether his client would ever be seen again.

"I was curious whether he was smart enough to disappear," Mr. Fonkalsrud says.

Would he go, get across the border, never pick up the phone, never refer to himself as Daniel Wolfe again? Or would he end up back in Winnipeg? Well, we know what happened.

Eventually someone betrayed him: An informer's tip led police to the Winnipeg house where Daniel was hiding. They nabbed him in a car in the North End. He went quietly.

A year later, there was a heavy police presence, including snipers on rooftops, when Daniel's murder trial began at the Regina courthouse. The gang's penchant for intimidating witnesses was by now well known. The Saskatoon police chief said it's not uncommon in Saskatchewan courts to see gang members gesturing that they're going to slash the throat of a witness as he or she takes the stand.

In delivering the verdict, the judge said Daniel convicted himself with his own words.

"This case is evidence of Wolfe's callous disregard for human life. There are no mitigating circumstances," the judge said. "But for some luck, many more people would have been killed. It ranks as one of the worst of its type in the history of this province."

Daniel received five life sentences.

2010: The Last Stand of Daniel Wolfe

In January of 2010, Daniel's mother was driving along a snow-swept prairie road when she saw a white owl perched near the shoulder. "In our spirituality, owls give messages," Ms. Creeley says. "As I passed, he just turned his head and followed the car. I thought, 'This is not good.'"

She was worried about Daniel. He had called to say things were crazy in jail. She pulled over to the side of the road and made an offering of tobacco.

At 12:40 p.m. that day in the federal penitentiary at Prince Albert, Sask., a group of six prisoners launched a choreographed attack on two inmates. In the surveillance video, Daniel can be seen at the back of the room, apparently unaware of what was happening. Senior Crown Attorney John Morrall, who later prosecuted the case, says Daniel was obviously not the target.

But when he noticed the attack, Daniel moved to help one of the victims. He was physically blocked by another inmate. He approached a second time and one of the attackers lashed out at him. A single stab—Mr. Morrall calls it a "get the hell out of here" stab—pierced his chest. Less than a minute later, prison guards fired tear gas to break up the melee. The attackers retreated. As the gas cleared, the two targets lay on the floor bleeding from more than 20 wounds.

Daniel appeared calm on the surveillance video. He sat down at a table near the wounded men and sipped a cup of coffee. He put his slippers back on. After a few minutes, he slumped over and fell to the floor. The wound had sliced a coronary artery. He was dead at 33.

2011: Wrestling with Daniel's Ghost

Daniel's death weighs heavily on his older brother. Richard questions the decisions he and his brother made more than two decades ago when they founded the gang.

"I keep going back, thinking, 'If we didn't make this, would he still be alive?'" he says. "Sometimes I look back and it overwhelms me."

But he also can't conceal his lingering regard for what they built. "We did feel pride, me and Danny. He always used to tell me, 'Be proud of who you are.' And I knew he was talking about, right away. No matter what, when we pass away, 50 years down the road, when they bring up the Indian Posse, they're going to remember our names."

Pride, in the end, led Daniel to commit the murders that precipitated his downfall. He couldn't allow a rival gang member to disrespect him in public. His life revolved around reputation and ego, and using violence to get what he wanted.

In an interview with the Winnipeg Free Press in 1994, Richard offered a kind of manifesto of the Indian Posse, in which he compared the gang to native warrior societies and talked about spilling the blood of racists.

In the context of the late 1980s and early 1990s—with the armed standoffs at Oka in Quebec and Ipperwash provincial park in Ontario and the death of native leader J.J. Harper at the hands of Winnipeg police—you can see how the rise of the Indian Posse and other native gangs fit an impression of indigenous youth in revolt.

In his letters from prison, Daniel would sometimes sign off with lines such as "Fuck Canada, this land is our people," or he would draw a Canadian flag upside down.

But the vague political ideas of the gang's early years, Richard admits, took a back seat to basic survival. And, he adds, those ideas have no role in the gang today.

Sgt. MacKinnon of the Winnipeg police dismisses the political rhetoric as a convenient way of dressing up brutal crimes committed for personal gain. "If you look at the victims of their homicides, the girls they force into prostitution and the people they sell drugs to, they're victimizing their own people," he says. "There is nothing cultural about the Indian Posse. The only cultural thing is a gang subculture."

But the gang's history and the Wolfe brothers' story are significant for what they reveal about the roots of violence and dysfunction in many prairie communities: Richard and Daniel were born into a family that suffered generations of pain as a result of residential schools. Their parents were addicted to alcohol and drugs. They had little supervision or care as children. Their home was violent. Daniel, as his mother acknowledges, almost certainly had fetal-alcohol-spectrum disorder, which impairs judgment and impulse control.

The cost of what they started is almost incalculable. It's a plague that stalks neighbourhoods west from Winnipeg to B.C. and north to the most remote and desolate reserves. The direct, measurable impacts, according to a report by the Saskatchewan Criminal Intelligence Service, are mostly financial: The gang's presence, or even perceived presence, drives down property values, boosts insurance costs and generally diverts resources to crime prevention.

The gang also erodes confidence in public institutions—not only in police and the courts, but in schools and the general possibility of making a living legitimately. It preys on poor people by getting them hooked on drugs or the fast money of prostitution.

And then there are the immense indirect costs, the wasted potential of so many young people who end up dead or in prison when they are capable of so much more—including, no doubt, the Wolfe brothers themselves.

Coda: 'We Have to Make That Change Now'

Daniel's letters to Richard from 1997 to 2007, written in a bubbly script, document the ups and downs of their relationship and the gang. He gives Richard updates on who is locked up and who is dead. There's always news about their family, particularly their younger brother, Preston. Although he was just following in their footsteps, Daniel was critical of Preston's bad behaviour as something that had to be stamped out.

There are also references to Daniel's two children with former girlfriends, whom he rarely saw. The mother of one of his children committed suicide on the Valentine's Day after his death, saying she couldn't live without him. Their child now lives with a grandparent.

The letters also make reference to their father, Richard Wolfe: "I haven't seen dad yet, but that's nothing new," Daniel wrote from prison in 1998. Later, he wrote that their father was in a Saskatchewan paper because he stabbed a friend to death after a day spent drinking hairspray. According to the report, it was his 55th conviction.

Toward the end, Daniel began reassessing his life. He talked about leaving the gang. In 2007, he wrote to Richard from the Regina Correctional Centre: "We're not getting any younger bro. We have to make that change now. I told mom to show me the way on that road, so now I have to chill on all that other shit!"

He never made those changes.

Sgt. MacKinnon says that although Daniel is dead, and although there have been a number of high-profile Indian Posse members sent to jail recently, the gang remains a top priority for police. And that's not likely to change.

"We'd be naive if we thought the IP was going to go away," he says. "Here we are 20 years later, you've got in some cases grandsons of original members who now see themselves as IP."

Chapter 3

Prison Gangs

I. Prison Gangs—
An Introduction

Criminal gangs such as street gangs, prison gangs, and outlaw motorcycle gangs are the primary retail distributors of drugs in the United States (NDIC, 2005). The 2011 National Gang Threat Assessment concluded that: "The most notable trends for 2011 have been the overall increase in gang membership, and the expansion of criminal street gangs' control of street-level drug sales, and collaboration with rival gangs and other criminal organizations" (National Gang Intelligence Center, 2011). This statement is true for all criminal gangs, including prison gangs. Compounding the prison gangs' criminal threat is the significant amount of violent behavior they engage in as the gangs compete for control of drug markets in and out of the prison or other correctional facility. Furthermore, in recent years many prison gangs have increased their cooperation with drug trafficking organizations, particularly the extremely violent Mexican drug trafficking organizations. The National Gang Intelligence Center reports that at least 33 U.S.-based criminal gangs have ties with the Mexican drug trafficking organizations and 10 of the 33 are prison gangs—Arizona New Mexican Mafia, Aryan Brotherhood, Barrio Azteca, Black Guerilla Family, California Mexican Mafia (EME), Hermanos de Pistoleros Latinos, La Nuestra Familia, Tango Blast, Texas Mexican Mafia (Mexikanemi), Texas Syndicate) (National Gang Intelligence Center, 2011). Unlike in the U.S., the gangs in Canadian prisons are just street gangs or outlaw motorcycle gangs that come together in the prison setting when the members are incarcerated, except for Aboriginal gangs that were formed for protection on the inside and continued their existence when members are released. Therefore, our prison gang discussion will be confined to U.S. prison gangs.

Prison gangs are an anomaly among criminal gangs, because they have their origin in prison, influence crime in the community, and commit their crimes and exert their influence from within a country's supposedly most secure institutions—prisons and other correctional facilities. Prison gang members are all criminals and engage in more crime than other criminal gangs even though they are for the most part incarcerated and supposedly under the control of the criminal justice system. Prison gang members, as individuals and groups, are more violent than other criminal gang members. The Aryan Brotherhood, although they make up one percent of the nations inmate population, are responsible for 18% of all prison murders (Gang Task Force, nd). Most prison gangs have a "blood in, blood out" policy meaning that prospective members must kill to join and die to leave the gang. "Once you're in, you're in till death!" (Morales, 2011).

How are prison gangs able to exert such control in a "controlled" setting? Prison gangs commit their crimes and control the prison environment through intimidation and violence. It is reasonable to expect to see gang members in prison, and we would also expect them to clique up in prison with other members of their gangs; however, the prison gangs that we discuss—Aryan Brotherhood, Barrio Azteca, Black Guerrilla Family, Hermanos de Pistoleros, Mexikanemi aka The Texas Mexican Mafia or EMI, Mexican Mafia aka La EME, Nuestra Familia, Public Enemy Number One, and the Texas Syndicate—originated in prison or other correctional facilities and moved into the community.

Prison gangs are a crime problem and security threat for the correctional institution. Prison gangs interfere with the ability of prison administrators to maintain order and discipline. They increase inmate violence against prisoners and staff members. Prison gangs and their members commit numerous crimes in prison. They engage in narcotics and drug trafficking and in protection rackets, extort money and valuables from non-gang members, and commit homicides against their own members who violate gang rules or non-gang members who do not pay their debts or are members of rival gangs. Prison gangs are also a problem for the community. Many prison gangs influence and control criminal street gangs in the community, up to and including extorting fees (taxes) from these gangs from their criminal activities. For example, the Mexican Mafia and the Nuestra Familia direct criminal activity through their control of criminal street gangs in the community throughout California. Prison gang leaders order "hits" for those who do not pay their "taxes" or otherwise disrespect the prison gang or its members. The contact with gang members on the outside makes contraband cell phones particular problems for prison administrators. Smuggled cell phones and smartphones make it possible for gang members to influence and control street gangs through unrestricted access and unmonitored conversations via voice calling, internet access, text messaging, email, and social networking websites (see Box 3.1). Prison gang members exercise control outside the prison because the majority of street gang members are career criminals who will continue to engage in crime until they are dead or reincarcerated. Therefore, sooner or later, they will be sentenced to prison where they will clique up or join a prison gang for protection. If they join they are members forever because of the blood oath taken. If released, prison gang members are expected to collect taxes for the gang and kickback money or drugs to their brothers behind bars; disobedience or disrespect of a prison gang leader, in or out of prison, is punishable by death. "For he who runs the inside controls the outside" (Mexican Mafia saying quoted in Morales, 2011).

Prison gangs exist in both state and federal prisons; however, prison gangs are particularly troublesome in California and Texas correctional institutions. These two states have the largest prison systems and the most prison gang members. Trulson, Marquart, and Kawucha (2006) opine that California and Texas account for 70 percent of all prison gang members in the United States. Prison gang expert, Gabriel Morales, says that the California Department of Corrections (CDC) is the "mother that gave birth to all the major prison gangs" (Morales, 2011) (see Box 3.2).

Box 3.1 Illegal Cell Phones in California Prisons

Visitors or correctional staff smuggle the majority of illegal cell phones into California prisons. Many cell phones have also been discovered in legal mail and quarterly packages. In 2010, more than 10,000 illegal cell phones were confiscated from prisoners in California. Historically, correctional staff who have been caught smuggling have been successfully prosecuted only when the phone possession was connected to a more serious charge such as drug distribution, and district attorney offices rarely prosecute unless a more serious offense is involved. In March 2011, legislation was approved in the California State Legislature to criminalize the use of cell phones, including penalties for both smugglers and inmates.

Source: NGIC, 2011: 31.

Box 3.2 Origin Of Selected U.S. Prison Gangs

Gang	Where Formed	When Formed
Mexican Mafia	California	1957
Texas Syndicate	California	1958
Nuestra Familia	California	1965
Black Guerilla Family	California	1966
Aryan Brotherhood	California	1967
Mexikanemi (Texas Mexican Mafia)	Texas	1984
Hermanos de Pisteleros Latinos	Texas	Mid-1980s
Public Enemy Number 1	California	1986
Barrio Azteca	Texas	1987

II. Selected Prison Gangs

Aryan Brotherhood

Source: The Department of Justice (www.justice.gov/criminal/ocgs/gangs/prison.html).

White inmates established the Aryan Brotherhood (AB) in San Quentin in 1964 or 1967 (both dates are cited in the literature) as a protection group against the depravations of black and Hispanic inmates. Black Guerilla Family members would kill and beat white inmates at random whenever they caught them out of their cells. The original AB members were violent white supremacists of Irish descent and biker gang members. An inmate of Irish descent, Jack Mahoney, persuaded the AB, also known as "The Brand" to adopt the Shamrock, the "Rock," as a symbol (Morales, 2011). The 666, the mark of the beast, in the shamrock is earned by committing a murder. The AB is well known in and out of prison for its violence. Members are expected to read *The Art of War* by Sun Tzu and Machiavelli's works, to exercise vigorously to stay in shape, and to read *Gray's Anatomy* to know where to stab enemies and inflict killing blows (Gang Task Force, nd).

Since its founding the AB, a prison gang following the white supremacist ideology, has spread to other states and prison systems including the federal prison system. The AB now operates inside and outside of prisons. There are two AB factions composed of members who are inmates in federal prisons and a second faction made up of inmates in the California prison system. In 1980, the federal AB faction formed a three-man "Commission" to oversee AB members in federal prisons. The California Commission and Council was formed in 1982. These Commissions approve prospective members, make decisions on gang rules, and resolve disputes among members (Morales, 2011). The Commissions issue orders for "hits" or "contracts." In 1997, two AB Commission leaders, Barry Byron "The Baron" Mills and TD "The Hulk" Bingham, in solitary confinement at the Federal ADX supermax prison, ordered a race war at a federal prison in Lewisburg, Pennsylvania, resulting in the deaths of two black inmates. The "race war" was actually instigated by murderous attacks on members of the DC Blacks, a black prison gang, by the pathologically violent AB member, Thomas "Terrible Tom" Silverstein. If Commission orders are not carried out, the result is death.

Women have assisted the AB since its establishment, acting as couriers for information from the prison to the community and smuggling drugs into the prison and money out; they have also worked in sensitive positions in law enforcement agencies and the Department of Motor Vehicles, or other statistical gathering departments where they can access information. There has always been a close relationship between the AB and outlaw motorcycle gangs. Allies of the Aryan Brotherhood are the Mexican Mafia, Hells Angels, Public Enemy Number One, and the Nazi Low Riders. Their enemies include Nuestra Familia, Black Guerilla Family, and the DC Blacks.

Box 3.3 Aryan Brotherhood Code and Pledge

Code
I will stand by my brother
My brother will come before all others
My life is forfeit should I fail my brothers
I will honor my brother in peace as in war

Pledge
The Aryan brother is without a care,
He walks where the weak and heartless won't dare,
And if by chance he should stumble and lose control,
His brothers will be there, to help reach his goal,
For a worthy brother, no need is too great,
He need not but ask, fulfillment his fate,
For an Aryan brother, death holds no fear,
Vengeance will be his, through his brothers still here.

Barrio Azteca

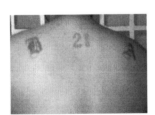 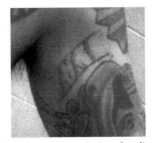

Source: The Department of Justice (www.justice.gov/criminal/ocgs/gangs/prison.html).

Barrio Azteca (BA) that began as a violent prison gang in 1986 has now expanded into a transnational criminal organization working with the Mexican drug cartels on both sides of the Mexican-United States border. Five X14 street gang members from El Paso, Texas formed the gang in the Coffield Unit of the Texas Department of Criminal Justice. Their original purpose was to gain control of the drug trade in the Coffield Unit. As the gang expanded in the Texas prison system, the gang recruited street gang members in jails and prisons who hated and sought protection from other Texas prison gangs such as the Mexikanemi and the Texas Syndicate. Originally, most of the gang members were from West Texas, but today BA members can be found in Arizona, California, Colorado, Illinois, New Mexico, and New Mexico.

The gang has grown into a 1,000- to 2,000-member violent transnational criminal organization working with Mexican drug cartels. A 2011 federal indictment alleges that 12 BA members and associates engaged in kidnappings, extortions, drug trafficking, and the 2010 murders of a U.S. Consulate employer, her husband, and the husband of another U.S. Consulate employee in Juarez, Mexico (FBI, March 09, 2011). The charges allege crimes committed in the United States and Mexico. The indictment alleges that the Barrio Azteca and the Vincente Carillo-Fuentes (VCF) drug trafficking organization formed a criminal alliance. Barrio Azteca members conduct enforcement activities, including murders, against VCF rivals, and in return the VCF pays the Barrio Azteca or provides them with drugs at a discounted price. In addition to the sale of drugs, the Barrio Azteca, like all other prison gangs that operate in the community, charge a 10% tax on all drug sales by street gangs that operate in their territory.

The Black Guerilla Family

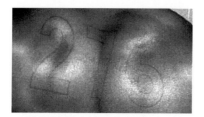

Source: The Department of Justice (www.justice.gov/criminal/ocgs/gangs/prison.html).

The Black Guerilla Family (BGF), a regional prison gang that operates primarily in California, Georgia, Maryland, and Missouri, is considered to be the most politically oriented prison gang. Black Panther member George Jackson recruited other militants from the Black Liberation Army, Symbionese Liberation Army, and the Weatherman Underground Army to form the BGF in San Quentin prison in 1966. According to the National Drug Intelligence Center (NDIC), the gang is highly organized along paramilitary lines with a supreme leader and a committee (National Drug Intelligence Center, 2008). The BGF has an established national charter, code of ethics, and oath of allegiance (see Box 3.4).

The BGF's major source of income comes from the sale and distribution of drugs. In California, the drugs are obtained from the prison gang, Nuestra Familia, Norteno street gang members, or local Mexican drug traffickers. In Maryland the BGF, the largest prison gang in the state, arranges to have drugs, tobacco, cell phones, food, and other contraband smuggled into Maryland prisons (FBI, May 02, 2011). The prison gang recruits and employs employees of prison facilities, including corrections officers, to assist BGF members in the smuggling of contraband and collecting intelligence.

Box 3.4 The Black Guerilla Family Oath

If I should ever break my stride, or falter at my comrade's side, this oath will kill me

If my word should ever prove untrue, should I betray the chosen few, this oath will kill me

If I submit to greed or lust or misuse the people's trust, this oath will kill me

Should I be slow to take a stand or show fear of any man, this oath will kill me

If I grow lax in discipline, in time of strife refuse my hand, this oath will kill me

Long live the spirit of George Jackson, long live the spirit of the Black Guerilla Family

Source: Morales, 2011.

Hermanos de Pistoleros Latinos (HPL)

Source: The Department of Justice (www.justice.gov/criminal/ocgs/gangs/prison.html).

Alfredo "Chino" Soto formed this Hispanic prison gang in the Texas Department of Criminal Justice (TDCJ) in the mid-1980s (Morales, 2011). The gang operates in prisons and in the community in both the United States (Laredo) and in Mexico (Nuevo Laredo). This violent gang has close connections to several Mexican DTOs and is involved in the trafficking of cocaine and marijuana from Mexico into the United States for distribution. HPL is reported to have at least 1,000 members.

Mexican Mafia (EME)

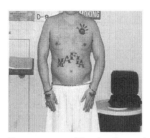 

Source: The Department of Justice (www.justice.gov/criminal/ocgs/gangs/prison.html).

The Mexican Mafia (MM), also known as La EME, Spanish for the letter M, is the first "validated" prison gang in America (Morales, 2011). It was formed by Louis Jesse "Huero Buff" Flores at the Deuel Vocational Institute in Tracy, California in 1957–1958. The majority of the members were previously Southern California street gang members, a tradition that exists today. By 1966, the extremely violent prison gang had gained control of San Quentin and Folsom prisons. According to prison gang expert Gabriel Morales (2011), the Mexican Mafia, operating on the principle "he who runs the inside, controls the outside," attempted to take over drug trafficking in Southern California through the control of the street gangs operating in southern California through the Sureno Alliance which we discussed earlier. This control was exercised by means of the indiscriminate murder of street gang members, inside the prison or in the community, who disrespected MM members, did not follow MM orders or pay a "tax" for their illegal activities to incarcerated MM leaders. The Federal Bureau of Prisons in 2010 listed 50 Mexican Mafia members from California controlling an estimated 2,500+ hard core Sureno (gang members who swear allegiance to EME) street gang members (Morales, 2011).

Box 3.5 Control of the Outside

The Mexican Mafia, the first prison gang, perfected the system of outside control of street gangs. "Members," or "brothers" of the Eme exert control over trusted "right-hand" men known as "shot callers." The shot callers are members of local gangs [Sureno alliance], but they assert authority and control over their particular gangs at the behest of a Mexican Mafia member. Below the shot callers are "soldiers," who are essentially local gangsters aspiring to become Mexican Mafia members. Soldiers are required to "put in work" which means that they must commit a variety of illegal activities for the benefit of the Mexican Mafia to earn the trust of a "brother."

Source: Agnifilo, Bliss, & Riordan, 2006:15.

Mexikanemi (The Texas Mexican Mafia or EMI)

Source: The Department of Justice (www.justice.gov/criminal/ocgs/gangs/prison.html).

The Texas Mexican Mafia (TX-EMI) is not to be confused with the California Mexican Mafia (EME), although they have close ties with one another. The TX-EMI, the largest prison gang in Texas, was founded by Heriberto Huerta to oppose the Texas Syndicate, another Texas prison gang to be discussed later. Huerta is currently serving time in the Federal ADX maximum-security prison in Florence, Colorado as a result of RICO convictions in 1994. The 1984 TX-EMI constitution written by Huerta clearly indicates the criminal nature of the gang, it states, "In being with a criminal organization, we will function in any respect or criminal interest for the benefit or advancement of La EME [sic]. We will traffic in drugs, contracts of assassinations, prostitution, robbery of high magnitude, and anything we can imagine!" (Morales, 2011:127). True to their criminal proclamations, the TX-EMI engages in a wide range of criminal activities, including alliances with other criminal organizations such as Mexican drug cartels and criminal street gangs like the Latin Kings. As is common with all prison gangs that operate in the community, their largest sources of revenue comes from a 10% "street tax" on drug dealers in the areas they control. In 2003, the TX-EMI adopted three rules to ensure the criminal nature of new recruits and improve the "quality" of prospective members. The rules state: 1) Prospects must commit a serious assault/kill with a weapon. (Also known as a "cameo" (a direct order to a gang member.)) 2) If the probationary member does not fulfill his obligation, his sponsor is responsible for making sure he is killed. 3) If a sponsor recruits an "undesirable" into the organization, he will be forbidden to recruit any more for a set period of time (Morales, 2011:133). The TX-EMI operates both in the Texas and federal prison systems. According to Morales (2011), there are approximately 1,400 members in the Texas prison system and on the street and another 175 members and over 500 associates in the federal system.

Nuestra Familia

Source: The Department of Justice (www.justice.gov/criminal/ocgs/gangs/prison.html).

By the late 1960s, the Mexican Mafia (MM) controlled most of the California prisons and was victimizing Northern California inmates and Southern California inmates who would not join the MM. Some Mexican Mafia members were against this treatment of fellow Mexicans and formed the Nuestra Familia Mejicana—NFM—(Our Mexican Family) (Morales, 2011). The Nuestra Family and the later alliances of Norteno (Northern) and Sureno (Southern) grew out of the NFM. By 1967, Morales (2011) states that many NFM members were being sent to San Quentin and dissatisfaction with the MM was increasing along with NFM membership. After several wars between the two groups, September 9, 1968, is seen as the official beginning of the Nuestra Familia and the start of the war between the two prison gangs. Morales (2011) says that the name of Nuestra Familia Mejicana was officially changed to Nuestra Familia when the gang began to accept non-Mexicans.

Along with the name change and increased membership came an increase in criminal activities by the NF. The 1998 federal and state three-year $5 million investigation, Operation Black Widow, into the Nuestra Familia was, at the time, the most expensive investigation into a U.S. prison gang (Trulson, Marquart, and Kawucha, 2006). The investigation and trial revealed that Nuestra Familia gang leaders locked down 23 hours a day in the state's highest security prison, the Security Housing Unit of Pelican Bay State Prison, were able to control thousands of Nortenos (Northern California gang members pledging allegiance to the NF) from Bakersfield, California to the Oregon State line (Reynolds and Sanchez, November 29, 2003). Using an elaborate communication system—coded messages disguised as love letters, urine used as invisible ink, letters marked "legal mail" sent to a nonexistent San Francisco law firm—gang leaders ordered crimes and hits and collected "taxes" from robberies and the selling of methamphetamines, heroin, and marijuana from the Norteno gang members.

Public Enemy Number 1

According to the National Drug Intelligence Center (2005) and the Department of Justice (http://www.justice.gov/criminal/ocgs/gangs/prison.html), Public Enemy Number One (PEN1), a white supremacist prison gang, is the fastest growing Caucasian prison gang, with an estimated membership of 400–500 persons. PEN1 operates primarily in the prison systems and communities in California; however, they also have a presence in locations throughout the northeastern, Pacific southwestern, southeastern, and west central regions of the country. PEN1 have alliances with other white supremacist prison gangs such as the Aryan Brotherhood and the Nazi Low Riders. Their primary source of income is the mid-level and retail-level of methamphetamine inside and out of prison. This extremely violent prison gang also engages in assaults, murders, auto theft, burglary, identity theft, and property crimes.

Texas Syndicate (TS)

Source: The Department of Justice (www.justice.gov/criminal/ocgs/gangs/prison.html).

Inmates from Texas who were incarcerated in the California Department of Corrections (Morales, 2011) formed the Texas Syndicate (TS) in San Quentin and Folsom Prison during the early 1970s. The TS began to show up in the Texas Department of Criminal Justice-Corrections Division in 1975–1976. Originally, both Hispanic and white inmates were allowed to join, but beginning in 1995 whites were excluded from membership. Today, the Texas Syndicate operates on both sides of the U.S.-Mexico border and is one of the largest and most violent gangs in the southwestern United States. The gang smuggles multi-kilogram quantities of powdered cocaine, heroin, and methamphetamine, and multi-tons of marijuana from Mexico into the U.S. for distribution inside and outside of prisons. TS members work closely with Mexican DTOs in these smuggling operations. The highly structured gang is estimated to have 1,300 members.

References

Agnifilo, M., Bliss, K. and Riordan, B. (2006). Investigating and Prosecuting Gangs Using the Enterprise Theory. *United States Attorneys' Bulletin.* May, 2006:15–22.

FBI. (March 09, 2011). El Paso, Division Press Release. Federal, State, and Local Law Enforcement Round UP Barrio Azteca Members Racketeering Charges Allege Responsibility for Murder of a U.S. Consulate Employee in Juarez on March 13, 2010.

FBI. (May 02, 2011). FBI Baltimore Division. Press Release.

Gang Task Force. (nd). Aryan Brotherhood. http://gangtaskforce.blogspot.com.

Morales, G.C. (2011). La Familia—The Family: Prison Gangs in America. 2nd ed.

National Drug Intelligence Center (NDIC). (2005). Special Issue: Gangs in the United States. *Narcotics Digest Weekly.* October, 4, 2005.

National Drug Intelligence Center. (2008). Attorney General's Report to Congress on the Growth of Violent Street Gangs in Suburban Areas. April, 2008.

National Gang Intelligence Center (NGIC). (2011). 2011 National Gang Threat Assessment: Emerging Trends. GPO.

Reynolds, J. and Sanchez, G. Center for Investigating Reporting. (November 29, 2003). Prison gang case puts role of FBI informants under scrutiny/Investigation results in 13 guilty pleas; 9 more defendants face trial next year. *SFGate.com.*

Trulson, C.R., Marquart, J.W. and Kawucha, S.K. (April, 2006). Gang Suppression and Institutional Control. *Corrections Today.*

Readings

1. Brook, J. L. (n.d). Blood In, Blood Out: The Violent Empire of the Aryan Brotherhood. *Crime Magazine.* http://crimemagazine.com.
2. ADL. (2007). *PEN1: Public Enemy Number 1—California's Growing Racist Gang.* Anti-Defamation League.
3. Mock, Brentin (2007). Vicious Cycle: Aryan Circle Blamed for Two Cop Killings. *Intelligence Report.* Southern Poverty Law Center. Winter.
4. STRATFOR. (November 19, 2008). The Barrio Azteca Trial and the Prison Gang-Cartel Interface. *Global Security Intelligence Report.*

Reading 1.
Blood In, Blood Out: The Violent Empire of the Aryan Brotherhood*

John Lee Brook

The Aryan Brotherhood: The First Woe

January 16, 1967: Nazi prison-gang associate Robert Holderman was stabbed and then battered to death by Black Guerilla Family gang members at San Quentin.

January 17, 1967: 1,800 black inmates and 1,000 white inmates clashed on the main yard at San Quentin over the death of Robert Holderman. Prison guards broke up the brawl by firing shots into the mass. Five inmates were wounded by the shots. One inmate suffered severe head trauma from the beating he received from opposing gang members. Two other inmates suffered non-fatal heart attacks.

---

* Reproduced with permission of *Crime Magazine;* Pat O'Connor, Editor and John Lee Brook, author.

August 27, 1967: Nineteen-year-old Barry Byron Mills was arrested in Ventura, California and held for transfer to Sonoma County, where he had boosted a car. Sonoma had issued an arrest warrant in his name for grand theft auto.

December 12, 1967: Barry Mills requested and was denied probation. Instead he was sentenced to one year in the Sonoma County Jail.

January 29, 1968: Barry Mills and Buddy Coleman escaped from the Sonoma County Honor Farm.

February 17, 1968: Barry Mills was arrested in Windsor, California, and held on a warrant charging escape without force.

March 12, 1968: Barry Mills sentenced to one year and one day in prison for escape without force from the Sonoma County Jail.

March 13, 1969: Barry Mills was released from prison.

January 13, 1970: Soledad State Prison Aryan Brotherhood leader Buzzard Harris, along with fellow Aryan Brotherhood members Smiley Hoyle, Harpo Harper and Chuko Wendekier, and Mexican Mafia members Colorado Joe Ariaz, John Fanene, and Raymond Guerrero battled with Black Guerilla Family gang members on the exercise yard at Soledad prison. Tower guard Opie Miller opened fire with his high-powered rifle, killing Black Guerilla leader W.L. Nolen, Cleveland Edwards and Alvin Miller. Aryan Brotherhood leader Buzzard Harris was wounded in the groin by a rifle bullet.

January 30, 1970: Barry Mills and William Hackworth were arrested after robbing a Stewarts Point convenience store.

February 3, 1970: Barry Mills convicted of first-degree armed robbery after co-defendant William Hackworth testified for the prosecution. Barry Mills sentenced to 5 years to life in prison.

April 21, 1972: Aryan Brotherhood members Fred Mendrin and Donald Hale murdered Fred Castillo by stabbing him to death at the Chino Institute for Men. Castillo was the leader of the Nuestra Familia gang. The Aryan Brotherhood murdered Castillo as part of a contract with the Mexican Mafia.

December 15, 1972: Aryan Brotherhood members Fred Mendrin and Donald Hale sentenced to life in prison for the murder of Fred Castillo.

1973: The Aryan Brotherhood was officially formed in the federal prison system.

October 18, 1977: Aryan Brotherhood member Little Joe O'Rourke engaged in a vicious gun battle with campus police at El Camino Community College. The gun battle erupted when the police, as part of a routine check, disrespected Little Joe by asking him for his student I.D. Little Joe was wounded and arrested.

November 25, 1977: Aryan Brotherhood members David Owens and New York Crane robbed the Bank of America in Agoura, California. They got away with $9,000.

December 2, 1977: New York Crane named as the prime suspect in the murder of fellow Aryan Brotherhood member Hogjaw Cochran.

December 29, 1977: Barry Mills released from San Quentin State Prison.

January 11, 1978: Aryan Brotherhood member David Owens arrested and charged with robbing the Bank of America in Agoura, California. Owens had $3,844 on him when arrested.

March 13, 1978: David Owens convicted of bank robbery. He was sentenced to federal prison. His co-defendant "New York" Crane was held over in Orange County Jail and charged with the murder of Hogjaw Cochran.

March 31, 1978: Little Joe O'Rourke, who opened fire on the El Camino Community College campus, sentenced to seven years in prison.

June 1978: Barry Mills sentenced to 20 years in federal prison for planning a bank robbery in Fresno, California. The bank was robbed by the Aryan Brotherhood in June 1976. Barry Mills did not participate in the robbery, but provided the blueprint for it.

The Second Woe

May 20, 1979: Barry Mills murdered Aryan Brotherhood associate John Sherman Marzloff in the United States Prison Atlanta, Georgia.

1980: The Aryan Brotherhood set up a commission to run the operations of all Aryan Brotherhood members in the federal prison system. The commission was composed of three men. Barry Mills assumed command of the commission.

June 8, 1980: Aryan Brotherhood associate Robert Hogan was murdered. The order to kill him came from Barry Mills.

September 27, 1982: Aryan Brotherhood Commissioner Thomas "Terrible Tom" Silverstein murdered Cadillac Smith, who was the leader of the D.C. Mob, at the United States Prison, Marion, Illinois.

December 9, 1982: Aryan Brotherhood member Neil Baumgarten (#20586-148) was murdered by members of the D.C. Mob. Baumgarten's murder was payback for the murder of Cadillac Smith.

January 13, 1983: Aryan Brotherhood member Blinky Griffen convicted of the murder of T-Bone Gibson.

February 13, 1983: Aryan Brotherhood member Richard Barnes was murdered. The order to kill Barnes came from Aryan Brotherhood Councilman McKool Slocum.

September 23, 1983: Aryan Brotherhood associate Gregory Keefer was stabbed to death by another Aryan Brotherhood associate. Keefer owed tax money from drug sales to Mills. When Keefer neglected to pay the tax, Mills ordered the hit.

October 6, 1983: Aryan Brotherhood member Richard "Rhino" Andreasen provided information to the feds about a bank robbery in Santa Ana, California. Rhino gave the feds the name of an Aryan Brother who was one of the bank robbers. For this transgression, Barry Mills ordered Rhino killed. An Aryan Brother stabbed Rhino to death at the United States Penitentiary Leavenworth, Kansas.

October 6, 1983: At the United States Penitentiary Marion, Illinois, Aryan Brotherhood Commissioner Thomas Silverstein, aka "Terrible Tom," stabbed Officer Eugene Clutts 40 times for "disrespecting him." Officer Clutts died. At the same prison a few hours later, Officer Bob Hoffman was stabbed 35 times by Aryan Brother Clayton Fountain, who "didn't want Terrible Tom to have a higher body count than me." Officer Hoffman died.

January 30, 1984: An Aryan Brotherhood associate stabbed and killed Officer Boyd Spikerman at the Federal Correctional Institution, Oxford, Wisconsin.

February 7, 1984: Aryan Brotherhood member Robert Scully assaults a fellow inmate at San Quentin. Scully was in a bad mood and "the bastard pissed me off."

March 13, 1984: Aryan Brotherhood member Rick Rose defected. His name was placed "in the hat."

April 12, 1984: Aryan Brotherhood member Jesse Brun sets fire to a black inmate at Folsom prison. The victim suffered burns over 25 percent of his body.

April 27, 1984: Aryan Brotherhood member Robert Scully was once again in a bad mood. Scully attacked and tried to stab a prison guard.

April 28, 1984: Robert Scully gases two guards at San Quentin. No charges were filed. No disciplinary action was taken.

May 1, 1984: Robert Scully stabbed a guard at San Quentin. Scully was held and searched. The searchers found three hacksaw blades in his rectum and two .22 caliber bullets inside his stomach. Scully had swallowed the bullets. All charges against Scully were dismissed.

May 29, 1985: Robert Scully assaulted another inmate at San Quentin. Scully's shank was confiscated and he was charged with possession of a deadly weapon. Scully received six additional years for assault.

September 1985: Tyler "the Hulk" Bingham was officially named to the three-man Federal Commission.

October 10, 1987: Aryan Brotherhood member Rodney Ross stabbed and killed 33-year old Gordon Gaskill at Folsom prison.

June 22, 1987: Aryan Brotherhood member Art Ruffo attacked a black inmate. Ruffo had a shank and tried to murder the black gang member. Officer David Pitts thwarted Ruffo's attempt at murder by shooting Ruffo in the hip. At the same time, Aryan Brotherhood member Cornfed Schneider attacked another black inmate. The attacks were planned and orchestrated as part of a hit on the D.C. Blacks at Folsom prison. The hits were ordered by Blue Norris, an Aryan Brotherhood councilman. This was the beginning of "Hell Week" at Folsom prison.

July 7, 1987: During a strip search, Cornfed Schneider stabbed Officer Carl Kropp in the throat. Councilman Blue Norris ordered the hit on Officer Kropp as payback for the shooting of Aryan Brotherhood member Art Ruffo. Officer David Pitts, who shot Art Ruffo, was wounded by a shotgun blast as he drove to his home in West Sacramento.

October 10, 1987: Aryan Brotherhood member Robert Scully, who was usually in a bad mood, had been moved to Tehachapi Prison. While there Scully was charged with possession of a deadly weapon. The charge was later dropped.

November 25, 1987: Judith Box was arrested by authorities. Box was the girlfriend of Wildman Fortman, who was a member of the Aryan Brotherhood. Box was charged with providing the Aryan Brotherhood with the home addresses of prison guards.

March 15, 1988: Aryan Brotherhood member Robert Rowland defected, providing authorities with information about a plot to murder prison guards. Rowland's name went "into the hat."

August 28, 1988: Judith Box was convicted of identity theft and conspiring to commit assault. Box obtained the requested information (home addresses of prison guards) from her job at the Franchise Tax Board.

February 15, 1989: Judith Box sentenced to three years in prison.

June 5, 1989: Aryan Brotherhood member Marvin Stanton was assaulted and shot with a 37mm block-gun while fighting with a member of Nuestra Familia. The battle occurred on one of the exercise yards at Corcoran State Prison.

June 14, 1989: During his trial, Aryan Brotherhood member Cornfed Schneider testified that he stabbed Officer Kropp in the throat because he thought the guards were coming to attack him.

July 24, 1989: The jurors, who were terrified, failed to find Cornfed Schneider guilty of attempted murder. Cornfed Schneider sentenced to an additional five years in prison for possession of a deadly weapon. Cornfed Schneider stabbed his attorney Phillip Couzens four times. The two men were talking in the hallway of the Sacramento County Courthouse.

April 18, 1990: Aryan Brotherhood member Todd Ashker convicted of second-degree murder in the death of a Folsom inmate. A hit had been ordered on the inmate by the commission. Ashker sentenced to 21 years to life in prison.

December 13, 1990: Aryan Brotherhood member Robert Scully, he of the bad attitude, was transferred to the new maximum security prison at Pelican Bay. Scully was transferred because of "his history of violence."

December 16, 1992: Aryan Brotherhood member Victor Carrafa, who had just been paroled, was arrested in Stockton, California. He had a six-inch Buck Knife and a .38 caliber semi-automatic pistol on his person.

March 14, 1993: Aryan Brotherhood member Termite Kennedy shot and killed Glenn Chambers of Oregon. Chambers had been supplying the Aryan Brotherhood with chemicals for the manufacture of crystal meth.

May 11, 1993: While being escorted to the dentist, Aryan Brotherhood member Victor Carrafa escaped from the custody of the Sacramento County Sheriff's Department. The escape had been planned. Aryan Brotherhood member Gerard Gallant helped Victor Carrafa escape. Gallant shot deputy Steve Fonbuena in the face and stomach.

February 26, 1994: Robert Scully released from Pelican Bay prison. Scully's parole stipulated drug and alcohol testing. It also prohibited him from associating with members of the Aryan Brotherhood or any other known felons.

March 24, 1994: Robert Scully was arrested in Newport Beach. He was carrying a .25 caliber pistol and displayed false identification. Scully was sent back to Pelican Bay prison for one year.

June 1, 1994: Aryan Brotherhood member Joseph Barrett assaulted a prison officer who confiscated a television from his cell.

March 23, 1995: Robert Scully released from Pelican Bay prison. Brenda Moore, who was the girlfriend of Cornfed Schneider, picked him up in front of the prison.

March 26, 1995: Robert Scully and Brenda Moore murdered Frank Trejo, who was a deputy with the Sonoma County Sheriff's Department. The murder took place in the parking lot of a bar in Sebastopol, California.

The Third Woe

1996: Barry Mills proposed that the Aryan Brotherhood absorb the prison gang known as the Dirty White Boys.

February 7, 1996: Aryan Brotherhood member Art Ruffo was strangled by his cellmate Brian Healy, who was an Aryan Brotherhood member. The murder took place at Pelican Bay prison and was ordered by the commission.

April 9, 1996: Aryan Brotherhood member Joseph Barrett, who was incarcerated at Calipatria Prison, received a message from the commission. The message instructed Barrett to "squeeze and hug his cellmate." Barrett's cellmate was Aryan Brotherhood member Thomas Richmond. Barrett obeyed the instructions and killed Richmond.

November 1, 1997: As a favor to the Mexican Mafia, the commission ordered Pelican Bay inmate Felipe Cruz hit. Cruz was strangled by Aryan Brotherhood member James Ellrod.

February 22, 1998: Aryan Brotherhood member Brian Healey told the feds he was willing to testify against the Aryan Brotherhood.

February 23, 1998: In an ordered hit, Pelican Bay inmate Timothy Waldron was strangled by Aryan Brotherhood member Steve Olivares.

March 10, 1998: Aryan Brotherhood member William Stanton was stabbed to death by two inmates. The murder took place on Pelican Bay Prison's A yard.

February 2, 2000: Aryan Brotherhood member Joseph Barrett was strip searched at Tehachapi State Prison. A shank and six razor blades were found in his rectum.

January 30, 2001: Aryan Brotherhood members Cornfed Schneider and Dale Bretches, both incarcerated at Pelican Bay, were discovered to be running a dog-fighting ring on the outside. Two of their pit bulls killed Dianne Whipple of San Francisco.

September 5, 2001: The Northern California office of the U.S. District Attorney announced it was indicting six members of the Aryan Brotherhood and one associate.

October 16, 2002: A federal indictment unsealed in Los Angeles charged 40 members and associates of the Aryan Brotherhood with several RICO violations, including murder. The indictment included Rafael Gonzalez-Munoz, who was a high-ranking member of the Mexican Mafia, and Joseph Principe, who was a federal prison guard.

April 7, 2003: Aryan Brotherhood member Blue Norris was found stabbed to death at Calipatria State Prison. He had defected from the Aryan Brotherhood and provided information to prison officials. His murder was ordered by the commission.

September 4, 2003: Aryan Brotherhood member Cornfed Schneider pled guilty to conspiracy, racketeering and smuggling. He was sentenced to life in prison. This was his third life sentence.

April 4, 2004: Brenda Jo Riley, who was the wife of an Aryan Brotherhood member, sentenced to serve 21 months in prison for acting as a message courier for the Aryan Brotherhood.

November 29, 2004: Aryan Brotherhood member Wade Shiflett was shot and killed by a prison guard on B yard at Sacramento State Prison. Shiflett was attempting to murder another member of the Aryan Brotherhood. The commission had ordered the hit because the brother had defected and was going to testify against them.

July 22, 2005: U.S. District Judge David Carter set a date for the federal trial against the Aryan Brotherhood. Judge Carter ruled defense attorneys could call Thomas "Terrible Tom" Silverstein as a defense witness. But Terrible Tom would remain shackled in court.

The Indictment

Specific crimes cited in the indictment against Barry Mills, Tyler Bingham and Thomas Silverstein:

The murders of:
John Marzloff in prison in Atlanta, Georgia.
Robert Hogan in Illinois.
Richard Barnes in California.
Gregory Keefer in Illinois.
Richard Andreasen in California.
Thomas Lamb in Illinois.
Arva Lee Ray in California.
William McKinney in California.
Charels Leger in Kansas.
Arthur Ruffo in California.
Aaron Nash in California.
Frank Joyner in Pennsylvania.
Abdul Salaam in Pennsylvania.
Terry Walker in Illinois.

The Baron and The Hulk, December 2002

They came for them while it was still dark. Shortly after 4:00 in the morning, a convoy of vehicles turned off the main highway. U.S. Marshal Clarence J. Sugar sat in the passenger seat of the lead vehicle. A tall man, Marshal Sugar was also heavily muscled. He carried himself with a swagger, and an air of menace hung from him like a cloak. Today he was strapped to the max: pepper spray, a Taser, and a Glock 9mm all rode on his Sam Browne belt. In his lap rested a MAC-10 machine gun. Next to his right leg, an M-16 assault rifle rested against the door of the SUV. Black body armor encased his upper torso making him appear even thicker than he was.

Spread out among the other vehicles, Marshal Sugar had a total of 19 Deputy Marshals accompanying him. All of them wore black fatigues, black body armor, and carried fully automatic weapons. All of them were hard men who knew how to handle themselves in combat situations.

It was cool and damp outside. A faint ribbon of blue arose from the western horizon to meet the darkness. Marshal Sugar looked out the window of his vehicle and shook his head. Even California had a Siberia, he decided, and this was it. 'It' was a remote forested area near a town called Crescent City, in Del Norte County, Calif. Up ahead he noticed a white glow that was definitely man made. As the convoy came around a final bend in the road, a huge, lighted compound became visible. Around the perimeter of the compound, which spread out over 275 acres, he could see miles of curlicued razor wire. Outside the wire stood electrified fences that would fry anyone who touched them.

The convoy arrived at the main entrance and the massive gate slowly opened. As the convoy roared inside, guards armed with high-powered rifles looked down from their watchtowers. Without hesitation, the convoy headed straight for a complex of white concrete buildings, which formed a series of X's when viewed from above. Screeching to a halt, the doors of the vehicles flew open and 20 U.S. Marshals jumped out. They moved in formation to the main door of the complex. The door was already open.

Inside the building, the marshals walked down a long gray corridor. An array of surveillance cameras looked disinterestedly down at them, recording every movement. The small army of marshals passed through a series of barred doors, which thunked closed behind them. After one more turn, they reached their destination: the Security Housing Unit of Pelican Bay State Prison. Called the SHU for short, it was also known as "the Hole" by those who worked and lived in it.

The SHU was a prison built inside a prison.

Pelican Bay State Prison was California's supermax prison. The place where California caged its most ferocious human animals. Some people called them criminals. Others called them prisoners. Still others called them inmates. They were beasts of the jungle, men who were so savage and so dangerous that they had to be separated from the other violent men.

Marshal Sugar and his deputy marshals were here to pick up and transport two of these violent men.

Arriving at the first cell, Marshal Sugar slammed the butt of his Mac-10 against the steel door. Inside the cell, a man jumped up from his bunk where he had been asleep. Standing in his white boxer shorts, he glared at the cell door, as if trying to burn a hole through it with his vision.

"Assume the position," said Marshal Sugar. "You're being moved."

"Fuck you," snarled the inmate. His name was Barry Byron Mills, but no one called him that. Everyone called him either The Baron or McB. The Baron nickname referred to his power and authority over other inmates. Those who called him McB did so because he was like McDonald's, worldwide and everywhere.

"Assume the position," repeated Marshal Sugar. This command meant The Baron should place his back against the inside of his cell door and put his hands through a slot in the door, so that his hands could be cuffed behind his back.

"No," said The Baron. Then he smiled and added, "Make me."

Marshal Sugar stepped aside and nodded at the Corrections Officer who stood beside him. The CO put his key in the doorlock and turned it. Heavy pneumatic bolts snapped back and the CO pulled the door open.

The Baron looked at Marshal Sugar. "Who the fuck are you and what do you want with me?" asked The Baron.

Marshal Sugar looked at The Baron, noting the man's massive muscles, tattoos and gleaming bald-head. "U.S. Marshals," said Sugar. "And like I just told you, you're being moved. And we're moving you right now." He paused. "We can do it the easy way or we can do it the hard way." Marshal Sugar smiled. "Or we can do it the semi-easy-hard way. The choice is yours."

Narrowing his blue eyes, The Baron said, "What's the semi-easy-hard way? I'm not familiar with that one."

"The easy way is that you act like a civilized human being and we'll treat you like one. The hard way is that my deputies rush you and take you by force. Sometimes—in the chaos that occurs in this particular method—you get a little roughed up," explained Marshal Sugar. He gave The Baron a fat smile. "The semi-easy-hard way is that I simply shoot you with this thing"—he held up his Taser—"and after you do the funky chicken for about 30 seconds, we search your body cavities and bundle you up."

Marshal Sugar shrugged. "I don't really care how we do it, because in the end the result is the same." With a dramatic flourish, he raised his forearm up to his eyes and looked at his wristwatch. "You have 10 seconds to decide."

The Baron clenched his fists, as if checking his energy levels. After a few seconds, he winked and turned around, clasping his hands at the small of his back. Deputy Marshals quickly surrounded him. One cuffed his hands, while others probed his ears and nose with flashlights. They were looking for anything that might be used as a weapon or as a key to unlock handcuffs.

"Open your mouth, please," said one of the marshals.

The Baron opened his mouth wide and the marshal shined his flashlight in it. "Touch the roof of your mouth with your tongue, please," said the marshal, peering into The Baron's mouth.

"Okay. Thank you." The marshal stepped back and The Baron snapped his mouth shut, thrusting his head forward a little bit like he was a shark biting into flesh.

A deputy marshal pulled a yellow jumpsuit from a bag he had been carrying. Stenciled across the back of the jumpsuit in bold, black letters was the word PRISONER.

"Put these on, please," said the deputy marshal, holding the jumpsuit out to The Baron. "But before you do, please squat down three times. Then we'll remove the cuffs so you can dress."

The Baron hissed a little between his teeth, shaking his head. If he had a shank—which was a crude, handmade knife—hidden up inside his rectum, squatting three times would cause the shank to move and probably pierce his intestines. He didn't have one. So he squatted three times.

When he finished the last squat, a marshal uncuffed his hands. While he pulled on the yellow jumpsuit, three deputy marshals pointed their Tasers at him. All three were big, beefy men, who gazed wishfully at him. Then they cuffed his hands behind his back, and shackled his feet. The final touch was a waist chain, like a steel belt, which they threaded through his handcuffs and locked snugly around him.

"What about shoes?" demanded The Baron.

"You'll get socks and slippers once you're in the van," Marshal Sugar told him.

The Baron glared at him.

"They'll get cold, but they won't freeze," the marshal informed him. "Park him over there," pointed Marshal Sugar, indicating a bench with large metal rings welded to it.

Deputy marshals escorted The Baron to the bench, where they ran heavy chains through his ankle shackles and waist chain. These they ran through the rings on the bench, pulling them tight, forcing The Baron to sit hunched over.

"Okay," said Marshal Sugar, "let's get the other one." Five deputy marshals remained with The Baron, while the others moved down the hallway to another cell.

This cell was the home of Tyler Bingham, who was also known as "The Hulk" and "Super Honkey." Both nicknames referred to his physique, he was almost as wide as he was tall, and he could bench press over 500 pounds.

The Hulk was waiting for them. He had heard voices, voices he didn't recognize, coming from the vicinity of The Baron's cell. Dressed in his yellow jumpsuit, which indicated his Hole-status, he stood against the back wall of his 7-foot by 10-foot cell.

Marshal Sugar nodded for the CO to open the cell door. Rolling his eyeballs, the CO did as instructed. As the CO pulled the cell door open, The Hulk launched himself at the marshals. Growling deep in his chest, he shot out the door as if out of a cannon. Grabbing one of the deputy marshals around the waist, The Hulk pulled the man to the ground. As the two men crashed to the floor, The Hulk tried to grab the marshal's pistol from its holster. He had his fingers on the butt of the 9mm Glock when five marshals grabbed him: one on each limb, and one trying to batter his head off with a flashlight.

Although partially stunned by the rapid blows to his head, The Hulk roared and fought like a demon possessed maniac. But only for about five seconds. Then the probes from two Tasers caught him, sending an arcing current of hot lightning through his massive body. Screaming, The Hulk wriggled, arched and bounced like he was having an epileptic fit, a grand mal seizure.

Grim faced, the deputies watched The Hulk do the funky chicken. They took no pleasure in the spectacle. They were only doing what the circumstances demanded. The Hulk had made his choice. After 30 seconds, Marshal Sugar raised his hand and the Tasers were switched off.

Marshals quickly stripped The Hulk naked. Flashlights appeared, and his body cavities were examined. Coating the index finger of his latex-covered hand with KY Jelly, one of the marshals did a quick rectal exam of The Hulk.

Marshal Sugar noted The Hulk's luxuriant gray walrus moustache, his shaved head, and the tattoos on his arms. On one arm was a tattoo of the Star of David, on the other arm a black swastika. Marshal Sugar wondered about that for a moment. Was it sarcasm, mockery, or some odd hodgepodge of white supremacist thinking?

Shrugging, Marshal Sugar said, "Get him dressed and shackled." He started to walk away, then had a second thought. "Put a restraint on his elbows. This guy is strong and his attitude sucks."

The deputy marshals smiled at the words "attitude sucks." That was an understatement.

When The Hulk finally regained consciousness, he found himself hog-tied: leg shackles, waist chain, his hands cuffed behind his back and, like a ribbon on a Christmas present, his elbows pulled close together behind his back by a plastic tie.

"Get him up," said Marshal Sugar.

Four marshals lifted The Hulk to his feet, where they steadied him for a few seconds. Getting Tasered was hard on the body's nervous system, and short-circuited the brain.

The Taser was invented in 1969 by a NASA researcher whose name was Jack Cover. He named the device after Tom Swift, the comic book hero: Thomas A. Swift's Electric Rifle. Kind of like a ray-gun in a sci-fi movie, the Taser was a great way to drop anyone, even a man with body armor, in a non-lethal manner.

"Okay," said Marshal Sugar, "let's go."

The parade of marshals moved back to The Baron's cell, two of the marshals almost dragging The Hulk along.

The Baron was quickly released from his bench and, like a black phalanx with two yellow figures in the middle, the procession walked back the way they had come.

Outside, the two yellow figures were placed in separate vans, where they were chained to ring bolts, which sprouted from the floor like alien fingers. The Hulk's elbow restraints were removed and his hands were double-cuffed in front. The Baron received the same treatment. Marshal Sugar was not a malicious man. He didn't pull the wings off flies, and he didn't torture criminals. He said anyone who did that was lost already.

The engines of the vehicles roared to life, headlights were turned on, and the cavalcade drove out through the main gate.

Pulling a cell phone from his pocket, Marshal Sugar speed-dialed a number. "We're on our way," he said into his phone. "ETA 10 minutes." Then he closed the phone and put it back in his pocket.

Five miles away, at the Crescent City airport, which was nothing more than a landing strip with a few small offices and a couple of old hangars, the pilots of an unmarked Boeing 727 began their final take-off check.

The Boeing 727 was a JPATS aircraft. JPATS stood for Justice Prisoner and Alien Transportation System. One of eight full-sized aircraft operated by JPATS, this plane was engaged in a high-priority transport flight for the Department of Justice. Its location was known only by a select few individuals, so that anyone who had an interest in sabotaging the flight could not do so. And since its convict-passengers would all be taken by surprise, none of them could plan their own escape or make arrangements for outside help in escaping.

Most of JPATS employees, including the U.S. Marshals, called it Con Air, even before the Nicholas Cage movie made the name famous.

Nine minutes later, the convoy arrived at the landing strip. The Baron and The Hulk were escorted onto the plane and seated. The Baron was seated six rows directly behind The Hulk, so that he could not communicate by means of hand signals. Both criminals received triple locked waist chains.

While the triple locking was taking place, Marshal Sugar told the two prisoners how it was going to be. "As long as you behave, you'll only be restrained by handcuffs, waist chains and shackles. If you decide to act like buttholes, then we will treat you like buttholes. You'll wear reinforced mittens"—he held up a pair of what appeared to be cyborg-like, mechanical mittens, which most of the marshals called "Dr. No hands" after the bad guy in the first James Bond movie—"and if you spit, bite or use abusive language, we will strap your head in this." He held up what looked like a baseball catcher's mask, one that had been specially modified to isolate and disable the wearer's mouth.

"And if we have to," continued the marshal, "I will shove a gag in your mouth and then duct tape your mouth closed." He squinted at the two criminals. "So. The choice is yours." He looked around at his deputy marshals. "We're big believers in free will around here. You do as you choose. In response to your choice, we do as we choose."

The deputy marshals nodded in agreement. They were highly-trained professionals, most of whom had served in the military before joining the U.S. Marshals Service.

The most important part of their marshals training was psychological. They were taught how to remain detached, cool and professional under the most provocative conditions. They didn't lose their tempers and react violently, nor did they allow their personal prejudices to influence their treatment of prisoners. In other words, no petty abuses took place, as was often the case at correctional institutes.

Marshal Sugar said, "Okay. Let's get this show on the road. We got places to go, people to see, things to do."

The deputy marshals who worked with Sugar had heard that line a thousand times. It always made them smile. It meant they had more prisoners to pick up. In this particular case, it meant 18 more prisoners to collect. All of them extremely violent. One of the men they would pick up was called "the most dangerous man in prison."

It should be an exciting day.

It was called Operation Arrow. No one knew who came up with the name, but the name caught on quickly. Now everyone involved referred to it by that name—Operation Arrow.

Phase One was underway and involved the surprise collection and transportation of 20 brutal criminals, who were being held in maximum security prisons all over the United States. After collection, the plane would fly back to Los Angeles International Airport, where the prisoners would be escorted to various holding facilities in the area, where they would be held until it was their turn for trial.

All together, 40 prisoners were to be tried, 23 of whom faced the possibility of the death penalty, if convicted. They were on trial for 32 murders and over 100 attempted murders, including stabbings, strangulations, poisonings, contract hits, and conspiracy to commit murder, most of which occurred inside prisons in the United States. But some of the murders had been committed outside prisons, in the real world.

Along with murder, other charges facing the 40 criminals looked to extortion, robbery, and narcotics trafficking.

The indictment had been filed by Assistant U.S. Attorney Gregory Jessner. At 110 pages, the indictment was long, the result of many years' worth of investigation.

Gregory Jessner was 42 years old and slender. He wore his brown hair short and appeared mild-mannered and soft-spoken. However, never judge a book by its cover. For a magnetic energy pulsed inside the man, an energy which powered the heart of a lion and the tenacity of a bulldog. Plus, Jessner was smart as God.

Jessner had filed his lengthy indictment against these 40 savage criminals for one simple reason: the death penalty appeared to be the only answer. Isolating these criminals in solitary confinement was ineffective, because they always found ways to communicate with each other. They bribed guards, used hand signals to talk to one another, or wrote in coded messages. In one instance, acting as their own defense attorneys, they had subpoenaed each other to appear at court hearings where they could speak with each other. Such men, men who were already destined to spend the rest of their lives in small, concrete boxes, merely laughed when the authorities added more time their sentences. Who cared? It was like beating a dead horse or talking to a wall.

So Jessner had decided the time had come to use his last resort—execute these supercriminals. "Capital punishment is the one arrow left in our quiver," said Jessner. "I think even a lot of people who are against the death penalty in general would recognize that

in this particular instance, where people are committing murder repeatedly from behind bars, there is little other option."

Prosecutor Jessner was used to handling murder cases. It was part of his job. Yet he
was struck by dismay when he considered the total indifference with which these men
killed again and again. The slaughter of other human beings meant so little to them
that they called it "taking care of business." Which meant they thought of murder the
same way anyone else thought of buying a pack of gum at the local 7-11 or a coffee-of-
the-day at Starbuck's. Murder was nothing more than a normal, everyday activity of life.

So Prosecutor Jessner decided to pursue these men using RICO. RICO would be the
arrow he drew from his quiver. RICO stood for the Racketeer Influenced and Corrupt
Organizations Act, which was a federal law for going after criminal organizations. RICO
came into being in 1970. G. Robert Blakely was the author of the RICO Act. He named
it after the character in the movie Little Caesar, whose name was Rico. Edward G. Robinson played Rico in the movie. And Robinson was one of Blakely's favorite movie stars.

Under the RICO Act anyone guilty of two or more of 35 stipulated crimes could be tried
as a racketeer. The penalties imposed by the RICO act were severe. Thus between the
death penalty on the one hand, and the RICO Act on the other hand, Prosecutor Jessner
hoped to write "the end" on the murderous activities of these 40 super-criminals.

"I suspect they kill more than the Mafia," said Prosecutor Jessner. "They kill more than
any single drug trafficker. There are a lot of gang-related deaths on the streets, but they
are usually more disorganized and random." Pausing, he thought about what he had just
said. "I think they may be the most murderous criminal organization in the United
States."

When Prosecutor Jessner used the word "they" he meant the Aryan Brotherhood. The
most violently ruthless gang in the world, the Aryan Brotherhood came to bloody birth in
San Quentin Prison in 1964. The prison population of San Quentin—called the "Q"—began
choosing sides based on skin color. Blacks only socialized with other blacks. Hispanics refused to speak with anyone who wasn't Hispanic. To protect themselves against the blacks
and Hispanics, a few outlaw bikers—who were white—doing time in the "Q" formed
their own clique. Back then the cliques weren't called gangs. Instead they were called "tips."

The black tip was called the Black Guerilla Family, and had ties to the Black Panthers
and the Nation of Islam. Mexican Mafia or La Eme was the name the Hispanics chose.
The white boys called their tip the Diamond Tooth Gang, which referred to their teeth.
To add an aura of fear and terror to their persons, the white guys glued bits of broken
glass to their teeth. When they smiled, the sunlight glittered off the glass in their teeth.
It looked as if they had diamonds in their teeth.[1]

For some reason, after a while they changed the name from the Diamond Tooth
Gang to the Blue Bird Gang. No one seems to know exactly why. Whatever the origin
of the name, the Blue Bird Gang began to attract other white members at the "Q." Soon
this gang of "white warriors", as they called themselves, dropped the Blue Bird name and
designated themselves the Aryan Brotherhood—a direct reference to their skin color.

---

1. A number of gangsta' rappers later adopted this 'jailhouse' dental fashion. The rappers put real
diamonds in their teeth. And the current trend of wearing baggy pants real-low on the buttocks—called
'sagging'—also began in prison and carried over into popular culture.

The Aryan Brotherhood recruited only the biggest, the baddest and the toughest white inmates. It was an exclusive order of white warriors. Their motto was "blood in, blood out." This meant that each potential member had to "make his bones" before he became a full-fledged member. "Making one's bones" meant spilling blood in hand-to-hand combat. Either the blood of another prisoner from a rival gang, or the blood of one of the guards. It didn't matter which, but blood had to be spilled.

Once accepted, the member was branded with a tattoo. The idea of the "branding" was taken from the Louis L'Amour western novel of the same name—*The Brand*. It was a very popular novel among white inmates.

Usually the brand or tattoo was that of a green shamrock or 666, which was the mark of the beast in the last book of the Bible, or the letters AB. Whichever brand it was it meant that person was owned by the Aryan Brotherhood. This was why the Aryan Brotherhood was sometimes called "the brand" or "the rock," because all its members were literally branded. The term "the rock" referred to the shamrock brand[2] that many members wore on their white skin.

Each new member of the Aryan Brotherhood had to take the pledge:

"An Aryan brother is without a care,
He walks where the weak and heartless won't dare,
And if by chance he should stumble and lose control,
His brothers will be there, to help reach his goal,
For a worthy brother, no need is too great,
He need not but ask, fulfillment's in his fate.
For an Aryan brother, death holds no fear,
Vengeance will be his, through his brothers still here."

Although the author couldn't confirm it, this pledge appeared to be similar to religious vows taken by Japan's kamikaze pilots in World War II, and the Thugs of India, who murdered and robbed in the name of Kali, a god of destruction.

In the beginning, each member of the Aryan Brotherhood had a vote in all things, in every decision. So if some snitch was to be murdered, or a defector was to be killed as an example to what happened to such traitors, everyone voted and the majority ruled. But the democracy didn't last long, because the Aryan Brotherhood was growing like a cancer. Within a few years, it had members in all of California's prisons and many of the federal prisons in the United States. Older members realized that it was time for a change.

A three-man commission was set up. The commission functioned as a blasphemous Father, Son and Holy Spirit of violence, murder and death. Commissioners made the big, strategic decisions for the Brotherhood. Under them were councils, which had five

---

2. This shamrock brand was taken from the Arabian 'shamrakh', which symbolized the Persian Triad. Triads, unlike 'trinities' which are three-in-one, have three distinct members. In this case, Heaven-Man-Earth, that is the divine, the human and the natural, with man the mediator between the celestial and the terrestrial. The human mediators are 'white-warriors.' The shamrock is the mark of the white warrior and symbolizes the sunwheel or the black sun. According to Michael Thompson, an AB member who defected, the shamrock brand refers to the AB's antipathy toward the Christian concept of the Trinity as presented by St. Patrick in Ireland.

to seven members. The councils ran the day-to-day operations of the gang. They could even order hits and contract murders, if necessary. Each prison system had its own council. For example, all the prisons in the state of California were governed by one five-man council. Texas had a council; Arizona had a council and so on.

Barry Mills, aka The Baron and Tyler Bingham sat on the Commission of the Aryan Brotherhood. The third commissioner was Thomas Silverstein, who was sometimes called "Terrible Tom." More about him later.

These three men were the shot callers, the Terrible Triumvirate of the Aryan Brotherhood. They decided who would live and who would die. Who would run drugs, who would rob banks, who would extort money, who would do their evil bidding. Their power was absolute. Anyone who stood in the way was killed. The long arm of the Aryan Brotherhood reached anywhere and everywhere.

Reading 2.
PEN1: Public Enemy Number 1 —
California's Growing Racist Gang*

*Anti-Defamation League***

Introduction

Nearly 300 police officers from more than two dozen federal and local law enforcement agencies fanned out across Southern California on December 14, 2006, to execute a series of search and arrest warrants at some 75 different locations. The extensive sweep resulted in the arrest of 67 alleged members of the large and violent white supremacist gang known as Public Enemy Number 1 (PEN1).

The raids capped a 10-month long investigation into PEN1 led by the Anaheim Police Department that had already resulted in a number of PEN1-related arrests in the week before the mid-December raids. Authorities took action after learning in November of an alleged PEN1 "hit list" that contained the names of an Orange County prosecutor and five police officers in several different departments. The suspects were arrested on a variety of charges, including conspiracy to commit murder, possession of illegal weapons and narcotics, forgery, probation violations and identity theft.

* © 2007 Anti-Defamation League; Reproduced with permission from Anti-Defamation League. Copies of this publication are in the Rita and Leo Greenland Human Relations Library and Research Center.

** The Anti-Defamation League is particularly grateful to the following law enforcement agencies and departments for their assistance and cooperation in preparing this report: the Costa Mesa Police Department, the Huntington Beach Police Department, the Office of the Orange County District Attorney, the California Department of Justice, the California Department of Corrections and the Orange County Probations Department.

Across California, authorities struggle to deal with problems caused by PEN1. An unusual hybrid of a racist skinhead gang, a street gang, and a prison gang, PEN1 has grown considerably in California, where it originated, and has even spread to nearby states.

California law enforcement and prison officials are increasingly faced with a wide range of problems caused by the organization, ranging from the illegal methamphetamine trade to white collar crime that includes identity theft and counterfeiting. In addition, PEN1 members have been convicted for violent crimes, including assaults, attempted murder and murder.

The group has also raised its profile in the California prison system, where incarcerated members attempt to gain more recruits and influence. PEN1's increasing strength stems to a large degree from its ability to position itself as a white power criminal organization capable of operating both on the streets and in the prison yards as foot soldiers for older, more established white supremacist prison gangs, such as the Aryan Brotherhood.

In the past several years, Public Enemy Number 1 has grown considerably in size. As it has expanded, so too has the threat that it poses. Heavily involved in the drug trade, PEN1 members also have a strong history of violence, both in the prisons and on the streets. Its mercenary and criminal nature, coupled with a white supremacist ideology and a subculture of violence, makes it a triple threat, both to law enforcement and to the public at large. Even people far removed from the worlds of narcotics and gangs may become victim to the PEN1 through white collar crimes ranging from fraud to counterfeiting to identity theft.

PEN1 is currently strongest in California, where it has caused many problems in recent years. However, if its growth is not stopped, it is likely to become increasingly problematic in other states as well—the Pacific Northwest and the Southwest being the most likely areas of PEN1 expansion. PEN1 may not be the nation's "number one public enemy," but they have more than proven themselves a violent, hateful, and dangerous threat—one that needs to be contained.

Origins

Public Enemy Number 1's (PEN1) original membership consisted largely of white, middle-class youths active in the punk music subculture popular in southern California in the mid-1980s. In fact, the name of the group comes from the 1980's British punk band *Rudimentary Peni* (there is no other connection between the band and the gang).

Music venues offered a variety of alternative music that appealed to both racist and non-racist skinheads, and some featured explicitly white power bands. People came from a wide geographic area, including Long Beach and the Inland Empire, to hear the music, drink, meet, network and form groups. A number of white street gangs emerged from this scene, including, among others, PEN1, Los Angeles Death Squad, Norwalk Skins and Orange County (OC) Skins.

PEN1 began as a white power gang, but without a single clear purpose or orientation. Almost from the outset, PEN1 was divided into two camps—one faction emphasized maintaining an ideologically oriented white power organization while the other faction championed carrying out more criminal activities. Brody Davis, an influential member of PEN1's original cadre, allegedly encouraged members to follow a more traditional path of promoting white power and racist skinhead ideology and to reject drug use and criminal activity. Initially, the group followed this path and members distributed leaflets that promoted white supremacy while also engaging in typical skinhead activities like heavy drinking and fighting.

However, another PEN1 leader, Donald Reed "Popeye" Mazza, reportedly used his own influence to steer the group in a different direction and as Davis's leadership position waned, many of the disenfranchised white youths in PEN1 turned to drugs. By the late 1980s, PEN1's activities resembled those of other criminally active gangs. The drug habits of Mazza and other PEN1 members drove a shift towards drug trafficking and crime to support the habits. To this day, drug use remains prevalent among PEN1 members.

PEN1's membership gradually increased as it expanded geographically from Long Beach to Orange County and expanded its criminal enterprises from drug distribution to also include auto theft, burglary, property crime, witness intimidation and identity theft. This in turn led to an increased PEN1 presence in California's prison system. Prison-based PEN1 members used the prisons as sources of recruitment, and PEN1 began to grow behind bars.

Prison Activities

Unlike the more notorious Aryan Brotherhood (AB) and Nazi Low Riders (NLR), Public Enemy Number 1 (PEN1) is not technically a prison gang according to California Department of Corrections guidelines. A prison gang is defined as a group that developed in prison and exists for the most part only behind bars, although it may in fact have counterparts on the outside. Prison gang members can automatically be assigned a Secure Housing Unit (SHU) sentence and segregated from the rest of the population; a regular inmate can only be sentenced to a SHU if he is a threat to institutional security or has been rigorously proven to be an associate of a prison gang (Donald Mazza, Nick Rizzo and Devlin Stringfellow, three top PEN1 leaders, were all given SHU sentences in this way). However, PEN1 members play an important role in California's prison gang structure, thanks in large part to the Aryan Brotherhood.

By the late 1970s, California prison officials attempted to limit the growing problem of the Aryan Brotherhood by subjecting it to increasingly closer scrutiny and locking its members in the SHU. In reaction, the AB reached out to NLR members to serve as middlemen for the Brotherhood's various criminal enterprises. At the same time, NLR filled a vacuum left by the AB by attracting white inmates who had previously turned to the AB for protection or who did not want to be documented as associates of prison gang members and confined in the SHU. The NLR's membership and criminal reputation grew tremendously after AB members were isolated in secure housing. However, in 1999, California prison authorities officially recognized NLR as a prison gang; as a result, members are now given automatic SHU sentences and segregated from the rest of the prison population. The NLR now suffered from many of the same limitations that the AB did.

During this period, an increasing number of NLR members dropped out of the gang and some joined PEN1. Most known PEN1 members entering prison are placed initially in the "mainline" or general population, where they have relative freedom to congregate and associate with other inmates and can more easily conduct criminal business without being monitored as closely as validated prison gang members. Given the limitations placed on their members' movements, the AB and NLR were forced to forge alliances with smaller groups that could help them maintain their position in the drug trade. The Aryan Brotherhood, in particular, realized PEN1's potential and inducted the group's members into its criminal operations both in and out of the prison, including drug trafficking (primarily the methamphetamine trade), property crimes, identity theft and murder. This was not without controversy; some NLR members were resentful that AB essentially gave the "keys" or control of the streets to PEN1. In an unsuccessful attempt to be independent of AB, a few NLR members broke away and formed another group. Most NLR members, however, maintained their allegiance to Aryan Brotherhood. NLR members may work on an individual basis with PEN1, but overall cooperation between the two groups has been limited.

Expanding Roles

Public Enemy Number 1 (PEN1) has grown steadily since the early 2000s. In 2003, the membership was estimated by law enforcement to be about 200; by 2005, the group had grown to 350–400 members documented by prison officials, although a substantial number of members and associates are unknown to authorities. Its total membership, including associates, could be as much as twice its documented membership.

PEN1's growing clout in the prison system and control over criminal activities makes it attractive to some white inmates from the general population who seek protection from ethnic and criminal gangs and other prisoners. Some members of white supremacist street gangs join PEN1 while incarcerated, then resume an association with their own street gang after their release. Due to a shared ideology, PEN1 members can easily blend in with other white racist gangs. This kind of dual membership makes it difficult for law enforcement to assess PEN1's size or attribute crimes to its members. However, because PEN1 members often "tier up," or cluster around one particular residence, which then becomes their main gathering place, it is easier for law enforcement to detect the group's presence in certain areas.

Individual PEN1 members have been documented throughout the country and even abroad. However, according to the California Department of Justice, approximately 300 of the group's documented members operate in southern and northern California. They appear to be most heavily concentrated in Orange County, where they are active in almost every city of the county, particularly in Anaheim, Costa Mesa, Garden Grove, Huntington Beach and South Orange County. They also have a strong presence in the Inland Empire, especially in Riverside and San Bernardino and exist in smaller numbers in San Diego and Los Angeles counties.

PEN1 is less active in northern California, where it lacks strength in numbers, but according to law enforcement, it does have a presence in Sacramento, Redding and Shasta. More recently, the group has begun to recruit in Arizona, near Lake Havasu and Bullhead City. There are as of yet only a handful of documented PEN1 members in the Arizona prison system, however.

Structures and Symbols

Unlike the Nazi Low Riders, Public Enemy Number 1 (PEN1) has strong leadership but it is loosely structured. And in contrast to the Aryan Brotherhood and many other prison-based gangs, the group does not appear to have a written constitution, defined code of behavior, or clearinghouse for approved actions.

PEN1's structure is largely based on personalities. Senior PEN1 members who are highly respected carry weight ("juice") within the organization and can decide on a course of action or who can join the organization. According to law enforcement, one ex-member cynically noted that the rules can change day to day depending on Donald Mazza's whims and self-serving interests.

PEN1 claims to adhere strictly to a racist skinhead philosophy and ideology; however, in practice, the group's mercenary interests allow PEN1 members to associate at times with Asians and Hispanics while maintaining a strict "whites only" policy when it comes to membership. There are members with Hispanic-sounding surnames; however, they identify themselves as Caucasian. In addition, some members have non-white girlfriends, but the group generally frowns on such relationships.

PEN1 members routinely associate or spend time with other white racist gangs. Bars, biker clubs and white power concerts that attract a variety of other white power gangs will often also attract PEN1 members. Other racist skinhead groups such as the Orange County Skins and Insane White Boys can often be seen together with PEN1 at both informal and planned activities. Some years ago, PEN1 was a driving force in an unsuccessful attempt to unite with those gangs and others (including La Mirada Punks, Norwalk Skins, and Southern California Skinheads) into a unified group called the Southern California Skinhead Alliance. However, some other white gangs, such as the Sacromaniacs and Wolfpac, have clashed with PEN1 members whom they view as both criminals and gangsters.

PEN1 members often tattoo themselves with numbers or letters that refer to the group. Members may have tattoos that spell out Public Enemy Number 1 or simply their version of its initials, PEN1. They may also refer to other terms or acronyms for the group, including Pen1, Peni Death Squad, PDS and Pen9. Peni Death Squad is just an alternate name for the group and does not signify the enforcers within the gang or a more violent sect within the organization. The number most commonly associated with the group is 737, which refers to the letters PDS on telephone touch pads: 7 = P, 3 = D, 7 = S. Often these references appear among other racist and non-racist images, including common neo-Nazi tattoos, Viking imagery and Odinic symbols. Like many gang members, PEN1 tend to be heavily tattooed.

Key Leaders

Donald Reed "Popeye" Mazza, Public Enemy Number 1's (PEN1) "shot caller" or leader, has a violent criminal history, including drug use (he was a heavy heroin user) and an attempted murder conviction. In April 1999, according to prosecutors, only 10 hours after being released from prison, Mazza stabbed an associate, William Austin, while Dominic (Nick) "Droopy" Rizzo, the number two leader in PEN1 (and godfather to Austin's child), held Austin down. Austin was a member of the Los Angeles Death Squad, another white supremacist gang, and an active participant in PEN1 and NLR activities. Austin was said to have been attacked in this "prison-ordered hit" because fellow gang members believed that he was working with law enforcement as an informant. According to prosecutors, an Aryan Brotherhood member is believed to have overseen the attack.

In 2003, Mazza was convicted of attempted murder and is currently serving 15 years in state custody at Pelican Bay, a high security state prison for hardcore gang members. In the summer of 2005, Mazza reportedly earned his Aryan Brotherhood "dancing shoes," which means that he was inducted into the AB ranks. He has now been validated by prison officials as an AB associate. Mazza's new membership in AB is likely to boost PEN1's position and power in California's prison system.

Dominic Peter "Droopy" Rizzo was given a life sentence for his attempted murder conviction and is locked up at West Valley Detention Center in Rancho Cucamonga. Prior to the conviction, Rizzo had been released from the Santa Ana Orange County Jail on July 17, 2002, on a $500,000 bond paid with a cashier's check, which later turned out to be bogus. His use of a forged document is not uncommon for PEN1 members, who are often involved in counterfeit schemes and identity theft.

In November 2003, while being transported, Rizzo slashed the neck of another inmate, a convicted child molester, with whom he was shackled in line. Rizzo pleaded guilty on July 17, 2006, to assault with a deadly weapon; his sentence was added to the life term he was already serving for the attempted murder of Austin. Prison personnel have since validated Rizzo as an AB associate.

Another key player in the PEN1 leadership is Devlin "Gazoo" Stringfellow, whose mother married Reuben Pappan, a significant Aryan Brotherhood member convicted in 2003 of conspiracy to commit murder. She later allegedly divorced Pappan so that her son could spend his parole at her home and not violate his terms of probation for affiliating with other gang members.

Female Members

With many of the male members of Public Enemy Number 1 (PEN1) locked up, its female members and associates often become the "worker bees" of the group. Women are given monikers and may participate in criminal activity. In fact, according to law enforcement, some within PEN1 view it as preferable for female members to carry out certain criminal activities precisely because they can better hide their affiliation with PEN1 and blend in more easily with the general population. In contrast with male PEN1 members, women often have tattoos that are hidden or small in size and do not adhere to a specific manner of dress or hairstyle.

Women are expected to provide income to the gang, often through menial jobs, and to rent apartments for gang members to help them hide from authorities when needed.

Some have served as drug couriers; others have worked at or have applied for jobs that might help gang-related activities, such as at a bail bond business or pharmacy, or as non-sworn law-enforcement personnel.

Key female members of the group can be crucial in facilitating PEN1 activities, especially by acting as links for incarcerated PEN1 members to the outside world by keeping up contacts outside of prison. Women play a key role in helping jailed PEN1 members circumvent restrictions on prisoners' telephone and written communications in a variety of ways, including facilitating three-way calling between members in prison to third parties, coordinating conference calls between inmates and gang members on the street, receiving collect calls from an inmate, using "call forwarding" to transfer the call to another individual, and helping inmates communicate with each other using mail dumps. Additionally, a female gang member may conceal the true source of a letter by various means, such as giving it the appearance of a legal document sent by an attorney.

Women also raise money to place on the inmates' prison "books." Inmates are allowed access to this money to use in prison convenience stores (male PEN1 members will also sometimes do this for incarcerated members). One PEN1 associate, in a 2001 television interview, described her caretaking and support role for PEN1 members as being akin to a "den mother." Simone Lawrence, another PEN1 associate, was convicted in March 2006 of committing identity theft for the sake of benefiting PEN1.

The status of individual women within PEN1 is typically based on their male partner's position within the organization. For example, the wives of PEN1's key leaders are considered to have the highest status level, which grants them respect, protection and monetary provisions. Nonetheless, PEN1 does not officially induct women into the organization nor can women hold leadership positions.

Law enforcement authorities have warned that even though the number of arrests of female members is small, women can be just as dangerous and criminally active as male members. For example, one woman, Monica "Mouth" Witak, was convicted of witness intimidation in association with PEN1. While housed at the Orange County Jail, Witak wrote a letter to a PEN1 member in another prison facility, requesting an assault against an individual who witnessed her cellmate's murder case. Witak received a five year sentence for the incident. Another woman, Kim Arrighi Fanelli, Nick Rizzo's sister-in-law, was convicted of possession of a shotgun and pseudo-ephedrine to make methamphetamines and sentenced to five years.

Drug Trade Involvement and Violent Crimes

Drug Trade Involvement

Public Enemy Number 1 (PEN1) members have sometimes been given the nickname "needle Nazis," due to their heavy drug usage and racist ideology. Because of their involvement with illegal drugs, both as users and sellers, many of their encounters with law enforcement on the streets revolve around drugs. On March 16, 2006, for example, law enforcement officials from various agencies in Orange County arrested 23 suspected members leaders and associates of PEN1 who were allegedly involved in drug sales, identity theft and other crimes. All the suspects had criminal records and more than half of those arrested were women. Most of the suspects were arrested on parole and probation violations. Officials also confiscated 12 weapons and recovered small amounts of heroin and methamphetamine from the gang.

Like the AB and the NLR, PEN1 members often have working relationships with Hispanic street gangs and non-white prison gangs such as the Mexican Mafia, due to a shared interest in criminal activity, particularly the drug trade. Even though PEN1 sells methamphetamine and, to a lesser extent, other drugs, it is not involved in the production of drugs. PEN1 members get most of their drugs from other illegal manufacturers; in some cases they may also "tax" or steal from other drug users and their associates. PEN1 members also use drugs as a means to entice and recruit others into the organization. They have sometimes allegedly supplied addicts with drugs, eventually coercing them, through force and intimidation, to commit crimes for the gang.

PEN1 members are also active in bringing drugs into the prison system, often through novel means. In August 2004, drugs were allegedly introduced into a Southern California prison by PEN1 members through dirty diapers brought into the facility by a member of an outside landscaping crew.

PEN1 members have managed to find ways to organize around the drug trade both in and out of prison. For example, law enforcement officers recently discovered that there are a few sober living homes or half-way homes in Orange County that have a reputation for being "PEN1 friendly." Some employees of the homes allegedly turn a blind eye, permit or, in some cases, may even be involved with drug sales and other criminal activity. PEN1 members have reportedly been able to take advantage of the fact that there is little licensing or regulation of these homes by government agencies, making them potentially easier targets for criminal activity.

Violent Crimes

In addition to drug related criminal activity, PEN1 members have committed a number of violent crimes, including assault, murder and attempted murder. In 2003, for example, PEN1 member Chad Studebaker, involved in a traffic altercation in Orange County, ran the victim's car off the road, sliced his neck with a knife, and yanked a Star of David hanging from the victim's neck. Studebaker then fled to a PEN1 safe home in Riverside County before being arrested; he was later convicted of attempted murder and sentenced to 21 years to life in prison.

A more gruesome incident occurred in April 2004, when a group of PEN1 attacked a 26-year-old Laguna Nigel resident because they thought he had stolen $12,000 from a stripper and PEN1 associate. Although they apparently intended only to torture him to extract a confession and the location of the money, their brutal attack with blows from a claw hammer to his skull killed the victim. Police arrested nine members and associates of PEN1 on various charges in connection with the slaying, including PEN1 leader Billy Joe Johnson of Huntington Beach and Jason Karr of Costa Mesa. In June 2006, Johnson pleaded guilty and was sentenced to 45 years to life; six other defendants also pleaded guilty and received lesser sentences. A mistrial was declared in October 2006 in the trial of the two remaining defendants when a juror used an internet search engine to research Johnson; they will have to be retried.

Authorities believe PEN1 members may also have been behind other unsolved murders that involved punishing members believed to have betrayed the group's trust. Orange County law enforcement officers discovered the dead body of Scott Miller, a PEN1 member, in an alley behind a housing complex in March 2002. Authorities suspect Miller had been punished for participating in a revealing television interview about PEN1 in February 2001 and because other PEN1 members suspected he was stealing drug money from the gang.

Similarly, in June 2002, Lake Elsinore police discovered the severely beaten body of an 18-year-old girl stuffed into a 55-gallon drum in an open field. The men charged with her murder, Jeffree Buettner and Glen Joseph Jones, were reportedly PEN1 gang members who allegedly believed the victim had been talking to law enforcement. They still await trial.

PEN1 members have also committed violent crimes in prison. Like other white supremacist prison gangs, PEN1 follows certain codes of behavior. The members will "take care of their own," meaning white prisoners, but will kill white sex offenders, who are considered unworthy of being white. The inmate whose throat Dominic Rizzo slit in 2003, for example, was a known sex offender.

Other Criminal Activity

In recent years, Public Enemy Number 1 (PEN1) members, like those of some other racist prison gangs, have become increasingly involved in white collar crime, including computer fraud, credit card fraud, counterfeiting and identity theft. PEN1 members sometimes solicit friends, relatives and associates who have access to personal records to steal that private data from institutions where they work, including banks, mortgage businesses, dental offices, hospitals or even the Department of Motor Vehicles. PEN1 members will also engage in stealing personal data via auto burglary, mail theft, purse snatching and trash diving. They can provide this data to people who can use it to create false identities. Documents that have been replicated have included drivers' license, bank statements, Social Security cards, notarized documents, duplicate checks and even W-2 forms, as well as counterfeit money.

In one case, PEN1 member Brian "Bullet" Mitchell was arrested for making counterfeit $50 bills by bleaching lower denomination currency with oven cleaner spray and running the paper through a color printer. He was later convicted of having equipment for the purpose of counterfeiting money for the benefit of financing the prison accounts of PEN1 members. In another case, law enforcement confiscated the computer of a PEN1 associate and found a laundry list of types of documents that could be falsified for a specified price.

Identity theft and stolen information have also been used by PEN1 members for their own personal pleasure. There have been reports of PEN1 members using stolen credit cards to check into hotels and hold parties. Law enforcement was only alerted when a security risk emerged at the hotel, such as PEN1 "guests" refusing to leave at the hotel's check-out time or stolen credit cards setting off an alert. In another case, a group of PEN1 members were kicked out of a hotel before check-out. They later received a refund check from the hotel. They allegedly took the check and made duplicates of it numerous times, cashing them in various drugstores.

Targeting Law Enforcement

As the criminal investigation into a possible Public Enemy Number 1 (PEN1) hit list of officers and prosecutors in Southern California suggests, PEN1 members can pose officer safety threats to law enforcement.

PEN1 members caught in criminal activity have a history of fleeing on foot and in their vehicles and have displayed aggressive and violent resistance to arrests by law enforcement. Like members of other drug-using criminal street gangs, PEN1 members can be unstable, irrational and unpredictable. In addition, many members have become habitual offenders, and may become combative to prevent re-arrest and lengthy incarceration under the "three strikes" law in California.

According to law enforcement sources, PEN1 members have also attempted to use a range of weapons against officers, including handguns, sawed-off shotguns, revolvers, semi-automatics and rifles. In one case, a vehicle was used as a weapon. On May 13, 2003, a PEN1 member wanted for a parole violation fled on foot when a California Highway Patrol officer attempted to stop his vehicle. The officer pursued the gang member, who allegedly doubled back to his vehicle, placed the car in reverse, struck the officer with the car door and knocked him to the ground. The suspect's car also injured the officer's canine. The suspect was arrested five days later at a local park.

In a February 2001 televised interview, PEN1 member Scotty "Scottish" Miller boasted that PEN1 members listen to police scanners, which allows them eventually to recognize officers by their voices, radio call signs and work shifts. He also bragged about owning "over 300 guns." California records revealed that Miller had no firearms registered to him. Since many PEN1 members have felony records, they must purchase their weapons illegally on the street or steal them during residential burglaries.

Reading 3.
Vicious Circle: Aryan Circle
Blamed for Two Cop Killings*

Brentin Mock

Shawn Hornacek lifts the sleeves of his Alabama Department of Corrections inmate uniform to reveal spider web tattoos on both elbows. The one on the right contains a swastika. Hornacek claims it represents "peace." But there's nothing peaceful about the spider web on his left elbow. At its center are two lightning flashes, or "cracker bolts," orbited by three rings. Hornacek explains that one ring is added to his loosely sketched web every time he attacks a black or gay person.

The tattoos—spider web, rings, cracker bolts—are membership patches, indicating that Hornacek belongs to the fastest growing and lately the deadliest white supremacist prison-based gang in the country.

"Aryan Circle," Hornacek says. "In it for life."

Once concentrated solely in Texas, the Aryan Circle currently operates inside and outside prisons in at least 13 other states, according to law enforcement officials as well as Aryan Circle websites and publications. The gang is more ideologically driven by a white nationalist revolutionary agenda than other racist prison gangs—and just as violent, if not more so. In recent months, it has been making a name for itself with a string of murders and other attacks, both inside the nation's prisons and in its communities, that have officials seriously worried.

Two police officers were killed in August in a shoot-out with Aryan Circle members in Louisiana. In Texas, law enforcement investigators believe the gang is responsible for a string of shootings last year, including at least three murders.

Hornacek, 31, is currently serving a 10-year sentence at Ventress Correctional Facility in Clayton, Ala., for, he says, stealing a trailer of guns. He told the Intelligence Report in a recent interview that he joined Aryan Circle in 2003 while incarcerated for possessing a crack pipe in Corpus Christi, Texas.

Circle leaders inside jails and prisons typically screen potential recruits by instigating fights between the prospective member and a "toad," a black inmate. Hornacek calls this exercise a "heart check."

"If he don't fight, that shows he's a little weak, and we weed him out," he says.

"Lotta cowards hide behind shit," Hornacek says in justifying the Circle's sadistic induction procedures. "They wanna be a part of something in prison to protect themselves, and one of Aryan Circle's laws is this ain't a tool for protection."

Circle leaders portray the gang as a nationwide clan of race warriors fighting for a grand cause. "In the beginning, the organization centered on the preservation of the race within a hostile prison environment," reads a history chapter in The Official Handbook of the Aryan Circle. "Today, it has expanded to much more than that."

Now, according to this official history, the goal of the Circle is to violently promote white nationalism, "both in prison and in the world throughout."

Smash Hits

The Aryan Circle is often confused with the Aryan Brotherhood, the older, wider spread and vastly more infamous rival. Although the two gangs have similar names and iconography—including swastikas and distinctive but subtle variations of lightning bolt tattoos—there are substantial differences in their history, organizational structure and ideology.

White inmates at the maximum-security prison in San Quentin, Calif., founded the Aryan Brotherhood in 1964. When the Aryan Brotherhood in Texas attempted to renounce crime and refashion itself as a "church," inmates started the Aryan Circle in

1985 to preserve radical white supremacist beliefs and remain on the defense against black and Hispanic prison gangs.

The Circle was built, as its history says, "on a prospective confidential basis. At no time will there be a membership rally held. In this way each member knows that the next member in line was a hand picked prospect."

Gang leaders often recruit white convicts who are serving relatively short sentences, because the sooner a Circle member is released, the sooner he can expand the gang's network outside prison. A "prospect" or "recruit" who passes the heart check is subject to a 12-month probationary period including a "hit" or "smash" against a gang enemy ordered by Circle leaders in order to "blood in" as a full member. New recruits swear allegiance until death. There's no quitting the Aryan Circle without going "blood out," meaning violently.

Circle prospects and members, or "patch holders" (each member has an identifying "patch number"), are ruled by hierarchical structures, which exist in geographical regions carved out both within the Texas state prison system, and also in federal penitentiaries across America. The gang leader who oversees a national region is called a "Leaf."

According to Aryan Circle documents obtained by Intelligence Report, the Leaf for Region One—which consists of federal and state prisons in Arkansas, Arizona, Colorado, Florida, Indiana, Kansas, Oklahoma and Texas—is 48-year-old Danny "Danny Boy" Lee Bonham, who's currently serving a life sentence in the Coleman federal prison near Orlando, Fla., for conspiracy to distribute narcotics.

The Leaf for Region Two—which includes prisons in Louisiana, Pennsylvania, South Carolina and West Virginia—is 42-year-old Tracy "Blayze" Kenyon Sexton, who's serving a 105-month sentence in the Allenwood federal penitentiary in central Pennsylvania for illegally possessing and transporting firearms.

The Circle produces a bimonthly magazine called The Circular, which has a post office box in Carnegie, Okla., and a mailing address in Lubbock, Texas. The editor-in-chief of the publication is Aryan Circle founder Mark Cooper Gaspard, also known as Mark Cooper Patterson. According to the Texas Department of Public Safety, Gaspard is currently under parole supervision until 2010. Arrested five times on burglary, armed burglary and drug charges, Gaspard has been in and out of Texas state prisons since 1979. In 1985, the year he started Aryan Circle, Gaspard was serving time in a Huntsville state prison, according to Texas DPS records.

Gaspard is a small man—just 5 foot 7 inches and 132 pounds. What he lacks in physical stature, though, he makes up for in charisma, according to Sigifredo Sanchez, head of the Texas Department of Criminal Justice gang department, and the official who confirmed Gaspard as the Aryan Circle founder. "He could talk people into doing things," Sanchez said. "He's a very smart and conniving individual."

According to Sanchez, Gaspard never wanted the lead role, despite his formulating the group's precepts, including the ideas that all who oppose the white race are sworn enemies and that all crimes against the white race are punishable by death.

"The people who are the innovators all were white. They generally had the freedom to be inventive without ZOG [Zionist Occupational Government] breathing down their neck," reads one article in an undated copy of The Circular. "It is clear that for many years these people have been trying to destroy us culturally and genetically. This is the reason the media promotes interracial marriage and racial integration."

When the Aryan Circle attempted to give Gaspard the rank of general, "he tossed it back," Sanchez said, because the group had grown too radical.

14 Whys

Norman Smith, who identifies himself as a vice president of the Aryan Circle inside the federal prison in Leavenworth, Kan., maintains a website where he castigates white inmates who socialize with black inmates. "To see White boys trying to act like, dress like and talk like 'Africans' sickens me. I watch as they turn their backs on their own kind figuring they are going to be part of the dark in here. But in there they are used as bitches, passed around like candy, humiliated, their stuff taken, used as fall guys to keep their 'brothers' out of the hole, or beaten."

"I will HONOR my heritage, my culture, my race," Smith proclaims. "I AM PROUD TO BE AN ARYAN."

This ongoing intra-gang reinforcement of a white nationalist belief system, as crudely expressed as it may be, further sets the Aryan Circle apart from the Aryan Brotherhood. The Brotherhood long ago placed illegal commerce above ideology by doing business with the Mexican Mafia, a non-white prison gang. The Brotherhood is still a race-based gang, but as the saying goes among prison gang investigators, the only color that really matters to the Brotherhood these days is green.

The Aryan Circle signed a peace treaty with the Mexican Mafia in 1996, ending a four-year gang war in the "TDC," or Texas Department of Corrections, that resulted in 13 murders. The Aryan Circle and Aryan Brotherhood gangs are also under a peace treaty in Texas. But outside that state, the rivalry between the two "has metastasized into its own beast," Sanchez said. Reports from the Federal Bureau of Prisons say the Aryan Circle has vastly improved its numbers and is in deadly conflict with the Aryan Brotherhood.

Hornacek told the *Intelligence Report* that the two gangs maintain uneasy truces with Aryan Brotherhood and Mexican Mafia in Texas, mainly due to their shared hatred of black prison gangs such as the Gangster Disciples and the Black Guerilla Family.

"If you got caught talking to a black [inmate], other whites would stay away from you," Aryan Circle member Johnny Bravo said in a February 2006 interview with Gorillaconvict, an authoritative blog run by incarcerated prison gang researcher Seth Ferranti. "We don't house with them [blacks], period."

A widely distributed Circle leaflet titled "14 Whys," a play on the famous "14 Words" white nationalist catchphrase, details the gang's strict opposition to any form of race-mixing, whether behind prison walls or in the world outside. "WHY does the media repudiate the historically proven fact that racial integration is cultural and biological genocide?" it asks. "WHY do the Christian churches promote adoption of colored children from all over the world by White families, when the result is genocide of the White race? WHY does the U.S. Government advance White genocide through forced busing of our school children?"

Family Circle

Aryan Circle's concern for white children extends to a hard-line stance against drug abuse by its own members. One recent article in *The Circular* reads like an anti-drug public service announcement for white supremacists: "More of our white brothers are being arrested and sent to prison with drug addictions. The outcome is ... a weaker white population, less protection for our white women ... and our lost sense of 'Family Values.' Our white sisters are left carrying the load of a 'household' we helped create. Often she is then forced into low-income housing and welfare lines where she becomes surrounded and overwhelmed by the black community who share these facilities. Then our children, the only hope for the future of our race ... never grow with a sense of moral separateness.

"The choice is clear: Your Race, Your Family, Your Freedom ... or your favorite drug."

Despite such pious admonishments, Circle members frequently engage in large-scale distribution of illegal narcotics, particularly methamphetamine, and many of them can't resist getting high on their own supply. In 2004, 29 Aryan Circle members were arrested in Texas for taking part in a methamphetamine ring that produced and sold more than 30 kilograms of meth in west Texas beginning in January 2000.

Prosecutors argued that Michael Curtis "Bones" Lewis, co-founder of the Odessa chapter of the Circle, was the ringleader. But several witnesses testified over the course of a three-week trial that Lewis was virtually incapacitated by a severe meth habit. Defense attorneys argued that Lewis and his supposed underlings were incapable of masterminding the complex black market operation described by prosecutors because of the Odessa gang's "disorganization, internal rivalries and [their] own drug addictions."

The jury didn't buy it. All 29 defendants were convicted.

After the 2004 methamphetamine bust, the Aryan Circle maintained a relatively low profile beyond prison walls. But that ended last January, when 20-year-old Circle member Ronald David Dickinson, who'd joined the gang while serving time for grand theft auto, was stomped to death by 52-year-old fellow Circle member John Michael Hays, who explained in a videotaped confession that Dickinson had called Hays' daughter a "Mexican whore."

In August, the same month Hays was sentenced to 99 years in prison, another Aryan Circle internal dispute flared into violence in Texas when Bryan "Bone" Aiken and three gang associates allegedly set out to assassinate Danny Covington, a Circle member since the 1980s. Covington, who lived in upscale North Richland Hills, near Fort Worth, was rumored to be abandoning the gang.

When the four hit men appeared at a drug house where Covington was believed to be, Covington and his friend Bryan Shuler showed up and found themselves in a shootout. Shuler was hit in the hand. Covington escaped in his car, but was chased down and shot in the arm by Aiken, who was only a few weeks out of prison.

At the time of the assassination attempt, Aiken was also a suspect, along with four other Circle members, in the July 18 home invasion robbery, beating and execution-style shooting of Randall Whatley, who survived.

According to prison officials, Aiken left the Aryan Circle after completing a "Gang Renouncement and Disassociation Process" in June 2004. But then he rejoined.

"It's rare that happens," Michelle Lyons of the Texas Department of Criminal Justice told the *Fort Worth Star-Telegram*. "He is one of only two people who completed the program and then went back into a gang."

Louisiana Shootout

Four days before the failed hit on Covington, two teenagers in Victoria, Texas, were killed and a third man was injured in a shootout with Circle member Dennis Leighton Clem, 24, who had just completed a four-year sentence in the TDC for "deadly conduct."

Clem fled the state with his girlfriend, Tanya "Little Feather" Smith, a reported member of the Aryan Circle Women's Branch, a division for female Circle members whose mission statement asserts: "As women of the Aryan Circle we strive to stand behind our men for the support they need against our foes. We will stand beside them when they are backed to the dooryard in battle. And we will fight for them should they become incapacitated by force."

One month later, Clem, Smith and Donald Alex Brendle, a member of the Louisiana chapter of Aryan Circle, were holed up in a Budget Inn motel room in Bastrop, La. Responding to a Crimestoppers tip, Bastrop Police Department detective sergeants John Smith and Charles Wilson approached the room from the parking lot. Clem immediately opened fire, killing Smith and Wilson. Minutes later, Clem shot and injured two ambulance workers. Clem died in a final exchange of gunfire with police.

Brendle and two other Louisiana Circle members were arrested the next day and charged with accessory to first-degree murder, attempted first-degree murder and obstruction of justice. Smith escaped but was later apprehended in Houston.

Clem will no doubt be hailed as a martyr within the Aryan Circle as the gang continues to cultivate new strongholds, especially in prison systems where the power of the Aryan Brotherhood is waning in the aftermath of federal racketeering indictments. Sanchez says the two are now even in numbers and power, both in Texas and abroad. The Aryan Circle's correspondence with Nazi gangs in Europe has enhanced their network.

"They're dealing with people out of France," says Sanchez. "If you're dealing with any European groups, it's always about the hate."

Hornacek, the Circle member incarcerated in Alabama, disavows any knowledge of the Circle's regions or Leafs. He claims to be "inactive," though he admits to maintaining contact with Circle members in California and Texas. Prison officials suspect he's under orders to establish the Circle within Alabama's state prisons, adding another ring to the gang's expanding web of violence and hatred.

"It's been brought to my attention that they are one gang to be observed and that we should definitely document and monitor them," says Eric Bascomb, the Alabama DOC security threat group coordinator. "They are very methodical and secretive about their process, and they are also more organized and radical than the Aryan Brotherhood."

According to Sanchez, dissension in the ranks of the Aryan Circle could deplete the gang. But he also warns that it could grow stronger. "You never know with these guys," says Sanchez. "All it takes is one guy who has the charisma to pull it all together, and he may be right around the corner."

Reading 4.
The Barrio Azteca Trial and the Prison
Gang-Cartel Interface*

Fred Burton & Ben West

On Nov. 3, a U.S. District Court in El Paso, Texas, began hearing a case concerning members of a criminal enterprise that calls itself Barrio Azteca (BA). The group members face charges including drug trafficking and distribution, extortion, money laundering and murder. The six defendants include the organization's three bosses, Benjamin Alvarez, Manuel Cardoza and Carlos Perea; a sergeant in the group, Said Francisco Herrera; a lieutenant, Eugene Mona; and an associate, Arturo Enriquez.

The proceedings represent the first major trial involving BA, which operates in El Paso and West Texas, New Mexico and Arizona. The testimony is revealing much about how this El Paso-based prison gang operates, and how it interfaces with Mexican drug cartel allies that supply its drugs.

Mexico's cartels are in the business of selling drugs like marijuana, cocaine and heroin in the United States. Large amounts of narcotics flow north while large amounts of cash and weapons flow south. Managing these transactions requires that the cartels have a physical presence in the United States, something a cartel alliance with a U.S. gang can provide.

Of course, BA is not the only prison gang operating in the United States with ties to Mexico. Prison gangs can also be called street gangs — they recruit both in prisons and on the street. Within the United States, there are at least nine well-established prison gangs with connections to Mexican drug cartels; Hermanos de Pistoleros Latinos, the Mexican Mafia and the Texas Syndicate are just a few such groups. Prison gangs like BA are very territorial and usually cover only a specific region, so one Mexican cartel might work with three to four prison or street gangs in the United States. Like BA, most of the U.S. gangs allied with Mexican cartels largely are composed of Mexican immigrants or Mexican-Americans. Nevertheless, white supremacist groups, mixed-race motorcycle gangs and African-American street gangs also have formed extensive alliances with Mexican cartels.

Certainly, not all U.S. gangs the Mexican cartels have allied with are the same. But examining how BA operates offers insights into how other gangs — like the Latin Kings, the Texas Syndicate, the Sureños, outlaw motorcycle gangs, and transnational street gangs like MS-13 — operate in alliance with the cartels.

Barrio Azteca Up Close

Spanish for "Aztec Neighborhood," BA originated in a Texas state penitentiary in 1986, when five inmates from El Paso organized the group as a means of protection in

---

* The Barrio Azteca Trial and the Prison Gang-Cartel Interface is republished with permission of STRATFOR (http://www.stratfor.com/weekly/20081119_barrio_azteca_trial_and_prison_gang_cartel_interface?fn=9814707329).

the face of the often-brutal ethnic tensions within prisons. By the 1990s, BA had spread to other prisons and had established a strong presence on the streets of El Paso as its founding members served their terms and were released. Reports indicate that in the late 1990s, BA had begun working with Joaquin "El Chapo" Guzman's Sinaloa Federation drug trafficking organization, which at the time controlled drug shipments to Ciudad Juarez, El Paso's sister city across the Rio Grande.

According to testimony from several different witnesses on both sides of the current trial, BA now works only with the Juarez cartel of Vicente Carrillo-Fuentes, which has long controlled much of Mexico's Chihuahua state and Ciudad Juarez, and broke with the Sinaloa Federation earlier in 2008. BA took sides with the Juarez cartel, with which it is jointly running drugs across the border at the Juarez plaza.

BA provides the foot soldiers to carry out hits at the behest of Juarez cartel leaders. On Nov. 3, 10 alleged BA members in Ciudad Juarez were arrested in connection with 12 murders. The suspects were armed with four AK-47s, pistols and radio communication equipment—all hallmarks of a team of hit men ready to carry out a mission.

According to testimony from the ongoing federal case, which is being brought under the Racketeer Influenced and Corrupt Organizations (RICO) Act, drugs are taken at discount from the supplier on the Mexico side and then distributed to dealers on the street. These distributors must then pay "taxes" to BA collectors to continue plying their trade. According to testimony from Josue Aguirre, a former BA member turned FBI informant, BA collects taxes from 47 different street-level narcotics operations in El Paso alone. Failure to pay these taxes results in death. One of the murder charges in the current RICO case involves the death of an El Paso dealer who failed to pay up when the collectors arrived to collect on a debt.

Once collected, the money goes in several different directions. First, BA lieutenants and captains, the midlevel members, receive $50 and $200 per month respectively for compensation. The bulk of BA's profit is then transferred using money orders to accounts belonging to the head bosses (like Alvarez, Cardoza and Perea) in prison. Cash is also brought back to Ciudad Juarez to pay the Juarez cartel, which provided the drugs in the first place.

BA receives discounts on drugs from the Juarez cartel by providing tactical help to its associates south of the border. Leaders of Carrillo Fuentes' organization in Juarez can go into hiding in El Paso under BA protection if their lives are in danger in Juarez. They can also order BA to track down cartel enemies hiding in El Paso. Former BA member Gustavo Gallardo testified in 2005 that he was sent to pick up a man in downtown El Paso who had cheated the Juarez cartel of money. Once Gallardo dropped him off at a safe house in El Paso, another team took the man—who was bound with rope and duct tape—to Ciudad Juarez, where Gallardo assumes he was killed.

BA and the World of Prison Gangs

Prison gangs are endemic to prison systems, where safety for inmates comes in numbers. Tensions (usually along racial lines) among dangerous individuals regularly erupt into deadly conflict. Prison gang membership affords a certain amount of protection against rival groups and offers fertile recruiting ground.

Once a prison gang grows its membership (along with its prestige) and establishes a clear hierarchy, its leader can wield an impressive amount of power. Some even wind up taking over prisons, like the antecedents of Russian organized crime did.

It might seem strange that members on the outside send money and answer to bosses in prison, since the bosses are locked up. But these bosses wield a great deal of influence over gang members in and out of prison. Disobedience is punishable by death, and regardless of whether a boss is in prison, he can order a hit on a member who has crossed him. Prison gang members also know that if they end up in prison again—a likely outcome—they will once again be dependent on the help of the boss to stay alive, and can perhaps even earn some money while doing time.

BA's illegal activities mean its members constantly cycle in and out of prison. Many BA members were involved in smaller, local El Paso street gangs before they were imprisoned. Once in prison, they joined BA with the sponsorship of a "godfather" who walks the recruit through the process. BA then performs a kind of background check on new recruits by circulating their name throughout the organization. BA is particularly interested in any evidence that prospective members have cooperated with the police.

Prison authorities are certainly aware of the spread of BA, and they try to keep Mexican nationals separated from known BA members, who are mostly Mexican-American, to prevent the spread of the gang's influence. BA has organizations in virtually every penitentiary in Texas, meaning that no matter where a BA member is imprisoned, he will have a protection network in place. BA members with truly extensive prison records might personally know the leader of every prison chapter, thus increasing the member's prestige. Thus, the constant cycling of members from the outside world into prison does not inhibit BA, but makes its members more cohesive, as it allows the prison system to increase bonds among gang members.

Communication challenges certainly arise, as exchanges between prisoners and those on the outside are closely monitored. But BA seems to have overcome this challenge. Former BA member Edward Ruiz testified during the trial that from 2003 to 2007, he acted as a clearinghouse for jailed members' letters and packages, which he then distributed to members on the outside. This tactic ensured that all prison communications would be traceable to just one address, thus not revealing the location of other members.

BA also allegedly used Sandy Valles New, who worked in the investigations section of the Office of the Federal Public Defender in El Paso from 1996 to 2002, to pass communications between gang members inside and outside prison. She exploited the access to—and the ability to engage in confidential communications with—inmates that attorneys enjoy, transmitting information back and forth between BA members inside and outside prison. Taped conversations reveal New talking to one of the bosses and lead defendants, Carlos Perea, about her fear of losing her job and thus not being able to continue transmitting information in this way. She also talked of crossing over to Ciudad Juarez to communicate with BA members in Mexico.

While BA had inside sources like New assisting it, the FBI was able to infiltrate BA in return. Josue Aguirre and Johnny Michelleti have informed on BA activities to the FBI since 2003 and 2005, respectively. Edward Ruiz, the mailman, also handed over stacks of letters to the FBI.

BA and the Mexican Cartels

As indicated, BA is only one of dozens of prison gangs operating along the U.S.-Mexican border that help Mexican drug trafficking organizations smuggle narcotics across the border and then distribute them for the cartels. Mexican drug trafficking organizations need groups that will do their bidding on the U.S. side of the border, as the border is the tightest choke point in the narcotics supply chain.

Getting large amounts of drugs across the border on a daily basis requires local connections to bribe border guards or border town policemen. Gangs on the U.S. side of the border also have contacts who sell drugs on the retail level, where markups bring in large profits. The current trial has revealed that the partnership goes beyond narcotics to include violence as well. In light of the high levels of violence raging in Mexico related to narcotics trafficking, there is a genuine worry that this violence (and corruption) could spread inside the United States.

One of the roles that BA and other border gangs fill for Mexican drug-trafficking organizations is that of enforcer. Prison gangs wield tight control over illegal activity in a specific territory. They keep tabs on people to make sure they are paying their taxes to the gang and not affiliating with rival gangs. To draw an analogy, they are like the local police who know the situation on the ground and can enforce specific rules handed down by a governmental body—or a Mexican cartel.

Details emerging from the ongoing trial indicate that BA works closely with the Juarez cartel and has contributed to drug-related violence inside the United States. While the killing of a street dealer by a gang for failure to pay up on time is common enough nationwide and hardly unique to Mexican drug traffickers, apprehending offenders in El Paso and driving them to Ciudad Juarez to be held or killed does represent a very clear link between violence in Mexico and the United States.

BA's ability to strike within the United States has been proven. According to a Stratfor source, BA is connected to Los Zetas—the U.S.-trained Mexican military members who deserted to traffic drugs—through a mutual alliance with the Juarez cartel. The Zetas possess a high level of tactical skill that could be passed along to BA, thus increasing its effectiveness.

The Potential for Cross-Border Violence

The prospect for enhanced cross-border violence is frightening, but the violence itself is not new. So far, Mexican cartels and their U.S. allies have focused on those directly involved in the drug trade. Whether this restraint will continue is unclear. Either way, collateral damage is always a possibility.

Previous incidents, like one that targeted a drug dealer in arrears in Phoenix and others that involved kidnappings and attacks against U.S. Border Patrol agents, indicate that violence has already begun creeping over from Mexico. So far, violence related to drug trafficking has not caused the deaths of U.S. law enforcement officials and/or civilians, though it has come close to doing so.

Another potential incubator of cross-border violence exists in BA's obligation to offer refuge to Juarez cartel members seeking safety in the United States. Such members most likely would have bounties on their heads. The more violent Mexico (and particularly Ciudad Juarez) becomes, the greater the risk Juarez cartel leaders face—and the more pressure they will feel to seek refuge in the United States. As more Juarez cartel leaders cross over and hide with BA help, the cartel's enemies will become increasingly tempted to follow them and kill them in the United States. Other border gangs in California, Arizona and New Mexico probably are following this same trajectory.

Two primary reasons explain why Mexican cartel violence for the most part has stopped short of crossing the U.S. border. First, the prospect of provoking U.S. law enforcement does not appeal to Mexican drug-trafficking organizations operating along the border. They do not want to provoke a coordinated response from a highly capable federal U.S. police force like the Drug Enforcement Administration, Bureau of Alcohol, Tobacco, Firearms and Explosives, or FBI. By keeping violence at relatively low levels and primarily aimed at other gang members and drug dealers, the Mexican drug-trafficking organizations can lessen their profile in the eyes of these U.S. agencies. Conversely, any increase in violence and/or the killing of U.S. police or civilians would dramatically increase federal scrutiny and retaliation.

The second reason violence has not crossed the border wholesale is that gangs like BA are in place to enforce the drug-trafficking organizations' rules. The need to send cartel members into the United States to kill a disobedient drug dealer is reduced by having a tight alliance with a border gang that keeps drugs and money moving smoothly and carries out the occasional killing to maintain order.

But the continued integrity of BA and its ability to carry out the writ of larger drug-trafficking organizations in Mexico might not be so certain. The Nov. 3 trial will undermine BA activity in the crucial trafficking corridor of El Paso/Ciudad Juarez.

The indictment and possible incarceration of the six alleged BA members would not damage the gang so badly—after all, BA is accustomed to operating out of prison, and there must certainly be members on the outside ready to fill in for their incarcerated comrades. But making BA's activities and modus operandi public should increase scrutiny on the gang and could very well lead to many more arrests.

In light of the presence of at least two FBI informants in the gang, BA leaders have probably moved into damage control mode, isolating members jeopardized by the informants. This will disrupt BA's day-to-day operations, making it at least temporarily less effective. Stratfor sources say BA members on both sides of the border have been ordered to lie low until the trial is over and the damage can be fully assessed. This is a dangerous period for gangs like BA, as their influence over their territory and ability to operate is being reduced.

Weakening BA by extension weakens the Juarez cartel's hand in El Paso. While BA no doubt will survive the investigations the trial probably will spawn, given the high stakes across the border in Mexico, the Juarez cartel might be forced to reduce its reliance on BA. This could prompt the Juarez cartel to rely on its own members in Ciudad Juarez to carry out hits in the United States and to provide its own security to leaders seeking refuge in the United States. It could also prompt it to turn to a new gang facing less police scrutiny. Under either scenario, BA's territory would be encroached upon. And considering the importance of controlling territory to prison gangs—and the fact that BA probably still will be largely intact—this could lead to increased rivalries and violence.

The Juarez cartel-BA dynamic could well apply to alliances between U.S. gangs and Mexican drug-trafficking organizations, such as Hermanos de Pistoleros Latinos in Houston, the Texas Syndicate and Tango Blast operating in the Rio Grande Valley and their allies in the Gulf cartel; the Mexican Mafia in California and Texas and its allies in the Tijuana and Sinaloa cartels; and other gangs operating in the United States with ties to Mexican cartels like Mexikanemi, Norteños and the Sureños.

Ultimately, just because BA or any other street gang working with Mexican cartels is weakened does not mean that the need to enforce cartel rules and supply chains disappears. This could put Mexican drug-trafficking organizations on a collision course with U.S. law enforcement if they feel they must step in themselves to take up the slack. As their enforcers stateside face more legal pressure, the cartels' response therefore bears watching.

Chapter 4

Outlaw Motorcycle Gangs

I. Outlaw Motorcycle Gangs—
An Introduction

The term outlaw motorcycle gangs (OMGs) was first used by Kentucky native and gonzo journalist Hunter S. Thompson in his 1966 seminal work on the Hells Angels Motorcycle Club—*Hell's Angels: The Strange and Terrible Saga of the Outlaw Motorcycle Gangs*. As documented in several biker autobiographies of the 1960s period, the formerly hell-raising and non-conforming motorcycle clubs such as the Hells Angels moved into criminal activity, particularly drug dealing, and became more like gangs (organized for crime as profit) than clubs of motorcycle enthusiasts (Barker, 2007). Following their evolution into crime, the major controversy surrounding these deviant clubs has been are they clubs or gangs?

Motorcycle clubs can be divided into conventional and deviant clubs (Barker, 2007). Conventional motorcycle clubs are those that represent all races and sexes, ride all makes of motorcycles, and behave according to the norms of society. These clubs join together based on a common interest in motorcycling and ride for pleasure and companionship. Historically, the members of these conventional clubs have come from different social strata and dress differently and act differently from deviant club members. Most motorcycle clubs are conventional clubs. Sociologically speaking, deviant motorcycle clubs are those who engage in non-conformist or norm-violating behavior, including anti-social and criminal behavior. These clubs cannot join or would not join traditional motorcycle associations such as the American or Canadian Motorcycle Association (AMA or CMA). Deviant clubs are not AMA or CMA sanctioned, of all one race, sex or sexual orientation, or those labeled outlaw motorcycle clubs/gangs. The deviant motorcycle clubs are a small percentage of all motorcycle clubs, but they receive the most attention.

Groups of deviant motorcyclists have evolved into a subculture of bikers called by others and themselves One Percent bikers (1%ers). Although there are various definitions of the One Percenter label, there is agreement that it includes male bikers who ride American-made iron; who, for the most part, engage in "in your face" opposition to conventional norms and values, seeing themselves as outsiders and seeing others "citizens" as outsiders. Outlaw motorcycle clubs are one percent clubs. A recently published book, *The One Percenter Encyclopedia: The World of Outlaw Motorcycle Clubs*

Box 4.1 One Percenter's Creed

One Percenters are the one percent of us who have given up on society and the politician's one-way law. We're saying we don't want to be like you. So stay out of our face. It's one for all and all for one. If you don't think this way, then walk away, because you are a citizen [outlaw bikers make a distinction between themselves and non-bikers—citizens] and don't belong with us.

Source: Statement attributed to Bandido Motorcycle Gang founder Donald Eugene Chambers (Winterhalder and De Clerco, 2008: xv).

From Abyss Ghosts to Zombies Elite (Hayes, 2011), is the first attempt to list the One Percent clubs, but even this ground-breaking work does not include all the one percent clubs. All deviant clubs are not one percent clubs (such as those of one race, one sex, gay or lesbian clubs), and all one percent clubs are not gangs. Outlaw motorcycle gangs are any outlaw/deviant clubs that operate outside society's laws and commit crimes for profit. Outlaw motorcycle gangs can be categorized into the "Big Five" outlaw motorcycle gangs, puppet/support OMGs, independent OMGs, and black/interracial OMGs. They are also classified as three-piece patch clubs, referring to the patch on the back of their "cut" (vest). The three-piece patch, "colors," consists of a top rocker, signifying the club's name, a bottom rocker designating where they are from and the club logo in the middle. As we will see (Pagans MC and Sons of Silence MC), there are variations on this but the "cut" will always have the club's name and logo on it. For example, the three-piece patch on the Hells Angels cut below shows that the wearer is a member of the HAMC (top rocker) from California (bottom rocker) and the patented Hells Angels "Death's Head" club logo is in the middle. MC, for "motorcycle club," also appears on most cuts.

Source: The Department of Justice (www.justice.gov/criminal/ocgs/gangs/motorcycle.html).

II. Big Five Outlaw Motorcycle Gangs

The designation of the Big Five outlaw motorcycle gangs is, in many ways, an arbitrary judgment, first made by law enforcement authorities in the form of the Big Four (Hells Angels, Bandidos, Outlaws and Pagans) to designate the criminal potential of the gangs. The Sons of Silence were added later with the list now becoming the Big Five outlaw motorcycle gangs. One could certainly argue that other clubs, such as the Mongols, Vagos, and Warlocks, should be included in any ranking based on criminal potential and size; however, there is general agreement among law enforcement authorities and biker experts that the Big Five outlaw motorcycle gangs are the Hells Angels, Bandidos, Outlaws, Pagans, and the Sons of Silence.

Hells Angels MC (HAMC)—International OMGs

Source: The Department of Justice (www.justice.gov/criminal/ocgs/gangs/motorcycle.html).

The Hells Angels MC aka Local 81 (8th letter in the alphabet is H; 1st letter in alphabet is A), The Big Red Machine, and the Red and White (the gang's colors) was founded on March 17, 1948, in Fontana/San Bernardino, California by former members of the P.O.B.O.B. MC (Pissed Off Bastards of Bloomington). The P.O.B.O.B. MC members were disgruntled World War II veterans having trouble adapting to civilian life who had joined together to "let off steam." Thus began the oft-repeated explanation that disillusioned veterans are the major players involved in the formation of outlaw motorcycle clubs/gangs. Nomadic members of the fledgling Hells Angels formed other chapters throughout California. These chapters operated autonomously and independently of each other until one man brought them all together—Ralph "Sonny" Barger (Barker, 2007). Technically, Barger, at that time the president of the Hells Angels Oakland Chapter, and his vice-president, George "Baby Huey" Wethern, were veterans. Barger was discharged from the Army after it was discovered he had joined with a fake birth certificate. Wethern joined the Hells Angels after receiving an undesirable discharge from the U.S. Air Force. Barger, Wethern, and the other young toughs that made up the nucleus of the new Hells Angels were not in anyway comparable to the WW II vets who formed the early outlaw clubs.

Barger is often erroneously referred to as the founder of the Hells Angels; however, he was only ten years old when the HAMC was formed in 1948. Nevertheless, this charismatic leader who would go on to become a media celebrity, best-selling author, cocaine addict, drug dealer, convicted felon and ex-con, would bring all the California HAMC chapters together and expand the HAMC internationally. It was under Barger's leadership that the Hells Angels Motorcycle Club evolved into the Hells Angels Motorcycle Gang. Barger, in his autobiography, admits that he sold drugs and got into a "lot of shit" in what he describes as the "gangster era" of the Hells Angels (Barger, 2000). It appears that the Hells Angels are still in their "gangster era."

The U.S. Department of Justice (2011) estimates that the HAMC has between 2,000 and 2,500 members in 27 U.S. states and 26 foreign countries. Internationally, the HAMC are a criminal threat on six different continents. The DOJ reports that the OMG is involved in the production, transportation, and distribution of marijuana and methamphetamine. The international criminal gang is also involved in the transportation and distribution of cocaine, hashish, heroin, LSD, Ecstasy, PCP, and diverted pharmaceuticals. We examined several of the recent racketeering cases against the HAMC in Chapter 1.

Bandidos MC—International OMG

Source: The Department of Justice (www.justice.gov/criminal/ocgs/gangs/motorcycle.html).

There are at least two conflicting versions concerning the formation of the Bandidos Motorcycle Club/Gang. The most often quoted version following the disillusioned veteran theme says that former Marine and Vietnam veteran, Donald Eugene Chambers, formed the Bandidos Motorcycle Club somewhere in Texas in 1966 and chose the Marine Corps colors of red and gold and the "Fat Mexican" logo (Hays, 2011). A second version and, in my opinion, the most credible is posited by biker expert and former Bandido leader, Edward Winterhalder (2008). Winterhalder accepts that Chambers is a former U.S. Marine but states, "[Chambers] was anything but a disillusioned Vietnam vet. The closest he got to Vietnam was watching the news. Whether he [Chambers] was disillusioned or not is a moot point: it sounds good in print and gels with the clichéd portrayal of bikers. In society's collective consciousness, anybody who starts or joins an outlaw motorcycle club must be disillusioned, disturbed, antisocial, or rebelling against something—perhaps all of the above" (Winterhalder and De Clerco, 2008, xiv). Winterhalder also disputes the selection of colors by Chambers. He says that the original colors were red and yellow inspired by the poisonous coral snake and the Southern expression "red and yellow, kill a fellow." The colors were changed to red and gold years later.

Another area of controversy concerning the founding of the Bandidos, is their original purpose. Law enforcement authorities allege that the Bandidos was formed as an outlaw motorcycle gang, not club, to control drug trafficking and prostitution in Texas. Winterhalder disputes this explanation; however, he acknowledges that Chambers was convicted and sentenced to life for a drug-related double homicide in 1972. Chambers was paroled in 1983 and was not involved in Bandido activities after this. (He died in 1999.) Whatever the original purpose for forming the Bandidos MC, there is ample evidence to support that the Bandidos MC is a criminal gang. As a testament to the criminal nature of the Bandidos Motorcycle Gang, starting with Chambers, every national president of the Bandidos MC has been convicted of a felony, usually drug trafficking, and been sentenced to prison.

Since its founding in 1966, the Bandidos have expanded throughout the U.S. and internationally. The gang's first European expansion was in 1989 when the Bandidos "patched over" [assimilated] the Club de Clichy in Marseille, France, igniting a war with the Hells Angels. The DOJ (2011) estimates that there are 2,000 to 2,500 Bandido members in the U.S. and 13 other countries. According to law enforcement authorities, the Bandidos MC is involved in transporting and distribution of cocaine and marijuana and the production, transportation, and distribution of methamphetamine. This fast growing outlaw motorcycle gang is most active in the Pacific, Southeastern, Southwestern, and West Central regions of the United States.

Outlaws MC—International OMG

Source: The Department of Justice (www.justice.gov/criminal/ocgs/gangs/motorcycle.html).

According to their national website, http://www.outlawsmc.com/, the Outlaws MC is the oldest outlaw motorcycle club, having been established in 1935 as the McCook Outlaws Motorcycle Club "out of Matilda's Bar on old Route 66 in McCook, Illinois just outside of Chicago." This motorcycle club was quite different from the outlaws motorcycle gang of today. A picture of the original McCook Outlaws Motorcycle Club appearing on the Outlaws MC national website shows a benign group of young men and women, none of whom appear to wear colors. Danny Lyons, a famous photographer of the 1960 Civil Rights Movement, joined the Chicago Outlaws Motorcycle Club in 1965 and road with them until 1967. The photographs he took while riding with the Chicago Outlaws were published in *The Bikeriders,* first published in 1968 and republished in 2003 (Lyons, 2003). Lyons' account of the Outlaws MC history is quite different from what appears on the national website. Lyons says that the original 1930s McCook Outlaws disbanded in 1947, "when most of its surviving members became policemen in Chicago and its suburbs" (Lyons, 2003:6). In the early 1950s a new club, the Chicago Outlaws Motorcycle Club, was formed, and in 1968 this club split with half the members going with Johnny Davis, a transit truck driver. It is this group that evolved into the present one percent Outlaws Motorcycle Club (Lyons, 2003). During this same period, the skull and crossed pistons, affectionately called "Charlie," was chosen as the club's logo. Supposedly, this logo was inspired by the logo worn by Marlon Brando in the first biker movie, *The Wild One.* By the late 1960s, the Outlaws Motorcycle Club, like the Hells Angels, had evolved into the Outlaws Motorcycle Gang. The last three national/international presidents of this criminal gang are currently serving life without parole for their RICO convictions.

The DOJ (2011) estimates that this OMG is slightly smaller than the HAMC and the Bandidos MC with an estimated 1,700 members in 20 U.S. states and 12 foreign countries. The Outlaws MC also identifies itself as the American Outlaws Association (A.O.A) and the Outlaws Nation. This criminal motorcycle gang is the dominant OMG in the Great Lakes region. As is common with all OMGs, the Outlaws are involved in the production, transportation, and distribution of methamphetamine. They are also involved in the transportation and distribution of cocaine, marijuana, and to a lesser extent, ecstasy. The HAMC and the Outlaws MC are bitter enemies and have a long history of violence toward each other. This was not always so. Lyons (2003:53) has a picture of a Chicago Outlaw riding his bike with a smiling Hells Angel on the back. They would be shooting each other today.

Pagans MC—Regional OMG

Source: The Department of Justice (www.justice.gov/criminal/ocgs/gangs/motorcycle.html).

The Pagans MC, a fierce one percent biker gang with ties to organized crime groups in Philadelphia, Pittsburg, and New York, did not start out as a one percent club, and disillusioned veterans have no place in their early history. Lou Dobkins, a biochemist at the National Institute of Health, established the club in 1959 in Prince George's County, Maryland. Tradition says that the original 13 members wore white denim jackets with Surt the pagan fire giant carrying a flaming sword logo on the back. The original members rode Triumph motorcycles. Their benign beginning did not foreshadow what the club would evolve into. According to an early member and Long Island Pagan's chapter president who earned his college degree in prison and went on to become a journalist and college professor, by the 1960s the Pagans had become "the baddest of the ass-kicking, beer-drinking, hell-raising, gang-banging, grease-covered, roadkill-eating 1960s motorcycle clubs …" (Hall, 2008:7).

During the 1970s, the fierce fighting club became an extremely violent criminal organization under the leadership of John Vernon "Satan" Marron. The Department of Justice reports that the Pagans are the most prominent OMG in the Mid-Atlantic region and are involved in the distribution of cocaine, methamphetamine, and PCP (DOJ, 2011). Most Pagans chapters are in the Northeast United States—New Jersey, New York, Pennsylvania, Delaware, and Maryland. The Pagans MC are the only Big Five outlaw motorcycle gang that does not have any chapters outside the United States, although there are rumors that they are attempting to establish a presence in Canada.

Sons of Silence MC—International OMG

Source: The Department of Justice (www.justice.gov/criminal/ocgs/gangs/motorcycle.html).

The Sons of Silence MC (SOS MC), also did not start out as a one percent biker gang. The club was founded by Bruce "The Dude" Richardson in Niwot, Colorado in 1966. As was common in the 1960s during a time of the military draft and the Vietnam War, Richardson had been in the military, specifically the U.S. Navy; however, there is no evidence that he had ever been to Vietnam or was a disillusioned veteran. The club appears to have been formed as a "drinking" social club. As the club evolved into a gang, Richardson left the club. Today, the DOJ (2011) reports that the SOS MC is an outlaw motorcycle gang with 30 U.S. chapters and five chapters in Germany. Club members, according to the DOJ, have been involved in a wide range of criminal activities, including drug and weapons trafficking.

The SOS MC patch is unique and different from the traditional one-percenter three-piece patch. The patch is one big center patch with the Latin saying "*Donec Mors Non Separate*"—Until Death Separates Us—appearing on the bottom of the center patch. There is a bottom rocker with the chapter's location.

III. Puppet/Support Clubs

Puppet/support clubs are outlaw motorcycle gangs affiliated with a dominant OMG. The puppet/support clubs do the biding of the dominant club, serve as potential recruiting sources, and provide cannon fodder in the wars between clubs. As is common with prison gangs, the OMG puppet/support clubs give a portion of their illegal gains to the dominant OMG. The Nomads chapter of the Quebec Hells Angels required each member of their puppet club, the Rockers, to give a 10-percent tithing or a minimum of $500 (Sanger, 2005). The larger OMGs will handle the wholesale distribution of the drugs, and the puppet clubs will handle the more dangerous retail sale, thereby insulating the dominant club members from prosecution. On occasion if the subordinate club member is caught committing a crime and demonstrates that he "has class" (keeps his mouth shut and takes the fall), he will be rewarded by becoming a "prospect" for the dominant club.

The Red Devils MC is a well-known puppet/support club for the HAMC, and the Black Pistons MC and Forsaken Few are known as puppet clubs for the Outlaws MC.

Box 4.2 Puppet/Support OMGs in Canada

"… outlaw motorcycle gangs for example do have a formalized structure for dealing with its support crime groups [puppet clubs]. Essentially these supportive crime groups are used to train the younger generation, identify those candidates with the potential to become full-fledged members, as well as exclude undesirables. In this kind of relationship, the advantage for the dominant is that the subordinate one further insulates the dominant group's members from the day-to-day criminal activities that would bring them into direct contact with the authorities and/or their rivals. Other benefits for the dominant group include the payment of money, goods, and services they receive from members of the subordinate group."

Source: CICS (2005).

The Red Devils MC on their website proudly announce that they are an "Official 81 support club." The small local Undertakers MC of Lexington, Kentucky also proclaim on their website "We are a motorcycle club and are **PROUD SUPPORTERS OF THE OUTLAWS M/C AND THE BLACK AND WHITE WORLD … IF IT AIN'T BLACK AND WHITE, IT JUST AIN'T RIGHT!**" (emphasis in the original).

Source: The Department of Justice (www.justice.gov/criminal/ocgs/gangs/motorcycle.html).

The Outlaws Nation and the Bandidos Nation list their puppet/support clubs on their national websites. The Bandidos website lists 22 puppet clubs in the "Red and Gold World"; however, Winterhalder (2005), the only former Bandido to write an autobiography, lists 47 Bandido "support" clubs in 13 states with 929 members. The puppet/support clubs of the Pagans include the Tribe MC, Last Rebels MC, and the Shore Dogs MC. All of the Pagan MC subordinate clubs wear a "16" on their cuts. (The 16th letter in the alphabet is P.) Support clubs for the Sons of Silence MC are reportedly the Silent Few MC (Arkansas), Silent Rebels MC (Louisiana), Silent Thunder MC (North Dakota), American Iron MC (Denver, Colorado), and the Deuce's Wild MC (Greely, Colorado).

IV. Independent Outlaw Motorcycle Gangs

Independent outlaw motorcycle gangs are considered to be those that are not listed in the Big Five and are not a puppet/support club of a Big Five club. Because of the jealously of their territory by Big Five clubs it is not easy to be an independent club. Independent clubs operate in areas where there are no Big Five clubs, or in the same area with permission of the dominant club. They are on friendly or tolerated terms with the larger club but remain independent of them.

Other independent clubs, such as the Mongols MC (national and international), operate in the same areas due to their ferocity and willingness to use violence. The Mongols MC and the HAMC fought a 17-year war over the wearing of the California bottom rocker. The Hells Angels said that they were the only motorcycle club who could wear the California rocker. The Mongols objected and went to war. After 17 years of murder and mayhem between the clubs, a truce was signed in 1977. Under the terms of the truce, the HAMC retained their Southern California chapters (Monterey, Orange County, Riverside, Fresno, Ventura, San Diego [Dago], and the original chapter, San Bernardino [Berdoo]), and the Mongols promised not to establish chapters in Northern California. The Mongols MC were granted a free reign over the rest of Southern California and "allowed" to wear the California rocker. The truce has not stopped the violence between the gangs. Another longtime Southern California independent OMG, the Vagos MC (regional and international), established in 1965 in San Bernardino, California is currently challenging the HAMC in California, Nevada, and Arizona. Other major independent clubs include the Warlocks MC (national and international) and the Iron Horsemen MC (regional and national) and the smaller independents such as the Avengers MC, the Breed MC, and the Renegades MC who operate in limited geographical areas.

Source: The Department of Justice (www.justice.gov/criminal/ocgs/gangs/motorcycle.html).

V. Black or Interracial One-Percent OMGs

There are numerous One Percent bikers that vehemently insist that there are no black one percent bikers, insisting that, like women, blacks are not welcome in the One Percent subculture. It is true that the One Percent subculture is basically sexist (women cannot be patch-holders in any one percent club) and racist, with some clubs/gangs being more racist than others; however, it is not true that there are no black one percent bikers or clubs. The Oakland, California Eastbay Dragons MC is an all black one percent club (Levington, 2003). The Wheels of Soul MC's website says that they are "an Outlaw Motorcycle Club, was founded in 1976 and is the only one of its kind.... we have a make-up of black, white, Latino, and Asian members" (www.wosmc-trenton.com/history.html). The Ching-a-Lings MC in Queens, New York City, are also interracial. According to a State of New Jersey Commission 1989 Report, the black Ghetto Riders MC of Camden County was founded in the late 1970s and has approximately 30 members and 20 associates (www.mafianj.com/mc/sg.html). Winterhalder reports there is a black, nationwide one percent club, the Hell's Lovers (Winterhalder, 2005).

References

Barger, R., with Zimmerman, K and Zimmerman, K. (2000). *Hell's Angels: The Life and Times of Sonny Barger and the Hell's Angels Motorcycle Club.* New York: William Morrow.

Barker, T. (2007). *Biker Gangs and Organized Crime.* Cincinnati, Ohio: LexisNexis/Anderson Publishing.

CICS. (2005). *2005 Organized Crime in Canada.* Ottawa: Criminal Intelligence Service Canada.

DOJ. (2011). *Motorcycle Gangs.* U.S. Department of Justice. http://www.justice.gov/criminal/oggs/gangs/motorcycle.

Hayes, B. (2011). *The One Percenter Encyclopedia: The World of Outlaw Motorcycle Clubs From Abyss Ghosts to Zombies Elite.* Minneapolis, MN: Motorbooks.

Hall, J. (2008). *Riding on the Edge: A Motorcycle Outlaw's Tale.* Minneapolis, MN: MBI Publishing Company and Motorbooks.

Levingston, T.G. with Zimmerman, K. and K. (2003). *Soul on Bikes: The East Bay Dragons MC and the Black Biker Set.* St. Paul, MN: MBI Publishing Company.

Lyons, D. (2003). *The Bikeriders.* San Francisco, CA: Chronicle Books.

Sanger, D. (2005). *Hell's Witness.* Toronto: Penguin Group.

Thompson, H.S. (1966). *Hell's Angels: The Strange and Terrible Saga of the Outlaw Motorcycle Gangs.* New York: Ballantine Books.

Winterhalder, E. (2005). *Out in Bad Standing: Inside the Bandidos Motorcycle Club—The Making of a Worldwide Dynasty.* Owasso, OK: Blockhead City Press.

Winterhalder, E. and De Clerco, W. (2008). *The Assimilation: Rock Machine Become Bandidos—Bikers Against the Hells Angels.* Toronto, Canada: ECW Press.

Readings

1. Barker, T. and Human, K.M. (2009). Crimes of the Big Four Motorcycle Gangs. *Journal of Criminal Justice.* 37: 174–179.

2. Quinn, J.F. and Forsyth, C.J. (2011). Coordinated Chaos: The Psychology and Structure of Organized Crime among One Percent Bikers. (Written for inclusion.)
3. Barker, T. (2011). American-Based Bikers: International Organized Crime. (Written for inclusion.)
4. Morselli, C. (2009). Hells Angels in Springtime. *Trends in Organized Crime.* 12: 145–158.

Reading 1.
Crimes of the Big Four Motorcycle Gangs[*]

Thomas Barker & Kelly M. Human

Abstract

Motorcycle clubs (MCs) can be divided into conventional and deviant clubs. The most deviant clubs are those known as 1 percent or outlaw motorcycle gangs (OMGs). The Big Four OMGs are the Hells Angels MC, the Outlaws MC, the Bandidos MC, and the Pagans MC. The first three, although American based, have international chapters and are the largest motorcycle gangs in the world. All four are known for their criminal activity and violence toward each other. There has been little scholarly research on these secret and dangerous motorcycle clubs. This research, utilizing a LexisNexis newspaper search classified the criminal activity of each of the Big Four gangs using a biker criminality typology developed by Quinn and Koch. The study found that the members of the Big Four gangs are involved in a wide range of criminal activities with the most common being ongoing enterprises/organized crime such as drugs and weapons trafficking. There were also numerous instances of spontaneous and planned violent acts against rivals and others. The study added to the limited body of knowledge on these deviant groups and suggests further areas of research.

Introduction

Riding motorcycles, a recreational activity for many, has become a deviant subcultural way of life for some. Riders join together in groups, clubs, and interest associations. One can divide motorcycle clubs into conventional and deviant clubs (Barker, 2007). Conventional club members, representing all races and sexes and riding all makes of motorcycles foreign and domestic, behave according to the norms of society and join together based on their common interest in motorcycles, riding together for pleasure and companionship. They join traditional motorcycle associations such as the American Motorcycle Association (AMA). Historically, they come from different social strata and dress differently and act differently from deviant club members. Deviant clubs,

---

   * Reproduced with permission. *Journal of Criminal Justice* 37 (2009) 174–179.

i.e., norm violating clubs from a sociological standpoint, include clubs not AMA sanctioned; of all one race, sex, or sexual orientation; or those labeled as outlaw motorcycle clubs (OMCs). Deviant clubs have always represented a small percentage of the motorcycle riding public, but they receive the most attention and publicity.

Over time, groups of deviant motorcyclists evolved into a subculture of bikers labeled by others and themselves as 1 percent bikers or outlaw motorcycle clubs (Barker, 2007). The 1 percent bikers are also a small percentage of all deviant motorcyclists. Furthermore, it is possible for clubs to be considered a deviant club and not be a 1 percent club, e.g., motorcycle clubs based on the same sex, race, or sexual orientation. Members of outlaw motorcycle clubs engage in unconventional behavior, often criminal behavior. In fact, many OMCs are more like gangs than clubs and are labeled outlaw motorcycle gangs (OMGs) by national and international law enforcement agencies. OMG members are males, primarily White and ride American Iron, mainly Harleys and Harley facsimiles of at least 750 cc engine sizes. They wear three-piece patches signifying the club/gang and its territory. Outlaw motorcycle gang members live for the club and make the club's priorities their own, even to the extent of committing illegal acts for the club. The threat of criminal activity by OMGs has been recognized as a problem by law enforcement officials since the early 1960s. Research and data on these clubs, however, is lacking. The purposes of this research were to provide empirical data on their criminal activity and examine the utility of the Quinn and Koch (2003) typology of biker criminality to classify the criminal behavior of selected OMGs.

There were few empirical studies of outlaw motorcycle clubs/gangs and no official records are kept on their crimes (see Barker, 2004, 2007; Dulaney, 2005). The usual research methods of surveys, interviews, and field study were not applicable to these deviant and dangerous groups; therefore a content analysis of newspaper articles was chosen to collect data. The authors recognize that a content analysis of newspaper articles is an imperfect measure of the behavior of any deviant group, particularly outlaw motorcycle groups who have received an inordinate amount of print and nonprint media attention since their founding in the 1950s. Editors make decisions based on what is newsworthy; therefore, often the most notorious crimes or behaviors are printed, leaving an unknown "dark figure" of crimes and behavior for the group. Recognizing these imperfections and given the purposes of this study, the authors conducted a LexisNexis search on what was known as the Big Four outlaw motorcycle clubs/gangs. The Big Four (Hells Angels, Outlaws, Bandidos, and Pagans) are considered to be "the largest and most consistently radical [criminal] of all one percent clubs" (Quinn, 2001, p. 380).

The Hells Angels, Bandidos, and Outlaws motorcycle clubs, although American based, have expanded internationally and are the largest motorcycle clubs/gangs in the world. The actual number of chapters and members of these secretive clubs/gangs is unknown and unknowable. There are, however, estimates and information on their size. The official Web site of the Hells Angels Motorcycle Club (HAMC) lists 256 charters (chapters) with 65 charters in the U.S. and 191 HAMC charters in twenty-seven other countries (Argentina, Australia, Austria, Belgium, Brazil, Bohemia/Czech Republic, Canada, Croatia, Chile, Denmark, England/Wales, France, Finland, Germany, Greece, Holland, Italy, Lichtenstein, Luxembourg, New Zealand, Northern Ireland, Norway, Portugal, Russia, South Africa, Sweden, Switzerland) (hells-angels.com/charters.htm—accessed

February 25, 2008). This is a constantly changing listing as new charters/chapters are established and others disbanded. Furthermore, the Web site says and the authors are personally aware of HAMC charters/chapters that are not listed. The Bandidos Nation lists 72 chapters in fourteen U.S. states and 81 chapters in twelve countries outside the United States (Australia, Bangkok, Channel Islands, Denmark, Finland, France, Germany, Italy, Luxembourg, Norway, Sweden) (Barker, 2007, pp. 78–79). The Outlaws Motorcycle Club claims to have 80 chapters in twenty states and 116 chapters in fourteen countries outside the U.S. (Australia, Belgium, Canada, England, France, Germany, Ireland, Italy, Norway, Poland, Russia, Sweden, Thailand, Wales) (Barker, 2007). These clubs, or chapters of these clubs, have engaged in organized crime activities since the 1960s (Barker, 2007). The Pagans Motorcycle Club, the most secretive of the clubs, does not list their chapters and does not have chapters outside the United States. There are larger outlaw motorcycle clubs/gangs than the Pagans in the U.S. and internationally, however, the Pagans are included in the Big 4 designation because of their propensity toward violence and criminal activity. The Pagans have always been heavily involved in criminal activity, including organized crime activities with traditional organized crime groups such as the Italian Mafia (Barker, 2007). There are also ties between the Pagans and the notorious White supremacists prison gang, the Aryan Brotherhood (Holthouse, 2005).

Literature Review

As stated, the scholarly literature on outlaw motorcycle gangs (OMGs) was limited (nineteen articles and four books—Barker, 2007; Harris, 1985; Veno, 2003; Wolf, 1991). The majority of the OMG literature came from journalists: Auger, 2001 (Canada); Bowe, 1994 (U.S.); Charles, 2002 (U.S. and England); Detroit, 1994 (U.S.-California); Kingsbury, 1995 (U.S.); Lavigne, 1987, 1996, 1999 (world); Lowe, 1988 (Canada); Mello, 2001 (U.S.); T. Reynolds, 2000 (U.S.); Sher & Marsden, 2003 (Canada); Sher & Marsden, 2006 (U.S.); Simpson & Harvey, 2001 (Australia); Thompson, 1966 (U.S.-California). There are also autobiographies from members or former members of outlaw motorcycle club/gang members that provide an "insider's" view of this world/lifestyle and its criminal activity (Barger, Zimmerman, & Zimmerman, 2000; Kaye, 1970; Levingston, Zimmerman, & Zimmerman, 2003; Mandelkau, 1971; Martineau, 2003; Mayson & Marco, 1982; Paradis, 2002; F. Reynolds, 1967; Wethern & Colnett, 1978; Winterhalder, 2005; Zito & Layden, 2002).

Among the limited scholarly works, Quinn and Koch (2003) proposed a typology to characterize biker criminality. These categories were used to examine the newspaper articles. The categories were:

> Spontaneous expressive acts usually involve one or a few members in violent crimes directed at rivals or other actors from within the saloon society milieu (e.g., bar fights) (emphasis added).
>
> Planned aggressive acts are generally directed at rival groups and are either planned by established cliques or chapter/regional/national officers or tacitly reflect the priorities of the chapter or club (emphasis added).

Short-term instrumental acts usually involve one or a very few members in thefts that take advantage of unique opportunities or are designed as a response to the particular needs of one of the involved members (e.g., motorcycle thefts, prostitution). They may vary along the continuum from planned to spontaneous (emphasis added).

Ongoing instrumental enterprises involving the fairly consistent attention of one or more cliques and designed to supply large amounts of money to the members and are usually planned well in advance of their execution (drug production/distribution) (emphasis added) (Quinn & Koch, 2003, p. 296).

Quinn and Koch (2003) described ongoing instrumental acts as generally involving several members of the club, specifically for financial purposes. Therefore, ongoing instrumental crimes are examples of organized crime. In the late 1980s, law enforcement authorities and academic experts began to recognize that outlaw motorcycle gangs were, along with indigenous Black street gangs and Hispanic gangs, becoming the new faces of United States organized crime (Delattre, 1990; see also Barker, 2007). Quinn and Koch (2003) commented on the structural tiers of motorcycle gangs that lead to the criminal networks that make these productive national and international criminal enterprises possible. Quinn (2001) also discussed the importance of club loyalty as a major catalyst of organized criminal involvement. This loyalty led to many gang wars. The gang wars could become quite expensive and required heavy flows of cash, and the quickest way to make the cash was through illegal means, often organized crime.

The one category that creates most problems for local police is the spontaneous expressive acts because they occur in public settings and often involve non-gang members. Outlaw motorcycle gang members consume large quantities of alcohol and frequently use methamphetamines, increasing the likelihood that fights and other violent acts will occur when members are in social settings such as bars. Members are usually armed, leading to the possibility of lethal encounters. Planned aggressive acts include specifically planned acts of violence which usually target rival clubs, are also a local police problem. The distrust and dislike common among rival outlaw motorcycle gangs increases the likelihood of violence. Clubs are very territorial and resist the incursion of other clubs and members of these clubs in their defined territories, increasing violence between clubs. Club members and clubs as a whole (short-term instrumental acts and ongoing instrumental acts) are also involved in profit-oriented crimes, including organized crime activities such as drug production and trafficking. Obviously, these acts often transcend local boundaries and create problems for state, federal, and international law enforcement agencies.

The Quinn and Koch (2003) typology rests on the premise that the full extent of outlaw motorcycle club criminal involvement varies from individual to club/gang involvement. Along this same line, Barker (2007, p. 126) says that there is a continuum of one-percent motorcycle clubs as criminal organizations with clubs or chapters of these clubs acting as voluntary associations built on a common interest in riding motorcycles on one end, and gangs organized for criminal profit on the other. The informal groupings of members in outlaw motorcycle clubs, or chapters, can encourage or discourage criminal activity; therefore, some clubs/chapters have few members involved in serious criminal behavior; in other clubs/chapters, small groups are involved in criminal activity, even organized crime such as drug enterprises, and operate with the club as a whole unaware of, or tacitly supporting, their activities (see Barker, 2007). On the other hand, many clubs/chapters or the leaders are fully aware of all incidents and operate as gangs oriented toward criminal profit.

Methodology

Published newspaper articles were chosen as data sources for this study and a content analysis was conducted on them. The selected newspaper articles were located in the LexisNexis data base. The search fields included all general news items in all available newspapers, for all available years. The searches included the terms Outlaws Motorcycle Club, the Hell's Angels Motorcycle Club, the Bandidos Motorcycle Club, and the Pagans Motorcycle Club. A total of 631 articles were obtained from the LexisNexis search: Outlaws MC (347), Hell's Angels (209), Bandidos MC (50), and Pagans MC (25). The articles spanned a twenty-five year period (1980–2005) and came from hundreds of different newspapers, domestic and international.

Several issues were considered during the content analysis process. The geographic location of the incident was identified. The authors did this because of the large international expansion of the three largest outlaw motorcycle clubs/gangs: the Hells Angels, Outlaws, and Bandidos. The clubs founded in the United States have more of an international than national presence. In fact, these three clubs/gangs now have more chapters and members outside the U.S. It was also necessary to separate criminal incidents from noncriminal incidents. Criminal articles were defined as those in which a criminal incident was the main focus, such as a gang member being arrested for individual, group, or club criminal activity (301 articles). Next each article was examined to determine if there were duplicative articles on the same incident. It was found that the 301 criminal articles actually dealt with 89 different incidents: 6 Pagan incidents, 16 Bandidos incidents, 26 Outlaws incidents, and 40 Hells Angels criminal incidents. Noncriminal incidents covered a wide range, including charitable works by members or the club or obituaries of a former or current member. Several noncriminal articles also discussed upcoming motorcycle rallies.

The next step was to determine if the articles related to crimes by or against the motorcycle club. Several articles contained information about criminal incidents perpetrated against the motorcycle club, such as clubhouse bombings or the murder of a member by a member of a rival club, not an uncommon event. Motorcycle clubs have participated in territorial wars since their inception. Another example of incidents against the club came in the form of police harassment. For instance, police conducting an illegal raid and destroying property belonging to motorcycle club members.

Some of the articles were not related to the Big Four motorcycle clubs and were excluded from analysis. This frequently occurred in the articles that referenced the general topic of outlaws motorcycle clubs. Confusion occurred because the term "outlaw" can refer to one specific club, the "Outlaws Motorcycle Club," or all clubs defined as outlaw motorcycle clubs. These articles concerned any number of outlaw motorcycle clubs, but were not specifically related to the Outlaws Motorcycle Club. An example included an article about a Warlocks Motorcycle Club member accused of murdering a police officer; the Warlocks are an outlaw motorcycle club/gang but not one of the Big Four.

All criminal articles were analyzed using the four categories of the Quinn and Koch (2003) typology. Spontaneous expressive acts—unplanned acts of violence by one or more club members against a club's rival included bar fights, fights with police officers, and menacing with a pit bull. Examples of planned aggressive acts—planned violent attacks generally against rivals included planned brawls by large numbers of members with their rivals, shoot-outs between two rival gangs, murder of an individual rival gang member, and the slaying of five members of a rival gang in order to shut the club down. Short-term instrumental acts—impulsive thefts that benefited one or more members of the gang included one member selling LSD for a short time to make money for motorcycle repairs, theft of vehicles, and possession of unlawful ammunition. The final category ongoing instrumental enterprises involved ongoing enterprises intended to supply money to the club or groups of club members. Examples included drug distribution networks, firearms trafficking, racketeering, an international luxury car theft ring, and illegal drug laboratories.

Results

Three hundred one of the 631 articles (48 percent) contained eighty-nine accounts of criminal incidents where a member or members of the Big Four motorcycle club committed an illegal act. The most common illegal acts involved drug trafficking, racketeering, brawling, various weapons charges, and murder. One incident with seventy-seven articles was a 2000 Milwaukee, Wisconsin racketeering trial of seventeen members of the Outlaws Motorcycle Club. Indicted in this trial were several regional leaders as well as members at large.

The Outlaws members were charged with several offenses, ranging from murder to bombing the clubhouses of rivals, to narcotics trafficking, racketeering, attempted arson, and dealing in stolen motorcycles. There were numerous victims, most of whom were unnamed. The investigations that led to this large number of indictments were precipitated by a gang war between the Outlaws Motorcycle Club and the Hell's Angels Motorcycle Club.

There were twenty-five articles related to the Pagans Motorcycle Club. Thirteen articles were crime related and dealt with six crime related incidents with four classified as ongoing instrumental enterprises. There was one incident classified as planned aggressive acts category and one spontaneous expressive act (see Table 1). There were no international incidents reported for this gang. Most incidents had more than one newspaper article, thus, the number in front of the article content in all tables is the number of articles that pertained to that incident.

The Bandidos Motorcycle Club had a total of fifty articles with twenty-five on criminal acts involving sixteen different criminal incidents (Table 2). Twelve of the articles covered four planned aggressive acts: three in Australia and one in Canada. There were seven articles on six spontaneous expressive acts: five in Australia and one in Texas. Five articles reported on five ongoing instrumental enterprises: three in Australia and one each in Texas and Colorado. One article dealt with a short-term instrumental act

Table 1. Pagans Motorcycle Club Criminal Activity

Criminal Incident	Location	Typology Category
(1) Distributing methamphetamines, marijuana and firearms	Virginia	Ongoing instrumental enterprises
(5) Selling cocaine to Amish youths	Pennsylvania	Ongoing instrumental enterprises
(2) Drug and racketeering charges	West Virginia	Ongoing instrumental enterprises
(2) Large-scale drug trafficking ring	Pennsylvania	Ongoing instrumental enterprises
(2) Brawl at tattoo expo with rival biker club	New York	Planned aggressive acts
(1) Murder in a sports bar brawl	New Jersey	Spontaneous expressive acts
N = 13 criminal articles.		

in Australia. There are numerous indigenous (Coffin Cheater, Commancheros, Gypsy Jokers, Finks, the Rebels—Australia's largest motorcycle gang with sixty-three chapters) and American based (Hells Angels, Bandidos, Outlaws) OMGs in Australia (Veno, 2003). They are a significant crime problem and extremely violent (Barker, 2007).

Table 2. Bandidos Motorcycle Club Criminal Activity

Criminal Incident	Location	Typology Category
(1) Drive-by shooting of rival gang member	Australia	Planned aggressive act
(3) Murder of infringing drug dealer	Canada	Planned aggressive act
(1) Murder of club rival	Australia	Planned aggressive act
(7) Shoot-out Father's Day massacre-gang war	Australia	Planned aggressive act
(1) Brawl with police officers after a bar explosion	Australia	Spontaneous expressive act
(1) Suspected murder over hidden money	Australia	Spontaneous expressive act
(1) Assault during a street altercation	Australia	Spontaneous expressive act
(1) Brawl in Darling Harbor pub	Australia	Spontaneous expressive act
(2) Carrying a loaded pistol	Australia	Spontaneous expressive act
(1) Knife murder during brawl	Texas	Spontaneous aggressive act
(1) Drug possession	Texas	Ongoing instrumental enterprises
(1) Drug and conspiracy charges	Colorado	Ongoing instrumental enterprises
(1) Drug charges, discovery of a pill press	Australia	Ongoing instrumental enterprises
(1) Trafficking of LSD	Australia	Ongoing instrumental enterprises
(1) Drug and weapons charges	Australia	Ongoing instrumental enterprises
(1) Possession of illegal weapons	Australia	Short-term instrumental act
N = 25 criminal articles.		

The Outlaws Motorcycle Club had 347 total articles with a majority (204 or 59 per-cent) related to twenty-six criminal incidents (Table 3). The most articles (176 or 51 per-cent) were on thirteen ongoing instrumental enterprises: six in Canada, two in Australia, and five in the United States. For the most part, Canadian 1 percent motorcycle clubs, indigenous and U.S. based, operate as criminal gangs and not clubs. This is especially true for the American-based clubs—the Hells Angels, Bandidos, and Outlaws (Barker, 2007). The next category with the most articles was spontaneous expressive acts with seventeen articles reporting on six criminal incidents: three in Australia and three in the U.S. There were three planned aggressive acts: two in Australia and one in Massachusetts, and six articles on three short-term instrumental acts: two in Australia and one in Canada.

The Hell's Angels Motorcycle Club had a total of 209 articles with fifty-nine that pertained to forty criminal incidents (Table 4). The most articles (thirty-seven) dealt with twenty-three ongoing instrumental enterprises: twelve U.S. incidents, six in Aus-tralia, and five in Canada. There were fourteen planned aggressive acts articles report-ing on ten criminal incidents: five U.S. incidents, four in Canada, and one in Australia. The eight-year biker war (1994–2001) in Canada between the indigenous Rock Ma-chine Motorcycle Club (later patched over to the Bandidos) is the worst organized crime war in history in terms of dead and wounded (Barker, 2007). The war resulted in 160 murders, including an innocent eleven year-old boy; 175 attempted murders; 200 peo-ple wounded, and the disappearance of fifteen bikers (Roslin, 2002). Four articles dis-cussed four spontaneous expressive acts that occurred in the United States. Four articles reported on four short-term instrumental acts: two in Canada and two in Australia.

Table 5 identifies the type of criminal activity by club/gang. As one can see, the data showed that the Hells Angels Motorcycle Club had the highest number of ongoing in-strumental enterprises (twenty-three of forty-nine or 47 percent of the criminal inci-dents). This was expected, as the Hells Angels here and abroad, have the reputation of being involved in organized crime activities. The Outlaws had thirteen instances and the Bandidos had five incidents of ongoing instrumental enterprises. Interestingly, the Pagans had the lowest number reported (four), but that was 67 percent of their total number of criminal incidents reported in the newspaper articles. The Hells Angels also had ten of the eighteen (56 percent) reported incidents of planned aggressive acts. Again, this was expected because the HAMC has been involved in violent wars over territory and drug markets with other outlaw motorcycle gangs since the present day Hells Angels were formed in Oakland, California in 1957 by Ralph "Sonny" Barger and his gang of young toughs (Barker, 2007). The reported incidents of spontaneous expressive acts and short-term instrumental acts were fairly evenly divided among the three largest gangs (Hells Angels, Bandidos, and Outlaws).

Discussion

The results provided empirical data on the criminal activity of the Big 4 motorcycle gangs. Such data was almost nonexistent on this underresearched topic. The data also contradicted the popular image of these groups. One percent biker clubs are a part of American pop culture with a genre of biker movies (The Wild One, Hells Angels on Wheels,

Table 3. Outlaws Motorcycle Club Criminal Activity

Criminal Incident	Location	Typology Category
(1) Drug conspiracy charges	North Carolina	Ongoing instrumental enterprises
(19) Racketeering and drug trafficking	Florida	Ongoing instrumental enterprises
(2) Conspiring to murder former enterprises	Australia	Ongoing instrumental
(14) Murder, fire-bombings, extortion and drug trafficking	Florida	Ongoing instrumental enterprises
(37) Drug racketeering, murder, extortion	Florida	Ongoing instrumental enterprises
(77) Racketeering, murder, bombings, narcotics trafficking	Wisconsin	Ongoing instrumental enterprises
(3) Distributing cocaine	Canada	Ongoing instrumental enterprises
(0) Distributing cocaine	Canada	Ongoing instrumental enterprises
(3) Drug trafficking	Canada	Ongoing instrumental enterprises
(2) Possession of drugs for sale	Australia	Ongoing instrumental enterprises
(17) Drug trafficking	Canada	Ongoing instrumental enterprises
(1) Drug trafficking, menacing	Australia	Ongoing instrumental enterprises
(1) Drug trafficking	Australia	Ongoing instrumental enterprises
(1) Attempted murder, criminal organization, possession of a weapon	Canada	Ongoing instrumental enterprises
(3) Hate crime against an African American	Massachusetts	Spontaneous expressive acts
(8) Fatal stabbing in party setting	New York	Spontaneous expressive acts
(1) Attempted murder, possession of weapons, fighting in clubhouse	New York	Spontaneous expressive acts
(1) Pub bashing	Australia	Spontaneous expressive acts
(1) Assault with a pool cue	Australia	Spontaneous expressive acts
(2) Knife confrontation with a police officer	Australia	Spontaneous expressive acts
(1) Bribery	Canada	Ongoing instrumental enterprises
(1) Looking for a brawl with rival gang members	Massachusetts	Planned aggressive acts
(1) Car bombing of rival	Australia	Planned aggressive acts
(1) Shoot-out with Odin's Warriors	Australia	Planned aggressive acts
(3) Beer store robbery	Canada	Short-term instrumental acts
(1) Auto theft	Australia	Short-term instrumental acts
(1) Drug possession (small amount of drugs)	Canada	Short-term instrumental acts
(0) Drugs and firearms	Australia	Short-term instrumental acts
N = 204 criminal articles.		

Table 4. Hells Angels Motorcycle Club Criminal Activity

Criminal Incident	Location	Typology Category
(1) Drug trafficking	Minnesota	Ongoing instrumental enterprises
(1) Shooting a rival gang member, racketeering	Illinois	Ongoing instrumental enterprises
(8) Selling methamphetamines, owning illegal firearms	Maryland	Ongoing instrumental enterprises
(1) Shoot-out with rival, racketeering, drugs	California	Ongoing instrumental enterprises
(1) Racketeering, drug, conspiracy charges	California	Ongoing instrumental enterprises
(1) Methamphetamine and cocaine ring	Massachusetts	Ongoing instrumental enterprises
(1) Murder of multiple rivals	Oregon	Ongoing instrumental enterprises
(1) Cocaine/weapons smuggling ring	Louisiana	Ongoing instrumental enterprises
(1) Five state drug trafficking ring	Massachusetts	Ongoing instrumental enterprises
(1) Drug labs and conspiracy to commit murder	California	Ongoing instrumental enterprises
(1) Drug trafficking and racketeering	Multiple states (11)	Ongoing instrumental enterprises
(7) Extortion	Canada	Ongoing instrumental enterprises
(1) Production and trafficking methamphetamines	Canada	Ongoing instrumental enterprises
(2) Conspiring to murder former members	Australia	Ongoing instrumental enterprises
(1) Illegal drug lab	Australia	Ongoing instrumental enterprises
(1) Stolen property ring	Australia	Ongoing instrumental enterprises
(1) Luxury car theft ring	Canada	Ongoing instrumental enterprises
(2) Possession of drugs for sale	Australia	Ongoing instrumental enterprises
(1) Drug trafficking	Canada	Ongoing instrumental enterprises
(1) Possession of ten marijuana plants	Australia	Ongoing instrumental enterprises
(1) Drug distribution network	Canada	Ongoing instrumental enterprises
(1) Weapons and drugs	Australia	Ongoing instrumental enterprises
(1) Methamphetamine trafficking	Nebraska	Ongoing instrumental enterprises
(3) Premeditated rival murder	California	Planned aggressive acts
(1) Providing explosives	California	Planned aggressive acts
(1) Death of fourteen-year-old boy, rival war	New York	Planned aggressive acts
(1) Murder of rival drug dealer	Washington	Planned aggressive acts
(1) Conspiracy to kill Outlaws rival with explosives	Kentucky	Planned aggressive acts
(1) Murder of rival Rock Machine member	Canada	Planned aggressive acts

(1) Pipe bomb detonation prank	Australia	Planned aggressive acts
(1) Cocaine territory fight	Canada	Planned aggressive acts
(1) Forty-three counts of manslaughter—rival members	Canada	Planned aggressive acts
(2) Murder of five rival members	Canada	Planned aggressive acts
(1) Beating and robbery	New York	Spontaneous expressive acts
(1) Gang rape	Massachusetts	Spontaneous expressive acts
(1) Assaulting an off-duty police officer	Massachusetts	Spontaneous expressive acts
(1) Kidnap, imprisonment, stalking, evading, and drugs	California	Spontaneous expressive acts
(1) Automobile theft	Australia	Short-term instrumental acts
(1) Strong arm debt collection	Canada	Short-term instrumental acts
(1) Murder of two prison guards	Canada	Short-term instrumental acts
(2) Rape	Australia	Short-term instrumental acts
N = 59 criminal articles		

Hells Angels Forever, Easy Rider, Wild Hogs), biker music and musicians (Steppenwolf, ZZ Top, Lynard Skynard, Marshall Tucker, Molly Hatchet, Billy Gordon, .38 Special, the Allman Brothers, Stevie Ray Vaughan, David Allen Coe, Willie Nelson), and numerous documentaries on Arts and Entertainment Network and the Discovery Channel. The movies and documentaries often portray 1 percent bikers as mythic figures rebelling against the norms of society and not criminals and violence prone individuals. The charismatic Hells Angels leader Ralph "Sonny" Barger is a media celebrity and best-selling author. Chuck Zito is also a well-known former Hells Angels chapter president, a former HBO actor, bodyguard to the stars, and best-selling author. There is a darker side to both of the individuals and the Hells Angels. Both men are convicted felons, ex-cons and have histories of violence (see Barker, 2007). In addition, Barger in his autobiography freely admits to being a former cocaine addict and drug seller (Barger et al., 2000). Other Angel autobiographies attest to the criminal and violent nature of the Hells Angels (Barker, 2007).

The continuing controversy surrounding 1 percent motorcycle clubs has been: are they clubs united by a love of biking and brotherhood or gangs predominated by criminals and criminal behavior (see Barker, 2007). The data provided support for the

Table 5. Types of Criminal Activity by Gang

Category	Hells Angels	Outlaws	Bandidos	Pagans	Total
Ongoing instrumental enterprises	23	13	5	4	45
Planned aggressive acts	10	3	4	1	18
Spontaneous expressive acts	4	6	6	1	17
Short-term instrumental acts	4	4	1	0	9

argument that the Big Four Clubs—the Pagans, the Bandidos, the Hell's Angels, and the Outlaws—or chapters of these clubs, often operate as gangs oriented toward criminal profit rather than motorcycle clubs. Utilizing the Koch and Quinn typology of motorcycle club crime, the study found that the most common type of criminal act identified in the newspaper articles was ongoing instrumental acts, with forty-five incidents recorded. These incidents were examples of organized crime. The data also provided evidence of the violent nature of these clubs/gangs. The next most common type of criminal act described in the articles was planned aggressive acts, which had eighteen incidents reported. These acts were violent acts directed at club rivals and often sanctioned by the officers of the clubs. As previous research has shown, motorcycle gangs do not tolerate rivals, either in the form of another club or an individual (Barker, 2007). There were several articles that pertained to clubhouse bombings and drive-by shootings that were for the sole purpose of ridding one club of a rival club.

The outlaw motorcycle culture focuses heavily on brotherhood and time spent in the saloon society milieu. According to Wolf's (1991) seminal study, the club bar was one of the most important and significant aspects of club life. The liberal flow of alcoholic beverages and methamphetamine use results in conflicts of an impulsive nature. The consequences of this motorcycle club trait became evident throughout the content analysis with seventeen incidents considered under the spontaneous expressive acts category, which was the third most common criminal category. Brawling and fighting both appeared quite frequently throughout each set of incidents for all four of the clubs.

The category with the fewest incidents was short-term instrumental acts with nine incidents. These offenses took place in the unique opportunities that occurred for the purpose of financial gain for only one member and not the club as a whole. One of the main reasons that only twelve articles pertained to this category could be a lack of reporting. According to Quinn and Koch (2003), the most common form of short-term criminal act was stolen motorcycles. A stolen motorcycle might not be reported due to the fact that it was stolen and chopped to begin with, causing trouble for the former owner. This crime is often successful because motorcycles are difficult to trace and almost impossible to return to their rightful owners. Some of these crimes are planned and some were simply carried out given the right opportunity. Also effecting the underreporting of short-time instrumental acts is the fact that the victims are often also members of the biker subculture who traditionally do not turn to the police for help.

This study contributed to the literature on outlaw motorcycle gangs and identified the need for further research. Some of the motorcycle clubs that began years ago as a release from strict societal standards have evolved into criminal organizations. Why has this occurred and for which ones? In some, particularly the Big Four, criminal activity, even organized crime, has become the norm rather than the exception. Are the American clubs and the members of the clubs similar to or different from their international brothers? Are other 1 percent biker clubs, nationally and internationally, different from or similar to the Big Four in their criminal activity? These are empirical questions that need research.

References

Auger, M. (2001). The biker who shot me: Recollections of a crime reporter. Toronto, Ontario, Canada: McClelland and Stewart.

Barger, R., Zimmerman, K., & Zimmerman, K. (2000). Hell's Angels: The life and times of Sonny Barger and the Hell's Angel Motorcycle Club. New York: HarperCollins.

Barker, T. (2004). Exporting American organized crime: Outlaw motorcycle gangs. Journal of Gang Research, 11, 37–50.

Barker, T. (2007). Biker gangs as organized crime. Cincinnati, OH: Anderson.

Bowe, B. (1994). Born to be wild. New York: Warner Book.

Charles, G. (2002). Bikers: Legend, legacy and life. London: Independent Music Press.

Delattre, E. J. (1990, May/June). New faces of organized crime. American Enterprise, 38–45.

Detroit, M. (1994). Chain of evidence: A true story of law enforcement and one woman's bravery. New York: Penguin Books.

Dulaney, W. L. (2005, November). A brief history of "outlaw" motorcycle clubs. International Journal of Motorcycle Studies.

Harris, M. (1985). Bikers: Birth of a modern day outlaw. London: Faber and Faber.

Holthouse, D. (2005, Fall). Smashing the shamrock: A massive federal indictment names the senior leadership of America's most frightening prison gang. But will it work? (SPLC Intelligence Rep. 119). Montgomery, AL: Southern Poverty Law Center.

Kaye, H. R. (1970). A place in hell: The inside story of 'Hell's Angels'—the world's wildest outsiders. London: New English Library.

Kingsbury, K. (1995). The snake and the spider. New York: Dell.

Lavigne, Y. (1987). Hell's Angels: Taking care of business. Toronto, Ontario, Canada: Ballantine Books.

Lavigne, Y. (1996). Hells Angels: Into the abyss. Toronto, Ontario, Canada: HarperCollins.

Lavigne, Y. (1999). Hells Angels at war. Toronto, Ontario, Canada: HarperCollins.

Levingston, T. G., Zimmerman, K., & Zimmerman, K. (2003). Soul on bikes: The East Bay Dragons MC and the Black Biker set. St. Paul, MN: MBI.

Lowe, M. (1988). Conspiracy of brothers. Toronto, Ontario, Canada: HarperCollins.

Mandelkau, J. (1971). Buttons: The making of a president. London: Sphere Books.

Martineau, P. (2003). I was a killer for the Hells Angels: The true story of Serge Quesnel. Toronto, Ontario, Canada: McClelland and Stewart.

Mayson, B., & Marco, T. (1982). Fallen Angel: Hell's Angel to heaven's saint. Garden City, NY: Doubleday.

Mello, M. (2001). The wrong man: A true story of innocence on death row. Minneapolis: University of Minnesota Press.

Paradis, P. (2002). Nasty business: One biker gang's war against the Hell's Angels. Toronto, Ontario, Canada: HarperCollins.

Quinn, J. F. (2001). Angels, Bandidos, Outlaws, and Pagans: The evolution of organized crime among the Big Four 1% motorcycle clubs. Deviant Behavior, 22, 379–390.

Quinn, J., & Koch, D. S. (2003). The nature of criminality within one-percent motorcycle clubs. Deviant Behavior, 24, 281–305.

Reynolds, F. (1967). Freewheelin Frank: Secretary of the Angels. New York: Grove Press.

Reynolds, T. (2000). Wild ride: How outlaw motorcycle myth conquered America. New York: TV Books.

Roslin, A. (2002, June 18). Quebec biker war: A Hells Angel chieftain named "mom" stands accused of running a $1 billion drug empire. High Times Magazine, 1–3.

Sher, J., & Marsden, W. (2003). The road to hell: How the biker gangs are conquering Canada. Toronto, Ontario, Canada: Alfred Knopf.

Sher, J., & Marsden, W. (2006). Angels of death: Inside the biker gangs' crime empire. New York: Carroll and Graf.

Simpson, L., & Harvey, S. (2001). Brothers in arms: The inside story of two bikie gangs. Crows Nest, New South Wales, Australia: Allen and Unwin.

Thompson, H. S. (1966). Hell's Angels: The strange and terrible saga of the outlaw motorcycle gangs. New York: Ballantine Books.

Veno, A. (2003). The brotherhoods: Inside the outlaw motorcycle clubs. Crows Nest, New South Wales, Australia: Allen and Unwin.

Wethern, G., & Colnett, V. (1978). A wayward Angel. New York: Richard Marek.

Winterhalder, E. (2005). Out in bad standing: Inside the Bandidos Motorcycle Club—The making of a worldwide dynasty. Owasso, OK: Blockhead Press.

Wolf, D. R. (1991). The rebels: A brotherhood of outlaw bikers. Toronto, Ontario, Canada: University of Toronto Press.

Zito, C., & Layden, J. (2002). Street justice. New York: St. Martin's Press.

Reading 2.
Coordinated Chaos: The Psychology and Structure of Organized Crime among One Percent Bikers

James F. Quinn & Craig J. Forsyth

Introduction

One percent (aka "outlaw") motorcycle clubs consist of men who "cannot or will not fit in to mainstream society, are alienated enough to exalt in the outlaw status the symbol infers, and fearless enough to defend that status against all challenges" (Quinn, 1987: 47). Law enforcement and political leaders on three continents have labeled them a serious form of organized crime (e.g., Davis, 1982 a, b; Barker, 2007; Veno & van den Eynde, 2007) that could pose a threat to national security (Royal Canadian Mounted Police [RCMP], 1999). This oversimplifies the structure and psychology of these complex and increasingly heterogeneous groups and, at least in Canada and Australia, exaggerates the power of these groups. We prefer a more nuanced view of criminality in these clubs framed by the interaction of gang-like "purism" and rational, corporate entrepreneurialism. We also incorporate the psychological dynamics that shape one-percenter behavior. Our goal is to examine the role of criminality in their internal structure and the impact of club structure on biker crime from the perspective of the subculture's members. It must be noted, however, that our discussion does not apply to all one percenters—some are law abiding tradesmen or business owners with limited awareness of their brothers' illicit profiteering.

One-percenters are a distinct subculture, but their individual and collective behavior is becoming less unique as clubs move from counter cultural gangs to a more rational subculture. (Countercultures cannot survive long without transforming into subcultures by moving their normative base closer to the surrounding society's norms, though often in caricatured form [Yinger, 1982].) Hedonistic purism and an unrelenting proclivity for violence remain core features of the subculture and are crucial to the intimidating power of its reputation (Quinn & Forsyth, 2007). All club members are drawn into internecine conflicts even if they avoid criminal profiteering. The use of violence was reflexive up through the 1980s; it is now questioned only on practical grounds—is this right time and place for its application, and if so, what venue and level of violence best suits the group's goals? Opportunistic and vengeful acts remain thematic; as Sonny Barger notes bikers love a fistfight. (2000). Nonetheless, "smartness" (Miller, 1958) increasingly wins out over impulsiveness in modern clubs. The economics of the subculture have come a long way from its early reliance on motorcycle thefts, small drug deals and prostitution by female companions. Their proclivity for trying to kill one another in events rooted in gang rivalry is actually where the club itself most clearly a party to criminal conspiracies but the majority of legal and scholarly attention is paid to their profiteering rackets.

Historical Background: Criminal Profits and Changing Biker Values

Immersion in criminal and marginally legal activities is a general characteristic of life in the saloon society milieu. Bikers are simply more extreme in their tactics and solidarity because their clubs provide them with the motives and capability for large sophisticated operations that are not readily available to most milieu denizens. These enterprises diverge from the subculture's original gang-like goals, but flow from the bikers' insatiable appetite for power. This adaptation to the threats posed by the mainstream during the formative and expansion phases of the subculture, roughly 1960 to 1975 (Quinn, 2001) helped form the modal organizational structure of the modern one percent club.

Early biker crimes were generally impulsive acts ranging from opportunistic thefts and spontaneous brawls to rapes and killings. Early clubs had few resources and little experience in dealing with the legal system but these prosecutions posed little threat to the existence of the clubs themselves. When avoidance and intimidation failed, thee bikers' siege mentality defined the threat as one directed at their very survival Quinn & Forsyth, 2011). The imagery of the misunderstood rebel that runs through much mainstream media was a poor salve for this fear, but little else was readily available. The fact that many "victims" grossly exaggerated their case against the bikers added to the one-percenter's sense of self-righteousness and victimization (Thompson, 1966).

After 1965, expansionist warfare among the larger clubs redirected the focus of one-percenter crimes from opportunistic acts of subsistence to operations guarded with wealth and paranoia (Quinn & Forsyth, 2011). The small time hustles typical of early one percenters were insufficient supplements to members' blue collar earnings once clubs had to support large scale, long term inter-group conflicts. The addictive qualities of wealth (Berry, 2002; Slater, 1983) unduly influenced some bikers as the subculture draws the great majority of its members from the lower middle class. The one-percenters' war mentality merged with greed and self-preservation to justify the absolute ruthlessness of their current power seeking.

The few statistics specifically describing one-percenters support the assertion that these clubs are composed of violent felons. An RCMP (2002) study of 73 high ranking HAMC members from 13 California chapters found that the average biker's criminal career lasted 15 years and included 10 major arrests. These figures refer only to the Hells Angels, but other clubs are similar if less extreme in this regard. Danner and Silverman (1986) underscore that idea that felonious violence is so endemic among these bikers that it statistically distinguishes one-percenters from other state prison inmates. In 1999, RCMP asserted that 83% of the known Canadian HA members had a criminal record, with over half of their convictions involving drugs, violence and weapons (RCMP, 1999). However, these statistics are dated and reflect only secondary data from law enforcement.

Alain's Quebec data suggest that as one-percent clubs started to become more entrepreneurial, drug arrests began to outstrip those for theft and violence. The odds of a 1%er being arrested and convicted rose from 22% in the early 1970s, to almost 1 in 3 by the late 1980s. He also asserts that, "biker criminality.... [was] not as violent or as organized and severe as the common view ... would lead us to believe" (Alain, 1993). These data were collected before the Hell's Angels and Bandidos absorbed the major Canadian clubs and made satellites of the rest, but capture vital truths about the origins of these clubs. Most crucial for understanding the relationship of organized crime to one percent clubs is the manner in which they are organized.

Modern one-percent clubs developed from a set of near-groups (Yablonski, 1973) operating largely confined to saloon society to an increasingly powerful underworld force. In the case of the one-percenters, that transformation was from raucous hedonism supported by homo-social camaraderie to a quest for control in their milieu by any means necessary. The older norms were not entirely lost, but often seem buried under the new ones. This evolution resulted from internecine warfare and the value changes it brought about within the subculture, but entailed the co-optation of some mainstream beliefs. Mainstream conflation of power, success and virtue was easily absorbed as the subculture consolidated into a few powerful clubs. The clubs quickly reached the pinnacle of power in saloon society, and became a hegemonic force in the underworld in some areas (Humphreys, 2001). Power, loyalty and respect are the overriding virtues of the subculture and milieu, but their meaning has been altered by the changing belief systems of the mainstream and subculture. Though fleeting, these values provide the only sense of safety available in the milieu.

Accommodation with the mainstream must be sought by any social form, if it is to survive (Yinger, 1982). For one-percenters, this means adopting an approach to legal issues similar to that of many corporations and political groups in that they hire top criminal attorneys to utilize all possible methods to use the legal system to their advantage. Their relations with the justice system are entirely adversarial and guided by the same ethos as their inter-club warfare (RCMP, 2000). This grew out of the realization that law enforcement would never leave them alone in their original milieu.

The imagery of the original bikers was both threatening and offensive to the mainstream and especially to the conservative mores of control agents. The basis of biker power shifted from fists and engines to sophisticated weapons and high tech security measures but their iconography and values have changed little. Acquiring power is seen as the best method of assuring respect by one-percenters. Success is respected as indicative of power, regardless of how it is obtained. Privacy is honored out of respect for underworld norms, as well as the need to keep information about various crimes and conspiracies compartmentalized in cliques.

Compartmentalization of information on criminal activities increased with the number and complexity of enterprises, motivated largely by fear of betrayal. Pressures to remain active within and loyal to the group increased as one-percenters became more sophisticated in organizing criminal activities within and beyond the club's formal parameters. Retirement from club life, once a privilege earned by years of service, became virtually impossible—membership is now theoretically for life or until the club decides to "pull the patch" of a member. This shift in ideology and practice attracted a new breed of men to club life, some of whom are willing to become informants if faced with serious charges. As the number of such betrayals grew, so also did willingness to invade members' privacy and insult their honor by investigating prospective and current members. These internal security measures alienate purists and accelerate the drift to entrepreneurial dominance. So also does the fact that impulse driven purists are much easier targets for arrest and prosecution than are rational entrepreneurs.

Clubs have adjusted their membership standards to eliminate those who they feel might later betray them (Alain, 1995; Queen, 2005). Betrayal generally means turning informant, but increasing concern with theft is an issue in some clubs as chapter treasuries grow. Thus, bikers are increasingly concerned with the accountability of the major players the club. Lavigne (1987) asserts that the fear created by this sort of internal security is instrumental in keeping club members and associates under control. He also feels it will be the critical factor in the eventual demise of the most powerful clubs. Lavigne's perspective is based heavily on events in "expansion franchises" in eastern Canada, especially the massacre of the HAMC "North Chapter" in 1985. The killings of most of the members of the Laval, Quebec chapter (located near Montreal) was motivated by their ostentatious lifestyle, refusal to account for profits in enterprises they operated jointly with the Montreal and Sherbrooke chapters, and interpersonal factors (Rubinstein, 2002).

Though commonly accepted by law enforcement (e.g., Southeast Connecticut Crime group, 2005), Lavigne's view fails to account for the depth of the internecine struggles between these clubs, nor does it take fully into account the strong camaraderie that unites many chapters and clubs. Nonetheless, informants and thieves are sometimes tortured to make sure the club knows all that they have revealed prior to killing them.

Three Dutch HAMC Nomads believed to have stolen millions, for example, were tortured before being killed by their brothers (Expactica News, 2004a, b).

The Savagery of Biker Violence

Just as pleasure is a powerful individual motivator, bikers focus on inflicting pain and death when angered. Club bikers spend much of their lives in each other's company and live by norms of hypermasculine competitiveness which provides great impetus for incredible savagery to develop. Savagery serves them well in dealing with other underworld players; they are one of the few American groups that can deal with Colombian and Mexican gangsters. When one-percenters feel betrayed, plans for annihilative vengeance are always laid, though sometimes in a delayed manner. Bikers also learn quickly from their mistakes: prosecutions and defeats almost always lead to new methods to protect the club from a recurrence.

Like other criminal groups, bikers know that their sanctions must be far more severe than those of the legal system to deter members from turning state's evidence when arrested. For example, as law enforcement began to penetrate one percent clubs in the 1970s and 1980s, probationary periods were lengthened and full background investigations of prospective members were initiated. The quality of intra-club savagery also increased noticeably as torture replaced a bullet to the brain. RICO and similar laws encouraged the creation of satellite clubs to more screen potential members. Concomitant subcultural pressures also encouraged the use of satellite clubs to test the feasibility of territorial expansion.

Many bikers study crime and police methods, and a few are interested in sadism and torture. This combines with their experience of past injuries to create a wealth of beliefs about torture and body disposal methods. These ideas multiply and spread in the isolated but intense and competitive atmosphere of club life. The savage lethality of the violence rises in proportion to the amount of money involved. Because the HAMC is the wealthiest of all one-percent clubs, such behavior would be expected to be most frequent within that club.

Modern Biker Criminality

Most one-percenters are immersed in multiple forms of criminality, and none can reasonably claim to be entirely unaware of the criminality within their clubs. However, many of the larger clubs increasingly favor members without criminal records in order to avoid police attention and improve their public image (Lavigne, 2000). The drift away from purism has also led to increasing reliance on legitimate sources of income and power. Lavigne, a vehement biker antagonist with a particular dislike for the Hells Angels Motorcycle Club (HAMC), admits that:

> "(n)ot all Hells Angels are rapists, drug traffickers and murderers. Many enjoy motorcycling and club camaraderie. They also run legitimate businesses" (Lavigne, 1987 p.108).

Extremes of violence and hedonism nonetheless remain hallmarks of subcultural behavior despite the shifting bases and demographics.

Multiple Hierarchies: The Overlap of Informal and Formal Power

Although details vary, the formal structure of a one-percent motorcycle club is similar to that of many conventional organizations; e.g., geographic tiers of organizational power, fairly standard offices. Each club has evolved a certain redundancy for key functions, such as dispute resolution, across their geographic divisions (i.e., local, regional, national/international). This formal hierarchy is generously supplemented with constantly shifting informal channels that keep each club's power structure dynamic. This combination of formal and informal power evolved to manage the contentious personalities that compose these clubs, while providing some insulation for the club itself.

While these groups are hierarchically organized, they do not have a unified chain of command. Power, the core subcultural value (Quinn & Forsyth, 2007), shifts along various dimensions and structures with each situation. It is thus more accurate to refer to the "hierarchies" of a club rather than a single "hierarchy." The roles and duties of club and regional officers are loosely defined, often overlap and shift with the situation and personalities involved. Nomads, nationals, and other elites have many internal control functions that seem duplicative when described formally. However, those functions mesh fairly well as specific personalities are chosen (or chose) to deal with various situations in different locations. Likewise, each club's dominant or mother chapter takes an active role in creating new chapters and coordinating inter-club warfare. These responsibilities are usually delegated to specially assigned members.

For example, the National Chapter and officers have exclusive power to grant and rescind "charters" for the club and determine internal discipline but the regional Nomads and/or state officers are the eyes and ears through which they generally operate. This variability is evident in two well-known Canadian cleansings or massacres. The 1985 massacre of the "North chapter" by the Quebec Angels upset, but did not alienate, the national leadership which was only informed after the killings had occurred (Lavigne, 1996; RCMP, 1999; 2002). The provincial leadership exercised what it saw as its prerogative over a rebellious subordinate group.

A more complex set of dynamics, involving both personalities and intraclub power struggles, led to the 2006 execution of eight Bandidos in Shedden, Ontario. The main conspirator in the Shedden case was not a particularly influential Bandido but was reputedly told to "Take care of it" when he complained to the club's international president about the Ontario chapter's behavior. Correcting a problem is a far cry from executing its source in cold blood but the (intentionally?) vague remark left the details of how to resolve the conflict to the people closest to the situation with the greatest concern about its resolution. The massacre could thus be defined as a response to the president's command while the president said that he meant only to bring about operational changes among the Canadian chapters. This mix of formal and informal power is found in other types of organizations, but has been finely tuned by the personalities of the one-percent subculture and the legal pressures it constantly faces. Informal structures encouraged these massacres while formal ones allowed the club to repudiate them with complete sincerity.

While national and regional officers technically out rank chapter leaders, few will publicly challenge an officer in a major chapter, especially while on his territory. This deference is rooted in a sense of concern for the club's welfare and sprang from the one-percenters' obsession with power. It is just one manifestation of the solidarity that motivates many one-percenters to choose beatings, imprisonment, and death over actions that might injure the club and their brethren. Like any value, this can be twisted to justify a wide variety of actions. This flexibility in values and power arrangements is required by the raucous nature of one-percenters and co-exists with their willingness to kill their fellow club members.

Internal killings are rarely if ever sanctioned by the club's uppermost levels unless the member is believed to have betrayed the club by cooperating with police or rivals. Most internal violence is organized by chapter or regional members guided by local concerns that are as much personal as club-related and demonstrate the retention of power at the local and regional levels as well as the propensity of cliques to act with little or no authorization from the club's hierarchy.

A shifting set of alliances and antagonisms among key personalities in each club and region determines how the group's organizational tiers interact at a particular place and time. The same principle holds for interclub relationships. The subculture numbers only a few thousand men nationally, so bikers from rival clubs often know one another personally which increases the emotional intensity of internecine wars. This loose, shifting and inconsistent maze of vertical and horizontal linkages within and beyond each club can perplex even members and is virtually inscrutable to outsiders. These linkages also function to keep illicit enterprises under the control of, yet partially independent of, the formal structure of the club.

This distribution of power frees members from many rational constraints while retaining a rational structure that partially supersedes personalities. It is a product of the fiercely independent men who have earned the one-percent diamond. Ironically, it seems to have some commonalities with social control mechanisms common to many large conventional organizations (i.e., office politics). Personal loyalties supplement those attached to the club as many leaders demand unwavering obedience, creating a paradox in these militaristic organizations composed of the most rebellious men in western civilization.

Bikers want to see their clubs as ruthlessly efficient paramilitary organizations and are likely to portray them in that manner, especially when it serves their interests in either asserting their own power or excusing their actions with a "Nuremberg defense." Thus law enforcement has acquired an image of the internal processes of these clubs that emphasizes their rationality and neglects their often fragmented decision making and poorly enforced discipline.

A member's status and official duties, along with his informal ties within and beyond the club, figure into a subjective calculus that determines his authority in a particular situation. So does his presence or absence when a decision is made. Club operations leave much to the interpretation and instincts of those "on the ground" when events unfold.

National and regional leaders are unlikely to second guess decisions taken at the local level unless the consequences are expected to be of great and far reaching magnitude.

Personal networks within and beyond the club facilitate the ascendancy of the most powerful men in each club as well as their criminal enterprises. The relationships between these men and their criminal activities are closely intertwined. Each region and club operates under a dynamic maze of formal power relationships that is balanced by informal, interpersonal ones. Any change in the personalities involved in a situation rearranges the balance of power within and across both the chapter and the enterprises of its members. There thus remain strong charismatic elements in the operation of one-percent clubs despite their drift to rational organization. Subculture participation must envelop one's life if one is to survive in club life.

Most critically, cliques, chapters and the club itself may have divergent interests in some situations, leading to internal power struggles. Thus a biker trying to build an illegal operation may undermine the efforts of others by underpricing products, manipulating suppliers or spreading gossip about competitors. He may also lure others (especially valuable non-members such as probationary members and valued associates) into his organization just to deprive a rival of their services. This benefits him and his clique but can undermine the club.

The Nature of One-Percenter Crime

The types of crimes committed by one-percenters are not especially unique, but the intimidating bravado they bring to these acts is distinctive: murder, rape, drug manufacture and distribution, prostitution/white slavery, weapons trafficking, extortion-protection, burglary, arson, loan sharking, theft/stolen property trafficking, and forgery are common rackets (Haut, 1999). Other police sources add biker explorations of insurance and stock frauds, pornography, (RCMP 1999, 2002), money laundering, and illicit internet gambling (Nathanson Center, 2001). These crimes are motivated by greed and readily understood by the public and law enforcement.

The drift toward entrepreneurialism transformed once recreational activities or private "hustles" into businesses as the need for wealth grows. The activities of the club as a formal organization and those of its members, as individuals or cliques, are often blurred by the extreme integration of club and personal lives that is typical of the subculture (Quinn & Forsyth, 2007). The justice system and media focus mainly upon the criminal syndicates that operate within clubs (Barker, 2005; Barker & Human, 2009) but it is in the area of inter club violence that the formal organization of the club is most directly involved. These acts make little sense outside of a gang-dominated milieu but are critical to retaining group honor. Most violence is planned to avoid mainstream attention but two public clashes between rivals 2002 illustrate the variability of club involvement in these dynamics. Like both of these events, most inter-club violence is face-to-face and employs guns, knives, clubs, boots and fists.

The Pagan's were infuriated when several members surrendered their colors to the Hells' Angels in exchange for membership in the rival club. The HAMC added insult to injury by choosing a Long Island venue for the HellRaisers' Ball, their annual tattoo and bike show. (Years of relative peace between the clubs in the NYC area were premised on Pagan dominance of Long Island countered by Angel control of Manhattan.) A specially assigned group studied the site and planned a strike against the event. Shortly thereafter, 10 vanloads of Pagans stormed the HellRaisers' Ball in an effort to retrieve the colors and/or exact vengeance. One biker was killed and 10 were injured in the melee which sent 73 Pagans from across the eastern seaboard to federal prison (Eltman, 2002a, b).

Also in 2002, a clique of Hells' Angels were offended when their arch-rivals, the Mongols, choose to party at Harrah's Resort in Laughlin, NV which had traditionally been used by the Angels during the River Run (a large motorcycling event that draws all variety of motorcycle enthusiasts). After garnering the support of other club members, they attacked the Mongols in the hotel bar in the wee hours of the morning when few "citizens" would be encountered. Forty two Angels and eight Mongols were indicted for the brawl that left two Angels and one Mongol dead (Rittman, 2006).

Acts of this nature are as typical of "organized crime" among bikers as the more frequently prosecuted profiteering operations. The Laughlin and Long Island fracases were unique mainly in their magnitude and public setting. More typical raids would have focused on bars, (now well fortified) clubhouses, and gathering points such as parking lots and most escape the attention of authorities and the media. The variability of formal club involvement degree in these two incidents illustrates that seen in all varieties of organized biker crime. The Pagan attack was officially mandated while the Laughlin melee displeased the upper echelons of the HAMC. These magnitude of these events fail, however, are understated compared with recklessness of the Bandidos/Rock Machine/Alliance's and the Hells Angels' use of explosives in Quebec which outraged Canada in the 1990s (Rubenstein, 2002; Sher & Marsden, 2003; Winterhalder 2005). In the last decade, however, little more than Molotov cocktails have been evident in biker warfare. The extremity of mainstream responses seems to have taught the subculture more care in avoiding "collateral casualties" because they generate restrictive laws and make it hard for illicit enterprises to flourish.

Biker Lifestyle and Profiteering

Most one-percenter criminal operations (e.g., control of bars) develop out of one type of crime (e.g., prostitution) and proliferate into a second (e.g., extortion) and third (e.g., drug sales) in a fluidly integrated manner that derives from their lifestyle (Quinn & Forsyth, 2007). Biker entry into various aspects of the sex industry is typical of this progression, in that it grew out of their penchant for strip clubs. (In the early days of the subculture, many biker women were sex workers [Quinn, 1987].) These enterprises often grow to include extortion of bars, employees, and patrons, as well as efforts to gather intelligence on police and rivals. Intimidation is implicit in most of their dealings with outsiders; the subculture's reputation for ruthlessness is a well-established tool that most wield with great skill.

The hallmark of the one-percent subculture is the manner in which bikers integrate crime and club duties with their private lives. Common one-percenter practices constitute a plethora of drug, alcohol and weapons offenses although the rate of alcoholism

	Impulsive	Premeditated
Expressive	Bar fights, domestic violence	Gangs wars, vengeance (response to insults against club)
Instrumental	Opportunistic thefts, drug sales, some extortion (especially of bars)	Sex, drug, theft rings, white collar crimes

and illegal drug use has declined as entrepreneurial values become more dominant. The scale of these more or less traditional rackets has expanded exponentially in the last quarter century, taking the subculture from a set of gangs to a constellation of activities many of which are felonious (Quinn, 2001; Quinn & Forsyth, 2007). However, focus on these criminal operations distorts the reality of crime within clubs and especially the role of the club in organizing that crime.

A Typology of One-Percenter Crime

Criminology has long recognized a division between expressive crimes driven mainly by emotion, and instrumental acts, which have practical, usually monetary, goals (Fesbac, 1969). Opportunistic acts take advantage of specific, often fleeting circumstances, such as serendipitous contact with a gun or drug supplier, or knowledge of a potential extortion victim's vulnerability.

Although its import has waned, spontaneity remains an important value among one-percent bikers but its manifestation varies across both clubs and individuals. Members of modern club members avoid impulsive crimes against non-bikers but will reflexively defend themselves, their brothers and their bikes from any perceived threat. Impulsivity, especially in defense of honor and power, is still tolerated to a large extent so long as it does not bring trouble to the group (e.g. Laughlin). In purist-leaning groups such as the Mongols, Outlaw and Pagans, some degree of impulsivity remains normative, respected and reinforced (Queen, 2005). Premeditated crimes include much gang warfare (e.g., HellRaisers' Ball) as well as typical criminal rackets. Thus a four part typology of biker crimes based on fundamental motivation (expressive or instrumental) and forethought is needed to delineate the nature of biker crime (Quinn & Koch, 2003).

These types are best conceptualized as continua of motivational and forethought dimensions. The subculture was originally associated mainly with expressive-impulsive acts which were easily sensationalized by the media. The modern media, due to its reliance on police sources, has come to emphasize the premeditated-instrumental aspects of club criminality. Obtaining interpretable data for quantitative comparisons of biker crimes across these dimensions is all but impossible. Expressive-impulsive acts are heavily obscured by saloon society's code of silence while organized criminal activity attracts the most law enforcement attention. Media and police reports routinely emphasize premeditated, instrumental criminality and the most outrageous examples of expressive violence while ignoring the mundane realities of these clubs. Veno and van den Eynde (2007) cogently describe the exaggeration of the bike threat to (Australian) society by police, media and politicians as a moral panic.

One-percenters are so skilled, ruthless and generally well-armed that a violent encounter with one can easily turn lethal. Further, they usually move about in small groups and follow an ethos of annihilative vengeance—All on one, one on all—meaning that companions never stand back and let a brother fight alone. In the event that a biker should lose a fight, revenge is requisite and premeditated violence will follow. This norm of annihilative retaliation explains much of the chronic hatred between certain clubs, but is also applied to individuals, especially within saloon society (Davis, 1982). Stealth and bravado are equally acceptable tactics in these situations which are unlikely to receive police attention unless a death results. As one-percenters become more involved in organized crime, the retaliatory norm adds to the power of the one percent image and underlies much of the subculture's most notorious acts.

Biker crimes very rarely involve entirely law abiding citizens. Bikers' instrumental crimes tend to be "silent" offenses, such as drug dealing and prostitution along with extortion of people operating in the margins of the law (Smith 2002). Indeed, Ontario's first use of organized crime laws for one percenters involved just such a case (Tyler, 2011). One-percenters have little direct contact with law-abiding mainstream citizens; one percent status is partly defined by a strong desire to live apart from the mainstream. Encounters do occur, however, such as when local residents stumble on a biker's illicit activities (e.g. marijuana field) (Davis 1982a, b; CISC, 1998, 1999). The reflexive response to such an interruption is intimidation, but many are discerning enough to co-opt citizens with generosity.

These clubs harbor a large number of organized criminal conspiracies alongside legitimate businesses. Both types of endeavors range from local to global in scope. The distinction between the endeavors of members and those of the club as a corporate entity is often difficult to delineate, but is as complete as any can be among one percenters.

Organized Crime and Organized Criminals

The critical question is the degree to which the club, rather than its individual members and their informal cliques, create and control these criminal events and enterprises. The internal processes that guide their decisions are unique to each event or enterprise, and the import of formal club guidance varies widely across situations. Alain (1993) notes that "crimes are activities of individuals, not of the group as a whole" (p. 56). While executives are often prosecuted for white collar crimes, their corporations are indicted far less. Perhaps because of their countercultural bases, one percent clubs are less often granted the same presumption of innocence. Saloon society norms discourage even curiosity about the activities of others (Queen, 2005), so it is often reasonable to presume that a biker's brothers are unaware of his crimes.

Chapter autonomy assures diversity in the types of crimes perpetrated, club loyalty provides an international network of well-vetted men, and multiple hierarchies give group assets a modicum of legal insulation. Each of these factors supports the diversification of crime within and across chapters. Some chapters of major clubs are increasingly identified with one or a few on-going enterprises (RCMP, 1999) but club dynamics also encourage legitimate enterprises. Members' wealth enriches the group thru dues, fee and shared personal resources.

One percent clubs are a unique social form that are organized and operate in a manner all-together different from most criminal organizations. A well-established La Cosa Nostra created fraternal organizations an effort to legitimate their public image. Conversely, bikers formed fraternal organizations in the 1950s and '60s that grew into social networks favoring certain types of felons and capable of planning at the international level. Traditional forms of organized crime rely on family or ethnic ties to assure members loyalties, while one-percent clubs use common interests, such as motorcycling, and experiences (e.g., club warfare, parties) to unite members. Mobsters use crime as a means of upward mobility into the mainstream society. Bikers revel in their status as outlaws.

The social insulation and emotional intensity of the experience provided by the club further bonds them to the group, which tacitly supports their illegal efforts. Each one-percent club is thus more a perpetually shifting set of cliques or "confederation of criminals" (RCMP 1999), than the directive power behind the actual enterprises.

Organizational Concerns in One-Percenter Criminal Enterprises

While the club provides technical, reputational and logistical support for members' enterprises, albeit in a generally indirect manner, the privileges of membership require complete immersion in group life and are financially costly. Dues, criminal defense funds, various special "one-time" fees, and intelligence gathering fees enrich the clubs (Clawson, 1983). Many also pay salaries or stipends to chapter and regional officers. In exchange, the club tries to assure its members local hegemony by supporting them without question in conflicts with both saloon society competitors and law enforcement (RCMP, 1999). As the costs of membership rise, so does the probability that bikers are successful entrepreneurs working on both sides of the law.

> "(M)embers call on other members for protection when their individual rackets are threatened, but they operate their businesses as individuals. Payments into a common treasury are not percentages of profits or tribute to the leader/godfather but rather are made to sustain group activities and to hire lawyers and bribe regulators" (Beare & Naylor, 1999).

The larger the network, the greater the territory, power and profits that can be derived from members' enterprises. Thus the imposition of fees can vary widely when imposed by regional leadership (e.g., Hells Angels' Canadian fees are reputedly greater than those in the U.S.). Along with some national fees, this is equivalent to taxation: leaders set expectations for members, support their efforts and then assure that the chapter and club treasuries remain healthy. Clubs, however, see the practice as a "quality control" mechanism that assures that all chapters contribute more or less equally to the club while all members meet its standards.

The relationship is reciprocal, with members of large clubs and powerful chapters being able to build, support and defend expansive enterprises. Furthermore, large networks allow better recruiting of new members and extended capabilities for interclub warfare. Nonetheless, the most basic unit of a motorcycle club is the local chapter, where most routine decisions and criminal activity occur. Threats posed by police, rivals, and other underworld competitors force club bikers' decision-making to handle multiple layers of concern. Rivals, the police and the club's hierarchies must be taken into account as crime, recreation or revenge is considered. The interests of partners within or beyond the club must also be noted, especially when one or a few criminal networks are frequently involved in enterprise. Links to traditional mobsters, foreign drug traffickers, and similar groups are the most sensitive of these, because they are among the few underworld entities that can resist biker domination.

Depending on the scale and complexity of the operation, officers (i.e., chapter, state, national, or nomad) may have some awareness of what members are doing, but in many cases avoid direct participation (McGuire, 1986a, b). This assures that the enterprises will contribute to the club while avoiding direct club involvement in the racket. Control of a few critical enterprises may loosely follow the club's command structure (Davis, 1982a; 1982b) especially when an officer or Nomad links a number of smaller operations (e.g., methamphetamine production & distribution) into a single entity. In a few cases, an operation is considered so important it is co-opted or at least partially guided by the club hierarchy. This may be due to the operation's inherent value to the club (e.g., weapons smuggling), the people involved (e.g., organized crime groups), or the geographic spread and logistical complexity (e.g., drug distribution) of the enterprise.

Clubs generally try to keep some distance between their organizational structure and their members' enterprises. Club leaders and formal structure are fairly well-known in the subculture and among police, but enterprises operate more or less as sets of isolated cells, linked only by a few key figures. This sort of insulated, cellular structure, in combination with the one-percenters' penchant for reckless violence, has earned them comparison with terrorist groups (Queen, 2005).

Clubs have, however, taken an increasing role in setting the prices of drugs that are widely manufactured and distributed by their members in order to minimize internal competition and friction. Methamphetamine is the most commonly regulated, but the price of cocaine, marijuana, and other drugs may also be set by leaders, usually at the regional level. Prostitution is similarly regulated in some metropolitan areas, based on the attractiveness of the women and the businesses in which they work. This sort of control helps assure good relations with other organized crime groups, but is primarily intended to reduce intra-club competition. Leaders may also mediate conflicts between distribution rings with then goal of preventing interpersonal animosities rather than controlling the enterprises, often leaving their culpability uncertain.

Club-Enterprise Interactions

By providing the networks that underlie members' businesses, rather than operating them, the bikers' hyper-masculine independence is sated, while then club retains some ignorance of the criminality of its members. The HAMC has the most tightly structured organization in this respect (Davis 1982b; CISC, 1998, 1999). While their entrepreneurial activities are largely controlled by individuals or small groups, cliques use the club's organizational sophistication and internal cohesion to limit rivals' growth and power while expanding their own. Thus, when threatened by competitors, offenses against a full patch member are insults to the group that require vengeance. Regardless of its perpetrator's motivation, any offense to a full patch biker is an offense against his club. To oppose a one-percenter in his private criminal behavior is to risk the wrath of his brothers.

Large modern M.C.'s are composed of intelligent sensation seekers bent on acquiring and enjoying power. Like many offenders, bikers are easily bored and tend to move from one activity to another. They seek adventure and novelty while being susceptible to boredom, and quite uninhibited in expressing themselves. These traits seriously limit the breadth and longevity of many enterprises. Members are largely on their own in running enterprises, so long as they obey club rules and do not cause too many problems. Enterprises tend to rise and fall as their participants unite, feud, and recombine in different forms with different foci over time. For example, a few bikers may import and distribute drugs for a time before tensions arise over the equality of profits and risks. One or two may withdraw from that operation to start a new venture focused on a different product, bringing others not involved in the first operation, into the new one. Alternatively, a key man in an operation may be jailed or killed, rendering the operation less profitable, or risky enough to warrant its dissolution in favor of a wholly new one.

The point is that only some operations are long-standing: most exist briefly in a specific form before shifting in focus and/or participants. Some are intermittent, serving mainly to finance a member's activities for a period of months. A "cooker" may thus manufacture drugs for a few weeks and then live off the proceeds while devoting himself to "club business" before returning to manufacture more drugs. Tracking such ephemeral patterns is difficult, even for subcultural insiders and few principles can be identified to predict them. A biker's collegiality and other personal traits, as well as the internal financial and "political" framework of the operation, are the main determinants of one percenters' activity patterns. They constantly weigh the various assets and liabilities of each situation with regard to police, rivals, and partners as well as personal gain and pleasure. The politics of the club and chapter must also be figured into this calculus, just as corporations must consider the responses of shareholders, customers, staff, competitors, and regulators. Any error in these calculations can result in consequences for the biker, his partners and even the chapter (Rubenstein, 2002).

The complexity of these issues makes it all but impossible to impose a linear hierarchy on bikers' activities. This is perhaps the most fundamental way in which these clubs differ from older criminal groups of comparable size. They are capable of acting in a highly concerted and disciplined manner, but it is instinctive to do so only as a gang in situations that threaten the group, its honor or its power. While one percenters have many conflicts among themselves, these animosities usually disappear the moment an external threat is perceived. Efforts to place one-percent clubs under a unified chain of command are usually attributable to an especially charismatic and power-hungry leader and are rarely retained because such leaders rapidly become targets for police and rivals while threatening members' autonomy. Likewise, enduring unity across these clubs is unfeasible for the same reason as well as the embittering experiences and traditions of inter-gang hatred.

Where purist sentiments remain strong, most criminal operations are one or two-shot endeavors, not designed for permanence. Conflicts among bikers, and between them and other underworld actors, are so common that long term investment in any single racket is unfeasible. A particular biker often brings specific skills or contacts to an operation, such as the ability to "cook" methamphetamine well, or a trusted contact within an ethnic drug cartel. The vagaries of his personal life (e.g., interpersonal tensions, more tempting opportunities, imprisonment) may discourage him from continuing the operation for a while, especially after sufficient profits have been earned. Thus, he can shut the operation down and do something else, or live on his earnings until he wants or needs to create another opportunity. The creation and dissolution of illegal enterprises within a one-percent club thus follows the social networks, needs and whims of the men involved (i.e., Personalities are often prioritized over profits.). The umbrella of club membership is more a context than a commanding influence on these enterprises. To bikers it is perfectly natural that their involvements in criminal enterprises include various combinations of their brothers or associates and are no more or less dependent on their membership than any other aspect of their lives.

Conclusions

As one percent clubs evolved from a purist gang ethos to a more entrepreneurial model, their crimes became more organized, lethal and profitable. Contact with other organized crime groups may have inspired a broader range of criminal activities (e.g., gambling, stock fraud) and increased the magnitude of some intergang violence (e.g., use of explosives). The violence endemic to the subculture was transformed from an expressive outlet to a method of supporting members' enterprises. The power of formal hierarchy of chapter, regional, national and international leadership increased to maintain a semblance of continuity within each club. That hierarchy is supplemented, and overshadowed by informal hierarchies based on personalities and expertise. These informal hierarchies are so fluid as to be all but untrackable.

This mode of organization originated in the bikers' need for a loose organization that would provide camaraderie and group pride while permitting the maximum amount of freedom for members and chapters. It evolved in the context of a gang based on common interests with an insatiable desire for power in all forms. The resulting modal organization is superb in meeting then practical and emotional requirements of uniting these men while insulating the club organization, and often its leaders, from prosecution. Most critically, these organizational traits evolved in response to subcultural and mainstream pressures. Whatever protection they may offer the group's leaders and assets were latent functions of such adaptations that were only later refined by club legal counselors. More attention to all of the factors involved in creating modal organizational forms can only benefit both criminology but inter group conflicts, police pressure and sanction severity are clearly critical evolutionary forces.

Biker crimes may be well planned and professionally executed or spontaneous; they may seek profit or emotional satisfaction and usually combine aspects of both goals to suit the participants' desires. Like the lives of their perpetrators, these crimes are almost entirely integrated into the dynamics of the club so it is inevitable that criminal (and legitimate) enterprises run by bikers rely on the club in some manner.

However, the club is more the network in which partnerships and cliques form and are regulated than the source of power and decision making for the enterprise. Clubs benefit indirectly from their members' businesses through fees, dues and fines. As prosecutions increase, so does pressure to solicit more money from members and this dynamic increasingly requires some degree of (generally illicit) potential for generating wealth as a prerequisite for membership. While the culpability of the club per se for any particular enterprise may be dubious, strong controls guide internecine warfare and it is in this realm that the club most clearly acts as an entity of organized crime.

References

Alain, M. (1995). The rise and fall of motorcycle gangs in Quebec. *Federal Probation*, 59 (2), 54–57).

Barger, R. "Sonny," with Keith and Kent Zimmerman (2000). *Hell's Angel.* New York: Harper Collins.

Barker, T. 2005. "One Percent Bikers Clubs: A Description." Trends in Organized Crime 9(1): 101–112.

Barker, T. 2007. *Biker Gangs And Organized Crime.* Florence, Kentucky: Anderson Publishing.

Barker, T. Human, K.M. 2009. Crimes of the Big Four motorcycle gangs. *Journal of Criminal Justice* 37 (2): 174–179.

Berry, C. (2002). Dreams of kindness, love and grace-wealth addiction. *Alternatives E-zine*, 23. Retrieved from http://www.alternativesmagazine.com/23/berry.html.

Clawson, P. (1983). Ex-hell's angel tells senators about corrupt police; describes drug trafficking by bikers. *Narcotics Control Digest*, 13(7), 2–5.

Criminal Intelligence Service Canada. (1999). *Annual Report on Organized Crime* in Canada, Ottawa, ON: Criminal Intelligence Service Canada.

Criminal Intelligence Service Canada. (1998). *Annual Report on Organized Crime in Canada*, Ottawa, ON: Criminal Intelligence Service Canada.

Danner, T.A., Silverman, I.J. (1986). Characteristics of incarcerated outlaw bikers as compared to nonbiker inmates. *Journal of Crime and Justice*, 9, 43–71.

Davis, R.H. (1982a). Outlaw motorcyclists: A problem for police (part I). *Federal Bureau of Investigations Law Enforcement Bulletin*, 51(10), 12–15.

Davis, R.H. (1982b). Outlaw motorcyclists: A problem for police (conclusion). *Federal Bureau of Investigations Law Enforcement Bulletin*, 51 (11), 16–22.

Expatica News. (2004a). *Secret hearing for Hells Angels murder suspects.* Retrieved from http://www.expatica.com/actual/article.asp?subchannel_id=19&story_id=5552.

Expatica News. (2004b). *Hells angels members shot dead in Holland.* Retrieved from http://www.expatica.com/source/site_article.asp?channel_id=1&story_id=4721.

Hells angels on trial for triple murder January 31. Retrieved from http://bikernews.org/news.php?extend.1985.

Eltman, F. (2002a). *Bikers made wills before attack: prosecutor.* Retrieved from http://www.canoe.com/CNEWSBikers0202/27_usap.html.

Eltman, F. (2002b). *73 Pagans indicted in fatal gang brawl: Hell's angels gathering scene of feb. 23 melee.* Retrieved from www.pittsburgpostgazette.com/localnews/20020313 pagansreg6p6.asp.

Fesbach, S. (1964). The Function of Aggression and the Regulation of Aggressive Drive. *Psychological Review*, 71, 257–272.

Haut, F. (1999). Organized crime on two wheels: Motorcycle gangs. *International Police Review*. 28: 474–5.

Humphreys, A. (2001). *Mafia begins unity drive: Canadian leaders face common threat from Hells Angels.* Retrieved from http://www.nicaso.com/pages/doc_page51.html.

Lavigne, Y. (1987). *Hells angels: Three can keep a secret if two are dead.* New York, NY: Carol Publishing.

Lavigne, Y. (1996). *Hell's angels: Into the abyss.* New York, NY: Harper Collins.

Lavigne, Y. (2000). *Hells angels at war: Hells angels and their violent conspiracy to supply illegal drugs to the world.* New York, NY: Harper Collins.

McGuire, P. (1986a). Outlaw motorcycle gangs: Organized crime on wheels. *National Sheriff*, 37(2), 10–20.

McGuire, P. (1986b). Outlaw motorcycle gangs: Organized crime on wheels. *National Sheriff*, 37(2), 68–75.

Miller, W. (1958). Lower class culture as a generating milieu of gang delinquency. *Journal of Social Issues*, 14, 5–19.

Nathanson Centre (2001). *Organized crime in Canada 2001.* Toronto, CA: Nathanson Centre, York University.

Queen, W. (2005). *Under and alone.* New York, NY: Random House.

Quinn, J.F. (1987). Sex roles and hedonism among members of outlaw motorcycle clubs. *Deviant Behavior*, 8(1), 47–63.

Quinn, J.F. (2001). Angels, outlaws, bandidos and pagans: The evolution of organized crime among the big four one percent motorcycle clubs. *Deviant Behavior*, 22(4), 379–400.

Quinn, J.F., Koch, S.D. (2003). The nature of criminality within one-percent motorcycle clubs. *Deviant Behavior*, 24(3), 281–305.

Quinn, J.F., Forsyth, C.J. (2011). The role of the war mentality in the development of the one percent motorcycle club; *American Journal of Criminal Justice.* Retrieved from http://www.springerlink.com/content/g111751866072677/.

Quinn, J.F., Forsyth, C.J. (2007). Evolving themes in the subculture of the outlaw biker. *The International Journal of Crime, Criminal Justice and Law*, 2(2), 143–158.

Quinn, J.F., Forsyth, C.J. (2009). Leathers and Rolexes: The symbolism and values of the motorcycle club. *Deviant Behavior*, 30(3), 235–265.

Royal Canadian Mounted Police (1999). Outlaw motorcycle gangs in Canada. *Royal Canadian Mounted Police Gazette*, 61(7–12), 1–25.

Royal Canadian Mounted Police (2002). In the streets and in the papers. *Royal Canadian Mounted Police Gazette*, 64(3), 13–15.

Ritter, K. (2006). *State trial to follow federal trial in wake of 2002 Nevada biker brawl.* Retrieved from http://www.tahoebonanza.com/article/20060802/Nevada/108020007.

Rubinstein, J. (2002). *Highway to hell.* Retrieved from http://www.julianrubinstein.com/articles/highway-to-hell.php.

Sher, J., Marsden, W. 2003. *The Road to Hell: How Biker gangs are Conquering Canada*. (Toronto, Vintage Canada Random House).

Smith, R. (2002). Dangerous motorcycle gangs: A facet of organized crime in the mid-Atlantic region. *Journal of Gang Research*, 9(4), 33–44.

Southeastern Connecticut Gang Activities Group (2005). Retrieved from http://www.segag.org/ganginfo/frmcgang.html.

Thompson, H. (1966). *Hell's angels*. New York, NY: Random House.

Tyler, T. (2009). Hells Angels' appeal tests anti-gang law. *The Star*, August 6, 2011 Retrieved from http://www.thestar.com/news/canada/article/656162.

Veno, A. and van den Eynde. J. 2007. Moral panic neutralization project: a media-based intervention. *Journal of Community & Applied Social Psychology*, 17(6), 490–506.

Winterhalder, Edward. 2005. *Out in Bad Standings: Inside the Bandidos Motorcycle Club—The Making of a Worldwide Dynasty*. Owasso, OK: Blockhead City Press.

Yablonski, L. (1973). *The violent gang*. New York, NY: Macmillan.

Yinger, J.M. (1982). *Countercultures: The promise and the peril of a world turned upside down*. New York, NY: Free Press.

Reading 3.
American-Based Biker Gangs:
International Organized Crime

Tom Barker

Introduction

The number one controversy in any discussion of one percent biker clubs, aka, outlaw motorcycle clubs (OMGs), is are they motorcycle clubs and a brotherhood built around the love of motorcycles, or criminal gangs whose members happen to ride motorcycles? Club spokesmen vigorously deny that the clubs are criminal organizations or gangs. These same spokesmen readily admit that some members commit or have committed criminal acts, however, they insist that there are a few bad apples in every organization, and the organization is not responsible or to be blamed for their behavior. However, many of these so-called "bad apples" are career criminals and psychopaths selected and recruited because of their known reputations for violence and/or criminal behavior. Australian biker expert, Arthur Veno, says, "Violence is central to club life. It's implicit in the rules, the way members live, and their interactions with other clubs" (p. 139, 2009). After selection, the prospective member is observed and scrutinized through a probationary period to ensure that they embody gang values that include the willingness to use violence and commit crimes for the club. Then, after the probationary period, the now totally committed club member becomes a part of a "brotherhood" that actively or tacitly supports the criminal behavior of other club members.

The supposed "brotherhood" of one percent bikers is actually more rhetoric than reality. One percent bikers have more to fear from their "brothers" than anyone else. The more enmeshed in criminal activities the club, now gang, becomes the more likely that greed will trump brotherhood. If a one percent biker, now a member of a criminal gang, is killed or injured, his assailant is most likely a fellow brother from his own "club" or another brother from the biker subculture. As outlaw motorcycle gang members engage in wars over territory and control of criminal markets, "brothers" kill and maim one another. At one time the original one percent motorcycle clubs may have been more clubs than gangs, but that has changed., especially since the clubs qua gangs became involved in drug trafficking in the 1960s (Barger, Zimmerman & Zimmerman 2002; Barker, 2007; Veno & Gannon, 2009).

Clubs to Gangs Evolution

Once the clubs evolved from the raucous "hell raising" misfits of the late fifties and early sixties documented by Hunter S. Thompson (1966) in his seminal work on the Hells Angels into the drug dealing outlaw motorcycle gangs of the 1960s, they have become criminal gangs organized for crime for profit. Thompson was actually the first person to use the term outlaw motorcycle gangs and recognize the criminal nature of the former outlaw motorcycle clubs. The criminal nature of the biker gangs serves to nurture and perpetuate itself. The nature, structure, and culture of the one percent biker subculture attracts bikers with criminal or potential criminal dispositions and facilitates and supports the criminal networks that arise in these clubs (Barker, 2007).

The selection and socialization processes common to all outlaw motorcycle gangs ensure the perpetuation of the deviant culture and values of crime and violence. Once identified as possible "righteous bikers" who would "fit in" and support club values, prospective members are invited to become prospects and begin their socialization process. Many clubs or club chapters only invite for membership prospects who demonstrate criminal propensities, some making the commission of crimes a prerequisite for membership. The end result of the probationary (socialization) process is the awarding of the club patch or "colors" a symbolic representation that the wearer is a member of the club and becomes his most cherished possession.

Over time this selection and socialization process with its accompanying peer group support facilitates the individual and group criminal behavior of its members and leads to the formation of gangs organized for profit through criminal activities, including organized crime. The patch or gang symbol worn on their "cut"—vest—as part of the club mystique also facilitates criminal activities of individual members and the group. A former secretary of the Hells Angels Oshawa, Canada chapter, who was also a paid police informant, testified that members join for the "power of the patch" which gives them protection when they engage in criminal activities. In addition to protection from other criminals in their milieu, the patch as a symbol of the gang is used to extort money from other criminals. A Brookville, Canada cocaine dealer admitted that Ontario's Hells Angels Nomads chapter used the "power of the patch" to collect a "tax" from all drug dealers within their territory (Seymour, 2010). This extortion technique is common among criminal street gangs, prison gangs, and traditional organized criminal gangs such as the Mafia. Patch holders themselves are subject to extortion from the club. They must pay the club a portion of their criminal proceeds and contribute monthly dues for a legal defense fund for members facing prosecution (Pazzano, December 12, 2008).

Examining the criminal history of OMG leaders provides evidence of the criminal nature of the motorcycle "clubs." A common characteristic of U.S biker club/gang leaders or officers is arrest or conviction of a felony. Every past national president of the Bandidos MC has been convicted and sent to prison usually for drug offenses. The same thing has happened to the last three national presidents of the Outlaws MC. Numerous Hells Angels MC national and chapter presidents, including the iconic leader, Sonny Barger, are convicted felons. Barger is a three-time convicted felon. In June 11, 2007 the Spokane, Washington Hells Angels chapter president was convicted of racketeering acts, including mail fraud and extortion. Two other current and former Angel leaders were convicted along with him. The federal prosecutor was quoted as saying the case "blows up the myth that (the Hells Angels) create — that they just get together to sell T-shirts and ride motorcycles" (Johnson, June 11, 2007). In July 2006, the former sergeant-at-arms of the San Diego Hells Angels chapter pled guilty to conspiracy to commit racketeering and conspiracy to commit and distribute methamphetamine and received a 14-year sentence. A Shasta County, California Hells Angels sergeant-at-arms, a registered sex offender, was arrested for the murders of two young girls — 12 and 15 — over 20 years ago (Herendeen, 2006). After finishing a 13-month sentence for drug and weapons possession his DNA was run against DNA found at the girls' murders and found to match. Members of the Washington Nomads Hell's Angels, including the chapter president and the former West Coast regional president where charged with racketeering offenses (Bowermaster, February 28, 2007). The government alleged that the Washington Hells Angels Nomads are a highly organized criminal organization.

In October 2006, the national and international Bandidos president was sentenced to a 20-month prison term after he pleaded guilty to conspiracy to commit racketeering (McDonald, March 12, 2007). The same federal judge one month later sentenced the 65 year-old president of the Bellingham, Washington Bandidos chapter to four years in prison after he pleaded guilty to racketeering.

In 2007, a combined investigation by federal, state, and local law enforcement agencies led to the indictments of 15 members and associates of the Outlaws MC in Massachusetts and 16 Outlaw members and associates in Indiana and Michigan (DOJ 1, August 15, 2007). The indictments charged the gang members with violent crime in aid of racketeering, illegal drug distribution, and gun violations. The indictments charged that Outlaws in Indiana, Massachusetts, and Michigan engaged in violent assaults on Hells Angels members resulting in beatings, shootings, and fatalities. The Massachusetts task force seized 18 guns, including an AR-15 assault weapon; 116 grams of cocaine, and $100,000 in cash. The Outlaws "Black Region" president who oversees Michigan and Indiana was also arrested along with two former vice presidents. The Indiana and Michigan cases were resolved by guilty pleas. Fourteen Outlaws from chapters in Fort Wayne, Indiana, Indianapolis, and the Detroit chapters of Eastside, Detroit Westside, Downriver, and Bay City pleaded guilty to violent crimes in aid of racketeering, illegal drug distribution, and firearms violations. One pleaded guilty to possessing a firearm following three prior felony convictions (DOJ 2, July 30, 2009).

In October 2009, 55 members and associates of the Pagans MC were indicted on 44 counts that included kidnapping, racketeering, robbery, extortion, and conspiracy to commit murder (DOJ 3, 2009). Five Pagan officers, including the national president and vice-president, were among those indicted. The biker gang members were accused of conspiring with a prison guard to murder a Pagan who was cooperating with the authorities. A 20-year friend of the national vice-president, an electrical contractor from Northern Virginia, was indicted because he asked for Pagan help in collecting two bad debts worth $30,000. The "respectable" businessman supplied the Pagan enforcers with the names addresses and physical descriptions of the two men who owed him money. Several of those indicted were accused of conspiring to murder an individual as requested by the president of the Avengers MC. Trafficking in cocaine and operating an interstate gambling operation—selling raffle tickets on a motorcycle—were included in the allegations. The illegal motorcycle raffle was an annual event earning the Mother Chapter [designated national headquarters] $50,000 a year. The robbery and extortion charges arose from a common practice among biker gangs, forcible taking of the colors [patch] from rival gangs. As of February 2010, 18 defendants have pleaded guilty to a variety of charges including stockpiling explosives to use in their war with the HAMC [Hells Angels Motorcycle Club], intimidating other clubs, extortion, and selling drugs. A Pagan vice president pled guilty to racketeering charges and conceded that the Pagans were, or were at one time, a criminal organization. The treasurer of the Charleston, West Virginia Pagans chapter pleaded guilty to setting up a plot with a prison guard to kill a Pagan in prison because it was believed he was cooperating with the authorities. He was also the second officer to admit that the "club" was involved in racketeering activities. The electrical contractor who asked for help in collecting bad debts pleaded guilty and received a 38-month prison sentence. He said in court that asking for the Pagans' help was "the worst decision and the biggest mistake of my life" (Clevenger, 2010).

Slightly less than a year later "Operation On The Road Again" by federal agents resulted in the arrests of 17 Pagans and their associates for racketeering, extortion, witness tampering, drug distribution, and firearms offenses. Those arrested were members or affiliates of clubs in Long Island, upstate New York, and New Jersey. Among the charges were allegations that the Rhode Island Pagans were going to attack the Hells Angels with home-made grenades in retaliation for an earlier attack.

In June 2010, 24 members of the Outlaws and four Pagans were indicted by a Virginia federal grand jury for a wide range of criminal activities including attempted murder of rival Hells Angels, kidnapping, assault, robbery, extortion, witness intimidation, narcotics distribution, illegal gambling, and weapons violations. The Outlaws national president Jack "Milwaukee Jack" Rosga and six chapter presidents and several vice-presidents, treasurers, and enforcers were arrested. Those arrested came from seven states—Maine, Montana, North Carolina, South Carolina, Tennessee, Virginia, and Wisconsin. Included within the allegations is a racially motivated assault on a black male in Fredericksburg, Virginia. The Pagan members are included in the indictment because allegedly they joined the Outlaws in an assault against rival gangs.

The Hells Angels and other well-known biker gangs, are not the only one percent biker gangs engaged in organized criminal activities. On the West Coast in 2006, "Operation Green 22" was carried out by 700 law enforcement officers against the Vagos MC. The coordinated effort involved officers from the BATF, and local police, and sheriff's departments. Twenty-five members and associates of the Vagos MC were arrested for charges ranging from murder, attempted murder, weapons, and drug violations. Those arrested included seven chapter presidents, one vice president, one secretary, one treasurer, and seven sergeants-at-arms (Risling, 2006). The Vagos are currently challenging the Hells Angels in Arizona, a state the Angels consider their territory. In the last two years there have been shootouts between the two gangs in Mesa, Prescott, Bullhead City, and Chino Valley. There is every reason to believe that this conflict will continue.

Four ATF undercover agents infiltrated the Mongols MC over a four-year period in "Operation Black Rain" in Southern California, resulting in a 2008 indictment. The federal racketeering indictment alleges 86 counts of murder, attempted murder, assaults, hate crimes, gun violations, and drug trafficking and led to the arrests of 61 Mongols (www.usdoj.gov/usao/cac/pressroom/pr2008/142). Among the allegations are that Mongols killed and assaulted numerous Hells Angels in California. The indictment alleges that senior Mongol members, including the national president traveled to Atlantic City, New Jersey to meet with Pagan members to form an alliance to allow for Mongol expansion into the Northeast. Furthermore, according to the indictment, the Mongols MC is ..."racist and hostile to the presence of African Americans in bars or clubs where Mongols are present, or African Americans in the presence of females associated with Mongols or Mongols members." As of September 2009, 34 Mongols have pleaded guilty to a variety of crimes all involving the furtherance of a criminal enterprise and knowing that the criminal enterprise, the Mongols MC, and its members and associates would commit racketeering offenses. In effect, admitting that the motorcycle club is a gang.

As stated above, crime and violence are part of the OMG culture. The violence between one percent "brothers" here and overseas goes on unabated. The violence often results from long-standing feuds and hatred. The feud and hatred between the Hells Angels and Mongols in 2002 erupted on the floor of Harrah's Casino in Laughlin, Nevada when hundreds of bikers went after each other with hammers, wrenches, four-cell MAG flashlights (aka death lights), knives, and guns. Ball-peen hammers are one of the favorite weapons of biker gangs, especially the Hells Angels. Ball-peen hammers can inflict terrible injuries, but they are legal and can be carried openly. The bloody melee left one Mongol and two Angels dead with numerous injuries. After the police got things under control, they found 14 guns, 107 knives, two hammers, two wrenches, and nine flashlights. The incident was such bad publicity for the casino that Harrah's sent out a letter to previous guests that everything was under control and it was safe to return. There is nothing but pure hatred between the two gangs who vow to kill each other on sight. Members of the Hells Angels and the Mongols fought in a Las Vegas wedding chapel in December 2008 after both groups showed up at separate weddings. Two members of the Mongols were stabbed and the chapel was trashed.

Violence and hatred between the HAMC and the Outlaws has existed since the late 1960s. A favorite Outlaw patch reads ADIOS—"Angels Die in Outlaw States." Two Hells Angels, one a prospect of a Canadian chapter, were arraigned and later convicted of shooting five members of the Outlaws at Custer State Park in South Dakota (Walker, 2006). Both gangs were in the area for the annual Sturgis Motorcycle Rally. It was the first violence between one-percent biker gangs at the rally since 1990 when a bar brawl between the Outlaws and the Sons of Silence left an Outlaw shot and two Sons of Silence members stabbed.

In September 2008, the president of the San Francisco Hells Angels, Mark "Papa" Guardado, was shot to death outside a bar in the Mission District of San Francisco. His death was reported to be the result of gang warfare but no one was charged until 2009 when Christopher Ablett a 36-year-old member of the Mongols was indicted on federal and state charges. The July 26, 2009 federal indictment charges Ablett with murder in the aid of racketeering and use of a firearm in a murder. The assassination is just one more murder between the two violent gangs. Mongols and Hells Angels have been murdering each other for decades. Their rivalry and hatred for one another is well known and marked by violence and murder.

At times biker violence extends to non-bikers, particularly blacks who are often the targets of racist bikers. A member of the Massachusetts Outlaws was convicted of interfering by force with the federally protected rights of a black man in an Ashland, Massachusetts's restaurant (DOJ 4, July 29, 2009). Two outlaws attacked the man and beat him with fists and a ball-peen hammer for staring at them.

American Biker Gangs Outside the U.S.

> Italy gave the world the Mafia; Asia spawned the triads; Russia and the collapsing Soviet empire gave birth to the new eastern mob.
> But America gave the world the bikers.
>
> (Sher & Marsden, *Angels of Death*)

Outlaw motorcycle gangs have been called the "only organized crime group developed in the United States (without ethnic ties) that is being exported around the world" (Smith, 1998: 54). Many biker gangs have established ties and working relationships with international organized crime groups such as La Cosa Nostra, Colombian Cartels, and even the Chinese Triads. International organizations such as Interpol, Europol, and the United Nations recognize the criminal potential of American-based outlaw motorcycle gangs.

Interlocking networks with indigenous OMGs in other countries allowed American-based OMGs to link common criminal enterprises and the benefits derived from these, allowing these clubs (now gangs) to enter the global marketplace of crime. The law enforcement community first recognized the international implications of American-based OMGs in the early 1980s. Since that time, the Angels have expanded internationally and other U.S. OMGs have established chapters in countries outside the United States. As one experienced prosecutor of biker gangs put it:

Biker gangs like the Hells Angels are nothing more than multinational corporations—and they're certainly interested in pursuing business opportunities around
the world... (Pat Schneider, Assistant U.S. District Attorney, Phoenix, Arizona quoted in Sher & Marsden, 2006:421).

The business opportunities for these biker gangs are crimes for profit.

American-Based Biker Gangs with Chapters Outside the Continental United States

According to the official club/gang 2010 websites, there are seven American-based
biker gangs with 484 chapters located in countries outside the United States (see Table
1). They are the Hells Angels, Bandidos, Outlaws, Mongols, Vagos, Warlocks, and the
Sons of Silence. As testament to their international expansion, the Hells Angels, Bandidos, and Outlaws have more chapters outside the United States than in the U.S. Hells
Angels has 64 U.S. chapters, 183 outside the U.S.; Outlaws has 93 U.S. chapters, 161 outside the U.S.; and Bandidos has 102 U.S. chapters, 125 outside the U.S. (Table 2). These
chapters are located in 41 countries across the globe. Germany, with 116 chapters, has
the largest American-based biker gang presence with chapters of the Hells Angels, Bandidos, Outlaws, Sons of Silence, and the Warlocks. England/Wales is next with 40 chapters of Hells Angels and Outlaws and one Warlock chapter. Canada has 37 chapters of
Hells Angels and Outlaws. There were two Bandidos chapters until one chapter killed

Table 1. American-Based Biker Gangs Outside United States by Country

1. Argentina	3	22. Italy	6
2. Australia	30	23. Japan (Okinawa)	1
3. Austria	7	24. Liechtenstein	1
4. Belgium	20	25. Luxembourg	1
5. Brazil	3	26. Malaysia	1
6. Canada	37	27. Mexico	4
7. Channel Islands	2	28. Northern Ireland	1
8. Chile	1	29. New Zealand	2
9. Costa Rica	1	30. Norway	24
10. Croatia	1	31. Portugal	3
11. Czech Republic	2	32. Philippines	1
12. Denmark	23	33. Poland	7
13. Dominican Rep.	1	34. Russia	13
14. England/Wales	40	35. Singapore	1
15. Finland	10	36. South Africa	5
16. France	36	37. Spain	7
17. Germany	116	38. Sweden	25
18. Greece	1	39. Switzerland	6
19. Hungary	1	40. Thailand	7
20. Holland	9	41. Turkey	1
21. Ireland	9	**TOTAL**	**484**

Table 2. American-Based Gangs by Chapters—U.S. and Outside U.S.

Gang	United States	Outside US
Hells Angels	64	183
Outlaws	93	161
Bandidos	102	125
Mongols	76	3
Vagos	24	3
Sons Of Silence	13	6
Warlocks	13	2
Total	385	484

eight members of the other chapter and the U.S. Bandidos disbanded the surviving chapter members after they were convicted of the murders. The Mongols claim to have a chapter in Canada, but there is no evidence to support the claim. It appears to be a ploy to rattle the Canadian Hells Angels, the dominant biker gang in Canada. France has 36 chapters of Hells Angels, Outlaws, and Bandidos. Australia has 30 chapters of Hells Angels, Bandidos, and Outlaws. The remaining chapters are spread throughout Europe and Asia with a concentration of American-based biker gangs in the Nordic countries of Denmark, Finland, Sweden, and Norway.

Conclusion

American-based outlaw motorcycle clubs have evolved into outlaw motorcycle gangs and have expanded their reach and criminal activities outside the United States. The international expansion of the American-based biker gangs has had a profound effect on the nature and composition of many clubs, particularly the Hells Angels, Bandidos, and the Outlaws. Each of these gangs has more chapters and members outside the United States than they do inside the U.S. Often, new international members do not meet the established criteria for membership; for example, there are instances where some members do not even own motorcycles or are former police officers. The international chapters have gained in influence and power. All new Hells Angels full patch members must be approved by the Hells Angels world council meeting at the yearly international run. The U.S. Bandidos only approved the Canadian Bandidos chapters that were to cause the Bandido Nation so much grief after pressure from their European allies. The gangs hold regional, national, and international meetings attended by the key officers—presidents, vice-presidents, sergeant-at-arms, and secretary treasurers. At these meetings major policies and procedures are set, chapters are approved or disbanded, members are approved, and the criminal activities are planned.

The American-based biker gangs have become more criminal as they and their drug links expand beyond the U.S. borders. They have become more violent toward each other as they fight over territory and drug markets. The American-based OMGs have become serious organized criminal threats in their new hosts. This expansion and spread of organized criminal activities and violence is on-going and leading other American-based OMGs to consider establishing chapters outside the United States.

References

Barger, R. with K. Zimmerman and K. Zimmerman (2002). *The Life and Times of Sonny Barger and the Hell's Angels Motorcycle Club.* New York: William Morrow.

Barker, T. (2007). *Biker Gangs and Organized Crime.* Cincinnati, Ohio: LexisNexis-Anderson.

Bowermaster, D. (February 28, 2007). Hell's Angels case going to court. *Seattle Times.* (http://seattletimes.nwsource.com).

Clevenger, A. (April 14, 2010). Va. Contractor gets 38 months for turning to Pagan's for muscle. *Charleston Gazette.*

DOJ 1 (August 15, 2007). Members of "Outlaws Motorcycle Club" Indicted in Detroit on Violent Crime, Drug and Gun Charges. http://detroit.fbi.gov/dojpressrel/pressrel07.

DOJ 2 (July 30, 2009). Fourteen Motorcycle Gang Leaders and Members Plead Guilty in Detroit to Violent Crime, Drug and Firearms Charges. http://detroit.fbi/gov-dojpressrel/pressrel09.

DOJ 3 (October 6, 2009). Federal Grand Jury Indicts Fifty-Five Members and Associates of the Pagans Motorcycle Club. www.atf.gov/2009press.

DOJ 4 (July 29, 2009). Outlaw Motorcycle Member Sentenced. http://boston.fbi.gov/pressrel?pressrel09.

Herendeen, S. (2006). Murder suspect built life on the coast. (www.modbee.com).

Johnson, G. (June 11, 2007). Guilty Verdicts in Hells Angels Trial. *FoxNews.com.*

McDonald, C. (March 12, 2007). Hells Angels leaders on trial today: Biker gang charged with racketeering. *Seattle Post-Intelligencer.* (http://seattleepi.nwsource.com).

Pazzano, S. (January 29, 2009). Biker verdict causes uproar. *Toronto Sun.* (www.torontosun.com/news/canada).

Risling, G. (March 19, 2006). Vagos motorcycle club targeted in Southern California crime sweep. *SignOnSanDiego.com.*

Seymore, A. (April, 21, 2010). Brookville cocaine dealer gets seven-year prison term: *National Post.* (www.canada.com).

Sher, J & Marsden, W. (2006). *Angels of Death: Inside the Biker Gangs' Crime Empire.* New York: Carroll & Graf.

Smith, B.W. (1998). Interpol's "Project Rocker" Helps Disrupt Outlaw Motorcycle Gangs. *The Police Chief.* September, 1998: 54–56.

Thompson, H.S. (1966). *Hell's Angels: The Strange and Terrible Saga of the Outlaw Motorcycle Gangs.* New York: Ballantine Books.

Veno, A. with E. Gannon (2009). *The Brotherhoods: Inside the Outlaw Motorcycle Clubs.* Crows Nest, NSW: Allen & Taylor.

Walker, C. (2006). Hells Angels bikers indicted. *Rapid City Journal.*

Reading 4.
Hells Angels in Springtime[*]

Carlo Morselli

Abstract

This article presents a case study of the criminal market activities surrounding the Quebec Hells Angels between 1997 and 2001. The popular and law-enforcement depiction of the Hells Angels, and most notably its Nomad chapter, follows the stereotypical image of traditional organized crime (e.g., monopoly control of the criminal market; a clear hierarchical organization; strict control of the organization's members and associates). This general claim is tested in this article. The counter argument emphasizes that whereas the Hells Angels organization is a hierarchical structure with clear and explicit rules laid out for its members, there is no clear indication that this formal organizational structure is relevant when studying the criminal activities of members and associates. Quite differently, when it comes to participation in criminal markets, flexibility offers a better fit than the rigid confines of a formal organization. Data for the study was obtained from law-enforcement files that followed an important crackdown on the motorcycle club in Quebec during March 2001—this crackdown and the ensemble of investigations leading up to it have been commonly referred to as Operation Springtime. Through the use of electronic and physical surveillance transcripts that recorded a high volume of communications between members and associates who were targeted by law-enforcement investigators over a five-year period, a representation of the criminal network surrounding the Hells Angels in their criminal market activities was constructed and analyzed. The main objective of the analyses was to assess the extent to which the Hells Angels hierarchy fits the criminal market activities that were targeted. The working hypotheses guiding these analyses follow that if Nomad members were indeed domineering criminal market participants, we would expect them to be relatively high in degree centrality (hands-on participants) and/or high in betweenness centrality (strategic brokers). Findings indicate that while the Nomads were, on average, higher in brokerage capital when compared with other members within the organization, Nomads were not the most central participants in the overall network. Instead, network participants who were highest in degree centrality were amongst the mid and lower-level members of the Hells Angels organization (suggesting a vulnerable/visible position), while those with the highest brokerage capital participants who held no biker or gang status (suggesting that the strengths of the network lay beyond the formal organization). In sum, the case study highlights the necessary nuances that are needed when approaching organized crime from a scholarly and policy outlook.

It would be difficult to tell how crime would be like in Quebec throughout the past three decades without the Hells Angels.[1] Although not a criminal organization per se, the motorcycle club's members and associates have been so intrinsic in the province's criminal markets that they have had not only a key role in shaping the structure of such markets, but also in determining the policies and controls that were developed to contain organized crime in such activities.

As often happens in such contexts, the image of the Hells Angels as a social threat can be so consuming that, during certain periods, the club has become the embodiment of organized crime, particularly in political, law-enforcement, and media circles. As a result, Naylor's (1997, 2002) wise advice not to "confound an association of criminals with a criminal association" (p.40) is lost in the midst of repeated claims that the province's criminal markets (and primarily illegal drug distribution markets) are controlled within an infrastructure governed by the six Hells Angels chapters across Quebec.

Naylor's warning is indeed sound. It is unlikely that the Hells Angels' formal organizational structure is transferable to a criminal market of any scope. However, extensive law-enforcement investigations and recent trials of a large number of the club's members and associates lend some credence to this unlikely transfer. The present case study uses material from these investigations and trials to examine this possibility. The line of inquiry guiding this study examines the extent to which a criminal network mirrors the formal organization in which many of its participants are members and associates.

Hells Angels Inc.

At their official website, the Hells Angels qualify themselves as the "oldest and biggest 1% motorcycle club in the world". The 'one-percenters' status refers to those motorcycle clubs that are not registered with the American Motorcycle Association or the Canadian Motorcycle Association (see Barger 2000; Wolf 1991). With a history spanning more than half a century, the club has emerged into a vast organization, with chapters spanning across five continents. The organization's name and its skull logo are officially registered under the Hells Angels Motorcycle Corporation and protected by international law.

The onset and expansion of the Hells Angels in Quebec has been similar to their emergence elsewhere, but one feature that remains unique to the Quebec branch is the club's association with crime and violence from its arrival in the province during the late 1970s. Tremblay et al. (1989) and Alain (2003) scanned the evolution of

---

1. A previous version of this paper was published by Springer Science+Business Media in *Inside Criminal Networks* by Carlo Morselli, ISBN: 978-0-387-09525-7, © 2009. Pg. 32–33, 123–138.

the one-percenters biker groups in Quebec and identified three phases since the early 1970s. In the first phase, from 1971 to 1978, most of this one-percenters population was located in rural Quebec, increasing from a population of roughly 600 to 900 members of various gangs. During this period, many alliances were formed between small biker groups. This period was also marked by the arrival, in 1977, of the first Hells Angels chapter (in Sorel, Quebec) which immediately established itself as an overriding organization of the smaller biker groups. During the second phase, from 1978 to 1983, 800 individuals were identified within the one-percenters classification. This period was marked by increased violence between clubs and by the positioning of several groups within various illicit drug markets (particularly for synthetic drugs). According to Alain (2003), the population of one-percenters in Quebec dropped to 300 during the final phase from 1984 to 2001. This period also highlights the presence of the Hells Angels as a dominant group within this biker subpopulation.

Although these studies provide a helpful count of the Hells Angels and other bikers with one-percenters status, a clear change in the club's reach must be established as of 1994, the year in which the sixth chapter was created in the province. This last chapter was a Nomad chapter that was comprised of the most reputed Hells Angels members across the province. While Nomad chapters are not restricted to a specific geographical territory, this new group quickly became a heavy presence in the Montreal region. In Montreal, the predominant clubs preceding the creation of the Nomads included members of Hells Angels chapters from outside the city and a Montreal-based group, the Rock Machine. The Rock Machine was at the core of an amalgam of small biker groups and independent drug merchants who joined forces to form the Alliance during the latter half of the 1990s, largely in reaction to the overwhelming presence of the Hells Angels Nomads in the city's drug markets.

Between 1994 and 2001, the Hells Angels and Alliance were at the heart of a lengthy biker conflict that led to a substantial number of killings in and around the city. The claim in law-enforcement and popular media circles was that control of Montreal's illegal drug markets were at stake. Reports vary, but the most valid count maintains that, during this seven-year period, 261 victims were implicated in the confrontation between these two factions, leading to 126 murders and 135 attempted murders—55% of these victims were members or associates of the Hells Angels (for more details on these events, see Morselli et al. 2008). Previous periods (most notably the late 1970s and mid-1980s) were punctuated by important events and atypical levels in biker-related homicides, but no other period in Quebec or Canadian history has been marked by such consistent and clustered homicides over such an extended period of time and around a specific group.

The involvement of the Hells Angels in this lethal conflict increased their already public notoriety and their status as a prime target for law-enforcement controls in the province. Such attention was not new for the club. Fifteen years earlier, members of the Hells Angels were amongst the first group to warrant the attention of a public commission that focused on the criminal activities of its members and the club's expansion across the province (Commission de police de Québec 1980). During the mid-1980s, the perception of the Hells Angels threat became important enough to warrant the contracting of the province's most controversial killer-become-informant. The seven-year biker conflict between the Hells Angels and the Alliance was the most important in terms of its implications on organized crime policy and controls in both the Quebecois and Canadian context. In the fall of 1995, following the accidental death of a young boy who was struck by a fragment of a bomb that exploded and killed a Hells Angels' affiliate, the province's first specialized organized crime squad was put into operation to contain the escalating biker conflict in the Montreal region This squad (or task force), dubbed the Wolverines, combined the efforts of investigators from the Sûreté du Québec, the Montreal Police, and the Royal Canadian Mounted Police. The main target of the Montreal Wolverines was the criminal activities of the Nomad chapter members, their underlings within the Hells Angels, and an affiliated group (the Rockers—not to be confused with the enemy gang, the Rock Machine) that was sponsored by the Nomad chapter and whose members were suspected of being the main executors of the Nomads' commands. The specific focus on the Montreal region ended during the summer of 1996, when the Wolverine squad expanded to include the Quebec City region. The Montreal/Quebec Wolverine squad was active for another 2 years until May 1998, when it was decentralized and replaced with a province-wide infrastructure of six investigative squads (known as the Mixed Regional Teams), designed to mirror the six Hells Angels chapters across the province.

Aside from the changes that took place on law-enforcement approaches to organized crime, the Hells Angels threat also triggered the first anti-gang (or gangsterism) legislation in Canada. Canadian legislators had been traditionally reluctant to adopt such legislation in previous decades. Although public commissions from the late 1960s to the late 1980s had shown the spotlight on various criminal groups and organizations in illegal markets and legitimate industries, public policy was consistently restrained from mimicking the American neighbours who drafted their criminal enteprise (RICO) legislation in 1970 and applied it widely and with considerable impact throughout the 1980s and 1990s. This all changed with the Hells Angels threat of the last decade. The growing number of murders in Montreal's crime scene escalated to the point that citizens were increasingly victimized as bystanders to the biker conflict. In the spring of 1997, Canada adopted its gangsterism legislation. This legislation was modified less than 4 years later, in 2001, after two prison guards were murdered and a popular newspaper journalist was shot by individuals who were suspected to be following orders of Nomad chapter members.

The investigative efforts to contain the criminal activities of Hells Angels members and associates by the Wolverine squad and its expanded version, the Mixed Regional Teams, came to a sudden and successful halt at the end of March 2001, when close to 150 individuals across the province were arrested and charged in what was (and remains) "the biggest organized crime sweep in Canadian history" (Sher and Marsden 2004: 254). This major crackdown against the Hells Angels was named Operation Springtime. Criminal charges against those arrested ranged from weapons offences, money laundering, conspiracy, drug trafficking, murder, and gangsterism. These arrests led to Canada's first maxi-trials that spanned into 2004, when the last set of accused pleaded guilty.

The evidence assembled against Hells Angels members and associates was massive. This included the colossal collection of electronic surveillance transcripts intercepted throughout the task force investigation that led to the Operation Springtime crackdown. Also included in the ensemble of evidence were the affidavits that described the overall workings of the organization and the implication of each arrestee therein. By this point, the description of the Hells Angels' inner workings had become common "knowledge", with the daily coverage of the investigation and trials constituting the prime focus for most media outlets. The general formulation beginning each affidavit prepared for the Operation Springtime arrests described the Quebec Hells Angels, and particularly the Nomad-Rockers segment, as a tightly knit organization with a clear pecking order in its domination of the illegal drug distribution activities of its members and their underlings. The prosecution's line of argument throughout the case was the following (this description originally appeared in French—the translation is mine):

– The present investigation establishes that the members of the Nomads and Rockers organizations form one gang, in which all participate and contribute to an important extent.

– This gang exists only for the commission of lucrative crimes that serve to enrich the gang and its members. The most frequent of these crimes is illegal drug trafficking, but other crimes, such as intimidation, assault, use of explosives, conspiracy, and murder are also common.

– (...) The Hells Angels Nomads and Rockers carry emblems that they refer to as "patches" and that such emblems identify their membership status. (...) The wearing of patches or other objects that identify members in the motorcycle club are often used for purposes of intimidation and are proudly exposed by members and ambitious associates who aspire to gain official membership in the club. These symbols therefore serve as a mark of commerce and as tools of intimidation for facilitating the control of illegal drug selling territories.

– There exists, within the realm of the Hells Angels organization and its affiliated gangs, a well-established hierarchical structure and mode of function in which each individual has a role. There is also interdependence between members and the diverse crimes that they commit. Committing crimes under the Hells Angels banner has major advantages that are due to the criminal status and notoriety of the organization, the terror regime that it has developed and the rapport de force that it has demonstrated throughout recent years, as well as the national and international scope of the organization.

– All individuals who are part of this organization are sponsored by an official member and have to gain the approval of 100% of members in order to climb the hierarchy. All have to be useful to the ensemble of the group. Individuals at the lowest level of this structure serve those at the highest level—the contrary is never the case. Aspiring members climb the hierarchy in accordance with their utility, such as the volume of sales in illegal drugs, their contacts for importing illegal drugs, or their capacity to commit violent acts ranging from minor assaults to murder.

– For an affiliated gang, the structure of this organization is composed of Friends, Hang-Arounds, Strikers, and Full-Patched members. For the Hells Angels, the structure is composed of Friends, Hang-Arounds, Prospects, and Full-Patched members. In general, Hells Angels recruit members from affiliated gangs, but this is not an obligation in that some members do come from elsewhere. (…) The Full-Patched member of an affiliated gang must have the 100% approval of all other members of that gang. At this level, the member manages an illegal drug trafficking network, alone or with other members. He has acquired the trust of the group and commits, with or for them, different crimes. He takes part, at this level, in decisions that concern the group. The affiliated gang is also sponsored by a Hells Angels chapter and exists exclusively to serve and execute different tasks for members of this chapter, such as the distribution of illegal drugs and assuring their protection. All members and strikers must pay 10% of the profits generated from illegal activities to the Club. (…) Within a Hells Angels chapter, a Hang-Around has a superior status than full-patched members of an affiliated gang. A Hang-Around may order and direct them. A Hang-Around must also serve members of the two superior echelons in the chapter. At this level, the Hang Around has already proven himself as a criminal and is well known within the group. He is sponsored by a Full-Patched member. The Hells Angels Prospect is also sponsored by a Full-Patched member and has to have the approval of 100% of members in order to climb the hierarchy and hope to become a Full-Patched member. At this level, he manages criminal operations in partnership with another member or association of members. He climbs the hierarchy in accordance with his effectiveness, availability, loyalty, and contribution to the group. The Full-Patched Hells Angels member is autonomous in the criminal activities that he manages alone or in association with others, but he must respect the rules and philosophy of the chapter. This level is the highest in the illegal drug distribution pyramid. His role is to supply drug distribution cells. At this level, he orders and commands crimes rather than executes them himself. It is a fact that no one could climb the levels of this hierarchy without committing a crime. The members of this gang are therefore all criminal.

This well-regulated criminal system was the model professed by law-enforcement officials, prosecutors, and media outlets throughout the trials of the Hells Angels members and associates following the Operation Springtime crackdown in 2001. The key points that should be retained from this interpretation are that:

1) The Nomad chapter of the Hells Angels and its affiliate clubs existed only for criminal purposes (specifically, illegal drug distribution) and recruited only offenders.

2) Hierarchy was the governance model within the organization and of any criminal activities that extended from the organization.

3) Climbing the echelons within the hierarchy was the motivational force driving all to participate in criminal activities.

4) Top-ranked members were privileged in that they were able to order lower-level members, while remaining active in profitable criminal activities from a distant and secure position.

This description offers the claims against which the present case study is designed. Using the electronic and physical surveillance records that were gathered during the police investigations leading up to the Operation Springtime crackdown, subsequent analytical sections examine the extent to which the Hells Angels hierarchy smoothly translates into the ensemble of interactions between its members and associates, as seen by the network analysis of communications between participants. The following section presents the data and methods in more detail.

Data and Methods

The data used for this case study represent the wide range of criminal activities that revolved around a specific organization—the Quebec Hells Angels. While the network in this case was firmly entrenched within illegal drug distribution activities, the investigation that targeted it tapped into an ongoing system surrounding this organization. This system included not simply drug importation and domestic distribution channels, but also conduits revealing the management and movement of profits from the illegal drug trade.

Although the case carried the name of the final crackdown (Operation Springtime), this final ensemble of arrests was the result of a series of investigations conducted by the task-force team throughout the preceding 4 years. The task force included investigators and analysts from the Royal Canadian Mounted Police, the Sûreté du Québec, and the Montreal Police.[2]

The first investigation in this task force, Project Rush, began in 1997. Project Rush targeted the entire Hells Angels organization in Montreal, but more particularly the elite Nomad segment of the Hells Angels, their underlings (Prospects), and the ensemble of participants who were members or underlings of the affiliated gang, the Rockers. Initially, Project Rush was built on the work of a police informant who was a member of the Rockers and maintained close links with several members of the Nomads. Eventually, more informants would be incorporated in the investigation and new investigative projects would spawn from Project Rush.

The most important of these spin-off investigations was Project Ocean, which began in the fall of 2000 and was initiated when Project Rush investigators learned that one of the targeted participants was transferring money obtained from drug distribution profits to an apartment in Montreal's east end. Project Ocean focused on this money hideout and mainly targeted the money movement and management extending from profits in the Nomads' drug distribution activities. Investigators retrieved an ensemble of spreadsheets showing the transaction profits and costs extending from the Nomads' transactions with drug dealers in the Montreal region. One group of names found on these spreadsheets included a drug trafficker, who was reputed to have considerable resources for moving drug consignments and other contraband through Montreal's waterfront port, and his associate, who was responsible for carrying money from the east-end apartment to him. The money carrier eventually became an informant and revealed the drug distribution connection between his drug trafficking associate and the Nomads.

The third case that led to Operation Springtime was Project Hammer (Projet Marteau, in French). Project Hammer also began in 2000, after the completion of another investigation that targeted a cocaine distribution network in the Montreal region. The previous investigation centred on a reputed drug trafficker and revealed that his main supplier was an associate of one of the Nomads, who were under investigation in Project Rush during that time. Following the premise that 'everything that leads to a Nomad is governed by the Nomads', the task force initiated Project Hammer to monitor and eventually dismantle this extensive cocaine distribution route.

---

2. For further details on case selection, data access, and the limits of using law-enforcement data for social network analysis, see Chapter 2 in Morselli (2009).

The final network that is analyzed in this article was extracted from a massive set of electronic and physical surveillance records that were submitted as evidence during the trials of 131 individuals. Media reports revealing the scope of this evidence consistently stated that the police recorded 270 000 logs of interaction bits between individuals monitored during the ensemble of investigations leading up to the March 2001 crackdown. This number is indeed a fair assessment of the initial set of files that my research team and I were dealing with when we took our first steps toward reconstructing the network surrounding the Hells Angels during this investigation. A first extraction of all logs recording non-conversational interactions (e.g., pager alerts, unanswered calls, busy signals, wrong numbers) reduced this number considerably. After three test trials on random samples of 100 logs, we found that the cut-point in file size was 400 bytes, with non-conversational interactions falling equal to or under this file size. Applying this 400-byte filter thus eliminated all telephone logs that resulted in an empty file and decreased the number of logs to 20 502. These logs recorded interactions between 1,500 individuals. However, not all individuals falling in the surveillance net were participants in the criminal network.

The final network of 174 participants is the result of a selection process that excluded all individuals who were not targeted by the police and for whom no additional evidence could be provided to illustrate their participation in the criminal operations that were under investigation. Project Rush comprised 61 of these participants; Project Ocean added 81 participants; and Project Hammer added 32 participants.

This network is examined for various forms of centrality, which is arguably the most popular operational concept used by social network analysts.[3] Actor or node centrality measures tell us how the nodes within a network are positioned. The two most common centrality measures are degree centrality and betweenness centrality.

Degree centrality is the simplest of the centrality measures. It is a straightforward measure of the number of direct contacts surrounding a node. Nodes with high degree centrality are therefore those that possess a high concentration of direct connectivity within a network. Degree centrality scores are generally presented as percentages of the overall number of other nodes, thus, a node with 10 direct contacts in a 20 node network will have a degree centrality score of 10 / (20-1), equalling 53%. Expressed as such, degree centrality scores vary between 0 and 100%, with 0% indicating that the node is an isolate and 100% indicating that the node is in direct contact with all other nodes in the network.

Betweenness centrality extends from degree centrality and, like other alternative centrality measures, introduces the nuance that it is not the quantity but the quality of connections that is important. This measure incorporates the indirect contacts that surround a node. Betweenness centrality measures the extent to which a node mediates relationships between other nodes by its position along the geodesics within the network. A geodesic is the shortest path (or number of degrees) connecting a dyad (a pair of nodes). The greater a node is located along the geodesics in the network, the higher its betweenness centrality. This measure essentially represents the ability of some nodes to control the flow of connectivity (or communication) within a network. Controlling the flow within the network in this indirect manner is the broker's edge. The index for betweenness centrality for a given node is equal to the proportion of times that that node

---

3. All analyses were conducted with Ucinet 6 (Borgatti et al. 2002).

is positioned along the geodesics between dyads. The maximum number of geodesics is equal to the number of dyads not including the node or $(g-1)(g-2) / 2$, where g is equal to the total number of nodes in the network (Wasserman and Faust 1994). Thus, in a 5-node network, each node, in theory, will be able to mediate between six dyads. The minimum score is 0, which means that a node falls on no geodesic. The maximum results when a node falls on all geodesics (the star graph or pure broker configuration).

Analytical Scheme

Centrality measures help designate key participants in the overall network, but different types of centrality measures offer different interpretations of how a network is structured. On one hand, we may expect the highest ranked members (the Nomads) to be amongst the most central, particularly in terms of the number of direct contacts they maintain in the network (degree centrality). On the other hand, centrality measures based on direct connectivity (degree centrality) are more likely to indicate a participant's vulnerability to detection within the network—particularly in the case of criminal networks.

Emphasizing the last point in the prosecution's line of argument during the trial that followed Operation Springtime—that the Full-Patched Hells Angels member orders and commands crimes rather than executes them himself—, we would expect the highest ranked members to be relatively low in their direct connectivity in the network, thus confirming their ability to capitalize on others who manage and execute crimes in their place. This latter scenario, however, is not necessarily consistent with a straightforward command system. The prosecution's account also offered another interpretation in its emphasis on partnerships between members of different ranks in the organization. High-ranked members may have been active as partners in the criminal activities, but with different networking patterns than lower-ranked members. Centrality measures that capture a participant's capacity to broker between other participants represent strategic forms of networking. Such measures account for a participant's capacity to mediate along the shortest paths uniting disconnected participants in the network (betweenness centrality).

Thus, in the context of a criminal network structure, in which direct connectivity is an indication of visibility/vulnerability and brokerage is a more subtle and strategic positioning pattern, we should expect lower-ranked members of an organization to be more visible (more vulnerable) and higher-ranked members to be more brokerage-like (more strategic) in their networking patterns. Settling the issue of whether higher-ranked members are hands-on participants or perform strategic manoeuvres in criminal networks (and inversely for lower ranked members) will help us clarify not only the interpretation held during the prosecution of these Hells Angels members and associates, but also similar claims that (too) often appear in regard to the presence of organizational structures in criminal activities.

The Hells Angels Network in Operation Springtime

In this section, I examine the extent to which the organizational structure of the Nomad/Rockers organization is coherent with the communications that made up the

Figure 1. The Hells Angels Network in Operation Springtime

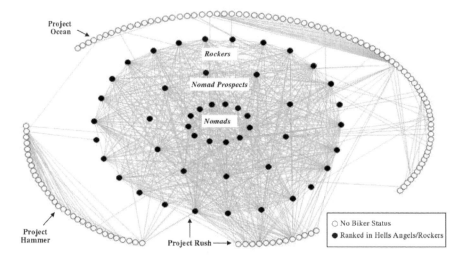

Fig. 1 The Hells Angels network in Operation Springtime

network intercepted during this extensive task force against these groups and the drug distribution operations that surrounded them. Figure 1 illustrates the intercepted communication patterns within and between the formal ranks that constitute the Hells Angels organization targeted during the investigations. The 48 participants who had formal status in the Hells Angels organization (black nodes) are distinguished from those who did not (white nodes).

Once again, formal rankings in the Hells Angels are as follows: Full-Patched members are at the top of the hierarchy; Prospects rank below full-patched members; and Hang-Arounds or Friends rank lowest within the organization. The Rockers' organizational structure is similar to that of the Hells Angels: Full-Patched members had the highest status, followed by Strikers, Hang-Arounds, and Friends. Regardless of their rank within the organization, Rockers are subordinates to all members of the Nomad chapter.

To follow the formal ranks, the sociogram in Figure 1 is best examined from the core outward. Some may argue that a graphic representation that illustrates the informal networking of members and associates within the formal hierarchy making up the organization should follow a vertical display. Figure 1 does present such a vertical display—just imagine that you are looking at a pyramid from above. The highest ranked Hells Angels—the 12 members of the elite Nomad chapter—are presented at the core. The layer surrounding the Nomad members presents the 10 Nomad Prospects. The third layer presents the 26 participants who had an official status with the Rockers. The outer layer of the network presents all participants targeted during the investigations but who did not have formal ranks in either the Rockers or the Hells Angels.

Figure 1 also illustrates how participants were targeted across the investigations that led to Operation Springtime. The 48 participants with formal ranks in the Nomads/Rockers and 13 participants without formal status (grouped at the bottom-center of the graph) were targeted during Project Rush. The 81 non-bikers that span the upper to right side of the graph were targeted during Project Ocean, which focused specifically on the financial routes extending in (profits) and out (costs) of the organization. The 32 participants positioned at the bottom-left of the graph were targeted during Project Hammer, which focused on a specific cocaine trafficking group that extended from the Nomad core.

Variations in Key Participant Status across the Network

If a bias taints this case study's data, it would be because most of the intercepted communications centred on the Nomads and Rockers who were at the center of investigations that generated this case study's main data sources. Nomads, in particular, were the most heavily targeted during the investigations. Thus, if there were a fundamental law-enforcement bias guiding the present analysis, we would expect Nomads to be amongst the most central participants, in terms of direct connectivity. This is not the case and the relative importance of Nomads as central participants varies. Figures 2 and 3 illustrate how degree and betweenness centrality are distributed across the overall network.

Figure 2 presents the network with an emphasis on those participants who had higher degree centrality. Aside from a few participants scattered across the Project Ocean and Project Hammer portions of the network, most participants with a high degree of direct contacts held an official rank within the Hells Angels organization. However, few of the Nomads had high degree centrality. This pattern was more concentrated amongst the Nomad Prospects and even more so amongst the lower-level Rockers.

Brokerage is a fundamental networking pattern in criminal networks (Morselli 2009). Figure 3 shows that brokerage is a pattern that is also more particular to Nomads in the Operation Springtime network—at least more so than for lower-level members in the Hells Angels. The participant with the highest betweenness centrality was a non-biker who was targeted during Project Ocean. Other participants with relatively high betweenness centrality were targeted elsewhere in Project Ocean and during Project Hammer. However, within the formal ranks of the Hells Angels (those targeted during Project Rush), the key participant status that was so vividly associated with the majority of Rockers and Nomad Prospects when assessing the degree centrality distributions substantially diminishes. Nomads, on the other hand, are amongst the few participants within the Hells Angels organization that are also identified as key participants from a betweenness centrality outlook.

Table 1 summarizes the patterns emerging from the previous figures.[4] The findings are telling in that average scores for the distinct ranks in the Hells Angels organization reflect the patterns that were typical of members in their networking. The two extreme

---

4. The results in Table 1 must be considered in the structural make-up of the overall network, which, according to the network centralization results, were relatively low for all centrality measures. Thus, the analysis involves a search for central participants in a network that was not heavily centralized to begin with.

Figure 2. The Hells Angels Network in Operation Springtime
(Key Players Designated by Degree Centrality)

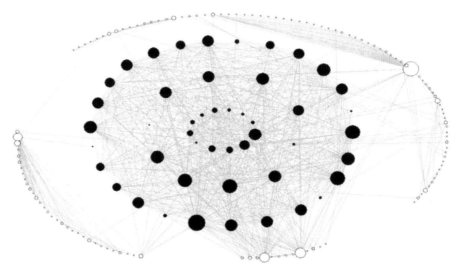

Fig. 2 The Hells Angels network in Operation Springtime (key players designated by degree centrality)

Figure 3. The Hells Angels Network in Operation Springtime
(Key Players Designated by Betweenness Centrality)

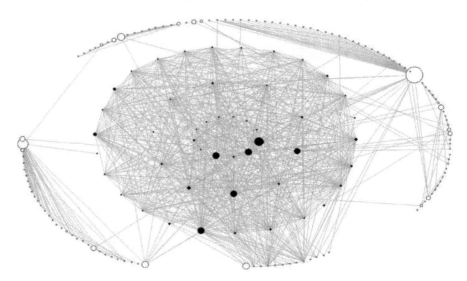

Fig. 3 The Hells Angels network in Operation Springtime (key players designated by betweenness centrality)

ranks in the organization networked in inversed patterns—members of the Nomads and Rockers—are at opposite ends for each of the measures. Whereas Nomads were relatively low in direct connectivity (degree centrality) and relatively high on brokerage-like connectivity (betweenness centrality), Rockers were high in direct connectivity and low

Table 1. Network Characteristics by Hells Angels
Organizational Rankings

	Nomads (n = 12)	Nomad Prospects (n = 10)	Rockers (n = 26)	Non-Gang Members (n = 126)	Network Centralization (n = 174)
Degree centrality	Low (7,95)	High (16,13)	High (15,30)	(2,15)	22%
Betweenness centrality	High (3,56)	High (3,18)	Low (1,30)	(1,35)	31%

in brokerage connectivity. Consistent with the formal organizational structure, Nomad Prospects find themselves somewhere in the middle of the elite Nomads and the bottom-level Rockers—they were high on both forms of networking.

Although the diverging patterns are consistent with the formal ranks within the Hells Angels organizational structure, these results do not necessarily represent a command hierarchy. As a group, members of the Nomad chapter were older (44 years of age, on average) than Nomad Prospects and Rockers (36 years of age for either subgroup). Criminal career experience and criminal maturity is therefore relevant and the relationships between a biker's age and the network measures are consistent with those found between formal ranks within the Hells Angels organization. Within the ensemble of participants who held an official rank amongst the participants targeted during the investigations making up this case study, age was negatively correlated with degree centrality and positively correlated with betweenness centrality.

Conclusion

The formal ranks in the Hells Angels organization do emerge in the communication patterns studied in this case study—the network, in short, did mirror the hierarchy to some extent. However, the network was not necessarily 'behaving' as a hierarchy. If we take formal rank within the organization to be an indication of prestige or reputation, the higher level gang members in this network were relatively low in the number of direct contacts they maintained. The more reputed members of this criminal network were therefore not 'hands-on' participants. They were indirectly involved, as suggested by their higher brokerage capital (betweenness centrality).

The results in this study do not clarify the causal order between networking and formal ranks. Two scenarios are possible. The first scenario reflects the law-enforcement and prosecutorial description of the Hells Angels' implication in the targeted drug distribution activities. In this description, Nomads had much authority and control over lower-ranked members and ranks within the organization defined how a member could position himself amongst others—in this sense, formal ranks define the network structure and members receive network privileges after reaching higher promotional levels. The second scenario would follow a tournament setting, as suggested by Levitt and Venkatesh's (2000) analysis of a Chicago gang's financial structure. If this is the case, promotions are an extension of what a member has proven to be capable of—strategic networking patterns should therefore precede promotion and a good indication of who the up-and-comers are within an organization's ranks and the network that mirrors it will be those lower-ranked members who network through patterns similar to high-level members. Rank, in this sense, is but a prize for knowing how to fit in amongst others and not a formal authorization to govern the actions of others.

References

Alain, Marc (2003). "Les bandes de motards au Québec: la distinction entre crime organisé et criminels organisés", Pp. 135–160 in M. Leblanc, M. Ouimet, and D. Szabo (eds.) *Traité de criminologie empirique*, 3rd Edition. Presses de l'Université de Montréal: Montreal.

Barger R (2000) *Hell's Angel*. Harper Collins, New York.

Borgatti SP, Everett MG, Freeman LC (2002) *Ucinet 6 for Windows*. Analytic Technologies, Harvard.

Commission de police de Québec (1980). *Rapport d'enquête sur les activités des groupes de motards de Havre-Saint-Pierre, Sept-Iles, Mont-Joli, Saint-Gédéon, Sherbrooke et Asbestos*. Enquête sur le crime organisé, Éditeur officiel du Québec.

Levitt SD, Venkatesh SA (2000) An Economic Analysis of a Drug-Selling Gang's Finances. *The Quarterly Journal of Economics* 115:755–789.

Morselli C (2009) *Inside Criminal Networks*. Springer, New York.

Morselli, Carlo, Dave Tanguay and Anne-Marie Labalette (2008). "Criminal Conflicts and Collective Violence: Biker-Related Account Settlements in Quebec, 1994–2001", Chapter 11 (pp. 145–164) in D. Siegel and H. Nelen (eds.) *Organized Crime: Culture, Markets, and Policies*. New York: Springer.

Naylor RT (2002) *Wages of Crime: Black Markets, Illegal Finance, and the Underground Economy*. Cornell University Press, Ithaca.

Naylor RT (1997) Mafias. Myths, and Markets: On the Theory and Practice of Organized Crime, *Transnational Organized Crime* 3:1–45.

Sher J, Marsden W (2004) *The Road to Hell: How the Bikers are Conquering Canada*. Vintage Canada, Toronto.

Tremblay P, Laisne S, Cordeau G, MacLean B, Shewshuck A (1989) Carrières criminelles collectives: évolution d'une population délinquante (les groupes motards). *Criminologie* 22:65–94.

Wasserman S, Faust K (1994) *Social Network Analysis: Methods and Applications*. Cambridge University Press, Cambridge.

Wolf DR (1991) *The Rebels: A Brotherhood of Outlaw Bikers*. Toronto, University of Toronto Press.

Chapter 5

Drug Trafficking Organizations

I. Drug Trafficking Organizations and Cartels

The U.S. Department of Justice (DOJ, 2010) makes a distinction between drug trafficking organizations and drug cartels:

> **Drug trafficking organizations (DTOs)** are complex organizations with highly defined command-and-control structures that produce, transport, and/or distribute large quantities of one or more illicit drugs. In March 2011, the U.S. Immigration and Customs Enforcement (ICE) Homeland Security Investigations (HSI) during Project Southern Tempest arrested 678 gang members and associates in 168 U.S. cities associated with ties to DTOs, including members of 13 gangs affiliated with Mexican DTOs (see Box 5.1).
> **Drug cartels** are large, highly sophisticated organizations composed of multiple DTOs and cells with specific assignments such as drug transportation, security/enforcement, or money laundering. Drug cartel command-and-control structures are based outside the United States; however, they produce, transport, and distribute illicit drugs domestically with the assistance of DTOs that are either a part of or in an alliance with the cartel.

There are numerous DTOs operating in the United States. Ethnic DTOs produce, transport, and distribute drugs into and within the U.S. Examples are Mexican, Asian, Colombian, Dominican, Cuban, and and several Italian criminal organizations (La Cosa Nostra, Sicilian Mafia, 'Ndrangheta, Camorra, and Sacra Corona). In addition, there are myriad organized criminal gangs (street, prison, OMGs) and single purpose criminal gangs that engage in some aspect of drug trafficking at the national, regional, or local levels. Canadian-based Asian (primarily Vietnamese and Chinese) DTOs produce and control a large portion of the wholesale and retail-level distribution of MDMA (Ecstasy) and high potency marijuana in at least 100 U.S. cities (DOJ, 2009). Colombian DTOs, once the largest supplier of illicit drugs to the U.S., have now been supplanted by the Mexican cartels; however, they still supply cocaine and heroin to 40 U.S. cities

---

Box 5.1 Project Southern Tempest

Project Southern Tempest was the largest ICE operation targeting gangs. The 678 gang members and associates came from 133 different gangs. There were 421 foreign nationals among those arrested coming from 24 countries in South and Central America, Asia, Africa, and the Caribbean. This operation was a part of Operation Community Shield, which began in 2005 as a global initiative in which ICE HSI partners with existing federal, state, local, and foreign anti-gang efforts to share intelligence on criminal gang organizations and their leadership, share resources, and combine legal authorities to identify, locate, arrest, prosecute, imprison, and/or deport transnational gang members [More on Operation Community Shield later].

Source: Department of Homeland Security Press Release (March 1, 2011).

(DOJ, 2009). Dominican DTOs distribute cocaine and heroin in at least 54 cities in 18 states, primarily in New York/New Jersey, New England, and the Mid-Atlantic regions of the United States (DOJ, 2009). Cuban DTOs distribute marijuana, cocaine, and methamphetamine in at least 25 cities in 11 states and the District of Columbia (DOJ, 2009). The U.S. Department of Justice reports that several U.S.-based Cuban DTOs have close affiliations to drug traffickers in Cuba, Peru, Venezuela, and Colombia. In addition, the Cuban DTOs are expanding their indoor cannabis cultivation operations and distribution networks into the Southeast and Mid-Atlantic Regions. The traditional American organized crime organization, La Cosa Nostra (LCN), operates as a DTO in 19 cities in 13 states, primarily in the New York/New Jersey and New England regions (DOJ, 2009). LCN works cooperatively with the Mexican DTOs and criminal street gangs and outlaw motorcycle gangs. According to the Department of Justice (2009), the U.S.-based Italian Criminal Organizations (IOC)—Sicilian Mafia, 'Ndrangheta, Camorra, and Sacra Corona United (Sacred Crown)—smuggle multitons of marijuana and cocaine into the United States for distribution in 19 states. These IOC DTOs also smuggle in lesser quantities of heroin and MDMA. Although the DTOs mentioned above are serious drug-trafficking threats, they are not the major drug trafficking threat to the United States.

The Mexican DTOs are the greatest drug-trafficking threat to the United States (see Box 5.2). They dominate because of their control of the smuggling routes along the 2,000-mile U.S.-Southwest Border, the principal route for drug smuggling into the United States, and their capacity to produce, transport, and/or distribute the major drugs in demand in the United States: cocaine, heroin, marijuana, and methamphetamine. Contributing to the dominance of the Mexican DTOs is their advanced communications capabilities, and strong ties to organized criminal gangs (street, prison, and outlaw motorcycle) in the United States. These criminal gangs smuggle and distribute Mexican DTO drugs, collect drug proceeds, and act as enforcers, thereby insulating DTO cell members from detection. The U.S Department of Justice (2009) reports that the Mexican DTOs maintain cross-border communication centers in Mexico that facilitate the coordination of cross-border smuggling operations.

Box 5.2 Selected U.S. Government Actions against Mexican Cartels

Operation Xcellerator (2009)

This multi-agency was against the drug networks of the Sinaloa Cartel which operates in Mexico, the United States, and Canada. The Sinaloa Cartel brings multi-tons of narcotics into the United States, through an enterprise of distribution cells in the United States, and Canada. The 21-month investigation resulted in the arrest of 755 individuals and the seizure of: $59 million in cash; more than 1,200 pounds of methamphetamine; 12,000 kilos of cocaine; eight kilos of heroin; 16,000 pounds of marijuana; 1.3 million dosage units of MDMA (Ecstasy); 169 weapons; 149 vehicles; three maritime vessels; and three aircraft. Those arrested were in California, Minnesota, and Maryland, and the drugs were distributed in southern California.

Source: Drug Enforcement Administration. Press Release, February 25, 2009.

Project Deliverance (2010)

Project Deliverance targeted Mexican DTOs operating in the United States, especially those operating along the Southwest border. In June 2010, 429 individuals in 16 U.S. states were arrested, and the following was seized: $5.8 million dollars; 2,951 pounds of marijuana; 112 kilograms of cocaine; 17 pounds of methamphetamine; 141 weapons; and 85 vehicles were seized. The 22-month operation led to the arrest of 2,266 persons, and the seizure of: $154 million; 1,262 pounds of methamphetamine; 2.5 tons of cocaine; 1,410 pounds of heroin; 69 tons of marijuana; 501 weapons; and 527 vehicles. Project Deliverance led to the arrest of individuals in 18 states: Arizona, California, Colorado, Florida, Georgia, Illinois, Maryland, Missouri, Montana, New Mexico, New York, North Carolina, Pennsylvania, Tennessee, Texas, Virginia, Washington, and Wisconsin.

Source: Department of Justice. Press Release, Thursday June 10, 2010.

Operation Delirium (2011)

Operation Delirium is a joint Mexican and United States operation against the La Familia Michoacana drug cartel. On July 21, 2011 the 20-month investigation into the operation of the cartel in 13 places (Alabama, California, Colorado, the District of Columbia, Georgia, Kansas, Michigan, Minnesota, Missouri, New Mexico, North Carolina, Tennessee, and Texas) resulted in the arrests of 221 individuals in the United States. In June 2011, Mexican authorities arrested the leader of La Familia in Mexico. Those arrested were charged with conspiracy to distribute methamphetamine, cocaine, and marijuana; distribution of methamphetamine, cocaine, and marijuana; conspiracy to import narcotics into the United States; money laundering; and other violations of federal law. The July 2011 operation seized $778,000; 635 pounds of methamphetamine; 118 kilograms of cocaine; and 24 pounds of heroin. Thus far, Operation Delirium has led to the arrests of 1,985 individuals, and the seizure of: $62 million dollars; 2,773 pounds of methamphetamine; 2,722 kilograms of cocaine; 1,005 pounds of heroin; and 14,818 pounds of marijuana.

Source: Department of Justice. Press Release, Thursday, July 21, 2011.

Table 5.1 Mexican Cartels: Primary Drugs and Areas of Operation

Cartel	Primary Drugs	Areas of Operation
Sinaloa Cartel	Cocaine, Heroin, Marijuana, MDMA, Methamphetamine	Florida/Caribbean, Great Lakes, Mid-Atlantic, New England, New York/New Jersey, Pacific, Southeast, Southwest, West Central
Los Zetas	Cocaine, Marijuana	Florida/Caribbean, Great Lakes, Southeast, Southwest
Gulf Cartel	Cocaine, Marijuana	Florida/Caribbean, Mid-Atlantic, New England, New York/New Jersey, Southeast, Southwest
Juarez Cartel	Cocaine, Marijuana	Great Lakes, New York/New Jersey, Pacific, Southeast, Southwest, West Central
BLO	Cocaine, Heroin, Marijuana	Southeast, Southwest
LFM	Cocaine, Heroin, Marijuana, Methamphetamine	Southeast, Southwest
Tijuana Cartel	Cocaine, Heroin, Marijuana, Methamphetamine	Great Lakes, Pacific, Southwest

Source: Adapted from U.S. Department of Justice (2011): Table 1 page 7.

The United Nations gang (UN) of British Columbia, Canada has been in direct contact with the Mexican cartels for at least five years (Wilson, 2012). The UN gang exports the potent B.C. marijuana into the U.S. Northwest and uses the profits to purchase Mexican cocaine and transport it back to the United States and Canada.

II. Mexican Drug Cartels

The Mexican DTOs in the United States are controlled by the seven main Mexican cartels (Sinaloa Cartel, Los Zetas, Gulf Cartel, Juarez Cartel, Beltran-Leyva Organization (BLO), La Familia Michoacana (LFM), and Tijuana Cartel) operating in over 1,000 U.S. cities (U.S. Department of Justice, 2011) (see Table 5.1). The Sinaloa Cartel is considered the preeminent cartel because of its ability to obtain multi-ton quantities of cocaine from South America, particularly Colombia, to produce or obtain large quantities of heroin, marijuana, and methamphetamine and its extensive distribution network to all regions of the United States. The cartels are in a constant struggle with each other for control of the smuggling corridors leading into the United States, leading to unprecedented levels of violence in Mexico and "spill over" violence in the United States (see Box 5.2).

Organized and single purpose drug trafficking organizations purchase smuggled drugs from the Mexican cartels and distribute them on their own. Cells that operate as

---

Box 5.3 City Deadlier Than Afghanistan

· The turf war between the Sinaloa and Juarez cartels in the Mexican border town of Ciudad Juarez, across the border from El Paso, Texas, has led to an estimated 10,000 homicides in the past four years. That is more than the civilian deaths in Afghanistan for the same period and more than double the number of U.S. troops killed in the Iraq war. There were 3,622 homicides in 2010, making Ciudad Juarez the city with the highest murder rate in the world at 272 per 100,000 residents.

Source: Rosenberg & Cardona, 2011.

---

extensions of the cartels in the U.S. provide warehousing, security, and/or transportation services for the cartels.

The National Drug Threat Assessment 2011 (DOJ, 2011) is not optimistic about the future of the United States drug problem and the threat presented by drug trafficking organizations, particularly the Mexican DTOs. The report opines that the overall drug demand is rising in the United States and that the DTOs are responding to government counterdrug efforts by modifying "their interrelationships, altering drug production levels, and adjusting their trafficking routes and methods." The report concludes that "The threat posed by the trafficking and abuse of illicit drugs will not abate in the near term and may increase." The abuse problem is a demand issue and should be addressed by increased prevention, treatment, and rehabilitation efforts. Dealing with the drug trafficking organizations and the criminal gangs that supply the drugs is a law enforcement issue and should be dealt with by increased prosecution efforts.

References

DOJ. (2009). Drug Trafficking Organizations: Overview. *National Drug Threat Assessment 2009.* National Drug Intelligence Center: U.S. Department of Justice.

DOJ. (2011). *National Drug Threat Assessment 2011.* National Drug Intelligence Center: U.S. Department of Justice.

Rosenberg, M. & Cardona, J. (2011). Inside Ciudad Juarez, the Border City That's Deadlier Than Afghanistan. *Reuters.*

Wilson, T. (2012). The UN Gang, and the Canada-Mexico Connection. *InSight: Organized Crime in the Americas.*

Readings

1. Shirk, D.A. (2010). Drug Violence in Mexico: Data and Analysis from 2001–2009. *Trends in Organized Crime.* 13:167–174.

2. Department of Justice. (2009). Fact Sheet: Department of Justice Efforts to Combat Mexican Drug Cartels.
3. Anon. (January 24, 2012). Polarization and Sustained Violence in Mexico's Cartel War. *Stratfor Cartel Report 2012.*
4. Hooper, K. (2011). The Mexican Drug Cartel Threat in Central America. *STRATFOR: Security Weekly.* November 17, 2011.

Reading 1.
Drug Violence in Mexico:
Data and Analysis from 2001–2009[*]

David A. Shirk

This is an excerpt from a 15-page report on violence related to criminal activity by drug-trafficking organizations in Mexico. The report was prepared for the Justice in Mexico Project (http://www.justiceinmexico.org/) which is hosted by the Trans-Border Institute at the University of San Diego. Endnotes appearing in the original document have been transformed into footnotes and renumbered.

This report provides an overview of the trends found in available data on drug-related killings in Mexico, and offers some brief observations about the causes of violence and the effectiveness of recent efforts to combat organized crime.

Measuring Drug-Related Violence

In terms of data, the Mexican government collects information on drug-related violence through various public security and intelligence agencies. However, its data are not widely accessible to the public. Recent media reports cite PGR and SEDENA figures which indicate that there were 7,724 drug-related killings in 2009.[1] However, these data are not reported by the government in regular intervals, which makes it difficult to evaluate trends over time. Moreover, state and local governments frequently report their own tallies, which often conflate both "ordinary" and drug-related homicides.

---

[*] Reproduced with permission from *Trends in Organized Crime* (2010) 13:167–174; Copyright of *Trends in Organized Crime* is the property of Springer Science & Business Media B.V.

1. These figures from PGR/SEDENA were reported on January 5, 2010 and obtained by the Trans-Border Institute from the news agency Imagen del Golfo (http://www.imagendelgolfo.com.mx/). According to this article, there were 560 killings in 2006, 3,537 in 2007, 5,903 in 2008, and 7,742 in 2009. The same report indicates that there were 195 females killed in 2008 and 425 in 2009; 535 police in 2008 and 470 in 2009; and 52 and 35 military personnel in 2008 and 2009, respectively. Meanwhile, a recent El Universal article reports the same figure for 2009, but different figures for all previous years: 1,573 in 2005, 2,221 in 2006, 2,673 in 2007, and 5,630 in 2008. Esther Sánchez, "Aumenta nivel de violencia del narco," El Universal, January 1, 2010.

The next best available source of information is violence documented by media sources, several of which have made an explicit attempt to categorize and track drug-related homicides. Although they report their data more regularly and openly, media sources have important limitations and exhibit wide disparities. For example, one major source of data on drug-related killings is the Mexican newspaper Milenio, which recently reported that there were 8,281 drug-related killings—nearly one every hour—in 2009.[2]

Another major media source that follows drug-related killings is the daily newspaper El Universal, which reported 7,724 drug-related killings in 2009. Finally, at year's end, Reforma newspaper reported that there were only 6,576 such killings in 2009.

The range of 1,705 deaths, a difference of roughly 25% between the lowest and highest estimates, is likely due to the use of different classifications for drug-related killings and different methodologies for data collection.[3] There is disagreement among the major media sources on the number of drug-related killings in almost every state. Indeed, the sole exception is Yucatán, where all three major media sources report no drug related killings in 2009.

In general, with the exception of Milenio, the major print media sources that document drug-related killings appear to be on par with or more conservative than the government in classifying and reporting drug-related homicides.[4] However, because it has the most conservative estimates and regular reporting of its data, Reforma has been the primary source of statistics on drug-related violence referenced by the Justice in Mexico Project of the Trans-Border Institute at the University of San Diego. Relying on these lower estimates helps to eliminate a type of data error known as a "false positive" or "type II" error.

Reforma is also a fairly reliable source because it has a large, national pool of correspondents who monitor and report the number of drug-related killings in their respective jurisdictions on a weekly basis. In terms of methodology, Reforma attempts to avoid the conflation of other homicides (e.g., those committed by drug users) that do not reflect the kind of high impact violence associated with organized crime. Instead, Reforma classifies drug-related killings as "narco-executions" (narcoejecuciones) based on a combination of factors related to a given incident:

- use of high-caliber and automatic weapons typical of organized crime groups (e.g., .50 caliber, AK- and AR-type weapons);
- execution-style and mass casualty shootings;
- decapitation or dismemberment of corpses;
- indicative markings, written messages, or unusual configurations of the body;
- presence of large quantities of illicit drugs, cash or weapons;
- official reports explicitly indicting the involvement of organize crime.[5]

---

2. "Un ejecutado cada hora durante 2009," Milenio, January 2, 2010.

3. Milenio, for example, reports nearly 700 cartel related killings in Baja California, a figure that appears to include virtually all homicides for the state.

4. This could reflect a lack of access to complete information from official sources, as well different classification systems by official sources, and even erroneous reporting on the part of either the government or the media.

5. These criteria were outlined for the Trans-Border Institute by a Reforma reporter who works closely with these data.

The Justice in Mexico Project has compiled Reforma's data on drug-related killings as reported at the state level on a weekly basis since November 2007, as well as the annual totals by state from 2006 to 2009. These Reforma data encapsulate the first 3 years of the administration of President Felipe Calderón (2006–2012), and are made available to interested researchers through the project's website (http://www.justiceinmexico.org/) as they become available.

Data on earlier trends in drug-related violence are less readily available, given that there was less media scrutiny on the phenomenon prior to recent years. One source, a recent report by Guadalajara-based researcher Marcos Pablo Moloeznik, draws on a combination of data reported by the PGR and Milenio to estimate the number of drug-related killings from 2001 to 2006, under Mexican President Vicente Fox Quesada (2000–2006), as ranging between 1,080 and 2,221 deaths annually.[6] While these figures are also referenced below, most data used in this discussion are drawn from the above-noted information provided by Reforma.

Major Trends in Drug-Related Violence in Mexico

There are a number of observable trends in the available data on drug-related violence. The first is that drug-related violence has become extremely elevated since 2005, with especially dramatic increases in the level of drug-related violence in 2008 and 2009. This violence took place in spite of—or perhaps, some would argue, as a result of—massive U.S. and Mexican government efforts to crack down on drug trafficking. The second is that there are important geographic dynamics to the distribution of violence; Mexico's drug violence is highly concentrated in just a few key states considered to be critical zones of production and trafficking. In terms of impacts, the extent to which drug-related violence affected public officials, police, women, and minors under the age of 18 was especially noticeable over the last year. Lastly, of significant concern to U.S. officials and citizens, is the perceived cross-border "spill over" of drug-related violence from Mexico, which is extremely difficult to quantify and outside the scope of this report.

The Number and Rate of Drug-Related Killings in Mexico

The two most immediately observable trends regarding drug-related violence in Mexico have to do with the growth in the absolute number and rate of drug violence (controlling for population). Media reports regularly reference the number of drug-related killings from 2006 to the present: over 16,000 killings, mostly concentrated in 2008 and 2009. However, taking a longer view from 2001 to the end of the decade, it is worth noting that the total number of drug-related killings exceeded 20,000 deaths.

(...)

---

6. Moloeznik, M. P. (2009). "Principales efectos de la militarización del combate al narcotráfico en México." Renglones (61).

While generally higher since 2008, violence spiked at different points in time. The earliest significant spike occurred in March 2008, the first time that the number of drug-related killings exceeded 400 in 1 month. However, after a 1-month lull in June 2008, drug related killings have consistently exceeded that number. While there are no clear patterns or cycles to the violence, there were major spikes in the fall and holiday season in both 2008 and 2009, as well as significant lulls at the start of each summer. In terms of major surges, September and December 2009 significantly surpassed the record number of drug-related killings observed in December 2008.

These absolute figures must be contextualized by controlling for population to determine the "rate" of drug-related killings. From 2001 to 2007, the rate of drug-related killings was relatively low, ranging between 1 to 2.2 drug-related killings per 100,000 people each year. However, the rate of drug-related homicides increased dramatically over the last 2 years of the decade; more than doubling to 4.8 per 100,000 in 2008 and growing by nearly 20% to 6.1 per 100,000 in 2009 (...).

According to conventional estimates, the total number of homicides in Mexico has steadily declined since the mid-20th century, and has ranged between 10 and 12 per 100,000 inhabitants over the last decade. Based on the above figures, drug-related killings represent perhaps 10–20% of all homicides nationwide for most of the 2000s. However, the dramatic increase in such killings in 2008 and 2009 suggests that they now represent a much larger proportion of intentional homicides, and have likely pushed Mexico's murder rate significantly higher.

Geographic Distribution of Violence

From the outset of the Calderón administration in 2006 to the present, there has been significant variation in the distribution of violence in Mexico. In 2006, violence was mainly concentrated in three Pacific coastal states: Michoacán, Sinaloa, and Guerrero. At that point, the national rate of violence was 2 drug-related killings per 100,000 people, while Michoacán's 543 killings (more than 25% of the national total) gave it a rate of 13 killings per 100,000 people. The following year, however, Michoacán saw a sharp decline to just 238 drug-related killings (10.5% of the national total), or 6 per 100,000; meanwhile, the national rate remained somewhat steady (2.2 per 100,000).

Meanwhile, Sinaloa became the state most intensely affected by violence, with a rate of over 13 drug-related killings per 100,000 people in 2007. At the same time, other states began to experience significant increases in the number and rate of drug-related killings (particularly in the northern border region).

By 2008, as Mexico's overall rate of drug-related killings more than doubled, three states experienced rates of violence far greater than in previous years. The state of Chihuahua, home to the traditionally lucrative smuggling corridor of El Paso-Ciudad Juárez, accounted for nearly a third of all drug-related killings, with a rate of 49.1 killings per 100,000. Meanwhile, the already embattled state of Sinaloa saw an increase to 25.7 killings per 100,000. Lastly, Baja California's rate of drug-related killings nearly quadrupled to 19.6 per 100,000. Far from a national phenomenon, these three states accounted for more than half of all of Mexico's drug-related killings that year.

In 2009, drug-related violence increased significantly at the national level, thanks partly to absolute increases in Chihuahua and the dispersion of violence to other states. Especially notable was the increase in drug-related violence in Durango and Sinaloa, Chihuahua's neighboring states in the so-called "Golden Triangle" region. Also significantly impacted were the central Pacific states of Jalisco, Guerrero, and Michoacán. Still, the overall concentration of violence remained in northern Mexico, particularly in states along the U.S.-Mexico border. These states saw a significant increase in the overall rate of violence, from 12.57 to 13.45 drug-related killings per 100,000 from 2008 to 2009, in large part due to the extremely high death toll in Chihuahua.

One notable exception along the border was Baja California, which saw a significant drop in both the number and rate of drug-related killings throughout most of the year. Baja California went from a rate of 19.6 per 100,000 in 2008 (nearly one in eight killings nationwide) to just 10.1 per 100,000 (about one in twenty nationwide). As a result of this apparent turnaround, some authorities and experts began to suggest that Tijuana was a success story in reducing drug-related violence. However, the relative calm in Baja California was broken in late 2009, as a spate of violence brought a dramatic increase in killings beginning in late November. In December alone, Baja California saw roughly 80 drug-related killings, compared to an annual average of about 27 per month. (...)

The Casualties of Drug-Related Violence in Mexico

Overall, the odds of being the victim of a drug-related killing in Mexico in 2009 were fairly low (around 1 in 16,300).[7] As noted above, this probability was significantly higher in certain states, notably Chihuahua (roughly 1 in 1,600), Durango (roughly one in 2,400), and Sinaloa (roughly 1 in 3,400). Still, the vast majority of drug-related violence occurs between and among organized crime groups. If you do not happen to be or have ties to a drug trafficker, the odds of being killed by one are extremely slim.

This said, drug violence has also impacted others. According to Reforma's data, an estimated 35 soldiers and nearly 500 police died as casualties of Mexico's drug violence in 2009. This represents roughly 7% of all drug-related killings. Presuming that innocent bystanders reflected a relatively smaller proportion of the total remaining (e.g., less than 3%), this suggests—as government officials have claimed in the past—that roughly 90% of drug-related killings in Mexico involve ranking members and foot soldiers of the DTOs.

While the profile of DTO operatives is not well documented. Government statements indicate that the average drug-related homicide victim is male and 32 years old, though there appears to be a growing number of female and younger casualties. Meanwhile, in addition to dedicated, highly paid enforcers, DTOs also appear to employ otherwise unaffiliated, untrained young men as part-time muscle for as little as $300 a job. It is likely that the latter are mainly drawn from among Mexico's low-income

---

7. In Mexico, a country of more than 100 million people, the odds of being killed in a drug-related homicide in 2009 were one in 16,328; almost three times less likely than being killed in an automobile accident in the United States (about one in 6,500). Bailey, Ronald. "Don't Be Terrorized: You're More Likely to Die of a Car Accident, Drowning, Fire, or Murder." Reason.com (http://reason.com/archives/2006/08/11/dont-be-terrorized).

neighborhoods, though middle- and upper-class families are not immune from participation in—or targeting by—organized crime.

Meanwhile, in 2009, Reforma also reported a greater number (424) and proportion of women (10% of all drug related killings) among the deceased compared to the previous year, when the 189 women reported dead represented just under 4% of all drug-related homicides. The growing prominence of women among the dead was noteworthy as several lady "capos" (bosses) and "narco-novias" (narco-girlfriends) have caught national attention in recent years. Also noteworthy in the final months of 2009 was the fact that several minors—in their early- and mid-teens—fell victim to drug-related violence, possibly a sign of changing tactics or recruitment strategies among DTOs.

Lastly, in recent years, investigative reporters and newsrooms have been especially targeted for drug-related threats and violence, making Mexico one of the world's most dangerous countries for journalists. Journalists perceived by DTOs to be a threat are harassed or even killed, often with overt messages warning other reporters to take note. Since 2000, as many as 60 journalists have reportedly been killed in Mexico (at least 17 in reprisal for their work), with the Christmas murder of Alberto Velazquez marking the 12th journalist killed in 2009. Meanwhile, some DTOs have reportedly deployed "press spokespersons" who direct messages to newsrooms in northern Mexico, often with instructions to portray the Mexican government and military in a negative light.

Causes and Evolution of Drug-Related Violence in Mexico

Based on available data and current research on drug-trafficking in Mexico, the recent escalation and varied geographic patterns of violence appear to be the result of several immediate factors:

- the fractionalization of organized crime groups;
- changing structures of political-bureaucratic corruption;
- recent government efforts to crack down on organized crime (through military deployments and the disruption of DTO leadership structures).

(...)

Overall, one thing that stands out about the evolution of drug-related violence in recent years is the extent to which it has been driven by the splintering of and competition among DTOs. As noted above, this competition was virtually non-existent as Mexican DTOs began to take over smuggling routes from struggling Colombian traffickers in the 1980s. Effectively, in the 1980s, Mexican DTOs operated primarily under a single hierarchy, with significant protection from the state. Many experts, therefore, speculate that the centralization of power and pervasive corruption under the long-ruling Institutional Revolutionary Party (1929–2000) contributed to the relative harmony and success of Mexican DTOs at this early stage.

Today, however, Mexico enjoys much greater political pluralism, and has experienced significant decentralization of power to state governors and mayors. By and large, this has been a positive development, since the lack of democratic competition and the excessive centralization of power in Mexico for most of the 20th century led to significant corruption and abuses. However, as a result of Mexico's contemporary political situation, the dynamics among DTOs have changed in ways that contribute to greater competition and violence.

Lacking a unified, overarching hierarchy of corrupt state officials to limit competition, the organization of drug trafficking has become more fractionalized. Competing organizations now vie for influence at both the national and sub-national level, sometimes competing to corrupt officials in different agencies within the same administration. As DTOs vie against each other they are rumored to have negotiated various pacts and truces; however, these appear to be short-lived. With the added effect of government counter-drug efforts—sometimes to the benefit of one DTO over another—the end result is a much more chaotic and unpredictable pattern of violent conflict among organized crime groups than Mexico has ever seen.

Final Considerations

The ultimate question is whether the Mexican government has a strategy that can achieve its frequently stated goal of breaking DTOs into smaller and more manageable pieces. Thus far, its de facto strategy has included four components: (1) the direct involvement of military personnel in combating organized crime groups; (2) the sequential targeting of specific organizations for the dismantling of leadership structures; (3) long term investments and reforms intended to improve the integrity and performance of domestic law enforcement institutions; and (4) the solicitation of U.S. assistance in terms of intelligence, material support, and the southbound interdiction of weapons and cash.

At least in the short term, this strategy appears to have had some success in dismantling organized crime networks, and seems to indicate a sea change in political will among Mexican government officials. Indeed, there have been disruptions of the top leadership structures of virtually every major DTO except for the Guzmán-Zambada organization. These efforts are in accordance with the Calderón administration's explicit agenda to breakdown the operational structures of organized crime, with the hope of turning a national security problem (i.e., DTOs capable of corrupting and directly challenging the state) into a local public security problem (i.e., disaggregated, essentially local criminal organizations). In the end, government officials hope to achieve a result similar to that seen in Colombia, which dismantled its major DTOs in the 1980s and 1990s.

(...)

Meanwhile, in Mexico and abroad, many have pointed to the on-going bloodshed as a reason to re-think current strategies and approaches to the war on drugs. In 2009, several leading Latin American leaders, including former Mexican President Ernesto Zedillo, spoke critically against the current policy emphasis on the criminalization of drugs, and called for a new approach centered on "harm reduction" through prevention and treatment. Along these lines, Mexico significantly revised its minor drug possession laws in 2009 to specify the quantities for which a person can be arrested by authorities. The measure—which has been criticized for effectively decriminalizing drugs—has not yet taken full effect, but is intended to reduce street-level corruption and facilitate treatment for habitual drug users. However, many in Mexico argue that, without changes in U.S. drug policy, efforts to combat DTOs or to address Mexico's own growing domestic demand for drugs will be futile.

Change may already be under way. The United States has shown increased willingness to recognize its shared responsibility for drug-related violence in Mexico, under both President George Bush and President Barack Obama. Both governments have pledged their support to help Mexico's counter-drug efforts through direct assistance—in the form of the three-year, $1.4 billion aid package known as the Mérida Initiative—and U.S.-side efforts to crack down on the southbound flow of weapons and the "iron river" of deadly firearms that supply Mexican DTOs. Some additional support has been directed to drug use prevention and treatment programs, though critics charge that much more support is needed in these areas to have any significant effect on U.S. drug demand.

At the same time, as in Mexico, there appears to be an emerging discussion on alternative approaches to managing illicit drug use in the United States. Over the last few years, several U.S. states have decriminalized minor drug possession by favoring fines over incarceration, and several states have legalized medical marijuana consumption. In March 2009, U.S. Attorney General Eric Holder signaled that his office would no longer focus on prosecuting medical marijuana dispensaries that are compliant with state law, despite federal prohibitions on all marijuana consumption. Meanwhile, at the urging of Congressman Eliot Engle, an ardent supporter of the Mérida Initiative, the lower chamber of the U.S. Congress approved a new commission to evaluate U.S. domestic and international counter-drug initiatives. The Western Hemisphere Drug Policy Commission Act (H.R. 2134) was debated and passed by the House of Representatives on December 8, 2009, and was referred to the Senate Foreign Relations Committee the next day.

Whether or not H.R. 2134 is approved, developments in Mexico in 2010 will no doubt play a significant role in the ongoing debate over the effectiveness of current U.S. drug policy. Given the extraordinary number of drug-related killings, 2009 was a year of unprecedented, high-profile violence in Mexico. Since recent blows against key DTOs may produce more turmoil over the ensuring months, the toll of drug-related violence remains high at the start of the new decade. Such violence must be taken in context, since drug-related killings are heavily concentrated in a few key states and very few members of the general population are casualties of this violence. However, the number of drug-related killings has clearly increased to unacceptable levels and creates serious concerns for both Mexican policy makers and citizens. While the problem of drug-related violence should not be exaggerated, it must be addressed. Identifying the best practices and strategies for both the short and long term must be a top priority for both Mexico and the United States.

Reading 2.
Fact Sheet: Department of Justice Efforts to Combat Mexican Drug Cartels

Office of Public Relations

WASHINGTON—The increased efforts and reallocation of personnel recently announced by the Department of Justice builds on the foundation of expertise and experience gained from ongoing efforts to combat Mexican drug cartels in the United States and to help Mexican law enforcement battle cartels in its own country.

Bureau of Alcohol, Tobacco, Firearms and Explosives (ATF)

ATF is on the frontline in the fight against violent crime, particularly firearms trafficking and gun-related violence associated with organized gangs and drug trafficking organizations. Working in conjunction with domestic and international law enforcement partners, ATF's efforts deny the "tools of the trade" to the firearms trafficking infrastructure of criminal organizations operating in Mexico and along the border.

ATF is relocating 100 personnel to the Houston Field Division to support the new ATF intelligence-driven effort, known as Gunrunner Impact Teams (GRITs). The teams will focus ATF's violent crime-fighting and firearms trafficking expertise, along with its regulatory authority and strategic partnerships, to combat violence along the U.S.-Mexico border.

Project Gunrunner

Cooperation among federal, state and local law enforcement agencies and the government of Mexico is the foundation of Project Gunrunner, ATF's national initiative to stem firearms trafficking to Mexico by organized criminal groups. Project Gunrunner has resulted in approximately 650 cases by ATF, in which more than 1,400 defendants were referred for prosecution in federal and state courts and more than 12,000 firearms were involved.

As part of the Recovery Act funding, ATF received $10 million for Project Gunrunner efforts, aimed at disrupting firearms trafficking between the U.S. and Mexico, to include hiring 25 new special agents, six industry operations investigators (IOIs), three intelligence research specialists and three investigative analysts. The funding will establish three permanent field offices, dedicated to firearms trafficking investigations, in McAllen, Texas; El Centro, Calif.; and Las Cruces, N.M (including a satellite office in Roswell, N.M.). Previously, approximately 148 special agents were dedicated to investigating firearms trafficking on a full-time basis and 59 IOIs were responsible for conducting regulatory inspections of federally licensed gun dealers, known as federal firearms licensees (FFLs) along the Southwest border.

As the sole federal agency that regulates FFLs, ATF's cadre of IOIs work to identify and prioritize for inspection those FFLs with a history of noncompliance that represent a risk to public safety; who sell the weapons most commonly used by drug trafficking organizations in the region; and have numerous unsuccessful traces and a large volume of firearms recoveries in high-crime areas. Along the Southwest border, ATF inspected approximately 1,700 FFLs in FY 2007 and 1,900 in FY 2008.

eTrace

The cornerstone of ATF's Project Gunrunner is eTrace, which allows law enforcement agencies to identify trends of drug trafficking organizations. In 2008, ATF deployed eTrace technology to the nine U.S. consulates in Mexico to facilitate the paperless exchange of gun crime data in a secure Web-based environment. eTrace allows law enforcement representatives to electronically submit firearms trace requests, to monitor the progress of traces, to retrieve completed trace results and to query firearm trace related data in a real-time environment. In FY 2008, Mexico submitted more than 7,500 recovered guns for tracing, most of which were traced to sources in Texas, California and Arizona.

ATF has analyzed firearms recovered in Mexico from 2005–2008 and has identified the following weapons most commonly used by drug trafficking organizations: 9mm pistols; .38-caliber revolvers; 5.7mm pistols; .223-caliber rifles; 7.62mm rifles; and .50 caliber rifles.

ATF is developing a Spanish-language eTrace to make firearms tracing easier and more accessible to law enforcement partners in Mexico and Central America. ATF's goal is to deploy the system to all 31 states in Mexico, giving law enforcement a better picture of firearms trafficking routes, trends and organizations throughout both nations.

Training and Awareness Efforts

In calendar year 2008, ATF trained more than 750 law enforcement officers from various Mexican federal and state agencies on firearms identification, firearms trafficking, firearms tracing, eTrace, explosives identification and post-blast investigation. With the assistance of ATF's Mexico City office and the Narcotics Affairs Section of the U.S. Department of State, ATF anticipates conducting numerous additional courses in these subject areas in 2009.

ATF will also concentrate training and industry awareness efforts on the Southwest Border. In partnership with the firearms industry association National Shooting Sports Foundation, ATF will conduct "Don't Lie for the Other Guy" seminars in southern Texas, Arizona and California. The campaign educates licensed firearms dealers about the straw purchase of firearms, which is a federal felony offense, and helps them identify potential straw purchase transactions so they can confidently deny the sales.

ATF in Mexico

ATF's activities in Mexico are coordinated through the ATF attaché office located in Mexico City. ATF Southwest field divisions (Dallas, Houston, Los Angeles and Phoenix) have established border liaison special agent contacts with representatives from the Mexican Attorney General's Office. The border liaisons meet regularly to coordinate firearms trafficking investigations. ATF has five personnel in Mexico at this time and will add an additional four personnel using a portion of the $10 million that ATF received in stimulus funding. The Mexican Attorney General's office also has a representative in ATF's Phoenix Field Division.

Drug Enforcement Administration (DEA)

In collaboration with Mexican law enforcement, DEA is actively working to systematically dismantle the cartels. As the largest law enforcement presence in Mexico with 11 offices, and a decades-long history of working with the Mexican government, DEA has a strategic vantage point from which to assess the drug trafficking situation in Mexico, the related violence, its causes and its historical context. DEA is placing 16 new positions in its Southwest border field divisions. With this increase, 29 percent of DEA's domestic agent positions (1,180 agents) are now allocated to its Southwest border field divisions. DEA is also forming four additional Mobile Enforcement Teams (METs) to specifically target Mexican methamphetamine trafficking operations and associated violence, both along the border and in U.S. cities impacted by the cartels. MET Teams will be placed in DEA's El Paso, Texas; Phoenix; Chicago; and Atlanta Field Divisions.

Shortly after Congress approved the Sensitive Investigative Unit (SIU) program in 1996, the Mexico City SIU was established, and DEA now works with a number of trusted counterparts throughout the country. DEA works closely with these vetted units to collect and analyze sensitive law enforcement information and to further the case development against and the prosecution of major drug trafficking organizations.

Working with Mexican counterparts, DEA and U.S. interagency partnerships have taken the offensive against Mexico-based cartels on their own turf and sought to systematically identify and dismantle U.S.-based cells of these Mexican cartels. Project Reckoning and Operation Xcellerator are recent examples of this U.S.-Mexico collaboration. Both actions were investigated and prosecuted in multiple Organized Crime Drug Enforcement Task Forces (OCDETF) cases, involving DEA and other OCDETF investigative agencies, state and local law enforcement, numerous U.S. Attorneys' Offices, and the Department's Criminal Division.

Special Operations Division

The mission of the Special Operations Division (SOD), a multi-agency task force spearheaded by the DEA, is to establish seamless law enforcement coordination, strategies and operations aimed at dismantling national and international narco-trafficking, narco-terrorists and other criminal organizations by attacking their command and control structure. SOD is able to facilitate coordination and communication across and among multiagency networks with overlapping investigations to ensure that tactical and strategic intelligence is shared between all of SOD's participating agencies, including the U.S. Attorneys' Offices and various intelligence centers such as the El Paso Intelligence Center and the OCDETF Fusion Center.

Project Reckoning

Project Reckoning was a 15-month operation targeting the Gulf Cartel and remains one of the largest, most successful joint law enforcement efforts ever undertaken between the United States and Mexico. Due to the intelligence and evidence derived from Project Reckoning, during 2008 the United States was able to secure indictments against Gulf Cartel leaders Ezekiel Antonio Cardenas-Guillen (brother of extradited Kingpin Osiel Cardenas-Guillen), Eduardo Costilla-Sanchez and Heriberto Lazcano-Lazcano, head of Los Zetas. Project Reckoning resulted in more than 600 arrests in the United States and Mexico, including 175 active Gulf Cartel/Los Zetas members, and the seizure of thousands of pounds of methamphetamine, tens of thousands of pounds of marijuana, nearly 20,000 kilograms of cocaine, hundreds of weapons, and $71 million.

Operation Xcellerator

Operation Xcellerator began in May 2007 from an investigation in Imperial County, Calif., and targeted the Sinaloa Cartel. Operation Xcellerator was recently concluded and resulted in more than 700 arrests, the seizure of more than $59 million in U.S. currency, 1,200 pounds of methamphetamine, 12,000 kilograms of cocaine, 1.3 million ecstasy pills, three aircraft and three maritime vessels.

El Paso Intelligence Center (EPIC)

Led by the DEA, EPIC is a national tactical intelligence center that focuses its efforts on supporting law enforcement efforts in the Western Hemisphere, with a significant emphasis on the Southwest border. Through its 24-hour watch function, EPIC provides immediate access to participating agencies' databases to law enforcement agents, investigators and analysts. This function is critical in the dissemination of relevant information in support of tactical and investigative activities, deconfliction and officer safety. EPIC also provides significant, direct tactical intelligence support to state and local law enforcement agencies, especially in the areas of clandestine laboratory investigations and highway interdiction efforts.

EPIC's Gatekeeper Project is a comprehensive, multi-source assessment of trafficking organizations involved in and controlling movement of illegal contraband through "entry corridors" along the Southwest border. The analysis of Gatekeeper organizations not only provides a better understanding of command and control, organizational structure and methods of operations, but also serves as a guide for policymakers to initiate enforcement operations and prioritize operations by U.S. anti-drug elements.

Implementation of License Plate Readers (LPR) along the Southwest border has provided a surveillance method that uses optical character recognition on images that read vehicle license plates. The LPR Initiative combines existing DEA and other law enforcement database capabilities with new technology to identify and interdict devices being utilized to transport bulk cash, drugs, weapons, as well as other illegal contraband.

The National Seizure System (NSS) consists of seizure information relating to drugs, weapons, currency, chemicals and clandestine laboratory seizures reported to EPIC by federal, state and local law enforcement agencies from Jan. 1, 2000, to the present. The NSS database contains approximately 400,000 records of seizure events.

In support of the Bulk Currency Program, EPIC established a depository for detailed bulk currency seizure information from both domestic and foreign law enforcement agencies. In addition, EPIC analyzes volumes of bulk currency seizure data and develops various reports such as state link reports which are routinely sent to federal law enforcement agencies throughout the country to provide investigative leads. EPIC also responds to requests for bulk currency seizure data from agents and officers in the field.

The ATF Southwest Border Unit, which also houses the EPIC Gun Desk, serves as the focal point for the collection, analysis, and dissemination of weapons related investigative leads derived from federal, state, local and international law enforcement agencies.

DEA Work with Mexico

DEA and the Department of State, Bureau of International Narcotics and Law Enforcement Affairs have provided training to Mexican officials on a variety of investigative, enforcement and regulatory methods related to methamphetamine trafficking and enforcement. This training included instruction on clandestine laboratory investigations, precursor chemical investigations and drug identification. During FY 2008, 1,269 Mexican federal, state and local counterparts were trained. DEA has also donated eight refurbished trucks used in clandestine laboratory enforcement operations to Mexico. DEA established a joint program with U.S. Customs and Border Patrol to monitor and investigate the importation of precursor chemicals into the United States, headed for Mexico. The program targets containerized cargo consignments and air cargo.

U.S. Marshals Service (USMS)

USMS has stepped-up its efforts along the Southwest border, deploying 94 additional Deputy U.S. Marshals during the last eight months and sending four additional deputies to Mexico City to assist the USMS Mexico City Foreign Field Office (MCFFO).

Twenty-five new Criminal Investigators-Asset Forfeiture Specialists have been placed in USMS asset forfeiture units in the field. The new positions are unique in that they will be solely dedicated to the USMS Asset Forfeiture Division and will support U.S. Attorneys' Offices and investigative agencies in investigations of cartels and other large-scale investigations.

International Fugitive Investigations

The USMS Investigative Operations Division (IOD) coordinates international investigations with USMS-led district and regional fugitive task forces, and other U.S. law enforcement, and provides guidance and direction on the international process.

In FY 2008, the USMS opened 790 international fugitive investigations, with 303 fugitive cases sent to Mexico. Of these cases, 206 were investigated and closed. For FY 2009 to date, the USMS has opened 376 international fugitive investigations, with 143 fugitive cases sent to Mexico. A total of 120 arrests have been made in Mexico through March 31, 2009.

Foreign Fugitive Investigations

Once a foreign fugitive is located, an investigation is conducted to determine if the fugitive is in the United States legally. In FY 2008, the USMS opened 707 foreign fugitive investigations, with 290 requests from Mexico. Sixty-six individuals were arrested and returned to Mexico. For FY 2009 to date, the USMS has opened 180 foreign fugitive investigations, with 69 requests from Mexico. A total of 37 have been arrested through March 31, 2009. There has been nearly a 250 percent increase in the number of fugitive arrests since 2003.

Mexico Investigative Liaison Program (MIL)

The Mexico Investigative Liaison Program (MIL) was created to address international fugitive matters along the Southwest border. The purpose of this district-based, cross-border violent crime initiative is to enhance the effectiveness of the USMS in the investigation and apprehension of U.S. fugitives located in Mexico and to coordinate the location and apprehension of foreign fugitives from Mexico.

The MIL currently has 33 Deputy U.S. Marshals assigned to the five Southwest border districts, as well as two adjoining USMS districts, who operate under the auspices of the MCFFO and Chief of Mission when conducting cross-border investigations. They were responsible for investigating more than 240 cross-border investigations and 50 arrests in 2008.

Mexico Foreign Field Office (MCFFO)

The MCFFO program helps to coordinate, support and train foreign law enforcement in an aggressive approach to apprehending and extraditing international fugitives—particularly those wanted in the United States—with special attention given to violent criminals and upper-level drug trafficking fugitives.

Located at the U.S. Embassy, the MCFFO is staffed by three full-time criminal investigators. Deputy U.S. Marshals in foreign field offices serve as the primary liaisons for fugitive investigations, provisional arrest warrants, extraditions and deportations, oversight of USMS cross-border investigations, and international law enforcement training.

The Marshals Service's chief law enforcement partners in Mexico are the Procuraduría General de la República (PGR—Mexico Attorney General's Office), the Agencia Federal de Investigación (AFI—Mexico Federal Law Enforcement Agency), the Instituto Nacional de Migración (INM—Mexico Immigration), and various state judicial police entities, including the Sonora State Police.

International Law Enforcement Training

USMS will also enhance efforts under the International Training Program to meet the training needs of Mexican law enforcement agencies on the federal and state level, in the areas of fugitive apprehension, tactical operations, judicial security and dignitary protection, witness protection, prisoner custody, housing and transportation and asset forfeiture. The next two training classes are scheduled for April and May 2009. The USMS has been providing training to its Mexican counterparts since 2001.

Eighteen officers from the Instituto Nacional de Migración (INM — Mexico Immigration), a Special Unit from the Mexico State of Tamaulipas, and the newly-formed Secretaría de Seguridad Pública del Distrito Federal (SSP) in Mexico were trained as part of this program during a two-week fugitive investigative course sponsored by IIB and the USMS Southern District of Texas, Laredo Division.

Since the inception of the Mexico Fugitive Investigators Training Program in 2001, 185 law enforcement officers from Mexico have been trained in fugitive apprehension techniques. As a result, there has been a 240 percent increase in the number of cross-border fugitive felon arrests since the inception of the program.

Domestic Fugitive Investigations — Southwest Border Districts

Currently, the USMS is the lead agency for 82 district-managed fugitive task forces, and seven Regional Fugitive Task Forces (RFTFs), including the following task forces in the five Southwest Border districts:

> The Pacific Southwest Regional Fugitive Task Force (Southern California)
> The District of Arizona High Intensity Drug Trafficking Area (HIDTA) Enforcement Agencies Task Force
> The District of New Mexico Southwest Investigative Fugitive Team
> The Western District of Texas Lone Star Fugitive Task Force
> The Southern District of Texas Gulf Coast Violent Offenders Task Force

The task forces operate in areas ranging from major metropolitan cities to rural, isolated areas along the Mexican border. Most of the district task forces operating directly on the Southwest border are partnered with all federal agencies and specifically support the Southwest Border HIDTA and the initiatives sponsored by the various partner agencies. These partnerships permit the USMS to act as a force multiplier well beyond the traditional fugitive apprehension role.

For FY 2009 to date, these five task forces have arrested 6,912 federal, state and local fugitives, including 208 alleged gang members, 143 individuals wanted for murder, 376 individuals wanted on weapons charges and 2,242 individuals wanted on narcotics charges. Through March 31, 2009, the five task forces have closed 8,335 warrants. They also have seized 114 firearms, 19 vehicles, more than $84,000 in cash, and approximately 240 kilograms of narcotics. In FY 2008, these five task forces arrested 15,564 federal, state, and local fugitives, closed 19,157 warrants, and seized 267 firearms, $648,333 in cash, and more than 2,730 kilograms of narcotics.

The USMS has apprehension authority for approximately 90 percent of all fugitives wanted under the OCDETF program, which is an important element of the Department's drug supply reduction strategy. Of the more than 7,200 active OCDETF warrants nationwide, more than 1,100 originate in the Southwest region. In FY 2008, the OCDETF Program along the Southwest border cleared 189 fugitive warrants. In FY 2009 to date, the OCDETF Program along the Southwest border has cleared 44 fugitive warrants.

The USMS task force network is supported by the Technical Operations Group (TOG), which provides critical, state-of-the-art electronic and air surveillance in fugitive investigations, judicial security investigations and protection details, and supports other USMS missions. To increase its intelligence-gathering capabilities, the TOG has designed a radio system in response to a critical needs assessment in the Southern District of Texas with plans to begin construction soon along the Texas-Mexico border.

Federal Bureau of Investigation (FBI)

The FBI is taking proactive measures to assess and confront this heightened threat to public safety on both sides of the U.S.-Mexico border, by creating a Southwest Intelligence Group (SWIG), which will serve as a clearinghouse of all FBI activities involving Mexico. The FBI will also increase its focus on public corruption, kidnappings and extortion relating to Southwest border issues.

In addition, the FBI is participating in multiple bi-lateral multi-agency meetings and working groups to hone strategies to address the problem. The FBI is well-equipped to deal with cartels, through established entities such as the National Gang Intelligence Center. The FBI has task forces throughout the country working to disrupt gang activity. The FBI's San Antonio division currently operates two Safe Street/Gang task forces addressing border violence in San Antonio, Texas, and the Rio Grand Valley.

In calendar year 2008, the FBI's offices in San Diego; Albuquerque, N.M.; Phoenix; El Paso, Texas; Houston; Dallas; Los Angeles; and San Antonio, Texas, maintained hundreds of Organized Drug Enforcement Task Forces Program (OCDETF) and criminal enterprise cases with a nexus to Mexican drug trafficking. The FBI has several hundred agents working these issues in these eight Divisions, resulting in thousands of arrests, indictments and convictions in FY2008.

The FBI has established six Border Corruption Task Forces focusing on drug and general border corruption tied to the southwest border, and is actively encouraging southwest border field offices to expand their use of Border Corruption Task Forces.

TAG Initiative

The Transnational Anti-Gang (TAG) Initiative was developed and implemented in October 2007 to enhance cooperation, coordination and augmenting investigative capabilities between the FBI and law enforcement agencies in El Salvador, Guatemala, Honduras and Mexico. The goal of the initiative is to aggressively investigate, disrupt and dismantle violent gangs whose activities rise to the level of criminal enterprises and who pose the greatest multi-jurisdictional threat.

Already, the TAG has seen successes, such as in September 2008, when TAG investigators arrested five MS-13 gang members who were transporting a cache of anti-tank weapons and military small arms. Also, FBI agents from Charlotte, N.C., worked with TAG investigators in actions that led to the indictment of 26 MS-13 gang members in June 2008, including Manual Ayala, who allegedly directed gang activities in the United States from his jail cell in El Salvador.

CAFÉ Initiative

The Central American Fingerprint Exploitation Initiative (CAFÉ), a criminal file/fingerprint retrieval initiative, was developed by the MS-13 National Gang Task Force and the Policia Nacional Civil (PNC) to store criminal fingerprints of gang members from Chiapas, Mexico, and the Central American countries of El Salvador, Guatemala, Belize and Honduras. This information is incorporated into the FBI's Criminal Justice Information Services database and is available to all U.S. local, state and federal law enforcement agencies. By incorporating these records into a searchable database, law enforcement agencies like the PNC can access the data through their own Automated Fingerprint Identification Systems.

Since 2006, the FBI has searched, processed and incorporated more than 72,000 criminal records from El Salvador, Guatemala, Belize, Honduras and Chiapas, Mexico, into the FBI's Integrated Automated Fingerprint Identification System.

Criminal Division

Office of International Affairs (OIA)

Mexico and the United States continue to make positive strides to increase the number of fugitives returned to the country where they committed serious crimes. Extradition records have been consistently broken for the past three years. In 2008, Mexico extradited a total 95 fugitives, 78 of whom were Mexican nationals, and 23 of whom were extradited for drug charges, to the United States. In addition, Mexico deported approximately 172 fugitives to the United States in 2008.

Extraditions from the United States to Mexico improved dramatically in 2008 as well. The United States surrendered 32 fugitives to Mexico in 2008, compared to 12 surrendered in 2007. Approximately 20 fugitives are currently undergoing extradition proceedings in U.S. courts.

In addition to achieving record numbers of extraditions from Mexico, OIA also increases the joint cooperation between Mexican and U.S. law enforcement authorities by responding to requests for mutual legal assistance from Mexico for evidence in hundreds of matters each year. OIA is represented at the U.S. Embassy in Mexico City by a Department of Justice attaché and deputy attaché.

Narcotic and Dangerous Drug Section (NDDS)

NDDS has a broad mission to combat domestic and international drug trafficking and narco-terrorism.

NDDS litigation unit attorneys prosecute those individuals and criminal organizations posing the most significant drug trafficking threat to the United States. NDDS attorneys recently indicted 17 members of the Gulf Cartel, including three leaders, for violations involving the extraterritorial manufacture or distribution of cocaine and marijuana destined for the United States. Also, in May 2008, NDDS attorneys were the first federal prosecutors to secure a conviction under the new narco-terrorism statute.

NDDS attorneys are responsible for the oversight of several classified projects, as well as the integration and dissemination of classified intelligence information to domestic criminal prosecutions. These attorneys coordinate the efforts of law enforcement and prosecutors worldwide to maximize the Department's effectiveness against international narco-traffickers. NDDS attorneys assisted with the coordinated takedowns in Project Reckoning and Operation Xcellerator.

Merida Initiative

The Merida Initiative was designed and presented to Congress as a U.S. interagency response to trans-border crime and security issues affecting the United States, Mexico and the countries of Central America. The Merida Initiative seeks to strengthen partner countries' capacities to combat organized criminal activities that threaten the security of the region. Merida assistance is focused three main areas: counter-narcotics, counterterrorism and border security; public security and law enforcement; and institution building and the rule of law.

Through the Criminal Division and law enforcement components, the Department is working now on Merida project planning, design, assessment and implementation. In fact, the Arms Trafficking Prosecution and Enforcement Strategy Session underway now is a bi-lateral Merida program, in which the Department of Justice, working with Mexican and U.S. interagency partners, played a substantial role in developing and presenting. Additional working-level assistance is anticipated to focus on effectively combating illegal arms trafficking.

The Department is working with Mexican counterparts on Merida projects designed to strengthen tracking and management of seized and forfeited assets; to enhance polygraph capability; and to review and strengthen internal integrity mechanisms. Additionally, the Department will be working with Mexican counterparts on prosecutorial capacity building programs; evidence collection, preservation and admissibility; forensics; extradition; and victim/witness protection.

Asset Forfeiture and Money Laundering Section (AFMLS)

AFMLS and its Mexican counterpart co-chair the Anti-Money Laundering and Asset Forfeiture SLEP sub-working group where cooperation to combat money laundering and enhance asset forfeiture cooperation between the countries is discussed. Most recently, AFMLS provided a detailed paper with comments on draft Mexican legislation that would allow for non-conviction based forfeiture in Mexico and would enhance Mexico's ability to cooperate on asset forfeiture matters with foreign countries, including the United States.

AFMLS is also working on a project to provide software and training to Mexican officials that will allow Mexico to better track and maintain assets it seizes and freezes so that it can maximize the value of those assets once it has lawfully forfeited them.

Office of Overseas Prosecutorial Development, Assistance and Training (OPDAT)

OPDAT has worked with Mexican counterparts since 2006 to develop greater collaboration and capacity in combating trafficking in persons. Most recently, an Assistant U.S. Attorney from Arizona has worked in Mexico City since October 2008 as an OPDAT Resident Legal Advisor (RLA) for Trafficking in Persons (TIP). The RLA is developing and coordinating workshops in collaboration with Mexican government officials and U.S. government partners (including DHS/ICE) to implement Mexico's newly passed anti-human trafficking law. Focus areas include greater cooperation between prosecutors and investigators on trafficking in persons cases; task force development concepts to include prosecutors, investigators, victim/witness specialists and members of relevant non-governmental organizations; and the importance of victim detection, rescue and protection in trafficking in persons cases.

The RLA has coordinated training for approximately 200 Mexican government officials in basic human trafficking law, victim identification, victim interviewing techniques, and trafficking case development. The Department and ICE have coordinated with the PGR to develop a training calendar for FY 2009, which includes more advanced trainings specifically tailored to human trafficking cases that focus on victim attention and assistance, evidence collection and preservation, crime scene management, and investigative techniques. Moreover, the RLA and ICE and the Government of Mexico regularly contact U.S. prosecutors regarding bi-national case coordination, as well as intelligence and information sharing related to ongoing investigations and prosecutions.

The Senior Law Enforcement Plenary (SLEP):

The SLEP is a U.S.-Mexico working group that consists of representatives from DHS, State Department and ONDCP, as well as DEA, FBI, USMS and ATF. SLEP working groups allow for information sharing between U.S. and Mexico representatives in the areas of: law enforcement and counternarcotics; interdiction; chemical controls; fugitives and legal issues; asset forfeiture and money laundering; organized migrant smuggling and trafficking in persons; arms trafficking; prisoner transfer; cyber and intellectual property crimes; and law enforcement training and technical assistance.

U.S. Attorneys' Offices

The U.S. Attorneys' Offices in the five Southwest border districts are on the frontlines of the national effort to prosecute criminal offenses arising at the border with Mexico, including the prosecution of narcotics trafficking, gun-smuggling, violent crimes and immigration offenses. The U.S. Attorneys' Offices also coordinate with Mexican prosecutors to share evidence in appropriate cases to ensure that justice is achieved either in U.S. courts or in Mexican courts.

Each of the Southwest border U.S. Attorneys' Offices work closely with ONDCP and federal, state, and local investigative agencies in initiatives such as the multi-agency Border Enforcement Security Task Forces, OCDETF Strike Forces, HIDTAs, and the Gatekeeper Initiative to attack complex criminal organizations; Project Gunrunner to reduce the smuggling of weapons across the border; bulk cash smuggling initiatives to restrict the flow of drug proceeds to Mexico; and the Border Fence Initiative, Tunnel Task Force, and maritime initiatives to detect illegal cross-border movement of people, drugs, money and guns.

Additional Programs and Funding

The Department's Office of Justice Programs and OCDETF will be investing $30 million in stimulus funding to assist with state and local law enforcement to combat narcotics activity coming through the southern border and in high intensity drug trafficking areas. State and local law enforcement organizations along the border can apply for COPS and Byrne Justice Assistance grants from the $3 billion provided for those programs in the stimulus package.

The OCDETF Fusion Center (OFC)

OFC is a comprehensive intelligence data center containing drug and related financial data. Through SOD, it provides critical support for long-term and large-scale investigations. OFC conducts cross-agency and cross-jurisdictional integration and analysis of drug related data to create comprehensive pictures of targeted organizations.

Reading 3.
Polarization and Sustained Violence in Mexico's Cartel War*

Anon

Editor's Note: In this annual report on Mexico's drug cartels, we assess the most significant developments of 2011 and provide updated profiles of the country's powerful criminal cartels as well as a forecast for 2012. The report is a product of the coverage we maintain through our Mexico Security Memo, quarterly updates and other analyses we produce throughout the year.

As we noted in last year's annual cartel report, Mexico in 2010 bore witness to some 15,273 deaths in connection with the drug trade. The death toll for 2010 surpassed that of any previous year, and in doing so became the deadliest year ever in the country's fight against the cartels. But in the bloody chronology that is Mexico's cartel war, 2010's time at the top may have been short-lived. Despite the Mexican government's efforts

---

* Reprinted with permission from STRATFOR, a provider of geopolitical analysis.

to curb cartel-related violence, the death toll for 2011 may have exceeded what had been an unprecedented number.

According to the Mexican government, cartel-related homicides claimed around 12,900 lives from January to September—about 1,400 deaths per month. While this figure is lower than that of 2010, it does not account for the final quarter of 2011. The Mexican government has not yet released official statistics for the entire year, but if the monthly average held until year's end, the overall death toll for 2011 would reach 17,000. Though most estimates put the total below that, the actual number of homicides in Mexico is likely higher than what is officially reported. At the very least, although we do not have a final, official number—and despite media reports to the contrary—we can conclude that violence in Mexico did not decline substantially in 2011.

Indeed, rather than receding to levels acceptable to the Mexican government, violence in Mexico has persisted, though it seems to have shifted geographically, abating in some cities and worsening in others. For example, while Ciudad Juarez, Chihuahua state, was once again Mexico's deadliest city in terms of gross numbers, the city's annual death toll reportedly dropped substantially from 3,111 in 2010 to 1,955 in 2011. However, such reductions appear to have been offset by increases elsewhere, including Veracruz, Veracruz state; Monterrey, Nuevo Leon state; Matamoros, Tamaulipas state; and Durango, Durango state.

Over the past year it has also become evident that a polarization is under way among the country's cartels. Most smaller groups (or remnants of groups) have been subsumed by the Sinaloa Federation, which controls much of western Mexico, and Los Zetas, who control much of eastern Mexico. While a great deal has been said about the fluidity of the Mexican cartel landscape, these two groups have solidified themselves as the country's predominant forces. Of course, the battle lines in Mexico have not been drawn absolutely, and not every entity calling itself a cartel swears allegiance to one side or the other, but a polarization clearly is occurring.

Geography does not encapsulate this polarization. It reflects two very different modes of operation practiced by the two cartel hegemons, delineated by a common expression in Mexican vernacular: "Plata o plomo." The expression, which translates to "silver or lead" in English, means that a cartel will force one's cooperation with either a bribe or a bullet. The Sinaloa Federation leadership more often employs the former, preferring to buy off and corrupt to achieve its objectives. It also frequently provides intelligence to authorities, and in doing so uses the authorities as a weapon against rival cartels. Sinaloa certainly can and does resort to ruthless violence, but the violence it employs is merely one of many tools at its disposal, not its preferred tactic.

On the other hand, Los Zetas prefer brutality. They can and do resort to bribery, but they lean toward intimidation and violence. Their mode of operation tends to be far less subtle than that of their Sinaloa counterparts, and with a leadership composed of former special operations soldiers, they are quite effective in employing force and fear to achieve their objectives. Because ex-military personnel formed Los Zetas, members tend to move up in the group's hierarchy through merit rather than through familial connections. This contrasts starkly with the culture of other cartels, including Sinaloa.

Status of Mexico's Major Cartels

Sinaloa Federation

The Sinaloa Federation lost at least 10 major plaza bosses or top lieutenants in 2011, including its security chief and its alleged main weapons supplier. It is unclear how much those losses have affected the group's operations overall.

One Sinaloa operation that appears to have been affected is the group's methamphetamine production. After the disintegration of La Familia Michoacana (LFM) in early 2011, the Sinaloa Federation clearly emerged as the country's foremost producer of methamphetamine. Most of the tons of precursor chemicals seized by Mexican authorities in Manzanillo, Colima state; Puerto Vallarta, Jalisco state; Lazaro Cardenas, Michoacan state; and Los Mochis and Mazatlan, Sinaloa state, likely belonged to the Sinaloa Federation. Because of these government operations—and other operations to disassemble methamphetamine labs—the group apparently began to divert at least some of its methamphetamine production to Guatemala in late 2011.

In addition to maintaining its anti-Zetas alliance with the Gulf cartel, Sinaloa in 2011 affiliated itself with the Knights Templar (KT) in Michoacan, and to counter Los Zetas in Jalisco state, Sinaloa affiliated itself with the Cartel de Jalisco Nueva Generacion (CJNG). Sinaloa also has tightened its encirclement of the Vicente Carrillo Fuentes (VCF) organization in the latter's long-held plaza of Ciudad Juarez. There are even signs that it continues to expand its control over parts of Juarez itself.

Los Zetas

By the end of 2011, Los Zetas eclipsed the Sinaloa Federation as the largest cartel operating in Mexico in terms of geographic presence. According to a report from the Assistant Attorney General's Office of Special Investigations into Organized Crime, Los Zetas now operate in 17 states. (The same report said the Sinaloa Federation operates in 16 states, down from 23 in 2005.) While Los Zetas continue to fight off a CJNG incursion into Veracruz state, they did not sustain any significant territorial losses in 2011.

Los Zetas moved into Zacatecas and Durango states, achieving a degree of control of the former and challenging the Sinaloa Federation in the latter. Both states are mountainous and conducive to the harvesting of poppy and marijuana. They also contain major north-south transportation corridors. By mid-November, reports indicated that Los Zetas had begun to assert control over Colima state and its crucial port of Manzanillo. In some cases, Los Zetas are sharing territories with cartels they reportedly have relationships with, including the Cartel Pacifico Sur (CPS), La Resistencia and the remnants of LFM. But Los Zetas have a long history of working as hired enforcers for other organizations throughout the country. Therefore, having an alliance or business relationship with Los Zetas is not necessarily the equivalent of being a Sinaloa vassal. A relationship with Los Zetas may be perceived as more fleeting than Sinaloa subjugation.

On the whole, Los Zetas remained strong in 2011 despite losing 17 cell leaders and plaza bosses to death and arrest. Los Zetas also remain the dominant force in the Yucatan

Peninsula. However, the CJNG's mass killings of alleged Zetas members or supporters in Veracruz have called into question the group's unchallenged control of that state.

In response to the mass killings in Veracruz, Los Zetas killed dozens of CJNG and Sinaloa members in Guadalajara, Jalisco state, and Culiacan, Sinaloa state. Aided by La Resistencia, these operations were well-executed, and the groups clearly invested a great deal of time and effort into surveillance and planning.

The Gulf Cartel

The Gulf cartel (CDG) was strong at the beginning of 2011, holding off several Zetas incursions into its territory. However, as the year progressed, internal divisions led to intra-cartel battles in Matamoros and Reynosa, Tamaulipas state. The infighting resulted in several deaths and arrests in Mexico and in the United States. The CDG has since broken apart, and it appears that one faction, known as Los Metros, has overpowered its rival Los Rojos faction and is now asserting its control over CDG operations. The infighting has weakened the CDG, but the group seems to have maintained control of its primary plazas, or smuggling corridors, into the United States. (CDG infighting is detailed further in another section of this report.)

La Familia Michoacana

LFM disintegrated at the beginning of 2011, giving rise to and becoming eclipsed by one of its factions, the Knights Templar (KT). Indeed, by July it was clear the KT had become more powerful than LFM in Mexico. The media and the police continue to report that LFM maintains extensive networks in the United States, but it is unclear how many of the U.S.-based networks are actually working with LFM rather than the KT, which is far more capable of trafficking narcotics. It appears that many reports regarding LFM in the United States do not reflect the changes that have occurred in Mexico over the past year; many former LFM leaders are now members of the KT. Adding to the confusion was the alleged late-summer alliance between LFM and Los Zetas. Such an alliance would have been a final attempt by the remaining LFM leadership to keep the group from being utterly destroyed by the KT. LFM is still active, but it is very weak.

The Knights Templar

In January 2011, a month after the death of charismatic LFM leader Nazario "El Mas Loco" Moreno, two former LFM lieutenants, Servando "La Tuta" Gomez and Enrique Plancarte, formed the Knights Templar due to differences with Jose de Jesus "El Chango" Mendez, who had assumed leadership of LFM. In March they announced the formation of their new organization via narcomantas in Morelia, Zitacuaro and Apatzingan, Michoacan state.

After the emergence of the KT, sizable battles flared up during the spring and summer months between the KT and LFM. The organization has grown from a splinter group to a dominant force over LFM, and it appears to be taking over the bulk of the original LFM's operations in Mexico. At present, the Knights Templar appear to have aligned with the Sinaloa

Federation in an effort to root out the remnants of LFM and to prevent Los Zetas from gaining a more substantial foothold in the region through their alliance with LFM.

Independent Cartel of Acapulco

The Independent Cartel of Acapulco (CIDA) has not been eliminated entirely, but it appears to have been severely damaged. Since the capture of CIDA leader Gilberto Castrejon Morales in early December, the group has faded from the public view. CIDA's weakness appears to have allowed its in-town rival, Sinaloa-affiliated La Barredora, to move some of its enforcers to Guadalajara to fend off the Zetas offensive there. The decreased levels of violence and public displays of dead bodies in Acapulco of late can be attributed to the group's weakening, and we are unsure if CIDA will be able to regroup and attempt to reclaim Acapulco.

Cartel de Jalisco Nueva Generacion

After the death of Ignacio "El Nacho" Coronel in July 2010, his followers suspected the Sinaloa cartel had betrayed him and broke away to form the CJNG. In spring 2011, the CJNG declared war on all other Mexican cartels and stated its intention to take control of Guadalajara. However, by midsummer, the group appeared to have been reunited with its former partners in the Sinaloa Federation. We are unsure what precipitated the reconciliation, but it seems that the CJNG was somehow convinced that Sinaloa did not betray Coronel after all. It is also possible CJNG was convinced that Coronel needed to go. In any case, CJNG "sicarios," or assassins, in September traveled to the important Los Zetas stronghold of Veracruz, labeled themselves the "Matazetas," or Zeta killers, and began to murder alleged Zetas members and their supporters. By mid-December, the CJNG was still in Veracruz fighting Los Zetas while also helping to protect Guadalajara and other areas on Mexico's west coast from Zetas aggression.

Vicente Carrillo Fuentes Organization/Juarez Cartel

The VCF, aka the Juarez cartel, continues to weaken. A Sinaloa operative killed one of its top lieutenants, Francisco Vicente Castillo Carrillo—a Carrillo family member—in September 2011. The VCF reportedly still controls the three main points of entry into El Paso, Texas, but the organization appears unable to expand its operations or move narcotics en masse through its plazas because it is hemmed in by the Sinaloa Federation, which appears to have chipped away at the VCF's monopoly of the Juarez plaza. The VCF is only a shadow of the organization it was a decade ago, and its weakness and inability to effectively fight against Sinaloa's advances in Juarez contributed to the lower death toll in Juarez in 2011.

Cartel Pacifico Sur

The CPS, headed by Hector Beltran Leyva, saw a reduction in violence in the latter part of 2011 after having been very active in the first third of the year. We are unsure why the group quieted down. The CPS may be concentrating on smuggling for revenue generation to support itself and assist its Los Zetas allies, who provide military muscle for the CPS and work in their areas of operation. Because of their reputation, Los Zetas receive a great deal of media attention, so it is also possible that the media attributed violent incidents involving CPS gunmen to Los Zetas.

Arellano Felix Organization

The November arrest of Juan Francisco Sillas Rocha, the AFO's chief enforcer, was yet another sign of the organization's continued weakness. It remains an impotent and reluctant subsidiary of the Sinaloa Federation, unable to reclaim the Tijuana plaza for its own.

2011 Forecast in Review

In our forecast for 2011, we believed that the unprecedented levels of violence from 2010 would continue as long as the cartel balance of power remained in a state of flux. Indeed, cartel-related deaths appear to have at least continued apace.

Much of the cartel conflict in 2011 followed patterns set in 2010. Los Zetas continued to fight the CDG in northeast Mexico while maintaining their control of Veracruz state and the Yucatan Peninsula. The Sinaloa Federation continued to fight the VCF in Ciudad Juarez while maintaining control of much of Sonora state and Baja California state.

We forecast that government operations and cartel infighting and rivalry would expose fissures in and among the cartels. This prediction held true. The Beltran Leyva Organization no longer exists in its original form, its members dispersed among the Sinaloa Federation, the CPS, CIDA and other smaller groups. As noted above, fissures within LFM led to the creation of two groups, LFM and the KT. The CDG also now consists of two factions competing for control of the organization's operations.

We also forecast that the degree of violence in the country was politically unacceptable for Mexican President Felipe Calderon and his ruling National Action Party. Calderon knew he would have to reduce the violence to acceptable levels if his party was going to have a chance to continue to hold power after he left office in 2012 (Mexican presidents serve only one six-year term). As the 2012 presidential election approaches, Calderon is continuing his strategy of deploying the armed forces against the cartels. He has also reached out to the United States for assistance. The two countries shared signals intelligence throughout the year and continued to cooperate through joint intelligence centers like the one in Mexico City. The U.S. military also continues to train Mexican military and law enforcement personnel, and the United States has deployed unmanned aerial vehicles (UAVs) in Mexican airspace at Mexico's behest. The Mexican military was in operational command of the UAV missions.

As we have noted the past few years, we also believed that Calderon's continued use of the military would perpetuate what is referred to as the three-front war in Mexico. The fronts consist of cartels against rival cartels, the military against cartels, and cartels against civilians. Indeed, in 2011 the cartels continued to vie for control of ports, plazas and markets, while deployments of military forces increased to counter Los Zetas in the states of Coahuila, Tamaulipas, Nuevo Leon and Veracruz; to combat several groups waging a bloody turf war in Acapulco, Guerrero state; and to respond to conflicts arising between the Sinaloa Federation and Los Zetas and their affiliate groups in Nayarit and Michoacan states.

While Los Zetas were hit hard in 2011, the Mexican government's offensive against the group was unable to damage it to the extent we believed it would. Despite losing several key leaders and plaza bosses, as noted previously, the group maintains its pre-eminence in the east. This is largely due to the ease with which such groups can replenish their ranks.

Resupplying Leadership

One of the ways in which Mexico's cartels, including Los Zetas, replenish their ranks is with defected military personnel. Around 27,000 men and women desert the Mexican military every year, and about 50 percent of the military's recruiting class will have left before the end of their first tour. In March 2011, the Mexican army admitted that it had "lost track of" 1,680 special forces personnel over the past decade (Los Zetas were formed by more than 30 former members of Mexico's Special Forces Airmobile Group). Some cartels even reportedly task some of their own foot soldiers to enlist in the military to gain knowledge and experience in military tactics. In any case, retention is clearly a serious problem for the Mexican armed forces, and deserting soldiers take their skills (and oftentimes their weapons) to the cartels.

In addition, the drug trade attracts ex-military personnel who did not desert but left in good standing after serving their duty. There are fewer opportunities for veterans in Mexico than in many countries, and understandably many are drawn to a lucrative practice that places value on their skill sets. But deserters or former soldiers are not the only source of recruits for the cartels. They also replenish their ranks with current and former police officers, gang members and others (to include Central American immigrants and even U.S. citizens).

2012 Forecasts by Region

Northeast Mexico

Northeast Mexico saw some of the most noteworthy cartel violence in 2011. The primary conflict in the region involved the continuing fight between CDG and Los Zetas, who were CDG enforcers before breaking away from the CDG in early 2010. Los Zetas have since eclipsed the CDG in terms of size, reach and influence. In 2011, divisions within the CDG over leadership succession came to the fore, leading to further violence in the region, and we believe these divisions will sow the group's undoing in 2012.

The CDG began to suffer another internal fracture in late 2010 when the Mexican army killed Antonio "Tony Tormenta" Cardenas Guillen, who co-lead the CDG with Eduardo "El Coss" Costilla Sanchez, in Matamoros, Tamaulipas state. After Cardenas Guillen's death in November 2010, Costilla Sanchez assumed full control of the organization, passing over Rafael "El Junior" Cardenas Vela, the Cardenas family's heir apparent, in the process. This bisected the CDG, creating two competing factions: Los Rojos, loyal to the Cardenas family, and Los Metros, loyal to Costilla Sanchez.

In late 2011, several events exacerbated tensions between the factions. On Sept. 3, authorities found the body of Samuel "El Metro 3" Flores Borrego, Costilla Sanchez's second-in-command, in Reynosa, Tamaulipas state. Then on Sept. 27, gunmen in an SUV shot and killed a man driving a vehicle on U.S. Route 83, east of McAllen, Texas. The driver, Jorge Zavala of Mission, Texas, was connected to Los Metros.

The Mexican navy reported the following month that Cesar "El Gama" Davila Garcia, the CDG's head finance officer, was found dead in Reynosa. Davila previously had served as Cardenas Guillen's accountant. Then on Oct. 20, U.S. Immigration and Customs Enforcement agents arrested Cardenas Vela after a traffic stop near Port Isabel, Texas. We believe Los Metros tipped off U.S. authorities about Cardenas Vela's location. (Los Metros have every reason to kill Los Rojos leaders, including Cardenas Vela, but cartels rarely conduct assassinations on U.S. soil for fear of U.S. retribution.)

On Oct. 28, Jose Luis "Comandante Wicho" Zuniga Hernandez, believed to be Cardenas Vela's deputy and operational leader in Matamoros, reportedly turned himself in to U.S. authorities without a fight near Santa Maria, Texas. Finally, Mexican federal authorities arrested Ezequiel "El Junior" Cardenas Rivera, Cardenas Guillen's son, in Matamoros on Nov. 25.

By December, media agencies reported that Cardenas Guillen's brother, Mario Cardenas Guillen, was the overall leader of the CDG. But Mario was never known to be very active in the family business, and his reluctance to involve himself in cartel operations appears to have continued after his brother's death. In addition, Costilla Sanchez is reclusive, choosing to run his organization from several secluded ranches. That he is not mentioned in media reports does not mean he has been removed from his position. Given his reclusiveness and Mario Cardenas Guillen's longstanding reticence to involve himself in cartel activity, it seems unlikely that Costilla Sanchez would be replaced. Because Los Metros seemingly have gained the upper hand over Los Rojos, we anticipate that they will further expand their dominance in early 2012.

However, while Los Metros may have defeated their rival for control of the CDG, the organizational infighting has left the CDG vulnerable to outside attack. Of course, any group divided is vulnerable to attack, but the CDG's ongoing feud with Los Zetas compounds its problem. Fully aware of the CDG's weakness, we believe Los Zetas will step up their attempts to assume control of CDG territory.

If Los Zetas are able to defeat the Los Metros faction—or they engage in a truce with the faction—they may be able to redeploy fighters to other regions or cities, particularly Veracruz and Guadalajara. Reinforcements in Veracruz would help counter the CJNG presence in the port city, and reinforcements in Guadalajara would shore up Los Zetas' operations and presence in Jalisco state. Likewise, a reduction in cartel-on-cartel fighting in the region would free up troops the Mexican army has stationed in Tamaulipas state—an estimated force of 13,000 soldiers—for deployment elsewhere.

Southeast Mexico

Some notable events took place in southeast Mexico in 2011. On Dec. 4 the Mexican army dismantled a Zetas communications network that encompassed multiple cities in Veracruz, Tamaulipas, Nuevo Leon, San Luis Potosi and Coahuila states.

In addition, Veracruz state Gov. Javier Duarte on Dec. 21 fired the city's municipal police, including officers and administrative employees, and gave the Mexican navy law enforcement responsibilities. By Dec. 22, Mexican marines began patrols and law enforcement activities, effectively replacing the police much like the army replaced the police in Ciudad Juarez in 2009 and in various cities in Tamaulipas state in August 2011. We anticipate that fighting between the CJNG and Los Zetas will continue in Veracruz for at least the first quarter of 2012.

We expect security conditions on the Yucatan Peninsula to remain relatively stable in 2012 because there are no other major players in the region contesting Los Zetas' control.

Southwest Mexico

In the southern Pacific coastal states of Chiapas and Oaxaca, we expect violence to be as infrequent in 2012 as it was in 2011. Chiapas and Oaxaca have been transshipment zones for Los Zetas and the Sinaloa Federation for several years; as such, clashes and cargo hijackings occasionally take place. However, direct and sustained combat does not occur regularly because the two groups tend to use different routes to transport their shipments. The Sinaloa Federation prefers to move its product north on roads and highways along the Pacific coast, whereas Los Zetas' transportation lines cross Mexico's interior before moving north along the Gulf coast.

Pacific Coast and Central Mexico

As many as a dozen organizations, ranging from the KT to local criminal organizations to newer groups like La Barredora and La Resistencia, continue to fight for control of the plazas in Guerrero, Michoacan and Jalisco states. Acapulco was particularly violent in 2011, and we believe it will continue to be violent through 2012 unless La Barredora is able to exert firm control over the city. Acapulco has been a traditional Beltran Leyva stronghold, and the CPS may attempt to reassert itself there. If that happens, violence will once again increase.

Security conditions worsened in Jalisco state at the end of 2011, and Stratfor anticipates violence there will continue to increase in 2012, especially in Guadalajara, a valued transportation hub. In November, Los Zetas struck the CJNG in Guadalajara in response to the mass killings of Los Zetas members in Veracruz state. The attacks are significant because they demonstrated an ability to conduct protracted cross-country operations. Should Los Zetas establish firm control over Guadalajara, the Sinaloa Federation's smuggling activities could be adversely affected, something Sinaloa obviously cannot permit. Given an increased Zetas presence in Zacatecas, Durango and Jalisco states, and Sinaloa's operational need to counter that presence, we expect to see violence increase in the region in 2012.

Unless a significant military force is somehow brought to bear, we do not expect to see any substantive improvement in the security conditions in Guerrero or Michoacan states.

Northwest Mexico

The cross-country operations performed by Los Zetas indicate that the group's growth and expansion has been more profound than we expected in the face of the government's major operations specifically targeting the organization. Such expansion will pose a direct threat not only to the Sinaloa Federation's supply lines but to its home turf, which stretches from Guadalajara to southern Sonora state.

In northwest Mexico, specifically Baja California, Baja California Sur and Chihuahua states (and most of Sonora state), the Sinaloa Federation either directly controls or regularly uses the smuggling corridors and points of entry into the United States. Security conditions in the plazas under firm Sinaloa control have been relatively stable. Indeed, as Sinaloa tightened its control over Tijuana, violence there dropped, and we expect to see the same dynamic play out in Juarez as Sinaloa consolidates its control of that city. Stability could be threatened, however, if Los Zetas attempt to push into Sinaloa-held cities.

Outside of Mexico

As we noted in the past three annual cartel reports, Mexico's cartels have been expanding their control of the cocaine supply chain all the way into South America. This eliminates middlemen and brings in more profit. They are also using their presence in South America to obtain chemical precursors and weapons.

Increased violence in northern Mexico and ramped-up law enforcement along the U.S. border has made narcotics smuggling into the United States more difficult than it has been in the past. The cartels have adapted to these challenges by becoming more involved in the trafficking of cocaine to alternative markets in Europe and Australia. The arrests of Mexican cartel members in such places as the Dominican Republic also seem to indicate that the Mexicans are becoming more involved in the Caribbean smuggling routes into the United States. In the past, Colombian smuggling groups and their Caribbean partners in places like Cuba, Puerto Rico and the Dominican Republic used these routes. We anticipate seeing more signs of Mexican cartel involvement in the Caribbean, Europe and Australia in 2012.

Government Strategy in 2012

There is no indication of a major shift in the Mexican government's overarching security strategy for 2012; Calderon will continue to use the military against the cartels throughout the year (a new president will be elected in July, but Calderon's term does not conclude until the end of 2012). This strategy of taking out cartel leaders has resulted in the disruption of the cartel balance of power in the past, which tends to lead to more violence as groups scramble to fill the resultant power vacuum. Mexican operations may further disrupt that balance in 2012, but while government operations have broken apart some cartel organizations, the combination of military and law enforcement resources has been unable to dislodge cartel influence from the areas it targets. They can break specific criminal organizations, but the lucrative smuggling corridors into the United States will continue to exist, even after the organizations controlling them are taken down. And as long as the smuggling corridors exist, and provide access to so much money, other organizations will inevitably fight to assume control over them.

Some 45,000 Mexican troops are actively involved in domestic counter-cartel operations. These troops work alongside state and federal law enforcement officers and in some cases have replaced fired municipal police officers. They are spread across a large country with high levels of violence in most major cities, and their presence in these cities is essential for maintaining what security has been achieved.

While this number of troops represents only about a quarter of the overall Mexican army's manpower—troops are often supplemented by deployments of Mexican marines—it also represents the bulk of applicable Mexican military ground combat strength. Meager and poorly maintained reserve forces do not appear to be a meaningful supplemental resource.

In short, if the current conditions persist, it does not appear that the Mexican government can redeploy troops to conduct meaningful offensive operations in new areas of Mexico in 2012 without jeopardizing the gains it has already made. The government cannot eliminate the cartels any more than it can end the drug trade. The only way the Mexican government can bring the violence down to what would be considered an acceptable level is for it to allow one cartel group to become dominant throughout the country—something that does not appear to be plausible in the near term—or for some sort of truce to be reached between the country's two cartel hegemons, Los Zetas and the Sinaloa Federation.

Such scenarios are not unprecedented. At one time the Guadalajara cartel controlled virtually all of Mexico's drug trade, and it was only the dissolution of that organization that led to its regional branches subsequently becoming what we now know as the Sinaloa Federation, AFO, VCF and CDG. There have also been periods of cartel truces in the past between the various regional cartel groups, although they tend to be short-lived.

With the current levels of violence, a government-brokered truce between Los Zetas and Sinaloa will be no easy task, given the level of animosity and mistrust that exists between the two organizations. This means that it is unlikely that such a truce will be brokered in 2012, but we expect to see more rhetoric in support of a truce as a way to reduce violence.

Reading 4.
The Mexican Drug Cartel Threat in Central America*

Karen Hooper

Guatemalan President-elect Otto Perez Molina told Mexican newspaper El Universal on Nov. 9 that he plans to engage drug cartels in a "full frontal assault" when he takes office in 2012. The former general said he will use Guatemala's elite military forces,

---

* Reprinted with permission from STRATFOR, a provider of geopolitical analysis.

known as Los Kaibiles, to take on the drug cartels in a strategy similar to that of the Mexican government; he has asked for U.S. assistance in this struggle.

The statements signal a shifting political landscape in already violent Central America. The region is experiencing increasing levels of crime and the prospect of heightened competition from Mexican drug cartels in its territory. The institutional weakness and security vulnerabilities of Guatemala and other Central American states mean that combating these trends will require significant help, most likely from the United States.

From Sideshow to Center Stage

Central America has seen a remarkable rise in its importance as a transshipment point for cocaine and other contraband bound for the United States. Meanwhile, Mexican organized crime has expanded its activities in Mexico and Central America to include the smuggling of humans and substances such as precursor chemicals used for manufacturing methamphetamine. Substantial evidence also suggests that Central American, and particularly Guatemalan, military armaments including M60 machine guns and 40 mm grenades have wound up being used in Mexico's drug conflict.

From the 1970s to the 1990s, Colombian cartels transited directly to Miami. After U.S. military aerial and radar surveillance in the Caribbean effectively shut down those routes, Mexico became the last stop on the drug supply chain before the United States, greatly empowering Mexico's cartels. A subsequent Mexican government crackdown put pressure on Mexican drug trafficking organizations (DTOs) to diversify their transit routes to avoid increased enforcement at Mexico's airstrips and ports. Central America consequently has become an increasingly significant middleman for South American suppliers and Mexican buyers of contraband.

The methods and routes for moving illicit goods through Central America are diverse and constantly in flux. There is no direct land connection between the coca-growing countries of Colombia, Peru and Bolivia. A region of swampy jungle terrain along the Panamanian-Colombian border known as the Darien Gap has made road construction prohibitively expensive and thus barred all but the most intrepid of overland travelers. Instead, aircraft or watercraft must be used to transport South American goods north, which can then be offloaded in Central America and driven north into Mexico. Once past the Darien Gap, the Pan American Highway becomes a critical transportation corridor. Honduras, for example, reportedly has become a major destination for planes from Venezuela laden with cocaine. Once offloaded, the cocaine is moved across the loosely guarded Honduran-Guatemalan border and then moved through Guatemala to Mexico, often through the largely unpopulated Peten department.

Though precise measurements of the black market are notoriously difficult to obtain, these shifts in Central America have been well-documented—and the impact on the region has been stark. While drug trafficking occurs in all Central American countries to some extent, most violence associated with the trade occurs in the historically tumultuous "Northern Triangle" of Guatemala, El Salvador and Honduras. No longer receiving the global attention they did when the United States became involved in their

Cold War-era civil wars, these countries remain poverty stricken, plagued by local gangs and highly unstable.

The violence has worsened as the drug traffic has increased. El Salvador saw its homicide rate increase by 6 percent to 66 per 100,000 inhabitants between 2005 and 2010. At the same time, Guatemala's homicide rate increased 13 percent to 50 per 100,000 inhabitants. Meanwhile, Honduras saw a rise of 108 percent to 77 per 100,000 inhabitants. These are some of the highest homicide rates in the world.

In comparison, the drug war in Mexico caused murder rates to spike 64 percent, from 11 to 18 deaths per 100,000 between 2005 and 2010. Conservative estimates put the number of dead from gang and military violence in Mexico at 50,000. These numbers are slightly misleading, as Mexican violence is concentrated in scattered pockets where most drug trafficking and competition among drug traffickers occurs. Even so, they demonstrate the disproportionate impact organized criminal groups have had on the societies of the three Northern Triangle countries.

Guatemala's Outsized Role

Increased involvement by Mexican cartels in Central America inevitably has affected the region's politico-economic structures, a process most visible in Guatemala. Its territory spans Central America, making it one of several choke points on the supply chain of illicit goods coming north from El Salvador and Honduras bound for Mexico.

Guatemala has a complex and competitive set of criminal organizations, many of which are organized around tight-knit family units. These family organizations have included the politically and economically powerful Lorenzana and Mendoza families. First rising to prominence in trade and agriculture, these families control significant businesses in Guatemala and transportation routes for shipping both legal and illicit goods. Though notorious, these families are far from alone in Guatemala's criminal organizations. Major drug traffickers like the well-known Mario Ponce and Walther Overdick also have strong criminal enterprises, with Ponce reportedly managing his operations from a Honduran jail.

The relationship of these criminal organizations to Mexican drug cartels is murky at best. The Sinaloa and Los Zetas cartels are both known to have relationships with Guatemalan organized criminal groups, but the lines of communication and their exact agreements are unclear.

Less murky, however, is that Los Zetas are willing to use the same levels of violence in Guatemala to coerce loyalty as they have used in Mexico. Though both Sinaloa and Los Zetas still need Guatemalan groups to access high-level Guatemalan political connections, Los Zetas have taken a particularly aggressive tack in seeking direct control over more territory in Guatemala.

Overdick facilitated Los Zetas' entry into Guatemala in 2007. The first indication of serious Los Zetas involvement in Guatemala occurred in March 2008 when Leon crime family boss Juan Leon Ardon, alias "El Juancho," his brother Hector Enrique Leon Chacon and nine associates all died in a gunbattle with Los Zetas, who at the time still worked for the Gulf cartel. The fight severely reduced the influence of the Leon crime family, primarily benefiting Overdick's organization. The Zetas most flagrant use of force occurred in the May 2011 massacre and mutilation of 27 peasants in northern Guatemala intended as a message to a local drug dealer allegedly tied to the Leon family; the Zetas also killed and mutilated that drug dealer's niece.

MS-13 and Calle 18

In addition to ramping up relationships with powerful political, criminal and economic players, Sinaloa and Los Zetas have established relationships with Central American street gangs. The two biggest gangs in the region are Mara Salvatrucha (MS-13) and Calle 18. The two groups are loosely organized around local cliques; the Mexican cartels have relationships at varying levels of closeness with different cliques. The U.N. Office on Drugs and Crime estimates that there are 36,000 gang members in Honduras, 14,000 in Guatemala and 10,500 in El Salvador.

They were formed by Los Angeles gang members of Central American origin whose parents had immigrated to the United States to escape the region's civil wars. After being arrested in the United States, these gang members were deported to Central America. In some cases, the deportees spoke no Spanish and had no significant ties to their ancestral homeland, encouraging them to cluster together and make use of the skills learned on the streets of Los Angeles to make a living in Central America via organized crime.

The gangs have multiplied and migrated within the region. Many have also returned to the United States: U.S. authorities estimate that MS-13 and Calle 18 have a presence in as many as 42 states. Though the gangs are truly transnational, their emphasis is on controlling localized urban turfs. They effectively control large portions of Guatemala City, Guatemala; Tegucigalpa, Honduras; and San Salvador, El Salvador. Competition within and among these gangs is responsible for a great deal of the violence in these three countries.

In a March statement, Salvadoran Defense Minister David Munguia Payes said that his government had evidence that both Sinaloa and Los Zetas are active in El Salvador but that he believes MS-13 and Calle 18 are too anarchic and violent for the Mexican cartels to rely on heavily. According to Honduran Security Minister Pompeyo Bonilla, Mexican cartels primarily hire members of these gangs as assassins. The gangs are paid in drugs, which they sell on the local drug market.

Though limited in their ties to the Mexican cartels, the prevalence of MS-13 and Calle 18 in the Northern Triangle states and their extreme violence makes them a force to be reckoned with, for both the cartels and Central American governments. If Central American street gangs are able to better organize themselves internally, this could result in closer collaboration, or alternately serious confrontations with the Mexican cartels. In either case, the implications for stability in Central America are enormous.

The U.S. Role

The United States has long played an important, complex role in Latin America. In the early 20th century, U.S. policy in the Western Hemisphere was characterized by the extension of U.S. economic and military control over the region. With tactics ranging from outright military domination to facilitating competition between subregional powers Guatemala and Nicaragua to ensuring the dominance of the United Fruit Co. in Central American politics and business, the United States used the first several decades of the century to ensure that Central America—and by extension the Caribbean—was under its control. After World War II, Central America became a proxy battleground between the United States and the Soviet Union.

On a strategic level, Central America is far enough from the United States (thanks to being buffered by Mexico) and made up of small enough countries that it does not pose a direct threat to the United States. U.S. interest in the region did not end after the Cold War, however, as it is critically important to the United States that a foreign global competitor never control Central America or the Caribbean.

The majority of money spent combating drug trafficking from South America to the United States over the past decade has been spent in Colombia on monitoring air and naval traffic in the Caribbean and off the Pacific coasts, though the U.S. focus has now shifted to Mexico. Central America, by contrast, has languished since the Reagan years, when the United States allocated more than $1 billion per year to Central America. Now, the region has been allocated a total of $361.5 million for fiscal years 2008–2011 in security, economic and development aid through the Merida Initiative and the Central America Regional Security Initiative (CARSI). The Obama administration has requested another $100 million for CARSI. Of this allocated funding, however, only 18 percent has been dispersed due to failures in institutional cooperation and efficiency.

The U.S. Drug Enforcement Administration (DEA) has facilitated most U.S.-Central American security cooperation. The DEA operates teams in the Northern Triangle that participate in limited counternarcotic operations. They are also tasked with both vetting and training local law enforcement, a particularly tricky—and most likely doomed—task. As the failure of Guatemala's highly vetted and lauded Department of Anti-Narcotics Operations shows, preventing local law enforcement from succumbing to the bribes and threats from wealthy and violent DTOs is a difficult, if not impossible, task.

The DEA's limited resources include five Foreign-deployed Advisory and Support Teams worldwide. These are the agency's elite operational teams that are equipped to train foreign law enforcement and military personnel and to conduct support operations. Originally established to operate in Afghanistan exclusively, the teams have been deployed to several countries in Central America, including Guatemala and Honduras. These teams are designed to be flexible, however, and do not represent the kind of long-term commitment that would likely be necessary to stabilize the region.

Central America's Challenge

Central America has no short-term escape from being at the geographical center of the drug trade and from the associated violence. Unless and until technologies shift to allow drugs to flow directly from producer to consumer via ocean or air transport, it appears likely that Central America will only become more important to the drug trade. While the drug trade brings huge amounts of cash (admittedly on the black market) into exceedingly capital-poor countries, it also brings extreme violence.

The billions of dollars drugs command create an insurmountable challenge for the regional counternarcotic campaigns. The U.S. "war on drugs" pits the Guatemalan elite's political and financial interests against their need to retain a positive relationship with the United States, which views the elites as colluding with drug organizations to facilitate the free passage of drugs and key figures in the drug trade.

For the leaders of Central America, foreign cartel interference in domestic arrangements and increasing violence is the real threat to their power. It is not the black market that alarms a leader like Perez Molina enough to call for greater involvement by the United States: It is the threat posed by the infiltration of Mexico's most violent drug cartel into Guatemala, and the threat posed to all three countries by further Central American drug gang destabilization, which could lead to even more violence.

Looking Forward

The United States is heavily preoccupied with crises of varying degrees of importance around the world and the significant budget-tightening under way in Congress. This makes a major reallocation of resources to Guatemala or its Central American neighbors for the fight against Mexican drug cartels unlikely in the short term. Even so, key reasons for paying close attention to this issue remain.

First, the situation could destabilize rapidly if Perez Molina is sincere about confronting Mexican DTOs in Guatemala. Los Zetas have proved willing to apply their signature brutality against civilians and rivals alike in Guatemala. While the Guatemalans would be operating on their own territory and have their own significant power bases, they are neither technologically advanced nor wealthy nor unified enough to tackle the challenge posed by heavily armed, well-funded Zetas. At the very least, such a confrontation would ignite extremely destabilizing violence. This violence could extend beyond the Northern Triangle into more stable Central American countries, not to mention the possibility that violence spreading north could open up a new front in Mexico's cartel war.

Second, the United States and Mexico already are stretched thin trying to control their shared 3,200-kilometer land border. U.S. counternarcotic activities in Mexico are limited by Mexican sovereignty concerns. For example, carrying weapons and operating independent of Mexican supervision is not allowed. This hampers the interdiction efforts of U.S. agencies like the DEA. The efforts also are hampered by the United States' unwillingness to share intelligence for fear that corrupt Mexican officials would leak it.

Perez Molina's invitation for increased U.S. participation in Guatemalan counternarcotic operations presents a possibility for U.S. involvement in a country that, like Mexico, straddles the continent. The Guatemalan choke point has a much shorter border with Mexico—about 970 kilometers—in need of control and is far enough north in Central America to prevent insertion of drug traffickers into the supply chain between the blocking force and Mexico. While the United States would not be able to stop the illicit flow of cocaine and people north, it could make it significantly more difficult. And although significantly reducing traffic at the Guatemalan border would not stop the flow of the drugs to the United States, it would radically decrease the value of Central America as a trafficking corridor.

Accomplishing this would require a much more significant U.S. commitment to the drug war, and any such direct involvement would be costly both in money and political capital. Absent significant U.S. help, the current trend of increased Mexican cartel influence and violence in Central America will only worsen.

Chapter 6

Dealing with Adult Criminal Gangs and Drug Trafficking Organizations

I. Introduction

Adult criminal gangs and drug trafficking organizations are the primary drug traffickers in North America (United States, Canada, and Mexico). As we have seen, large national and transnational street gangs, prison gangs, outlaw motorcycle gangs, and DTOs smuggle, transport, and distribute illicit drugs throughout North America. In the course of their criminal activities, these gangs routinely cross national and state borders. These criminal organizations are extremely violent as they compete for markets, territory, and maintain internal discipline. However, on occasion, gangs, even those who are bitter rivals, work together when needed to increase their illicit profits.

Criminal gangs have grown and expanded along with the opportunities and expanding criminal markets. Some local street gangs have morphed into criminal organizations that commit criminal acts locally, regionally, nationally, and in some cases across national borders. American-based outlaw motorcycle gangs have evolved into regional, national, and transnational drug distributors able to coordinate partnerships with international DTOs in the U.S., Canada, and Mexico. Prison gangs starting out as criminal organizations within the prison system now operate on the street and act as a link between DTOs, street gangs, and OMGs in criminal activities. Along the U.S.-Mexican border, U.S. prison gangs commit crimes on both sides of the border and liaison with Mexican DTOs and cartels. The seven Mexican drug cartels are a particular drug-trafficking problem in the United States because they operate in 3,000 American cities.

II. Investigation and Prosecution Strategies

The porous borders between the United States, Canada, and Mexico do not contain adult criminal gangs. Therefore, dealing with the criminal threats posed by these adult criminal gangs requires new thinking and new strategies. Unlike traditional intervention and prevention programs suggested for "youth" gangs, the response to adult criminal gangs requires a new theory of investigation and prosecution—the enterprise theory and prosecution under the RICO act in the United States. Under this theory, the gang as a criminal organization (enterprise) engages in a pattern of racketeering that affects interstate or foreign commerce and the defendant/s is/are members of the racketeering enterprise (Sheppard, 2007). The enterprise theory targets adult criminal gangs, particularly those with a hierarchical structure, and multiple gun and drug connections and seeks to incarcerate as many members as possible. Today's approach to gang investigations has as its ultimate goal "to dismantle the gang and appropriately punish its core members" (Agnifilo, Bliss and Riordan, 2006:15). Federal prosecution of gangs using RICO is extremely labor intensive often involving multiple agencies and requiring permission by the Department of Justice to proceed under the appropriate federal statues; therefore, not all adult gang prosecutions take the federal route. For that reason, 31 states have their own or similar RICO statues and use the enterprise theory and the appropriate statutes to prosecute gangs.

As stated, RICO prosecutions at the state or federal level are not always the best strategy. Smaller, less-established gangs, or sets of larger, established gangs could be dismantled by the more traditional approach of taking out the leadership for individual crimes. For example, the violent transnational street gang MS 13 has a federal task force organized to investigate and prosecute the gang; however, there are often incidents where action must be taken against individual members and not the gang (see Box 6.1).

Box 6.1 MS 13 National Gang Task Force

Mara Salvatrucha, or MS 13, continues to expand its influence in the United States. FBI investigations reveal that it is present in almost every state and continues to grow its membership, now targeting younger recruits more than ever before.

To counteract this growth, the FBI formed the MS 13 National Gang Task Force in December 2004. Based at FBI Headquarters, this intelligence-driven task force combines the expertise, resources, and jurisdiction of federal agencies that investigate this violent international street gang. It focuses on maximizing the flow of information and intelligence, coordinating investigations nationally and internationally, and helping state and local law enforcement improve operations and prosecutions targeting MS 13.

The task force has instituted the Central American Fingerprint Exploitation (CAFÉ) initiative to acquire criminal fingerprints from the Central American region and to merge those fingerprints and associated criminal records into our Integrated Automated Fingerprint System (AFIS) database.

Modified from: FBI.gov MS-13 National Gang Task Force.

For instance, a Salvadoran national and MS 13 gang leader was convicted of prostituting a 12-year-old female with clients throughout northern Virginia, Maryland, and Washington, D.C. The MS 13 leader, known as "sniper," joined MS 13 in El Salvador and was the leader of the Pinos Locos clique of MS 13. He met the young female runaway at a Halloween party. She asked for his help in finding a place to stay, and he began prostituting her out the next day (U.S. Department of Homeland Security, July 28, 2011). In another case, the leader of the Queens, N.Y. chapter of MS 13, known as "Diablito," and several other members drove the streets looking for rival members to shoot. They spotted three young men, mistakenly believing them to be rival gang members. Diablito jumped from the car and shot one to death (U.S. Department of Homeland Security, April 29, 2011).

Furthermore, gang prosecutions do not always involve racketeering offenses, especially those involving interstate or foreign commerce. A weekend crime spree by five members of the Sur-13, or Surenos 13, gang resulted in lengthy prison sentences ranging from 13 to 24 years. The defendants, three males and two females, went on an armed robbery spree that covered metro Atlanta, Georgia. Their crime spree included seven carjackings or attempted carjackings, the robbery of a small grocery store, and several pedestrian robberies. Officers from the U.S. Immigration and Customs Enforcement's (ICE) Homeland Security Investigations made the arrests (U.S. Department of Homeland Security, August 8, 2011). Often, the prosecution of one or more members can dismantle a local less-established gang. The Ivy Street Gangstas (ISG) operated in and around two areas of Newport News, Virginia. They were a local gang with no regional or national members or associates. Four members, including the leader, of the ISG gang pleaded guilty to two murders and coordinating with each other to commit robberies, distribute narcotics, and commit acts of fraud to obtain money and property for the gang's benefit (FBI, January 25, 2012).

III. RICO and VICAR Prosecutions of Criminal Enterprises

The enterprise theory of prosecution is the best weapon law enforcement can use against well-established gangs with a hierarchal structure and multiple gun and drug connections. According to Agnifilo et al. (2006), all assistant United States attorneys, outline two charging options using the enterprise theory of gang prosecutions. The first charging option uses the Racketeer Influenced and Corrupt Organization Act (RICO) and/or the Violent Crimes in Aid of Racketeering Act (VICAR). RICO/VICAR prosecutions are best used against broad-based, violent, and entrenched criminal gangs. The second charging option, the drug conspiracy/continuing criminal conspiracy (CCE), is appropriate to use against a drug trafficking organization. Agnifilo and his fellow U.S.D.A.'s opine that if the targeted gang is primarily a DTO whose members carry guns and engage in occasional violent acts that the continuing criminal conspiracy (CCE) is probably the best option. However, if the gang is structured and highly violent then the RICO/VICAR is the appropriate charging option because of the penalties (long sentences and VICAR murder is a death-eligible offense).

To prosecute a gang under RICO requires showing that: (1) an enterprise existed; (2) that the enterprise affects interstate commerce; (3) that the defendant was associated with the enterprise; (4) that the defendant engaged in a pattern of racketeering activity; and (5) that the defendant conducted or participated in the racketeering activity of the enterprise by committing at least two racketeering acts within 10 years of each other. The definition of enterprise is fairly liberal and includes any union or group of individuals associated in fact but not a legal group. Gangs clearly fit this definition. Local and state convictions may be used to satisfy the requirement of two criminal acts within 10 years of each other. The distribution of drugs not grown in the United States, such as cocaine, easily meets the requirement of affecting interstate commerce. A VICAR prosecution only requires one criminal act within 10 years; however, that act must be violent and carried out for personal monetary gain or for status in the gang.

Sheppard (2007) outlines three RICO and VICAR prosecutions to demonstrate how the actual RICO/VICAR investigation and prosecution moves forward. The first example involved the King Mafia Disciples (KMD), a street gang operating in Salt Lake City, Utah. Ten members of this gang were convicted of RICO/VICAR offenses. To prove that a enterprise existed, the prosecution at trial presented the KMD manual used by the gang, the hierarchy structure, photographs of the "jump in" ceremony for new members, the gang's colors (white and purple), tattoos showing membership in the gang (which included six-pointed stars, crowns, and pitchforks), photographs and videos of the gang's meetings to show that the members of the gang associated with each other to commit the crimes. Under the RICO statutes, gangs qualify as enterprises; therefore, once the prosecution proves that the group is a gang, the enterprise requirement of RICO is met. A pattern of racketeering activity was shown through evidence of the crimes committed (murder, aggravated assault, robberies, drug distribution) and the requirement that members had to commit these crimes to become a member. Evidence was presented to show that each member committed these crimes for personal gain and for the gang as a whole. Seven members of the gang were convicted of VICAR charges by proving a single act of homicide in furtherance of gang racketeering activities.

The second gang prosecution discussed was the RICO and VICAR charges against a Utah white supremacist prison gang, the Soldiers of the Aryan Culture (SAC). This violent gang originated in prison and expanded into the community as members were released from prison and began recruiting members from outside the prison. New members served a six-month probationary period during which they demonstrated their suitability for membership through the commission of criminal acts. Once the probate became a member, he received the gang's symbols/identifiers: tattoos of swastikas, lightning bolts, and the gang's initials (SAC). The gang's hierarchy consisted of general, lieutenant, sergeant, etc. RICO was used to prosecute six of the gang's leaders and the eight members were prosecuted under the VICAR statutes. At trial, the prosecution presented the gang's code of conduct, its associations, its meetings, the member's tattoos, and evidence of the completion of criminal orders to prove that the

Soldiers of the Aryan Culture was an enterprise as defined by RICO and VICAR. The pattern of racketeering activity was shown by the SAC manual, the commission of criminal orders by higher-ranking SAC members, and the fact that SAC members benefitted personally and the gang benefitted by the members' criminal activities. Twelve of the 14 SAC members were convicted and received sentences ranging from three to 20 years in prison.

The last RICO prosecution presented by Sheppard (2007) involved the Third Ward gang of Petersburg, Virginia. There were three factions or "sets/cliques" of this gang called "Top," "Spurs," and "Boston." Each of the sets/cliques engaged in drug distribution and violent crimes, including murder. Thirty-six members of the Third Ward gang were charged with conspiracy to violate the RICO act and conspiracy to distribute 50 grams or more of cocaine base.

In order to meet the RICO requirements, the prosecution proved that the gang was involved in criminal activities that affected interstate commerce—distributing cocaine that is not grown in the U.S. and must be shipped across state lines and national borders. The prosecution also proved that each defendant engaged in murder, attempted murder, and more than two acts of drug dealing. In order to prove that the defendants were members of a gang, the prosecution presented pictures of gang graffiti, testimony about the gang's territory, the white t-shirt and blue jeans each member wore as their "uniform" or colors, and pictures of the defendants' tattoos illustrating gang affiliation. Thirty-one of the defendants pleaded guilty and five were convicted at trial.

IV. Conclusion

We have discussed adult criminal gangs and illustrated the similarities and differences among street gangs, prison gangs, and outlaw motorcycle gangs. We have also provided information on drug trafficking organizations, particularly the Mexican cartels. As we examined the criminal enterprises, we presented the best available information on the gangs in North America. These criminal organizations represent a criminal threat for the United States, Mexico, and Canada. Throughout the book we have presented numerous examples of prosecutions of adult criminal gangs, primarily from the United States. The United States, under the enterprise theory and the RICO and VICAR statutes has taken the lead on the prosecution of these gangs because it is the country most affected and our laws apply to gangs that engage in foreign and interstate commerce. In addition to the FBI's MS 13 Task Force, other federal law enforcement agencies work with domestic (local and state) and foreign law enforcement agencies (Canada, Mexico, and Central America) in cooperative actions against adult criminal gangs (see Box 6.2).

Box 6.2 Operation Community Shield/Transnational Gangs

U.S. Immigration and Customs Enforcement (ICE) recognizes that violent transnational criminal street gangs represent a threat to public safety in neighborhoods and communities across the U.S.

In 2005, under the auspices of the national gang enforcement initiative Operation Community Shield (OCS), ICE established itself as the lead federal agency in the investigation of transnational criminal street gangs such as MS 13.

Operation Community Shield does the following:

- Works with federal, state and local law enforcement partners, in the U.S. and abroad, to develop a comprehensive and integrated approach to conducting criminal investigations and other law enforcement operations against gangs.

- Identifies violent street gangs and develops intelligence on their membership, associates, criminal activities, and international movements. Deters, disrupts, and dismantles gang operations by tracing and seizing cash, weapons, and other assets derived from criminal activities.

- Seeks prosecution and/or removal of alien gang members from the United States.

- Works closely with our attaché offices worldwide and foreign law enforcement counterparts in gathering intelligence, sharing information and conducting coordinated enforcement operations.

ICE's unique dual federal authorities, both criminal and administrative, have made the agency a leader in criminal investigations targeting street gangs, prison gangs, and outlaw motorcycle gangs that pose a threat to the public safety and national security.

[ICE actions under Community Shield have led to the arrests of more than 15,000 gang members and associates representing more than 1,000 different gangs. The following gangs were included in these ICE investigations and arrests: **Street Gangs:** Surenos 13, Avenues, MS 13, Surenos Trece, Latin Kings, La Raza 13, Black Disciples, Houstone, Bloods, Crips, Trinitarious, Gran Familia Mexicana, Los Pitufos; **Prison Gangs:** Aryan Brotherhood, Mexican Mafia, and Tango Blast; and **Outlaw Motorcycle Gangs:** Hells Angels and Warlocks. Those arrested included gang members from Mexico, Honduras, El Salvador, Argentina, Peru, Cuba, Vietnam, Afghanistan, Bahamas, Guatemala, Costa Rica, Philippines, and the Dominican Republic.]

Source: www.ice.gov/community-shield.

References

Agnifilo, M., Bliss, K. and Riordan, B. (2006). Investigating and Prosecuting Gangs Using the Enterprise Theory. *United States Attorneys' Bulletin.* May: 15–22.

Diaz, T. (2012). *No Boundaries: Transnational Latino Gangs and American Law Enforcement.* Ann Arbor, MI: The University of Michigan Press.

FBI. (January 25, 2012). Leader of IVY Street Gang sentenced to life for murders. FBI-Norfolk Division. Press Release.

Sheppard, P.H. (2007). Fighting Gangs with RICO and VICAR. *Swift & Certain.* 4(2).

U.S. Department of Homeland Security. (April, 29, 2011). New York MS-13 gang leader arraigned on murder charges. www.ice.gov.news/release.

U.S. Department of Homeland Security. (July 28, 2011). MS-13 Gang leader convicted of sex trafficking of a child. www.ice.gov/news/release.

U.S. Department of Homeland Security. (August 8, 2011). 5 "Sur-13" gang members sentenced for crime spree Weekend-long robbery and assault binge spanned 5 counties. www.ice.gov/news/releases.

Readings

1. McFeeley, R.A. (May, 2001). Enterprise Theory of Investigation. *FBI Law Enforcement Bulletin.*
2. Wheatley, J. (2008). The Flexibility of RICO and Its Use on Street Gangs Engaging in Organized Crime in the United States. *Policing: A Journal of Police and Practice.* 2(1): 82–91.
3. Bjerregaard, B. (2003). Antigang Legislation and Its Potential Impact: The Promises and the Pitfalls. *Criminal Justice Policy Review.* 14(2): 171–192.

Reading 1.
Enterprise Theory of Investigation*

Richard A. McFeeley

Although the media frequently focuses on the conviction of the leaders of major criminal enterprises, such as the Gambino crime family, the Columbian Cali Cartel, or the Sicilian Mafia, dozens of lesser-known individuals belonging to the same criminal organizations also often receive long prison sentences. Those who escaped prosecution or served their sentence may return to find the criminal enterprise to which they belonged extinct due to a powerful tool in the law enforcement arsenal—the Enterprise Theory of Investigation (ETI).

The ETI has become the standard investigative model that the FBI employs in conducting investigations against major criminal organizations. The successful prosecutions of major crime bosses serve as direct testaments to the benefits of this model. Unlike traditional investigative theory, which relies on law enforcement's ability to react to a previously committed crime, the ETI encourages a proactive attack on the structure of the criminal enterprise. Rather than viewing criminal acts as isolated crimes,

* Published with Permission. *FBI Law Enforcement Bulletin.* May 2001:19–25.

the ETI attempts to show that individuals commit crimes in furtherance of the criminal enterprise itself. In other words, individuals commit acts solely to benefit their criminal enterprise. By applying the ETI with favorable state and federal legislation, law enforcement can target and dismantle entire criminal enterprises in one criminal indictment.

Applying the ETI

By restructuring both their investigative resources and theory, many law enforcement agencies can use this model. Initially, some police agencies may hold a skeptical view of the use of the ETI because its application requires an increased time commitment, which may affect case-closure rates and also because they may perceive the ETI as more complex than traditional investigative models. However, the advantages of the ETI easily outweigh these presumed disadvantages, primarily because the ETI provides a highly effective method of targeting and dismantling criminal enterprises.

To recognize the value of the ETI, investigators must accept several main premises. First, while some major organized criminal groups commit crimes to support idealistic views, financial profit remains the underlying motive for most criminal enterprises.

Next, major organized criminal groups typically engage in a broad range of criminal activities to achieve this profit goal. While the nexus of these violations may be closely interrelated (e.g., drug trafficking and money laundering), major criminal enterprises historically rely on numerous criminal acts to support their existence and often divide the responsibility for committing these acts among their members and crews. The ETI capitalizes on this diversity by analyzing the enterprise's full range of criminal activities, determining which components allow the criminal enterprise to operate and exploiting identified vulnerable areas within each component. For instance, to accomplish their profit objectives, major drug trafficking organizations must establish four separate subsystems within their organization—narcotics transportation and distribution, financial, communication. The ETI identifies and then targets each of these areas simultaneously, especially those components viewed as the most vulnerable. The more diverse the criminal enterprise, the more potential for exploitation due to the existence of these types of subsystems.

A final premise of the ETI maintains that major organized criminal gangs have a pyramidal hierarchy structure where the lowest levels, consisting of more people, conduct the majority of the enterprise's criminal activities. Therefore, working a case "up the chain" proves beneficial because it starts the investigation at the level where most investigative opportunities exist.

Defining an Enterprise

What defines a criminal enterprise? Do two bank robbers committing serial robberies fall within the definition? How about employees of a government contractor engaged in systematic bid-rigging? Although these criminal groups might have a loose-knit organizational structure, application of the ETI probably would not prove beneficial in these instances.

The FBI defines a criminal organization as a group of individuals with an identified hierarchy engaged in significant criminal activity. These organizations often engage in a broad range of criminal activities and have extensive supporting networks. Generally, the ETI only proves effective when the organization engages in a myriad of criminal activities. In the case of the bank robbers, federal and state robbery laws, sufficiently address this group's single purpose criminal activity. However, if the bank robbers begin to diversify by stealing cars and guns to support their robberies, the ETI now offers advantages that traditional methods of investigation do not. The ETI supports the notion that the gang's new found diversity allows law enforcement more investigative opportunities by exploring the most vulnerable areas of their criminal activities. For example, introducing an undercover officer into a close-knit gang to obtain their robbery preparations may be practical. However, if the gang advances to criminal violations that require assistance from someone outside the gang, a department could expand its investigative opportunities and use an undercover officer to provide stolen vehicles.

Most state and federal general conspiracy laws define a criminal conspiracy as two or more individuals. The federal Continuing Criminal Enterprise statute,[1] applicable to major drug conspiracies, requires that the individual charged led five or more individuals while the federal Racketeering Influenced Corrupt Organization (RICO) statute requires only two or more individuals to comprise a criminal enterprise.[2] Law enforcement managers must decide which statutes to use when they form the investigative strategy to direct the evidence collection toward meeting the legal requirements of each statute. This type of advance decision making supports the proactive nature of the ETI.

Using the criminal statute as guidance, the investigation should focus continually on an essential part of the indictment proving who belongs to the criminal enterprise. Obviously, law enforcement can use traditional investigative techniques, such as physical surveillance, to show criminal associations. However, the act of showing criminal associations does not necessarily involve proactive evidence collection against the subjects and often uses historical information to prove this element.

Determining the Scope of the Enterprise's Criminal Activities

Once investigators confidently believe that an enterprise does exist, the next step involves determining the scope of its illegal activities. This step proves important because it will help define the investigative strategy.

Investigators always treasure any new intelligence regarding an enterprise's current activities; however, investigations can still progress with older information. For example, a review of past investigations, prosecutions, and criminal histories of suspected members, and even open-source information (e.g., newspaper accounts) can assist in this process. The task force concept allows instant multiagency searches of

---

1. 1 U.S.C. 1961 et seq.
2. 21 U.S.C. 848.

historical records and indices. In fact, during this stage, agencies can piece together information that they may have, but just could not link to the actions of a criminal enterprise.

While larger police agencies often use highly trained and specialized analytical support teams to assist with case analysis, those police agencies without this resource should not skip this important step. Investigators can create simple time lines that chart significant historical events based on previous intelligence. In doing so, they can help reveal patterns of criminal activity, and possibly predict future trends.[3] The investigative strategy that managers develop should anticipate the steps needed to counter these future trends, which remains the essence of the proactive nature of the ETI.

While traditional investigative theory targets individual criminals, the ETI can show they commit seemingly isolated crimes to benefit an entire criminal enterprise. The selection of favorable legislation, from simple state conspiracy laws to the more complex federal racketeering laws, will round out the investigative strategy by focusing the prosecution not only on the individual committing a crime but the leaders who order or benefit from it.

Developing an Investigative Strategy

Both historical and real-time evaluation helps form the investigative strategy. Because investigators should base this strategy on perceived weaknesses within the enterprise, they must conduct a thorough evaluation of the enterprise's activities. The investigators should obtain enough information to analyze to gain a basic understanding of the extent of the enterprise's criminal activities. Investigators should examine the full range of these illicit activities separate them into components, and draw an investigative strategy that attacks each component separately, yet simultaneously.

For example, a large and sophisticated burglary ring must have some form of each of the following components in place: methods of theft, resale of the stolen goods, and concealment of their illicit proceeds. Police can use a surveillance team to try to catch the actual burglars and, at the same time, use undercover officers to pose as a "fence" against the ring's efforts to resell the stolen property. A financial investigator could track purchases and asset acquisitions of each individual. As the case progresses, investigators can shift additional resources to the enterprise's most vulnerable areas. Because the ETI ultimately attempts to indict and convict all the members of an enterprise especially within the leadership ranks, the investigative strategy needs to address how each investigative method will advance the investigation "up the chain." At this point, the use of innovative and more sophisticated investigative techniques becomes invaluable because proving a case against the leader of a major criminal organization typically is more difficult than convicting a "player" of the organization. For example, deferring prosecution of low-level burglars in favor of cooperation or a court-authorized wiretap of the ring leader's telephone might support a hierarchical attack on the enterprise.

---

3. For additional information on the use of time lines in investigations, see Craig Meyer and Gary Morgan, "Investigative Uses of Computer: Analytical Time Lines," *FBI Law Enforcement Bulletin*, August 2000. 1–5.

Criminal Associations

Showing criminal associations does not does not necessarily involve proactive evidence collection against the subjects and often uses historical information to prove this element. Consider the following successful examples that focus on the members of criminal enterprises:

- A recent FBI investigation initially used gang graffiti to not only determine membership in the gang (enterprise), but to show its area of influence. Investigators also can use gang colors, clothing, and hand signals in this manner.

- Agencies can use intercepted telephone conversations, call-detail records, and pen registers to show associations.

- Officers executing warrants or processing prisoners should not overlook the more mundane collection of documentary evidence that can prove useful in showing associations. Some examples could include pagers and cellular telephones with stored numbers, or addresses books or scraps of paper with names and telephone numbers. Standard post-seizure practice should involve electronically capturing this type of information for later link analysis.

- Officers should include accomplice information when compiling a subject's biographical file, such as other individuals arrested and the location of the subjects (i.e., whose house or car) when the arrest took place. This information proves valuable in showing past criminal relationships.

Additionally, financial profit remains one of the main goals of most criminal enterprises. Virtually every major criminal organization uses a system to reward its members through monetary means. Often-times, successfully dismantling an organization relies solely on the ability of law enforcement to disrupt this financial component. Removal of a criminal enterprise's financial base usually disables the organization to the point where they cannot recover. This occurs because even the lowest members of the organization require prompt payment for their actions. Removing the ability of an enterprise to make payments generally takes away the incentive for those doing the work to continue. Although the enterprise can fill some positions of those incarcerated members through upward attrition, only a few trusted members of a criminal organization generally handle methods of dividing, shielding, and accounting for the profits. Successfully incarcerating those in such a position of trust can result in large voids within the criminal organization. By creating chaos and uncertainty within the financial component of the enterprise, members quickly look elsewhere for "employment" and financial reward.

Attacking the flow of money has become the norm in major federal organized crime and drug trafficking organizations. Strategic use of asset forfeiture and money laundering statutes removes not only the illegal proceeds (e.g., cars, houses, and jewelry), but, more important, it disables the systems that the enterprise has put into place to accom-

plish its profit goal. Some examples include fraudulent bank accounts used to shield illicit income and property used to facilitate the criminal activity, such as "legitimate" businesses.

The plan should remain aggressive, yet workable. For instance, case managers may
not include targeting the head of the criminal enterprise in the initial plan, but the investigative strategy should define the steps on how to achieve this objective.

Investigators, should interface with prosecutors as early as possible in the case. Because the investigative strategy essentially remains a start-to-finish blueprint for the
case, investigators must know from the outset which elements of the criminal statutes
they must prove and then tailor the investigative plan accordingly.

Finally, case managers should postpone any actions that might expose the scope of
the investigation until completion of the covert phase. This remains important because
opportunities to arrest subjects increase as the case proceeds, which may conflict with
those departments that gauge their effectiveness on raw arrest data and, therefore, might
not delay arresting individuals once sufficient evidence exists.

Using a Task Force

The use of a joint task force remains a necessity in the successful application of the
ETI. Any law enforcement officer who ever served on a multiagency task force recognizes the strength that combined resources provide in achieving objectives. Immediate
benefits include additional staff, access to more technical and investigative equipment
(e.g., different sets of surveillance vehicles), and the pooling of financial resources for
items, such as payment of informants and purchase of evidence. Another major advantage that directly supports the ETI model is that different police agencies bring the
potential to expand jurisdictions and expertise into all of the areas that a criminal enterprise engages. For example, while virtually every state and local police agency has counterdrug enforcement as part of its mission, very few of these agencies employ a criminal
tax investigator who specializes in tracking international money transfers. Thus, getting an Internal Revenue special agent involved in the investigation not only adds another individual to assist with general investigations, but adds an individual who can
provide an area of expertise that the task force might otherwise lack.

Many federal task forces employ a wide range of individuals, including nonsworn
personnel, with specialized skills not usually found in the law enforcement realm. Departments can retain bank examiners, accountants, and securities experts as either con-
sultants or an actual member of the task force. Many federal agencies invest considerable
effort in developing a class of nonsworn professionals, ranging from investigative assistants
to more specialized positions that employ an expertise in areas not typically found in
the realm of sworn personnel (e.g., link analysis, chart presentations, and legal research).

Because police agencies have differing missions and methods of measuring success,
the most important part of the task force formation involves complete agreement by the
participating agencies regarding the objectives and goals of the investigation and what
rules the task force will follow. Additionally, the participating agencies should complete a memorandum of understanding that addresses questions, such as the following:

- Which agency will maintain responsibility for the overall investigation?
- Are the lead agency's rules acceptable to the other participating agencies?
- Will the case be prosecuted in the state or federal courts?
- Will each participating agency use their forms or will the task force adopt one standard format for investigative reports?
- Who will maintain seized evidence?
- Will each agency agree to delay arrests and seizures if it may jeopardize the investigation?
- How much funding (including overtime) will each agency contribute to the investigation?
- Whose procurement rules will the task force follow to acquire equipment and supplies?
- Will each agency accept liability for the action of their assigned personnel?
- Will the state investigators need to be deputized or vice versa?
- Will the agencies divide the forfeiture share equally, regardless of the level of participation (e.g., one part-time officers versus three full-time officers)?

Implementing an Attack

In this stage, task force members follow the previously developed investigative strategy and merge traditional methods of evidence collection with investigative methods of evidence collection with investigative methods developed specifically to attack the identified component of the criminal enterprise. This often involves the largest commitment of personnel, time, and resources. Task force supervisors should consider assignments depending on the outline of the investigative strategy and the areas within the enterprise that remain vulnerable for exploitation, along with the area of each officer's expertise and experience. Investigators should use both traditional and sophisticated investigative techniques to receive optimal results. However, regardless of the original plan. The task force must adapt and shift investigatory resources as the case develops. For example, if the task force obtains a wire tap order to penetrate a criminal enterprise's methods of communication, case managers must consider temporarily reassigning personnel to meet the high resource requirements of operating wire taps.

An Example of the Enterprise Theory of Investigation

In a city plagued with chronic drive-by shootings, traditional investigative methods may focus on each shooting as an isolated incident. However, a task force suspecting gang involvement can develop a time line that shows that each time a member of a street gang was incarcerated, an increase in shootings against rival gang members occurred. Using this analysis and adopting an enterprise investigative theory, the task force can gather "traditional" evidence against the individual shooters and focus on developing evidence that shows the shootings as more than just random acts. At trial, the prosecutors can use the investigative efforts to show that gang leaders ordered the shootings to defend a perceived gap in their turf as a result of the incarceration factor and, therefore, prosecute not only the shooters but the gang leaders as well.

Careful coordination with prosecutors as the case develops ensures that all members of the criminal enterprise receive indictments and that the enterprise's established subsystems become permanently dismantled.

Conclusion

Oftentimes, larger criminal enterprises prove problematic for agencies to dissolve using traditional methods. However, with the enterprise theory of investigation, the larger the enterprise and the more diverse its illegal activities, the more investigative opportunities for law enforcement.

Because the use of conspiracy or criminal enterprise statutes form the baseline from which agencies develop their investigative strategies, the ETI requires that departments expand the traditional models of evidence collection. While these traditional models generally only attempt to identify individuals and the crimes they commit, the ETI requires that investigators broaden evidence collection to show that an individual conducted the criminal activity to benefit the enterprise as a whole. By using favorable statutes along with a carefully laid out, multipronged attack on each established component that a criminal enterprise uses to conduct its illegal business, investigators can expand criminal culpability for a single criminal act to all members of the enterprise, regardless of whether they actually committed the crime.

Reading 2.
The Flexibility of RICO and Its Use on Street Gangs Engaging in Organized Crime in the United States*

*Joseph Wheatley***

Introduction

Terms such as racketeering, criminal enterprises and organized crime conjure up images of the Mafia contending with federal agents and prosecutors. This crackdown continues, but in this article the author discusses how a different kind of organized

* Reprinted with Permission; © The Authors 2008. Published by Oxford University Press on the behalf of CSF Associates: Publius, Inc. All Rights Reserved.

** Joseph Wheatley is a Trial Attorney in the Organized Crime and Racketeering Section at the U.S. Department of Justice.

crime group has also emerged—street gangs. Just as perceptions of organized crime have evolved, so have the US government's laws and strategies to thwart crime. For instance, the Racketeer Influenced and Corrupt Organizations statute (RICO), originally enacted to dismantle the Mafia, has been successfully used against street gangs.

The first section reviews the history and statutory language of the Racketeer Influenced and Corrupt Organizations (RICO). The second section outlines the federal government's crackdown on street gangs; provides sample definitions of the term 'street gang'; analyzes how such gangs may be engaged in 'organized crime'; and discusses how members and associates of street gangs may qualify for prosecution under RICO. To be clear, definitions of 'street gangs' and 'organized crime' may help decision makers set priorities and allocate resources targeting certain entities, but the definitions do not dictate what conduct RICO itself criminalizes, since the law contains no such definitions, and is limited to no particular group. RICO's statutory language and the intent of Congress provide that flexibility. Finally, the article offers concluding remarks about how RICO's flexibility permits the federal government to respond to new and emerging forms of organized crime groups, such as street gangs.

The Origins and Statutory Language of RICO

In 1970, the Organized Crime Control Act established RICO, which heralded a new approach for conceptualizing and targeting organized crime.[1] To paraphrase, RICO's most often used provision prohibits participating in or conducting criminal enterprises, through a pattern of racketeering activity, or conspiracies to commit such conduct.[2] By focussing on criminal enterprises, RICO distinguishes itself from the various laws targeting organized crime that predated it.

RICO's use of the enterprise model broke new ground in the way that the government targeted organized crime groups. Before the enactment of RICO, federal criminal law did not penalize individuals for their conduct related to criminal enterprises *per se*. However, such a legal regime tended to be incomplete; the complex structure of some organized crime entities could shield certain members, such as bosses, from prosecution. Accordingly, with its leadership and assets largely intact, a criminal enterprise, such as the Mafia, could generally endure the loss of low-level members and then continue perpetrating crimes with new recruits.

Such challenges posed by the Mafia helped prompt Congress to enact RICO, which allowed the government to target members and assets of organized crime groups that may have otherwise eluded prosecution under previous laws.[3] Section 1962 of RICO states that it is unlawful for

> "any person"[4] to: (a) use income derived from a pattern of racketeering activity, or derived from the collection of an unlawful debt, to acquire an interest

1. 18 U.S.C. §§ 1961–1968 (2007).
2. 18 U.S.C. § 1962(c), (d) (2007).
3. S. Rep. No. 617, 91st Cong., 1st Sess. 36–43 (1969).
4. 18 U.S.C. § 1961(3) (2007).

in an enterprise affecting interstate commerce;[5] (b) acquire or maintain, through a pattern of racketeering activity, or through collection of an unlawful debt, an interest in an enterprise affecting interstate commerce;[6] (c) conduct or participate in the conduct of the affairs of an enterprise affecting interstate commerce through a pattern of racketeering activity, or through collection of an unlawful debt;[7] or (d) conspire to commit any of the violations listed above.[8]

RICO's complex provisions listed above contain several statutory elements that merit further explanation. First, 'racketeering activity' includes a variety of state and federal crimes. To paraphrase, the crimes covered by RICO include:

any act or threat involving murder, kidnapping, gambling, arson, robbery, bribery, extortion, dealing in obscene matter, or dealing in a controlled substance or listed chemical..., which is chargeable under State law and punishable by imprisonment for more than 1 year;[9]

various specified acts that are federally indictable under Title 18 of the United States Code;[10] and various other kinds of federal offenses.[11]

Second, RICO's requirement for a 'pattern of racketeering activity' may be satisfied by at least two acts of racketeering, such as two murders, provided that they comply with certain time requirements in the statute.[12] To establish the pattern, the government must show that the acts of racketeering are continuous and interrelated, and not merely isolated events.[13]

Third—and most importantly for the purposes of this article—RICO defines an 'enterprise' broadly to 'include[d] any individual, partnership, corporation, association, or other legal entity, and any union or group of individual associated in fact although not a legal entity'.[14] Since Congress mandated that RICO be construed liberally,[15] the courts have held that the statute's definition of an enterprise is not an exhaustive list, but rather a sample of the sorts of entities that can constitute an enterprise.[16] To qualify as an association-in-fact, as opposed to a readily identifiable legal entity, the association generally must satisfy requirements that the courts have read into the statute, such as

---

5. 18 U.S.C. § 1962(a) (2007).
6. 18 U.S.C. § 1962(b) (2007).
7. 18 U.S.C. § 1962(c) (2007).
8. 18 U.S.C. § 1962(d) (2007).
9. 18 U.S.C. § 1961(1)(A) (2007).
10. 18 U.S.C. § 1961(1)(B) (2007). To name just a few, the violations of Title 18 of the United States Code that are indictable under RICO include offenses such as bribery (Section 201), wire fraud (Section 1343), money laundering (Section 1956), and interstate transportation of stolen property (Sections 2314–2315).
11. 18 U.S.C. § 1961(1)(C)-(G) (2007).
12. 18 U.S.C. § 1961(5) (2007).
13. See Sedima, S.P.R.L. v. Imrex Co., Inc., 473 U.S. 479, 496 (1985).
14. 18 U.S.C. § 1961(4) (2007).
15. See 18 U.S.C. § 1961 (2007) (Congressional Statement of Findings and Purpose); see also *id.* (Liberal Construction of Provisions Clause).
16. United States v. Turkette, 452 U.S. 576, 580 (1981).

(1) 'continuity';[17]

(2) 'a common purpose';[18]

(3) a decision-making mechanism.[19]

The government utilized RICO to strike at the heart of a quintessential enterprise that existed solely for criminal purposes, the Mafia. Law enforcement authorities continue to undermine the crime families by frustrating their efforts to recruit and retain leaders and underlings, or secure assets—which in turn, hinders the families' capacity to commit crimes.

As shown by such RICO prosecutions, the Mafia represents a certain conception of organized crime. It is a hierarchical organization, characterized by continuity, a strict chain of command, membership requirements, and codes of conduct. Moreover, the Mafia has historically engaged in certain racketeering crimes that distinguish it as a criminal group, such as extortion, loan sharking, gambling businesses, manipulation of labor unions, sales of black-market goods, and money laundering. Although RICO did not single out the Mafia for prosecution, the group's characteristics and criminal preferences made the group an archetypal enterprise under RICO, which Congress passed with the intention of dismantling organized crime groups.[20] Investigations by Congress and law enforcement authorities had revealed the Mafia to be the most significant organized crime present in the United States. In keeping with that, early uses of RICO were primarily directed toward the Mafia. However, a different type of organized crime group, the street gang, has emerged since then, and prompted a similar crackdown by the federal government.

Street Gangs: Evolving Conceptions of Organized Crime and the Use of RICO and Government Crackdowns

In some urban and rural communities throughout the United States, street gangs have emerged as significant organized criminal groups. Although street gangs have existed as criminal groups for centuries,[21] their development into more sophisticated criminal groups is a relatively recent phenomenon. In response, the federal government has utilized RICO to prosecute street gangs.[22] The first subsection will outline the federal government's crackdown on street gangs. The second subsection will define the term 'street gang'. The third subsection will provide a sample of street gangs in the United States, compare and contrast them with the Mafia, and analyze how such gangs may fit the organized framework set by the President's Commission on Organized Crime in 1986. The fourth subsection will analyze how members and associates of street gangs

---

17. United States v. Gray, 137 F.3d 765, 772 (4th Cir. 1998).

18. See Bonner v. Henderson, 147 F.3d 457, 459 (5th Cir. 1998).

19. *Id.*

20. S. Rep. No. 617, 91st Cong., 1st Sess. 36–43 (1969).

21. See Taylor, C. S. (1990). *Dangerous Society,* Michigan State University Press, pp. 1–4.

22. See Kessler, R. E. (2006). "Gang Leader Sentenced." *Newsday,* Jan. 10, p. A29.

may qualify for prosecution under RICO, a flexible statute that contains no definitions of 'street gang' or 'organized crime.'

The Federal Government's Crackdown on Street Gangs

The federal government has resorted to various law enforcement strategies to combat street gangs, including charging defendants with firearms and narcotics violations, but this article will primarily discuss the use of RICO. Prosecutions of street gangs under RICO date back to at least the mid-1980s, but such prosecutions appear to have become more common in recent years. This subsection will briefly trace the federal government's crackdown on street gangs.

Federal prosecutions of gangs using RICO may be traced back at least to the mid-1980s, when prosecutors charged prominent gangs, such as the 'Westies' in New York City.[23] The gang primarily earned money from loan sharking, narcotics dealing, and extortion, at times in collusion with the city's Gambino Mafia family.[24] Trial began in 1987; all but one of the defendants were eventually convicted, including leader Jimmy Coonan, who was later sentenced to 60 years in prison.[25]

The RICO prosecution of the Westies in the 1980s, and other early federal RICO prosecutions of gangs, such as El Rukns in Chicago, were not part of a nationwide coordinated federal crackdown on gangs per se, but rather prosecutions of sophisticated criminal enterprises that were initiated on a case-by-case basis.

In recent years, RICO prosecutions have formed part of a broad and coordinated crackdown on street gangs, often in conjunction with state law enforcement authorities. In one of the prominent cases, Mara Salvatrucha, a street gang commonly known as MS-13, has been the target of a RICO conspiracy prosecution in Maryland; as of 5 June 2007, federal prosecutors in Maryland have obtained 14 convictions of MS-13 members for RICO conspiracy charges in that case.[26] Elsewhere, members of MS-13 and other gangs have been convicted of RICO violations.[27] Later in this article, MS-13 will be examined in greater depth.

The federal crackdown on gangs is a multi-front effort, composed of prevention, enforcement, and prisoner reentry programs. On 15 February 2006, US Attorney General Alberto Gonzales announced the creation of the Justice Department's Comprehensive Anti-Gang Initiative to combat gang violence.[28] As part of the Initiative, the Department provides anti-gang resources for

---

23. United States v. Coonan, 938 F.2d 1553 (2nd Cir. 1991).

24. *Id.* at 1556.

25. *Id.* at 1559.

26. U.S. Attorney's Office for the District of Maryland, *MS-13 Gang Member Sentenced to 35 Years on Racketeering Charges*, 5 June 2007.

27. See Robert E. Kessler, *supra* note 22; U.S. Attorney's Office for the Northern District of Georgia. *Members of 'K-E-S' Street Gang Plead Guilty to Federal RICO Indictment*, 24 March 2006.

28. U.S. Department of Justice, *Fact Sheet: Department of Justice Initiative to Combat Gangs*, 15 Feb. 2006.

(1) prevention programs to discourage gang membership;

(2) enforcement programs to prosecute violent gang members;

(3) prisoner reentry programs to reintegrate ex-convicts into society.[29]

As described by Roslynn R. Mauskopf, US Attorney for the Eastern District of New York, there are three general reasons why federal prosecution of gang members is 'the most effective strategy'.[30]

First, individual states, rather than the federal government, are 'limited to looking at discrete isolated crimes and defendants'.[31] In contrast, federal laws, such as RICO, target the gangs as a whole and diminish their capacity to function as an organization. Second, mandatory minimum sentences and the Federal Rules of Evidence provide 'leverage' against low-level gang members, which may induce their co-operation with the government against higher level gang members. Third, the federal government, at times in partnership with state law enforcement authorities, possesses additional personnel, expertise, and resources to build cases against gangs.[32]

For instance, the Department has established institutions that coordinate antigang efforts on a national level, gather intelligence, and prosecute the most significant gangs. First, led by the Department's Criminal Division and created in 2006, the Gang Targeting, Enforcement, and Coordination Center (GangTECC) coordinates investigations.[33] Second, the National Gang Intelligence Center (NGIC), created in 2004, integrates the Department's intelligence assets regarding gang activity.[34] Third, the Department's Criminal Division in 2006 created a Gang Squad, composed of experienced attorneys, who help prosecute the country's most significant gangs.[35]

Definitions of Street Gangs

This article examines street gangs from a legal perspective, and thus does not focus upon sociological definitions of street gangs, which may differ significantly from legal terminology and criteria related to the prosecution of members of a street gang. The United States Code does not contain a definition of a street gang that applies across the entire code; however, it defines a 'criminal street gang' in a sentencing enhancement, as an ongoing group, club, organization, or association of five or more persons formed for the purpose of committing a violent crime or drug offense, with members that have engaged, within the past five years, in a continuing series of violent crimes or drug law

29. U.S. Department of Justice, *Attorney General Alberto R. Gonzales Announces Expansion of Justice Department's Comprehensive Anti-Gang Initiative*, 27 April 2007.

30. Harris, A. (2005). "Gang Member Sentenced to 63 Years for Shooting that Left Three Injured." *New York Law Journal*, 15 Dec., p. 16.

31. *Id.*

32. *Id.*

33. U.S. Department of Justice, *Fact Sheet: Department of Justice Efforts to Stop Gang Violence in America's Communities*, 17 Jan. 2007.

34. *Id.*

35. *Id.*

violations that affect interstate or foreign commerce.[36] Mere membership in a gang is not illegal, and the statute makes no mention of 'organized crime'.

As with the term 'organized crime',[37] definitions of 'street gang' abound, and span academic disciplines.[38] Having reviewed the literature on gangs, a report by the Bureau of Justice Assistance at the US Department of Justice observed that most of the street gang definitions include a portion, or all, of the following factors:

> (1) three or more individuals associate periodically as an ongoing criminal group or organization, whether loosely or tightly structured, (2) the group has identifiable leaders, although the leader for one type of criminal activity may be different than the leader for another, (3) the group has a name or identifying symbol, (4) the organization's members, individually or collectively, currently engage in, or have engaged in, violent or other criminal activity and (5) the group frequently identifies itself with, or claims control over specific territory (turf) in the community, wears distinctive dress and colors, and communicates through graffiti and hand-signs among other means.[39]

Such definitions help inform an analysis of how a gang engages in *organized crime*, which the following pages will do. Bear in mind, however, that such definitions do not limit the application of RICO. As this article will argue in further detail, an entity does not have to be a 'street gang' or engaged in 'organized crime' for RICO to apply. Indeed, RICO contains no such definitions, which gives law enforcement authorities the flexibility to respond to varying and emerging threats.

Gangs: Do They Qualify as Organized Crime Groups?

The prosecutions of the Westies and other street gangs show that such gangs are not necessarily un-sophisticated groups of criminals engaging in low-level offenses. Indeed, a street gang may bear, or eventually bear, a resemblance to traditional organized crime groups, such as the Mafia, and commit crimes on par with such groups—murder, extortion, and loan sharking, for instance. The author of RICO, G. Robert Blakey, has observed that the Mafia itself was once less sophisticated and evolved over time: '[Gangs are] in the process of growing into Mafias ... The Mafia started out as a gang.'[40]

Consider an emerging gang in the United States that has begun to establish a national presence, Mara Salvatrucha, commonly known as MS-13.[41] *Newsweek* dubbed MS-13 the 'fastest growing' and 'most violent' street gang in the country.[42] Composed

---

36. 18 U.S.C. §521.

37. See generally Finckenauer, J. O. (2005). "Problems of Definition: What Is Organized Crime?" *Trends in Organized Crime* 8(3).

38. See North Carolina Criminal Justice Analysis Center of the Governor's Crime Commission. (2000). *Perceptions of Youth Crime and Youth Gangs: A Statewide Systemic Investigation*, pp. 1–4.

39. U.S. Department of Justice, Bureau of Justice Assistance. (1997). *Urban Street Gang Enforcement*. Washington, DC: Bureau of Justice Assistance.

40. Gibeaut, J. (1998). "Gang Busters." ABA Journal, January, p. 65.

41. Campo-Flores, A. (2005). "The Most Dangerous Gang in America." Newsweek, 28 March, p. 22.

42. Id.

primarily of Salvadorans and other Central Americans, MS-13 has approximately 8,000–10,000 members in 33 states around the country, and reputedly tens of thousands of members in Central America.[43] Although MS-13 initially presented itself as a nationally decentralized organization,[44] law enforcement authorities have observed increasing coordination between MS-13 chapters in Atlanta, Dallas, Los Angeles, New York, and Washington,[45] DC, which would be in step with the gang's high level of organization in El Salvador.[46] Paul McNulty, then-US Attorney for the Eastern District of Virginia, stated that 'in some of the violent crimes, there seems to be a kind of approval process in some kind of hierarchy beyond the clique'.[47] Among the gang's alleged crimes are smuggling of narcotics, primarily cocaine and marijuana, into the country; transportation and distribution of drugs; alien smuggling; assault; homicide; and robbery.[48]

In 1986, the President's Commission on Organized Crime released its report, which listed six characteristics for groups engaged in 'organized crime':

> The criminal group (in its various manifestations, 'cartel', 'corporation', 'family', 'gumi', 'triad', etc.) is a continuing, structured collectivity of defined members utilizing criminality, including violence, to gain and maintain profit and power. Thus, the six characteristics of the criminal group are *continuity, structure, defined membership, criminality, violence,* and *power as its goal.*[49]

The characteristics are not limited to a particular organized crime group, thereby leaving room for other groups to qualify. Using the six characteristics listed above, the following subsection will examine whether a street gang, particularly MS-13, may qualify as being engaged *in organized crime*, as opposed to being merely *organized at committing crime*, a distinction that was explored in a study of San Diego and Chicago gangs conducted by Deborah Lamm Weisel.[50]

The President's Commission on Organized Crime's six characteristics help inform an analysis of how a gang engages in organized crime, and may aid decision makers in setting priorities and focusing resources upon dangerous organized crime groups.

First, the President's Commission on Organized Crime's continuity characteristic requires that an entity operate with a criminal purpose over an extended span of time.[51] Although the criminal activity of gangs may differ from the criminal scope of the Mafia,

---

43. *Id.*
44. *Id.*
45. Gangs in the United States. (2005). Narcotics Digest Weekly,4 October.
46. Campo-Flores, A. supra note 41.
47. *Id.*
48. Gangs in the United States, supra note 45.
49. President's Comm'n on Organized Crime. (1986). "Report to the President and the Attorney General." *The Impact: Organized Crime Today,* pp. 25–29 (hereinafter President's Comm'n Report) (emphasis added).
50. See Weisel, D. L. (2002). "The Evolution of Street Gangs: An Examination of Form and Variation." In Reed, W. L. and Decker, S. H. (eds), *Responding to Gangs: Evaluation and Research,* The U.S. Department of Justice, p. 52.
51. President's Comm'n Report, *supra* note 49, at 26.

both entities engage in criminal activity that becomes the livelihood of the organization through-out its lifespan. For instance, Chicago's Black Gangster Disciple Nation (BGDN) gang demonstrates continuity, since the group has been operating criminally for several decades, although a gang may operate for less time and still qualify as an organized crime entity.[52] A gang does not have to operate criminally for decades in order to satisfy the requirement; such a bright-line rule would be unnecessarily rigid and limit the definition of 'organized crime' to all but the most mature groups. The principle underlying the continuity requirement is that a gang will not qualify as an organized crime group if its activity is sporadic and disconnected, disorganized in other words. Provided that a gang's activity appears connected over time, such as MS-13, it may satisfy the continuity requirement, whether the span of time is a year or 10 years.

Second, the structure characteristic requires that the entity have an established decision-making structure.[53] As is the case with the Mafia, the structure of gangs, such as the BGDN, may be complex and follow a strict chain of command.[54] For instance, the BGDN has a management structure that parallels the structure of a corporation, including a board of directors, as well as officials called governors and regents, who are responsible for ensuring the supply of narcotics into Chicago neighborhoods.[55] In contrast, MS-13 may not have such a clear hierarchy,[56] but that does not mean that it lacks structure altogether. Moreover, the structure requirement set forth in the report of the President's Commission on Organized Crime does not demand that the entity's structure be rigidly vertical, but merely that it should have some structure. A gang may have diffuse leadership and subgroups. In some respects, MS-13 may currently be such an organization, with diffuse leadership and subgroups, although it may evolve into a more bureaucratic organization, as a 2004 report by the National Drug Intelligence Center suspects.[57] Either way, its relatively fluid decision-making structure would satisfy the structure requirement.

Third, to qualify as a group engaged in organized crime, the gang must also restrict membership.[58] Although the membership requirements of a street gang may not be as elaborate as the Mafia's, their requirements relating to entry and participation effectively restrict the gang's membership.[59] For instance, MS-13 may require prospective members to be jumped in, meaning that the recruits must endure an assault to join the group; some prospective female members are reputedly required to have sex with male members to join the organization.[60] Moreover, MS-13's membership is largely composed of people with Salvadoran ethnicity, although other Central Americans have also joined the gang.[61]

---

52. Gibeaut, J., *supra* note 40, at 68.
53. President's Comm'n Report, *supra* note 49, at 26–27.
54. Gibeaut, J., *supra* note 40, at 68.
55. *Id.*
56. Campo-Flores, A., *supra* note 41.
57. *Id.*
58. President's Comm'n Report, *supra* note 49, at 27.
59. Cosby, R. (2006). "MS-13' Is One of Nation's most Dangerous Gangs." *MSNBC*, 13 Feb.
60. *Id.*
61. Campo-Flores A., *supra* note 41.

Fourth, members must use criminal activity to finance the organization.[62] The Mafia, for instance, first derived most of its revenue from loan sharking and gambling businesses.[63] The Mafia has also earned income from prostitution, labor racketeering, and sales of black-market goods.[64] By the 1980s, narcotics trafficking had become the most significant source of revenue for the organization.[65] According to law enforcement authorities, BGDN operated a $100 million annual narcotics business, with distribution franchises located outside of Chicago, which sustained the gang.[66] While likely less lucrative than BGDN and perhaps less motivated by profits than the Mafia, MS-13 finances itself using proceeds from, among other things, alien smuggling, narcotics distribution, and robbery.[67]

Fifth, a group must use violence in pursuit of its goals to fit the President's Commission's organized crime profile.[68] In the Mafia, for instance, the rules and penalties of the organization are strict; members face the risk of execution if they fail to abide by the commands of their superiors, or if they sponsor the membership of someone who disappoints or betrays the organization.[69] Similarly, the indictment of the Westies contained numerous allegations of violent crime. In a case in Virginia, federal prosecutors presented evidence that Brenda Paz was murdered by MS-13 members after she attempted to cooperate against the gang as a witness for the government; two defendants were convicted for her murder.[70]

Sixth, the organization must be motivated by power and profit.[71] The Mafia, for instance, secured power through the profits from illicit activities[72] and infiltration of legitimate businesses.[73] MS-13 similarly seeks power and profits by using criminal activity such as narcotics distribution and robbery, and by using violence, such as murdering witness Brenda Paz, to maintain its authority.[74]

Based on the six-part framework set forth in the report of the President's Commission on Organized Crime, street gangs such as MS-13 may indeed qualify as a new stage in the ever-evolving conceptions of organized crime groups. Undoubtedly, not every street

---

62. President's Comm'n Report, *supra* note 49, at 28.

63. The President's Comm'n on Law Enforcement and Admin. of Justice, Task Force Report: Organized Crime 2,4 (1967) (hereinafter Task Force Report); Report of the Senate Special Comm. to Investigate Organized Crime in Interstate Commerce, S. Rep. No. 307, 1st Sess., at 2 (1951) (hereinafter Kefauver Committee Report).

64. Kefauver Committee Report, *supra* note 63, at 1.

65. President's Comm'n Report, *supra* note 49, at 11.

66. Gibeaut, J., *supra* note 40, at 68.

67. Gangs in the United States, *supra* note 45.

68. See *Id.*; President's Comm'n Report, *supra* note 49, at 28–29.

69. *Organized Crime and Illicit Traffic in Narcotics: Hearings before the Permanent Subcomm. on Investigations of the Senate Comm. on Government Operations*, 88th Cong., 1st Sess. 80, at 2 (1963) (hereinafter *McClellan Committee Hearings*) (remarks of Senator John McClellan); President's Comm'n Report, supra note 49, at 42–43.

70. U.S. Attorney's Office for the Eastern District of Virginia, *News Release*, 17 May 2005.

71. President's Comm'n Report, *supra* note 49, at 29.

72. Task Force Report, *supra* note 63, at 2, 4; Kefauver Committee Report, *supra* note 63, at 2.

73. Task Force Report, *supra* note 63, at 4.

74. U.S. Attorney's Office for the Eastern District of Virginia, *supra* note 70.

gang would qualify as an organized crime group. As shown throughout this article, street gangs differ from the Mafia, the quintessential organized crime group, in a number of significant respects, such as the types of crimes they commit and their bureaucratic sophistication. However, were the characteristics of an organized crime group so limited as to include only the Mafia, the government would run the risk of overlooking dangers to society that did not fit the mold set by the Mafia.

The strength of the six-part framework is that the organized crime characteristics are not limited to just one group or organizational model. Thus, the framework provide a degree of flexibility in identifying and targeting new threats that may not have been contemplated when the six characteristics were first articulated.

Gangs: Do Their Members and Associates Qualify for Prosecution under RICO?

Although street gangs such as MS-13 may appropriately be called 'organized crime' groups, it is necessary to engage in a separate analysis to determine whether relevant RICO provisions apply to conduct committed by street gang members, and whether RICO prosecution is appropriate. While terms such as 'street gangs' and 'organized crime' may help decision makers set priorities and focus resources targeting certain entities, the terms do not determine what RICO criminalizes, since it contains no such definitions, and is not limited to such groups.

Just as the six-part framework for organized crime groups is not limited to a particular group, RICO does not limit its application to a given group. The author of RICO, G. Robert Blakey, once remarked that RICO is suited for gang prosecutions.[75] As shown in the previous subsection, street gangs such as MS-13 are sufficiently advanced to be called organized crime groups; but how do the provisions of RICO apply to street gangs, if at all? This sub-section will examine RICO's 'enterprise' and 'pattern of racketeering activity' elements to determine whether the statute would apply to a street gang such as MS-13.[76] Finally, it will examine whether such a prosecution would fall within the intent of RICO.

First, with respect to RICO's 'enterprise' element, the group must satisfy requirements that the courts have read into the statute, such as (1) continuity;[77] (2) a common purpose;[78] and (3) a decision-making mechanism.[79] As shown by the previous subsection, a street gang such as MS-13 (1) is motivated by power and profit; (2) is united in a common purpose, such as narcotics distribution and violence; (3) has demonstrated continuous, rather than sporadic, activity; and (4) possesses a fluid, albeit increasingly bureaucratic and vertical, decision-making mechanism.

Second, RICO's 'pattern of racketeering activity' element requires a 'relationship plus continuity';[80] namely, there must be a relationship between the acts committed and

75. Gibeaut, *supra* note 40.
76. 18 U.S.C. §§ 1961–1962 (2007).
77. United States v. Gray, 137 F.3d 765, 772 (4th Cir. 1998).
78. See Bonner v. Henderson, 147 F.3d 457, 459 (5th Cir. 1998).
79. *Id.*
80. United States v. Pungitore, 910 F.2d 1084, 1104 (3d Cir. 1990), cert. denied, 111 S. Ct. 2009 (1991).

continuity in the commission of the acts.[81] Since members and associates of an active and organized street gang, such as MS-13, may commit a significant number of offenses—narcotics distribution, for instance—on a regular basis, the 'pattern of racketeering activity' element is often readily provable.

Finally, a street gang such as MS-13 may indeed satisfy RICO's statutory elements, but does it comport with the intent of the statute? Congress enacted RICO with the intention of eliminating organized criminal entities and their destructive influence on the country.[82] Although they differ from the Mafia that helped spawn RICO, street gangs still exert a destructive influence on the country in their own way—by alien smuggling, distributing drugs in the streets, and robbing people, for instance. RICO's liberal interpretation clause readily accommodates evolving conceptions of organized crime groups—in this case, gangs such as MS-13 that pose evolving kinds of dangers to society.

Conclusions: Evolving Conceptions of Organized Crime and the Flexibility of RICO

This article has examined how street gangs qualify as organized crime groups, and separately, how their members and associates may qualify for prosecution under RICO. The statute possesses considerable flexibility to target criminal groups that arise, since it names no particular criminal group as liable for prosecution. In keeping with that, RICO does not criminalize *membership* (nor have previous statutes), lest it penalize status, which would run afoul of the Constitution; instead, RICO criminalizes *conduct* on behalf of a criminal enterprise. In fact, a federal court noted that, were RICO applied solely to members of organized crime, it would probably be unconstitutional.[83] RICO prohibits specific conduct, not the status of being a member of an organized crime group. This emphasis upon conduct, not membership in an organized crime group, similarly demonstrates the flexibility of RICO, which is not bound by a rigid list of banned groups.

Definitions of 'street gangs' and 'organized crime' may serve to aid decision makers in setting priorities and focusing resources upon certain organized crime groups, such as the MS-13 street gang. The federal government has made a crack-down on gangs a national priority, and may use the range of law enforcement tools at its disposal, including RICO, where applicable, to address such threats. RICO, through its liberal interpretation clause, contemplates its use in prosecutions of members and associates of new and emerging criminal organizations—street gangs, for instance. Granted, RICO may not be suited for the prosecution of members of each and every street gang. However, where such organizations fall within the intent and language of the statute, the use of RICO is an appropriate and effective means to prosecute crimes committed by gang members.

---

81. *Id.*
82. S. Rep. No. 617, 91st Cong., 1st Sess. 36–43 (1969).
83. See United States v. Mandel, 415 F. Supp. 997, 1018–1019 (D. Md. 1976).

Reading 3.
Antigang Legislation and Its Potential Impact:
The Promises and the Pitfalls*

*Beth Bjerregaard***

A number of state legislatures have developed new strategies for addressing the problems of gang-related criminal behavior. Legislatures have both enhanced traditional criminal laws and drafted new legislation aimed specifically at alleviating the gang problem. One of the most comprehensive approaches originated in California where the first statute aimed exclusively at prohibiting the activities of criminal street gangs was enacted. The California Street Terrorism and Enforcement Prevention Act's primary focus was to make it a criminal offense to engage in criminal gang activity. A multitude of other states quickly followed suit and passed similar legislation. The purpose of the article is to examine the approach taken by state legislatures to make participating in gang activities a substantive crime. This approach will be analyzed in terms of its potential effectiveness as well as its potential for abuse and discriminatory application. Last, suggestions for improving existing statutes will be offered.

Keywords: antigang legislation; street gang legislation; California Street Terrorism and Enforcement Prevention Act (STEP)

There is a growing perception that street gangs are becoming more powerful and aggressive and are infiltrating areas of the United States previously thought to be immune to the threat of gang activity. There is evidence that both the nature of gangs and their criminal activities have changed significantly in recent years (Quinn & Downes, 1993). Several theses have been advanced to explain these changes, such as the gangs' increased involvement in the drug trade, increased access to firearms, and increased sophistication. In conjunction, media coverage of gangs began to intensify during the 1980s (McCorkle & Miethe, 2002, p. 4). There is little doubt that these changes have resulted in an increased awareness of the problems associated with gangs. As a result, law enforcement personnel and policy makers began to focus on strategies to solve the emerging gang problem. Communities, whose social lives have been negatively affected by gangs and their criminal activities, also began to search out ways to effectively deal with gang-related activities.

Review of Legislative Approaches

There are essentially three primary strategies that have been developed to deal with gangs: prevention, intervention, and suppression. Prevention programs have been de-

* Reprinted with Permission *Criminal Justice Policy Review* 2003 14: 171.
** The author would like to thank M. Dwayne Smith for his helpful review of earlier drafts.

signed to identify and amend the factors associated with gang membership. Intervention programs are designed to direct youth out of the gangs. Suppression strategies, on the other hand, emphasize the supervision, arrest, prosecution, and incarceration of known gang members. In recent years, the growing conservatism that has emerged in the United States, coupled with the perceived failure of rehabilitation as an effective approach to crime control, has resulted in an increased emphasis on suppression techniques (Klein, 1995). This approach has been best developed in areas with established gang problems and has resulted in a variety of inventive policies. Police departments, in mainly large urban areas, have created specialized gang units designed to conduct surveillance and gather information about both gangs and gang members operating in their jurisdictions. Other strategies have included such things as conducting police sweeps, establishing special gang prosecution units, and incarcerating serious known gang members (for a summary of these approaches, see Spergel, 1995). However, research has suggested that these approaches have not been particularly successful (Klein, 1995; Oehme, 1997).

In conjunction with these approaches, a number of innovative approaches have emerged in recent years including the creation of new legislation aimed specifically at prosecuting gang members. Some jurisdictions have relied on traditional tactics utilizing antiloitering, public nuisance, curfew, and parental responsibility statutes to prosecute gang members. Additionally, legislatures have criminalized a variety of gang activities such as gang solicitation and recruitment, witness intimidation, and drive-by shootings. One of the most comprehensive approaches was initiated in the state of California. In 1988, the state enacted the California Street Terrorism Enforcement and Prevention Act (STEP) (1997). The STEP Act makes it a substantive crime to participate in criminal gang activity. The act states that any person who

> actively participates in any criminal street gang with knowledge that its members engage in or have engaged in a pattern of criminal gang activity, and who willfully promotes, furthers, or assists any felonious criminal conduct by members of that gang

is guilty of a criminal offense. Over the next several years, numerous states followed California's lead and enacted similar statutes (for a review of statutes, see Bjerregaard, 1999).

Most of these statutes are patterned after the California STEP Act and share several common features. To convict someone under these statutes, the state must prove a number of elements. First, they must demonstrate the existence of a criminal street gang. Although a variety of definitions are utilized by different states, the majority of states clarify that a gang should consist of at least three individuals, can have either a formal or informal organizational structure, and include members who have engaged in a pattern of criminal activity (e.g., STEP Act, 1997). Once the state has proven the existence of a criminal street gang, they must demonstrate that the defendant had "knowledge that [the gang] members engage in or have engaged in a pattern of criminal activity" and that he or she had the specific intent to "promote, further, or assist the criminal conduct of the gang" (e.g., STEP Act, 1997). Last, the state must demonstrate that the defendant is a member of that gang. There are a variety of definitions utilized by states to identify an individual as a gang member.

The purpose of this article is to examine these legislative responses by analyzing them in terms of their potential benefits and abuses. Particular emphasis will be placed on the potential discriminatory application of these legislative responses. Last, suggestions for improving such legislation will be offered.

Potential Benefits of the Legislation

Despite their rapid enactment, there were some legitimate rationales offered for the necessity of such laws. Both law enforcement agencies and the courts have expressed frustration at their attempts to address the gang problem by enforcing traditional criminal laws. Such officials recognize that dealing with gang-related criminal activity often presents unique challenges. Law enforcement officials were often confronted with situations where they were unable to act. The L.A. City Attorney Gang Prosecution Section (2001, p. 325) points out that gang activities frequently observed by uniformed police officers were oftentimes lawful behaviors (e.g., flashing and signs, hanging around particular territories) and that officers were unable to prohibit such behaviors without directly observing criminal activity such as drug selling. Challenges also exist in terms of prosecuting gang members. First, traditional criminal laws do not effectively deal with situations in which multiple offenders are prosecuted for the same incident (Dahmann, 1995, p. 301). Additionally, Dahmann (1995, p. 301) points out that oftentimes such prosecutions involve both adult and juvenile offenders traditionally necessitating that they be dealt with in different judicial systems. Furthermore, gang prosecutions often engender additional issues such as witness problems (e.g., reluctance to get involved, witness intimidation, etc.).

Legislation, such as the California's STEP statute is seen as a way to address many of these problems. Such legislation provides both law enforcement personnel and prosecutors with additional tools for addressing gang-related activities. Additionally, such legislation helps to serve as a deterrent by announcing to gang members that engaging in criminal activities will not be tolerated and that if one participates in these behaviors as a gang member, this will enhance the punishment received for the substantive criminal act. Perhaps most important, such legislation provides the community with a sense that something is being done to tackle the problem.

Initiation of Step Legislation

It is important to address the overall framework in which these antigang initiatives have been passed. The passage of the STEP Act in California coincided with a variety of more punitive measures delineated on the crime control agenda. Scholars such as Jackson and Rudman (1993), McCorkle and Miethe (2002), and Zatz (1987) have all addressed the recent responses to the "gang problem" as responses derived from a "moral panic." Moral panics are described as having three distinct characteristics. First, there is a focus on the behavior of threatening populations (Jackson, 1997, p. 147; McCorkle & Miethe, 2002, p. 15). These populations are then demonized and are referred to in exclusively negative terms. Last, McCorkle and Miethe (2002) state that a moral panic should fluctuate over time with the majority of the activity and concern occurring around the time of the discovery of the problem or condition.

Applying these criteria to the gang situation, McCorkle and Mieth (2002) delineate the growth of the gang problem throughout the 1980s and 1990s. They emphasize the role of both the media and law enforcement agencies in helping to create panic in the public regarding the potential threat generated by gangs. As a result of a perceived threat, which was not confirmed, policy makers found themselves forced to respond to the demands of multiple constituencies.

McCorkle and Miethe (2002) also discuss the role of claims makers in helping to generate this type of panic in the public. These individuals and organizations help to increase public awareness of the negative conditions and situations they believe provide cause for alarm.[1] To make their case, claims makers rely on a variety of techniques including the use of narrative stories, the manipulation of numbers, and metaphors. The use of all three of these methods is evident in the history of antigang legislation in the past two decades.

First, media coverage of gangs exploded simultaneously with a rise in awareness of gang-related problems in police departments across the country (McCorkle & Miethe, 2002). The media engaged in the use of narratives to help convey the danger associated with gang activities frequently relying on stories of drive-by shootings that killed innocent victims. Additionally, media portrayals of these offenses also helped to reinforce the notion of the predatory criminal—an "other" who presents the most danger. McCorkle and Miethe (1998, p. 61) believe that a necessary condition for a moral panic is that the public have some level of fear toward certain minority groups. This is particularly relevant to the gang problem because street gangs are predominantly lower class males who are either African American or Hispanic (Howell, 1994; Joseph, 1997; Oehme, 1997; Spergel, 1990). This is particularly disturbing as both the public and ultimately state legislatures were forced to rely on media accounts for the vast majority of their knowledge concerning gangs (Jackson & Rudman, 1993; McCorkle & Miethe, 2002).

The use of metaphors has also been prevalent in helping to define the social problems presented by street gangs. In large part, the "war" against gangs is a part of the larger "war on crime" in which the United States is engaged. Police in Los Angeles "have been utilizing military weapons and tactics, including helicopters, mass detentions and Checkpoint Charlies" (McKenzie, 1996, pp. 53–54). Focusing on suppression techniques and couching such approaches in terms of a military engagement has a number of adverse implications.

First, there is a heavy reliance on the criminal justice system and law enforcement in particular to solve these problems. There is ample evidence to suggest that the growth of gangs in urban communities coincides with the growth of the underclass in these same areas (Hagedorn, 1988; Huff, 1989; Jackson & Rudman, 1993). William J. Wilson (1987) defines the underclass as those who are effectively excluded from participation in the mainstream economy. For some youth, the gang represents a survival strategy. If this is the case, then this is a problem that cannot be adequately addressed

---

1. McCorkle & Miethe (2002, pp. 11–12) point out that the claims makers are often sincere and convinced they are pursuing noble goals.

solely by the criminal justice system. At best, the law enforcement agents are able to focus on the outward manifestations of the gang problem. They do not have the adequate tools or the ability to attack the root causes of the problem. Even more disturbing, this approach casts the criminal justice system into an us versus them mentality, where the need to identify the enemy is of the utmost importance. This in turn increases the risk that profiling may occur.

Because the majority of these enforcement efforts have taken place in minority communities, we are taking a very real risk that such approaches may backfire and actually exacerbate the problem rather than eradicate it. First, suppression techniques targeted at specific communities can lead to a highly adversarial climate in which communities and police view each other suspiciously. The danger is that police officers will rely on "ambiguous cues and stereotyping in trying to identify the enemies" (Skolnick & Fyfe, 1993, p. 114). When this occurs, the danger is that youth who have committed no crimes but were in the "wrong place at the wrong time" will be subject to these tactics (Burrell, 1990, p. 742). Regina Austin (1992) notes that greater surveillance of minority communities leads to "harassment of those black citizens who are most vulnerable to unjustified interference because they resemble the lawbreakers in age, gender, and class" (pp. 1773–1774). It was noted in *Chicago v. Morales* (1997) that opposition to the ordinance was especially intense in the African American community, as they feared that under the ordinance you were "guilty until proven innocent" (Austin, 1992, pp. 4–5). This perspective is not without justification. Researchers have found that police officers, when asked to indicate the locations they most expect to encounter hostile responses, put minority areas at the top of the list (Bayley & Mendelsohn, 1969). There is much evidence that minorities have historically been subjected to disproportionate harassment and excessive use of force by the police (Taylor-Greene, 1994). More recently, there have been complaints of continued harassment and inequitable applications of the criminal laws. Studies in both Maryland and Ohio have demonstrated that the police have utilized traffic codes in discriminatory manners by overwhelmingly targeting Black motorists (Harris, 1997). Ultimately, this can lead to hostilities among the very groups these laws were designed to protect. In minority communities, this can serve to further alienate residents from the police, which may result in inhibited cooperation and negative attitudes toward police.

Further exasperating this problem is the fact that research has also identified both the seriousness of the offense and the demeanor of the offender as the most important factors influencing police responses to juveniles (Quinn & Downs, 1993). Therefore, this may generate more severe police encounters, which simply serve to perpetuate the cycle. Also, as the frequency of contacts with the police increases, many youth will lose their fear of authority. Fear of the police may be replaced with an animosity, which serves to further intensify the problem. This can eradicate respect for the law and eventually confidence in our justice system. Eventually, this becomes a self-fulfilling prophecy. Greater surveillance will lead to more arrests, which in turn will justify the initial surveillance.

There is some evidence that this is a potential problem with gang-related legislation. McCorkle and Miethe (1998, p. 59) relay the comments of a gang unit officer who stated that "it is safe to assume that when you run across a young black drug dealer, he's probably a gang member." Likewise, Freed (1995, p. 290) states that officers of the

Community Resources Against Hoodlums (CRASH), a unit operating in Los Angeles, focusing on gang suppression activities, often prejudge all gang members. Additionally, the unit itself has been described as "hostile and adversarial" (Covey, Menard & Franzese, 1997, p. 265). This, coupled with the lack of clear definitional guidance in terms of what constitutes a gang member, has led to a situation in which officers argue that "they know a gang and a gang member when they see one ... [which] generally means young minority males in lower or working class neighborhoods who act, talk, and wear clothing associated with stereotypical gang images" (McCorkle & Miethe, 2002, p. 64). Again, because gang members are largely minority, the reality of the situation is that the fight against street gangs is a fight that is played out predominately in inner-city, minority communities.

An additional problem with suppression techniques is that official intervention leads to the official labeling of the youth. McCorkle and Miethe (1998) quote a federal public defender in Las Vegas as stating that

> minorities are often identified and entered into the record as gang members or associates, without being informed, simply because they happen to be in the company of a known gang member, and that member probably got labeled in a similar fashion (p. 59).

There is ample evidence that minorities comprise the vast majority of all gang databases. In fact, in Orange County, California, 92% of those listed were youth of color; similarly, in Cook County, Illinois, the database was found to be two-thirds Black (Pintado-Vertner & Change, 2000, p. 5). These databases identify youth as "suspects" before any crime has been committed (Pintado-Vertner & Change, 2000, p. 4).

Leading gang experts caution that such labeling may serve to increase group cohesion by drawing attention to the gang and increasing the alienation that exists between the gang and the community (Conly, Kelly, Mahanna, & Warner, 1993; Klein & Maxson, 1989). Malcolm Klein (1995) points out that focusing on gangs and gang members also gives status and identity to the gang.

Practical Difficulties with the Statutory Construction of the Legislation

Although antigang legislation was enacted with ambitious objectives, it is unclear that such legislation has been or will be an effective tool to address gang-related problems. Existing statutes present a variety of issues, which need to be addressed to enhance their effectiveness and to reduce the chance that such legislation will be utilized inappropriately.

Constitutionality of Statutes

All of these statutes were designed to provide states with a tool to attack gangs and gang members directly instead of simply addressing the resultant criminal activities. Since their enactment, several of these statutes have faced constitutional challenges. The most common method of attacking this legislation has been to challenge it as unconstitutionally vague. Cases have questioned specific terminology contained within the statutes such as "actively participates," "criminal street gang," and "gang member-ship" (Bjerregaard, 1998). These statutes have also been attacked for being overbroad and infringing on constitutionally protected activities such as freedom of association. Thus far, state antigang legislation modeled after the California STEP Act has with-stood these challenges and been upheld at the state appellate level. In upholding these statutes, the courts have recognized the importance of employing limiting elements. Specifically, the courts have emphasized the importance of requiring specific intent and knowledgeable active participation in the construction of these statutes. Similarly, they have applauded states for clearly defining key terminology within the statutes. All of these components operate to reduce discretion and act to ensure the fair and equitable application of the law.

In 1998, for the first time, the U.S. Supreme Court, in *City of Chicago v. Morales et al.* (1999), considered the constitutionality of a city ordinance prohibiting gang loiter-ing. In response to citizen complaints, the city of Chicago enacted an ordinance, which stated that

> whenever a police officer observes a person whom he reasonably believes to be a criminal street gang member loitering in any public place with one or more other persons, he shall order all such persons to disperse and remove themselves from the area. Any person who does not promptly obey such an order is in violation of this section (Chicago Municipal Code §8-4-015).

The key problem cited by the Supreme Court was the vagueness of the key terminology in the ordinance, which essentially gave the police officers the "absolute discretion to deter-mine what activities constitute loitering" (*City of Chicago v. Morales et al.*, 1999, pp. 32–33) and therefore potentially enforce the law in an arbitrary and/or discriminatory fashion.

Thus far, almost all of these statutes have withstood constitutional challenges at the state appellate level. Having been held facially valid, we need to turn toward the appli-cation of such laws.

Definitional Issues

Social scientists have been grappling with definitional issues since they first started studying gangs (see Ball & Curry, 1995). Although a consensus seems to exist among the STEP legislation, not all antigang statutes employ similar definitions. Most states' statutes are patterned after California's STEP Act (1997) and define a gang as

> any ongoing organization, association or group of three or more persons, whether formal or informal, having as one of its primary activities the commission of one or more of the criminal acts enumerated, having a common or common iden-tifying sign or symbol, and whose members individually or collectively engage in or have engaged in a pattern of criminal gang activity (STEP Act, 1997).

Perhaps most troubling, in terms of providing guidance for enforcement of these statutes, are the definitions of gang membership. Under existing legislation, law enforcement officers must have probable cause to believe that the alleged offender either is a gang mem-ber or has knowledge that he or she is assisting known gang members. A gang member is typically defined as "a person who engages in a pattern of criminal street gang activity and who meets two or more of a list of enumerated criteria," most often including self-admission, identification by a parent/guardian, information from a reliable informant or an informant plus corroboration, physical evidence, photographs, tattoos, clothing style, colors, residence in an area frequented by gang members, use of hand signs, and being stopped in the company of or arrested with gang members a number of times (e.g., Arizona Rev. Stat. Ann., 1996).

> Under Florida and South Dakota laws, a person could potentially meet the statutory definition of a gang member simply by living in a gang area, associating with known gang members, and being stopped in the company of gang members more than four times (Truman, 1995, p. 717).

There are several problems inherent in this type of definition. First, social science researchers recognize that there are varying levels of participation in gangs and that membership in some types of gangs is evasive (Covey et al., 1997, p. 12). Researchers have found that gang membership is relatively unstable and that many individuals drift in and out of gang involvement (Esbensen & Huizinga, 1993; Thornberry, Krohn, Lizotte, & Chard-Wierschem, 1993). Additionally, leading gang scholars have recognized that there are several different types of gang members whose participation and commitment to the gang vary (Klein, 1995). Core members are much more actively involved in the gang than fringe members or "wannabees" who are not considered to be true gang members by their peers. Therefore, identification of an individual by a third party and even self-identification may not be reliable indicators of gang members without more objective criteria.

Second, and even more problematic, is the fact that several of the enumerated gang indicators are extremely open to interpretation and provide law enforcement officers with little guidance and broad discretion in enforcing these statutes. Herein lies the crux of the problem. The flexibility provided by such broad definitions gives law enforcement officers a fair amount of discretion in enforcing these statutes. In fact, a certain amount of discretion is necessary for officers to be able to do their jobs efficiently and effectively. However, discretion also opens the door to the possibility of abuse. Racism in the criminal justice system has frequently hidden behind the cloak of discretion (Herman, 1993).

The race of a suspect may influence an officer's decision to stop and potentially arrest in a number of different ways. First, because the majority of gangs are composed primarily of minority members and because law enforcement efforts to eradicate gangs are primarily conducted in inner-city minority communities, they are the individuals who are most likely to be subjected to this law. Whereas police officers, as well as judges, would agree that approaching and/or detaining a suspect solely on the basis of his or her race would be illegal, police also admit that race is often a factor that contributes to their decision to detain a suspect (S. L. Johnson, 1983). African Americans and other ethnic minorities frequently "reside and work in areas associated with criminal activity thereby increasing the likelihood of [police contact]" (Harris, 1994, pp. 677–678).

The definition is constructed in such a way that it allows officers to compose profiles of potential or likely gang members. Race and/or ethnicity would likely be one of the factors included in such a profile. This practice has already been noted with drug courier profiling (Allen-Bell, 1997). There is evidence that suggests many police officers believe that minority status correlates with a general propensity to commit crime and that this belief can influence their decisions to investigate and/or detain a suspect (S. L. Johnson, 1983). One commentator has argued that using race as a proxy for criminality "results from a self-fulfilling prophecy: racial stereotypes influence police to arrest minorities more frequently than non-minorities, thereby generating statistically disparate arrest patterns that in turn form the basis for further selectivity" ("Developments in the Law," 1988, pp. 1507–1508). It also follows that if police make minorities more vulnerable to stops and questioning, then minorities will have "more reason to fear the police, regardless of their compliance with the law" (Maclin, 1998, p. 391). Examples are numerous. In Hartford, Connecticut, young Hispanic males who matched police profiles of gang members were subjected to frequent police stops and interrogations (Anonymous, 1994). In Denver, Colorado, police compiled a list of suspected gang members that included approximately two thirds of the African American males in the city between the ages of 12 and 24 (D. Johnson, 1993). There is evidence from other cities that some law enforcement gang sweeps resulted in virtually every Black male in the vicinity being arrested despite the fact that many were later proven not to be gang members (Burrell, 1990). Mayer (1993) points out that

> overbroad definitions will provide little more than a license to arrest or investigate youths for whom no other rational basis for an investigation exists. Given the disparate treatment of teenagers of different races, such a will result in the disparate classification of minority teenagers as gang members … regardless of their individual culpability (p. 972).

One result of these discriminatory practices is that minority youth often "become gang members based on law enforcement guesswork. A childhood nickname may be transformed into a gang 'moniker' and neighborhood playmates into 'homeboys'" (Burrell, 1990, p. 751). Identification of just one youth as a gang member could lead to all of his friends being identified as fellow gang members (Mayer, 1993). By definition, this practice has the potential to wrongly identify innocent citizens as gang members and to create gangs where no gangs exist. Unguided discretion simply heightens the risk of discriminatory enforcement, which, in turn, increases the risk of damaging already fragile police-community relations (Browning, Cullen, Cao, Kopache, & Stevenson, 1994).

Clothing, Colors, and Tattoos

Almost all definitions of gang members utilize clothing, colors, and/or tattoos as several of the criteria that can be utilized to demonstrate that a suspect is a gang member. The difficulty is that more and more of the clothing and styles associated with the gang culture have worked their way into teen fashions (Joseph, 1997; McCorkle & Miethe, 2002; Stover, 1986). Many of the fashions once thought to be reliable indicators of gang membership, such as baggy pants, oversized T-shirts, baseball caps worn backwards, and even tattoos are now considered fashionable (Salt Lake City Sheriff's Department, n.d.; Texas Youth Commission, n.d.). In fact, "gang attire" has become so popular that authorities from law enforcement to school officials in suburbs have noted the fact that many students are adopting this style of dress (Burrell, 1990). This has, in part, been fueled by the hip-hop culture, and shows such as MTV, which help to shape teen fashions. Arguably, even pagers and handguns can no longer be thought to distinguish gang members from nongang youth (Armor & Jackson, 1995).

This problem is further complicated by the fact that "many gangs adopt designer labels or insignia of sports teams" (Burrell, 1990, p. 754). Both professional and sports clothing items are now popular with gangs, and several gangs have adopted particular teams to symbolize their gang. The gangs are attracted to such clothing for several reasons. First, several of the sports teams have colors that match gang colors. For example, the Gangster Disciples have adopted Duke's blue and black colors ("Chicago Gangs Adopt Duke," 1999), and the Neighborhood Crips prefer U.N.C.'s light blue and white colors. Additionally, the Neighborhood Crips logo is used to symbolize their gang name (Etter, 1998). Likewise, certain designer clothes or brand names have been adopted by gangs. For example, Calvin Klein has been adopted by the Bloods and is said to denote "Crip Killer" whereas British Knights said to indicate "Blood Killer" are worn by Crips. This type of attire offers the added benefit that it is popular among all types of persons and therefore does not necessarily operate as a conspicuous identifier for police officers.

Utilizing these indicators of gang membership has great potential for abuse. First, because so many youth are using gang symbols and clothing to "fit in," it is difficult to say that these signs carry as much weight in today's society as they did several years ago. For example, in the state of Arizona, having a tattoo and wearing blue Adidas would identify one as a gang member (Pintado-Vertner & Change, 2000, p. 4). Second, wannabees or youth who hope to join the gang will frequently adopt the gang attire although they are not yet seriously involved in the gang or the gang's criminal activities ("An Urban Ethnology," 1999). Others may wear such clothing to obtain status or to protect themselves from other gangs (Burrell, 1990; Mayer, 1993; McCorkle & Miethe, 1998). Tattoos are left as a permanent legacy to a youth's gang membership even long after he or she has left the gang. As Susan Burrell (1990) points out, the "dangers of acting on appearance alone are particularly acute where gang membership is the sole basis for detention" (p. 754). It introduces the possibility that youth in inner cities will be subjected to regular investigation simply because they look like a gang member,[2] thus opening the door to possible discrimination (Burrell, 1990).

The primary problem with these definitions is that they have the possibility of being overly inclusive and identifying innocent juveniles or those who reside in criminally infested neighborhoods or who have social affiliations with criminals as gang members. Conversely, if the definitions are too narrow, they do little to advance the tools available to law enforcement agents beyond those of existing criminal statutes. The challenge facing both social scientists and practitioners is to develop a pragmatic, operational definition of gang membership.

---

2. An important notable exception to this is the recent Supreme Court decision, *City of Chicago v. Morales et al.* (1999) where the Court held that the definition of loitering used by the city of Chicago was impermissibly vague.

Pattern of Criminal Activity

Additionally, for a group to be defined as a gang, either the group or its members must have engaged in a pattern of criminal activity. Appellate courts have held that a pattern of criminal activity can be demonstrated by an individual committing a series of offenses or by multiple offenders committing one or more offenses in a single incident (*In re Leland D.*, 1990; *In re Lincoln J.*; 1990; *In re Nathaniel C.*, 1991). For example, if two gang members break into a home and steal a television (burglary and larceny), they have displayed a "pattern" of criminal activity. The courts have also held that the criminal activity does not even have to be gang related (*People v. Gardeley*, 1996, p. 716). Both of these judicial interpretations have essentially made it easier to define a group as a gang.

Suggestions for Improving Legislation

Although gang-related legislation has been extensively enacted and over 70% of all states now have some form of legislation related to gangs (National Youth Gang Center, n.d., p. 1), there is evidence that such legislation has not been the panacea it was once thought to be. McCorkle and Miethe (2002), studying the development of such legislation in the state of Nevada, examined court data to determine the extent to which this new legislation was being utilized. They found that, with a few exceptions, the new laws were "rarely and sometimes, never used" (p. 193).

Although the stated intent behind the antigang statutes is admirable, the swift reaction of the legislatures and the lack of reliance on established criminological theory and research leaves open the possibility that such legislation will ultimately fail in achieving its purpose. Even more disturbing is the possibility that these approaches could backfire and actually exacerbate the problem. We must be especially sensitive to the impact that these statutes will have in the minority communities inasmuch as these are the populations that will be most affected by these laws.

Carefully constructed laws that safeguard the constitutional rights of citizens and provide safeguards against inequitable application can be a valuable tool for both law enforcement agents and court personnel. These laws can provide criminal justice personnel with additional apparatus to address the problems facing many of these communities. Furthermore, they provide a way to attack the core problem of gang membership by facilitating the incapacitation of core gang members and of those who are engaging in criminal activities as a part of their gang membership. Such laws can, if drafted and utilized appropriately, assist communities in providing safer environments for its residents. The last section of this manuscript will provide suggestions for improving our current antigang legislation to address the issues discussed above.

Improving Definitions

First and foremost, we must strive to ensure that these statutes are not written in such a fashion as to be vague or overbroad. Although the appellate courts have almost unanimously held that the terminology defined within the existing statutes is not unconstitutionally vague, this is an area in which legislatures would benefit from consulting social science research and experts in the study of gangs. As one commentator noted, "for a statute to have a reasonable expectation of achieving its intended goal, those crafting it must have knowledge of the behavior that they are attempting to alter" (Holland, 1995, p. 278). At this point in time, law enforcement agencies, legislatures, and sociologists often employ vastly different definitions of gangs and gang-related activity. Although it is beyond the scope of this article to create the perfect definition, there are several ways in which existing definitions can be improved.

Gang Membership

First, there should not be an overemphasis on the social ties of the individual or on his or her area of residence. Although both of these factors may be related to gang membership, they should not by themselves define an individual as a gang member. By identifying youth as gang members if they meet two or more of the enumerated criteria, one can be identified solely on the basis of these criteria.

Likewise, there should be a tempered focus on the juvenile's attire. The Portland Police Department employs a definition that both recognizes that attire can be a sign of gang membership and narrows the criteria so that sole reliance on basic attire is not acceptable. Their definition states that "an individual [must] display clothes, jewelry, hand signs and/or tattoos *unique* to gang affiliation; clothing color alone is *not sufficient* for designation" [italics added] (quoted in Mayer, 1993, p. 973).

Definitions should attempt to focus on hardcore, committed gang members. Additionally, laws should be aimed toward groups with clear criminal agendas. Legislatures should be careful to restrict their definitions of gang membership to include only individuals who are actively and not peripherally involved in the gangs, thereby excluding wannabees and fringe members from their statutes. There are several ways that this could be accomplished. One is to examine factors such as the frequency of association. Commitment can also be demonstrated by emphasizing the individual's intent to further the criminal purpose of the group. Ensuring that the statute requires specific intent helps to ensure that only blameworthy individuals are targeted by the legislation. If legislatures are going to rely on an enumerated list of indicators, they should require the presence of at least three of these criteria so that no two factors such as clothing and area of residence are enough to identify someone as a gang member.

Gangs

In terms of defining a criminal gang, reconceptualizing the requirement of a "pattern of criminal activity" would help to ensure that the individual criminal behavior of one or two individuals does not become the shared responsibility of all youth who associate with them. This would reduce the risk of all members being treated as presumptively culpable. Furthermore, the enumerated offenses should be serious offenses. Similarly, to punish someone for his or her gang involvement, the enumerated offenses should be restricted to gang-related offenses. Finally, legislatures should clearly define this term to exclude concurrent activities and to require that this element can only be met by repeated violations of the law, demonstrated by at least two separate offenses.

The adoption of a narrower, more specific, definition of gang membership is beneficial for a number of reasons. First, it ensures that the legislation is targeting serious, involved gang members. This will help preserve police-community relations as well as guard against such possibilities as increasing gang cohesion and/or inappropriately labeling juveniles as gang members and potentially increasing their criminal involvement and perhaps contributing to a breakdown in respect for the law. Finally, narrow definitions operate to curtail police discretion and therefore reduce the possibility that the laws will be applied in a discriminatory fashion.

Additionally, any time the possibility of discriminatory application of a law exists, we should strive to employ stricter standards of review to ensure that this will not occur. The U.S. Supreme Court recognized as far back as their decision in *Terry v. Ohio* (1968) that certain investigative techniques resulted in tensions between urban citizens and the police. Whenever evidence exists that racial profiling might have occurred or that race played a significant role in the decision to label an individual as a gang member, courts should employ a heightened level of scrutiny to these cases. Judges should carefully screen these cases to ensure that independent evidence against the defendant exists. Kennedy (1997) suggests that race should be prohibited from entering into the decision-making process, except in those cases when the state can offer a compelling justification for its existence.

Antigang Legislation as an Effective Tool

Perhaps the biggest problem with these approaches is that they provide only temporary solutions and ignore the real problems that have contributed to the increase in both gangs and gang-related activity in our society. By focusing on gang suppression, we take the emphasis off of identifying and eradicating the ultimate causes of gang development and gang membership. Thus, these strategies fall short of offering meaningful solutions to the problem (Shelden, Tracy, & Brown, 1997). In many communities, gangs represent a survival strategy for some youth (Covey et al., 1997). Gangs are not created only to commit criminal acts. If gangs are eradicated in these neighborhoods, we need to think about what will replace the gang in these youths' lives. Likewise, gang suppression techniques may simply temporarily reduce membership in the gang. Without addressing the causes of gang involvement, other youth will be there to simply replace, or at least supplement, the incarcerated member.

Current gang initiatives should decrease the emphasis on suppression by increasing the commitment to prevention. It is vitally important to utilize research to identify the factors that place a juvenile at risk for gang involvement and to initiate programs to help control these factors. To effectively address the issue of gang membership, we need to focus on the root causes of gang membership rather than expending our efforts in trying to control gangs once they are formed. Inasmuch as the causes of gang membership are extensive and interrelated, dealing with gangs requires a comprehensive, multifaceted approach. We have a good deal of social science research to help guide policy in this regard. Although there is much that can be done at the individual level, such as providing youth with alternatives to gang involvement, strengthening of family ties, and educational commitment, to institute large-scale reforms, change must take place at the societal level. Hagedorn (1988) suggests deemphasizing the criminal justice system as a method of handling the gang problem. Instead, he suggests we should focus our efforts on providing meaningful employment opportunities and improving education. We need to develop programs that will address housing conditions in our inner cities, promote economic revitalization in minority communities, and primarily reduce economic and social inequality in our society (Joseph, 1997). McKenzie (1996) suggests that the best place to initiate these policies might be the inner suburban rings of metropolitan areas. Gang problems are not as well established in these areas and also these communities may have some of the features that would enhance successful implementation; these include substantial tax bases, a core group of residents with solid ties to the community and the proximity to the large city. These areas also have more heterogeneous populations that would allow for a multicultural approach.

To be successful, any intervention strategy will need to include systematic evaluation as a necessary component. A key problem is that there have been no real systematic evaluations of any of these strategies. What we currently know has been pieced together from a variety of sources. With appropriate evaluation, we can enhance and elaborate polices that are successfully meeting their goals, eliminate those that are not, and rework those that are struggling.

Programs designed to attack the root causes of gang membership are going to be complex and costly. Additionally, the results of these programs are not going to be realized immediately. Currently, there is a "deep-rooted reluctance to face up to the implications of the social context of gang life" (Covey et al., 1997, p. 313). In fact, Anonymous (1994, p. 1707) points out that by implementing our current strategies, we as a society have overreacted to the gang problem in what she also terms a moral panic. She feels that this panic is, at least in part, driven by our lack of empathy for the problems facing inner-city youth and our images of minorities as criminals. Moore (1993, pp. 28–29) also identifies some of the most common stereotypes concerning gangs. She states that these stereotypes contribute to our moral panic. These stereotypes, coupled with a lack of research to address their validity, contribute to our lack of ability to address the problem effectively. We should educate our law enforcement personnel so that they are not susceptible to these clichés and therefore not prone to typecast.

Prosecutors and police officers can also rely on existing legislation to attack the substantive crimes committed by gang members, deemphasizing the use of antigang legislation because its deterrent value is at the least questionable. This would move police officers away from the difficult and potentially dangerous task of having to identify gangs and gang members and would place the emphasis back on the substantive crime being committed by the individual, regardless of his or her status as a gang member. Most jurisdictions already have in place "three strikes you're out" legislation, which would allow prosecutors to attack offenders with subsequent offenses more harshly.

At a minimum, these issues should be taken seriously. We need to allocate the resources necessary to deal with these issues and be committed to developing and implementing long-term strategies that will benefit future generations. All of us, academicians, social science researchers, legislators, and practitioners alike should work together to address this issue. The gang problem needs to be addressed in a comprehensive and deliberate manner. For any solution to be ultimately effective, it must not only address the root causes of the problem, but it must also ensure that it operates in such a way as to protect the rights of innocent citizens. Although the task may seem overwhelming at first, it is one that we must tackle if we are to advance and improve our society.

References

Allen-Bell, A. A. (1997). The birth of the crime: Driving while Black (DWB). *Southern University Law Review*, 25, 195–225.

Anonymous. (1994). Juvenile curfews and gang violence: Exiled on main street. *Harvard Law Review*, 107, 1693–1710.

Ariz. Rev. Stat. Ann. §13-105 (8) (West Supp. 1996).

Armor, J. D., & Jackson, V. K. (1995). Juvenile gang activity in Alabama. *The Journal of Gang Research*, 2, 29–35.

Austin, R. (1992). The Black community, its lawbreakers, and the politics of identification. *Southern California Law Review*, 65, 1769–1817.

Ball, R. A., & Curry, G. D. (1995). The logic of definition in criminology: Purposes and methods for defining "gangs." *Criminology*, 33, 225–245.

Bayley, D. H., & Mendelsohn, H. (1969). *Minorities and the police: Confrontation in America*. New York: Free Press.

Bjerregaard, B. (1998). The constitutionality of anti-gang legislation. *Campbell Law Review*, 21, 31–47.

Bjerregaard, B. (1999). The Supreme Court and anti-gang legislation: The potential impact of the Morales case. *The Criminal Law Bulletin*, 35, 27–41.

Browning, S. L., Cullen, F. T., Cao, L., Kopache, R., & Stevenson, T. J. (1994). Race and getting hassled by the police: A research note. *Police Studies*, 17, 1–10.

Burrell, S. L. (1990). Gang evidence: Issues for criminal defense. *Santa Clara Law Review*, 30, 739–790.

California Street Terrorism Enforcement and Prevention Act, Cal. Penal Code §186.20-28 (West, 1997).

Chicago gangs adopt Duke, UNC clothing as uniforms. (October 13, 1998). *Daily News*. Retrieved June 17, 1999, from http://www.jacksonvilledailynews.com/stories/1998/10/13/hboh24.shtml.

Chicago Municipal Code §8-4-015.

Chicago v. Morales, U.S. Briefs 1121 (1997).

City of Chicago v. Morales et al., U.S. LEXIS 4005 (1999).

Conly, C. H., Kelly, P., Mahanna, P., & Warner, L. (1993). *Street gangs: Current knowledge and strategies*. Washington, DC: National Institute of Justice.

Covey, H. C., Menard, S., & Franzese, R. J. (1997). *Juvenile gangs* (2nd ed.). Springfield, IL: Charles C Thomas.

Dahmann, J. (1995). An evaluation of Operation Hardcore: A prosecutorial response to violent gang criminality. In M. W. Klein, C. L. Maxson, & J. Miller (Eds.), *The modern gang reader* (pp. 301–303). Los Angeles: Roxbury.

Developments in the law—race and the criminal process. (1988). *Harvard Law Review*, 101, 1472–1641.

Esbensen, F. A., & Huizinga, D. (1993). Gangs, drugs, and delinquency in a survey of urban youth. *Criminology*, 31, 565–589.

Etter, G. W., Sr. (1998). Common characteristics of gangs: Examining the cultures of the new urban tribes. *Journal of Gang Research*, 5, 19–33.

Freed, D. (1995). Policing gangs: Case of contrasting styles. In M. W. Klein, C. L. Maxson & J. Miller (Eds.), *The modern gang reader* (pp. 288–291). Los Angeles: Roxbury. Hagedorn, J. (1988). *People and folks: Gangs, crime and the underclass in a rust belt city*. Chicago: Lake View Press.

Harris, D. A. (1994). Factors for reasonable suspicion: When Black and poor means stopped and frisked. *Indiana Law Journal*, 69, 659–688.

Harris, D. A. (1997). Driving while Black and all other traffic offenses: The Supreme Court and pretextual traffic stops. *Journal of Criminal Law and Criminology*, 87, 544–582.

Herman, S. N. (1993). Why the Court loves Batson: Representation, reinforcement, colorblindness, and the jury. *Tulane Law Review*, 67, 1807–1853.

Holland, L. (1995). Can gang recruitment be stopped? An analysis of the societal and legal factors affecting anti-gang legislation. *Journal of Contemporary Law*, 21, 259–305. Howell, J. C. (April, 1994). Gangs: Fact sheet #12. Retrieved October 26, 1999, from http://www.ncjrs.org/txtfiles/gangsfs.txt.

Huff, C.R. (1989). Youth gangs and public policy. *Crime and Delinquency*, 35, 524–537.

In re Leland D., 272 Cal. Rptr. 709 (Cal. Ct App. 1990).

In re Lincoln J., 272 Cal. Rptr. 852 (Cal. Ct. App. 1990).

In re Nathaniel C., 279 Cal. Rptr. 236 (Cal. Ct. App. 1991).

Jackson, P. (1997). The police and social threat: Urban transition, youth gangs, and social control. In G. L. Mays (Ed.), *Gangs and gang behavior* (pp. 81–98). Chicago: Nelson-Hall Publishers.

Jackson, P., & Rudman, C. (1993). Moral panic and the response to gangs in California. In S. Cummings & D. J. Monti (Eds.), *Gangs: The origins and impact of contemporary youth gangs in the United States* (pp. 257–275). Albany: State University of New York Press. Johnson, D. (1993, December 11). Two out of three young Black men in Denver listed by police as suspected gangsters. *The New York Times*, p. A-8.

Johnson, S. L. (1983). Race and the decision to detain a suspect. *Yale Law Journal*, 93, 214–258.

Joseph, J. (1997). Black youth gangs. *Journal of Gang Research*, 4, 1–12.

Kennedy, R. (1997). *Race, crime and law*. New York: Vintage.

Klein, M. W. (1995). *The American street gang: Its nature, prevalence, and control*. New York: Oxford University Press.

Klein, M. W., & Maxson, C. L. (1989). Street gang violence. In N. A. Weiner & M. E. Wolfgang (Eds.), *Violent crimes, violent criminals* (pp. 198–234). Newbury Park, CA: Sage.

L.A. City Attorney Gang Prosecution Section. (2001). Civil gang abatement: A community-based policing tool of the Office of the Los Angeles City Attorney. In J. Miller, C.

L. Maxson, & M. W. Klein (Eds.), *The modern gang reader* (2nd ed., pp. 320–329). Los Angeles: Roxbury.

Maclin, T. (1998). Race and the Fourth Amendment. *Vanderbilt Law Review*, 51, 333–393. Mayer, J. J. (1993). Individual moral responsibility and the criminalization of youth gangs. *Wake Forest Law Review*, 28, 943–998.

McCorkle, R. C., & Miethe, T. D. (1998). The political and organizational response to gangs: An examination of a "moral panic" in Nevada. *Justice Quarterly*, 15, 41–64.

McCorkle, R. C., & Miethe, T. D. (2002). *Panic: The social construction of the street gang problem*. Upper Saddle River, NJ: Prentice Hall.

McKenzie, E. (1996). Suburban youth gangs and public policy: An alternative to the war on violence. *Journal of Emotional and Behavioral Problems*, 5, 52–55.

Moore, J. (1993). Gangs, drugs, and violence. In S. Cummings & D. J. Monti (Eds.), *Gangs: The origins and impact of contemporary youth gangs in the United States* (pp. 27–46). Albany: State University of New York Press.

National Youth Gang Center (n.d.). Analysis of gang-related legislation. Retrieved August 25, 2002, from http://www.iir.com/nygc/gang-legis/analysis.htm.

Oehme, C. G., III. (1997). *Gangs, groups and crime: Perceptions and responses of community organizations*. Durham, NC: Carolina Academic Press.

People v. Gardeley, 927 P.2d 713 (Cal. 1996).

Pintado-Vertner, R., & Change, J. (2000). The war on youth. *Color Lines*. Retrieved August 25, 2002, from http://www.alternet.org/story.html?storyid=285.

Quinn, J. F., & Downs, B. (1993). Predictors of the severity of the gang problem at the local level: An analysis of police perceptions. *Gang Journal*, 1, 1–10.

Salt Lake City Sheriff's Department. (n.d.). *Gangster clothing*. Retrieved February 20, 2002, from http://www.slsheriff.org/html/org/metrogang/clothes.html.

Shelden, R. G., Tracy, S. K., & Brown, W. B. (1997). *Youth gangs in American society*. Belmont, CA: Wadsworth.

Skolnick, J., & Fyfe, J. (1993). *Above the law: Police and the excessive use of force*. New York: Free Press.

Spergel, I. (1990). Youth gangs: Continuity and change. In M. Tonry & N. Morris (Eds.), *Crime and justice: A review of the research* (pp. 171–275). Chicago: University of Chicago Press.

Spergel, I. (1995). *The youth gang problem: A community approach*. New York: Oxford University Press.

Stover, D. (1986). A new breed of youth gangs is on the prowl and a bigger threat than ever. *American School Board Journal*, 173, 19–25.

Taylor-Greene, H. (1994). Black perspectives on police brutality. In A. T. Sulton (Ed.), *African-American perspectives on crime causation, criminal justice administration and crime prevention* (pp. 139–148). Englewood, CO: Sulton.

Terry v. Ohio, 392 U.S. 1 (1968).

Texas Youth Commission. (n.d.). *Gang related clothing*. Retrieved February 20, 2002, from http://www.tyc.state.tx.us/prevention/clothing.html.

Thornberry, T., Krohn, M. D., Lizotte, A., & Chard-Wierschem, D. (1993). The role of juvenile gangs in facilitating delinquent behavior. *Journal of Research in Crime and Delinquency*, 30, 55–87.

Truman, D. R. (1995). The Jets and Sharks are dead: State statutory responses to criminal street gangs. *Washington University Law Quarterly*, 73, 683–735.

An urban ethnology of Latino street gangs in Los Angeles and Ventura Counties. (n.d.). Retrieved October 26, 1999, from http://www.csun.edu/~hcchs006/table.html.

Wilson, W. J. (1987). *The truly disadvantaged: The inner city, the underclass, and public policy.* Chicago: University of Chicago Press.

Zatz, M. (1987). Chicago youth gangs and crime: The creation of a moral panic. *Contemporary Crisis*, 11, 129–158.

Index